CONTROVERSY

CONTROVERSY
And Other Essays in Journalism
1950-1975

William Manchester

Little, Brown and Company—Boston-Toronto

Many of these essays first appeared in magazines and are reprinted through the courtesy of the following: *Holiday, American Heritage, Reporter, New York Times Magazine, Harper's, Esquire, The Atlantic Monthly.*

*Published simultaneously in Canada
by Little, Brown & Company (Canada) Limited*

PRINTED IN THE UNITED STATES OF AMERICA

This book is for Don Congdon, who has been my literary agent for twenty-eight years, and the late Harry Sions, who was my editor for eighteen years. Both men contributed to these essays with ideas, encouragement, criticism, and immense moral support.

A writer works in a ball park all by himself. Sometimes he wonders whether there is anybody watching in the stands. Don and Harry always had season tickets, were always in their boxes, and were always cheering. Their hurrahs meant so much—my gratitude runs so deep—that the language is too feeble a vehicle to convey it.

It may be different elsewhere. But in a democratic society the highest duty of the writer, the composer, the artist is to remain true to himself and let the chips fall where they may. In serving his vision of the truth, the artist best serves his nation.

—John F. Kennedy
Amherst, Massachusetts
October 26, 1963

Contents

Controversy

In 1961 Arthur Krock reproached me for my enthusiasm over the new President: "Mencken would be mad as hell at you. Didn't he tell you that a newspaperman should look at a politician only one way—down his nose?" Mencken had, but it didn't matter; I couldn't disdain Kennedy. He was brighter than I was, braver, better-read, handsomer, wittier, and more incisive. The only thing I could do better was write. I never dreamed that one day I would write his obituary—the longest presidential obituary in history, and, in the end, the most controversial.

Neither did I dream that the controversy would pit me against old friends, nor that our estrangement would become a newspaper sensation dwarfing the donnybrooks of Mencken, who had at least gloried in them, as I could not. At the time I was hurt, baffled, and, I'm afraid, very sorry for myself. Only much later, when the dust had settled and I had returned to my quiet, donnish life, did I understand what had happened, and why. By then I wanted only to forget it all. I nearly succeeded.

Then, while going through my papers, I ran across the fat files of those years. I save everything, even memoranda of phone conversations, so I was in a position to set down a complete account of precisely what the controversy had been all about. Friends urged me to do it, arguing that the full story should be told. The result follows.

It may remind some of the Sartrian theater of the absurd. Certainly it cannot rank as great tragedy. There are a few hardy figures in it, there are more who were weak. Mostly it is a story of people whose perceptions were still warped by grief. "Do you think you've suffered more than Jackie and me?" Bob Kennedy cried out to me in anguish at one point during that dreadful summer of 1966. Of course I hadn't.

That was why I was slightly—but only slightly—more rational than they were.

So there were no stalwarts in the controversy. There were no villains, either. The only villain lay in a Texas grave. Even today I cannot willingly set down his name. His crime robbed us of everything which would have made the controversy impossible—not only the central fact, but the mind-set which followed. Norman Mailer summed it up the day after the assassination in Dallas. "It was our country for a while," he said. "Now it's theirs again."

A FTERWARD THERE WERE STORIES that I was not the Kennedys' first choice to write an authorized account of President Kennedy's death in Dallas, but I have been unable to verify any of them. The most persistent report was that an approach had been made to Theodore H. White, who had won the family's approval with *The Making of the President 1960*. Later I asked White; he had no memory of it. It is true that an aide to Attorney General Robert F. Kennedy sounded out Walter Lord. Lord was interested, and the aide promised to get back to him. Before this possibility could be explored with the family, however, Jacqueline Kennedy decided that she preferred me.

In the chaos after Dallas the President's survivors kept few records of their deliberations, but I know that his widow had made up her mind on this issue before Christmas, 1963, because Ed Kuhn, then editor-in-chief of McGraw-Hill, was in Washington the week before the holiday trying to win the assignment for one of his writers, Robert J. Donovan, author of *PT 109*. A Kennedy assistant told Kuhn and Donovan that Mrs. Kennedy had concluded that she wanted William Manchester to do it.

Kuhn telephoned me at my office on the Wesleyan University campus in Middletown, Connecticut, saying that he would like to publish the book I was going to write about the murder of the President. I told him that he was misinformed; I had no intention of doing any such thing. I had recently returned from Germany, where I had been researching a history of the Krupp munitions dynasty. The Krupp project, I said, would keep me busy for the next two years. Kuhn rang off without further explanation. It wasn't until February 5, 1964, after I had signed a contract for the Krupp book with Little, Brown and Company, my publishers, that Pierre Salinger phoned me, relaying the widow's request. I was noncommittal. Hanging up, I said to my secretary, "Mrs. Kennedy wants me to write the story of the assassination. How can I say no to her?" She said, "You can't."

Nor, I felt, could I, though I did wonder why she had chosen me. At that time I was forty-one, with a university appointment and what a *New York Times* reporter called "a small but secure literary reputation"—the qualifications, in short, of a considerable number of writers. None of my seven books had been on any best-seller list. I hadn't even met Jacqueline Kennedy; I knew only the men in the family.

Bob Kennedy subsequently told me that after one of my evenings alone with his brother at the White House the President had told his wife of his regard for me, and that she had recalled that in the days which followed his funeral. It is a good story, but I don't believe it. John Kennedy hadn't liked me that much. I think Jackie picked me because she thought I would be manageable. I had written a short book about her husband while he was still alive. National security not then being a discredited phrase, I believed that an incumbent President should have some control over the publication of remarks he had made privately, and so I had submitted galleys to him, specifying that he could alter only his own words. As it happened, he requested no changes, but Jackie may well have concluded that the incident proved that I would be infinitely obliging. It was a natural mistake.

Later I compounded it by giving the Kennedys manuscript approval of the assassination book, agreeing that it should not appear until the family or its representatives had read it and given me a green light. That is not how studies of historical events are ordinarily published, but this was not an ordinary publishing venture. It was conceived at a time when millions, me among them, were still mourning John F. Kennedy. None were more stricken than those who had been close to him. When I flew to Washington on February 26 for preliminary discussions with Bobby at the Justice Department, I was shocked by his appearance. I have never seen a man with less resilience. Much of the time he seemed to be in a trance, staring off into space, his face a study in grief.

Bob said of the book that the family was anxious to avoid flamboyance and commercialism. I replied that he should let me know what was acceptable to him. I did suggest that since the project had apparently originated with Mrs. Kennedy, it might be wise for me to discuss it directly with her. That would be unnecessary, he answered; he represented her. Later, when I came to know her, she was to tell me the same thing in other words: "Deal with Bobby." "Work it out with Bobby." "Let Bobby take care of it."

One of the things he took care of was the publisher. He wanted me to secure an option release from Little, Brown. Instead the book would be issued by Harper & Row and edited by Harper's chief editor, Evan Thomas, who had brought out John F. Kennedy's *Profiles in Courage* and Bob's *The Enemy Within*. In this, as in virtually everything else, I consented. Reluctantly but gracefully, Little, Brown agreed to let me go. At the same time, I resigned my post at Wesleyan and prepared to move my wife and three children to Washington.

At the end of our talks, Bob and I decided to set down the details of the project in a memorandum of understanding. At that point we assumed that Salinger would draft the memo, but when I returned to the capital on March 22 at Salinger's invitation, I discovered that he had flown off to California to run for the Senate. By phone he suggested that I draw up the memorandum myself. With Bobby's wishes in mind, I typed out a version in my room at Washington's University Club. This became the basis for revision during conferences between Bob, me, Evan Thomas, Ed Guthman, and Don Congdon, my gifted, debonair agent.

These were my first meetings with Guthman and Thomas. Ed, who had been awarded a Pulitzer Prize for his exposure of labor union racketeering in the late 1940s, was a kind of Jewish Abraham Lincoln. I have seldom admired a colleague more. Evan also left a first impression of candor, though as I came to know him better I learned that he was a highly complex man. The son of Norman Thomas, he was dour, sardonic, and possessed of a mordant wit, yet his air of crusty independence was misleading. Under it he was eager to be accommodating toward celebrated men and women, a trait which won him many famous friends but which could create problems if conflicts arose between his goals and those of the celebrities.

By March 25 the five of us believed that we had taken out insurance against every possible misunderstanding. The project, we agreed, would probably take from three to five years; publication was tentatively scheduled for November 22, 1968, with the understanding that the date might be advanced by two years if I finished earlier. The provision for manuscript review seemed to eliminate the possibility of luridness. To guarantee my independence, I would accept no money from the Kennedys. Instead I would pay all my own expenses. Safeguards against commercialism were more complex, not because there were any disagreements but because we had no way of knowing how popular the completed book might be. Evan proposed that Harper limit its profit to $35,000 and provide me with an advance, after commissions, of $36,000. Author's royalties after the first printing would be contributed to the John F. Kennedy Memorial Library.

Don Congdon was unhappy about this. I was giving up a great deal—my job, my plans for other books, my income from magazine writing—and it was obvious, even then, that my outlay for this new project would come to more than $36,000. Accordingly, the memorandum provided that I would receive royalties from a British edition and foreign translations, if any; one-quarter of any book club or paperback money; and, should there be any magazine serialization, the proceeds from that. The clause covering this specified that magazine rights "may be disposed of by William Manchester, with the approval of Mrs. John F. Kennedy and Robert F. Kennedy, though it is not the intention to prevent the sale of serial option rights to a responsible publisher." Don was still pensive—as a literary agent he thought that the reading public's interest in President Kennedy might have waned by the time I finished the book—but I told him I didn't want to bargain over a national tragedy, and he returned to New York.

On Wednesday, March 25, 1964, Bob and I signed seven copies of the memorandum. I asked for one of them but didn't get it; later a Xerox copy was mailed to me. Thursday morning Jackie and Bob flew to Sun Valley, Idaho, on a skiing vacation, and at 3 P.M. the Attorney General's office announced the project to reporters. "Because versions of what occurred November 20–25 already have appeared and because it is understood other articles and books are in the course of being prepared for later publication," the announcement read, "these arrangements have been made with Mr. Manchester in the interest of historical accuracy and to prevent distortion and sensationalism."

Friday Don received a telegram:

LOOK MAGAZINE WISHES TO DISCUSS POSSIBLE TERMS FOR WIL-
LIAM MANCHESTER BOOK ON THE ASSASSINATION OF PRESIDENT
KENNEDY. PLEASE TELEPHONE DAN MICH AT MU-9-0300 AS
SOON AS POSSIBLE. MIKE LAND BOOK EDITOR LOOK

Don quite properly replied that *Look* was premature. There was no need for him to consult me about the offer, and besides, I was too busy. I had leased an apartment at 800 Fourth Street SW in the capital and was commuting to New England weekends while signing up a house in Washington's Cleveland Park for my family. Meanwhile I had begun my research. My first two calls were on Bill Moyers at the White House and Chief Justice Earl Warren. It was essential that the new President, whose confidence Moyers enjoyed, know what I proposed to do. It was equally important that the presidential commission which the Chief Judge headed understand the nature of my inquiry. Warren recognized that while the lines of the two investigations might occasionally intersect, they were very different. The commission was conducting an inquiry into a crime. I was exploring the full sweep of events in late November 1963. They were focusing upon the assassin of a President, I upon the Presidency itself.

During the months which followed I approached every person who might shed light on those autumn days. I retraced President Kennedy's last journey from Andrews Field in Maryland to San Antonio, Kelley Field, Houston, Carswell Air Force Base, Fort Worth, Love Field, Dealey Plaza, Parkland Hospital, back to Love and back to Andrews, over the ambulance route to Bethesda Naval Hospital and then to the White House, the great rotunda of the Capitol, St. Matthew's Cathedral, and Arlington. Some evenings in Washington I worked in the Warren Commission offices on Maryland Avenue. In Texas I went over every motorcade route, searching for men and women who had been spectators. In Dallas I walked from Love Field to the famous overpass, looking for potential sniper's nests as well. Every scene which I would describe in the book was visited: the rooms in the White House, Bob Kennedy's home at Hickory Hill, Brooks Medical Center, the presidential hotel suites in Houston and Fort Worth, the Houston Coliseum and ballroom, the Paine garage and bedroom where Lee Harvey Oswald stayed, Marguerite Oswald's house, her son's tiny room in Dallas, Parkland's Major Surgery and Minor Surgery areas, Bethesda's seventeenth-floor suite and basement morgue, the pavements of Washington, the pews of St. Matthew's.

Jim Swindal, the pilot of Air Force One, led me back and forth through the compartments of the presidential aircraft. I crawled over the roof of the Texas School Book Depository and sat in Oswald's sixth-floor perch. I rode his Dallas bus, watch in hand. Before taxi driver Bill Whaley died in Dallas he picked me up at the spot where he had picked up Oswald, drove me over the same route in the same taxi at the same speed, and dropped me off at the same curb. I stood where Officer J. D. Tippit died. I darted over the last lap of Oswald's flight to the Texas Theater. In Dallas police headquarters I sat where the assassin had sat, rode down in the same elevator accompanied by Dallas patrolmen, and took notes in the headquarters garage while standing where

Oswald was killed. With a Secret Service agent and Dallas eyewit-
nesses as my guides, I went over the stretch of Elm Street where the
President was shot. I watched the so-called Zapruder film of the assassination seventy times and then went over it frame by frame. In Washington, Hyannisport, and elsewhere I studied each relevant office, embassy, and home—over a hundred of them. I even had the damaged
Dallas-to-Bethesda coffin uncrated for inspection. And I interviewed
Jacqueline Bouvier Kennedy, hour after hour, with a tape recorder in
her Georgetown home on N Street.

"Mr. *Man*chester!" she said in that inimitable, breathy voice as she
stepped into the living room, closed the sliding doors behind her with a
sweeping movement, and bowed slightly from the waist. It was a few
minutes before noon on April 7, 1964, the date of our first meeting.
She was wearing a black jersey and yellow stretch pants, she was beaming at me, and I thought how, at thirty-four, with her camellia beauty,
she might have been taken for a woman in her mid-twenties. My first
impression—and it never changed—was that I was in the presence of a
very great tragic actress. I mean that in the finest sense of the word.
There was a weekend in American history when we needed to be
united in our sadness by the superb example of a bereaved First Lady,
and Jacqueline Kennedy—unlike Eleanor Roosevelt, a more extraordinary woman in other ways—provided us with an unforgettable performance as the nation's heroine. One reason for this triumph was that
her instincts were completely feminine. If she met your plane at the
Hyannis airport, she automatically handed you the keys to her convertible. Men drive, women are driven: that was the logic of things to her,
and it is impossible to think of her burning a bra or denouncing romantic love as counterrevolutionary.

Before a taping session four weeks after we had met, she asked me,
"Are you just going to put down all the facts, who ate what for breakfast and all that, or are you going to put yourself in the book, too?" I replied that I didn't see how I could very well keep myself out of it.
"*Good,*" she said emphatically. And so, for better or for worse, I was to
be there. After the book appeared, Jerzy Kosinski told me that he
thought its greatest value was its duality: the way it described events
and, simultaneously, how people responded to them. Of the many
words which the book provoked, that was the most perceptive comment
I heard. Its implications explain why writing it was so great a strain.

The research was also difficult—about half the people I interviewed displayed deep emotional distress while trying to answer my

questions—though none of the other sessions were as affecting as those with Jackie. Future historians may be puzzled by odd clunking noises on the tapes. They were ice cubes. The only way we could get through those long evenings was with the aid of great containers of daiquiris. (Bobby wouldn't drink while being interviewed. His replies are abrupt, often monosyllabic—and much less responsive.) There are also frequent sounds of matches being struck. Before our first taping I had carefully put the Wollensak recorder where I would see it and she wouldn't. I didn't want her to worry about the machine. Also, I had to be sure that the little light on it was winking, that the reels were turning, that all this wasn't being lost. It was a good plan. Its defect was revealed to me when she took the wrong chair. Then the only way I could check the light was by hunching up. It was an odd movement; I needed an excuse for it. A cigarette box on a low table provided one. Before that evening I hadn't smoked for two years. At the end of it I was puffing away, and eight more years would pass before I could quit again.

Early in our acquaintance she made plain her feelings about another writer, Jim Bishop. His style, his taste, his standards, and his personality were, I gathered, all abominations to her. I didn't know Bishop, and, though I had once read a book by him, I had forgotten most of it. She told me not to bother looking it up. The important thing, she said, was that I had been asked to write a book about the assassination, while he quite definitely had not. She explained that he had continued to try securing her cooperation, and that of other members of the family and their friends, for a book which would be called *The Day Kennedy Was Shot*. He wouldn't get it, she said emphatically; by choosing me she had, so to speak, cut him off at the pass. From time to time she would express curiosity about whether or not he was still going ahead.

That fall, after she had moved to 1040 Fifth Avenue in New York, she learned that she had not, in fact, discouraged him, and on September 17, 1964, she wrote him, appealing to him to abandon his plans. She said in part:

> As you know—it was my fear as long ago as December—that all sorts of different and never ending, conflicting, and sometimes sensational things would be written about President Kennedy's death.
> So I hired William Manchester—to protect President Kennedy and the truth. He was to interrogate everyone who had any connection with those days—and if I decide the book should never be

published—then Mr. Manchester will be reimbursed for his time. Or if I decide it should be known—I will decide when it should be published—sometime in the future when the pain is not so fresh. I suppose I must let it appear—for I have no right to suppress history, which people have a right to know, for reasons of private pain.

She sent me a copy of this, and I was troubled. She had not "hired" me. I had not agreed to be "reimbursed" for my time, and I certainly had not consented to permit anyone to decide whether or not my book should be published. Had Bobby raised such a possibility during our discussions, I would have withdrawn immediately. Before I could point this out to her, however, she forwarded me a copy of a second letter to Bishop. He had again refused to drop his project, and now she wrote him:

I chose Mr. Manchester because I respect his ability and because I believe him capable of detachment and historical accuracy. . . . I exercise no surveillance over what he is doing, and I do not plan to. He will present his finished manuscript and it will be published with no censorship from myself or from anyone else. I have too much respect for history to tamper with the results of his research. . . . I have no wish to decide who writes history. Many people will write of last November for years—but the serious ones will wait until after Mr. Manchester's book appears. This book will be the one that historians will respect. . . . What I am dedicated to is the accurate history of those days and that will come from Mr. Manchester.

After that I felt easier, naively believing that all possibility of conflict between us was past. Actually the Bishop factor had complicated my work by introducing a new factor, speed. Friends in publishing told me that he was plunging ahead. I came to accept it as part of my mandate that I must beat him to the bookstores. On January 12, 1965, when I dined at La Caravelle on Manhattan's West Side with Bobby, we talked of that. I assured him that I would be finished well before the five years we had originally envisaged, and said that I might even be ready within three years. Meantime it had occurred to me that our original plan, for publication in 1968, could be a trap for Bob. I explained. That would be a presidential election year. If the book appeared on November 22, the prepublication excerpts in magazines would come out during the campaign. His political plans were then uncertain, but if he were running on the national ticket, and it was conceivable, the book might be construed as a plea for sympathy. So he, too, might have good reason for wanting it out earlier. He agreed. As we left matters that evening, I undertook to write a strong foreword assuming full responsibility for the text, while he in turn promised that either he or his agents would promptly read the completed manuscript for the purposes of approval.

The year 1965 was grueling for me. First in Washington and then, that autumn, back at my home in Middletown, I wrote fourteen or fifteen hours a day, seven days a week. Arthur Schlesinger, a friend as well as a colleague, told mutual friends that he was afraid I might be on the verge of a breakdown. And so I was. On November 26 I was admitted to a Connecticut hospital with nervous exhaustion. When I regained my feet after ten days and encountered Sander Vanocur at a cocktail party, he told me that rumors about my condition were "all over Washington," and that, according to one story, I had lapsed into catatonic schizophrenia. Sandy wanted me to appear at the National Press Club with him so that reporters could see for themselves that it wasn't true. I declined. I felt I had to get back to the book. Finishing it had become an obsession with me. By early February I had a complete draft, and on March 8 I wrote Jackie, Bob, Don, and Evan Thomas at Harper's that my secretary was typing the fair copy. Jackie replied March 14:

Dear Bill,
  I was very touched to receive your letter and am so glad for you that the book is finished. I know and appreciate all you went through in writing it. After Bob Kennedy and Evan Thomas have gone over the manuscript, I want you to know that I will read it too, whenever they think I should. Thank you, Bill, for all you did.

  Affectionately,
  JACKIE

Soon thereafter Evan Thomas, who had been conferring with Bobby, informed me that she wouldn't be reading it at all, because that would only reawaken agonizing memories for her. For the same reason, Bob wouldn't read it either. Instead he was delegating his and Jackie's right of approval to Ed Guthman, who had left the Justice Department to become National Editor of the *Los Angeles Times,* and John Seigenthaler, the blond, tough editor of the *Nashville Tennessean* and Bobby's best friend. Guthman, Seigenthaler, Evan, and Don made four readers. Just in case Jackie changed her mind about going over it, I made five copies of the 1,201-page manuscript and packed them in a suitcase. On Friday, March 25, 1966, I boarded a Middletown-to-New York Trailways bus. The suitcase weighed 77 pounds. It was the only time I have had to pay an excess-baggage fee on a bus.

My first stop was at Harper's, where I left the ribbon copy. Then, after I had dropped off Don's manuscript, Evan accompanied me while I delivered the three remaining copies to Bob's Manhattan office on East Forty-fifth Street, and he and I took Angie Novello, Bob's devoted private secretary, to lunch at Le Valois. Afterward Angie and I called on Pam Turnure, Jackie's private secretary, at her Park Avenue office. Pam, Angie, and I took a cab to the Kennedy suite in the Carlyle Hotel, where we toasted the completion of the book. I remember Pam marveling at the recent reconciliation between Jackie and Arthur Schlesinger; Jackie had been very cross with him when *A Thousand Days* had been serialized in *Life* the previous year, but now his book was winning awards, and she admired him again. At that point I had to leave to catch a 7 P.M. bus back to Middletown. Pam rode down in the elevator with me. As we passed through the lobby and out into the street, I asked her whether I should provide Jackie with one of the copies of the manuscript. She said I shouldn't, and told me to "work through Bob, who is representing Jackie."

The next morning I took my Krupp research notes out of the Wesleyan Library vault and picked up where I had left off on that project, partly out of a sense of obligation to Little, Brown, who had continued to advance me money on it while I was writing for another publisher, but also because I yearned for the change in material. Writing about the assassination had been anguish all the way. Now I was describing the Franco-Prussian War. It was fascinating. And I didn't give a damn who won it.

The weeks which followed were a euphoric time for me. I felt a sense of achievement over the task finished, the new book was going well, and I was seeing much more of my family, always my sheet anchor. Meanwhile I was reading about Jackie and Bobby in the newspapers. He was very active. At various times stories told of his marching in a Manhattan parade, delivering a speech in Mississippi, speaking to Alabama college students, campaigning for a reform candidate in New York, being cheered at the Calgary Stampede, laying a cornerstone in Ethiopia, being received by the Pope, marching in another Manhattan parade, and shooting some rapids on a raft in Idaho.

Jackie was, if anything, busier. Fully emerged from mourning now, she was photographed dancing, skiing, riding in a New Jersey hunt, cruising along the Dalmatian coast, greeting European nobility, and visiting Acapulco, the West Indies, and Spain, where, before donning a dashing Andalusian costume, she received the attentions of a hairdresser who had been flown from Madrid to Seville for the occasion. She was reported to be romantically interested in the Spanish ambassador to the Vatican. It was reported that she was not speaking to Princess Grace of Monaco. *Women's Wear Daily* reported that she had become one of the "REALGIRLS—honest, natural, open, de-contrived, de-kooked, delicious, subtle, feminine, young, modern, in love with life, knows how to have fun." Back in New York the first week in May, she encountered Richard Goodwin, formerly a Kennedy aide and now a neighbor of mine in Middletown. She told Dick that she felt "warmly" toward me, that she favored an early publication date, and that she hoped I understood why she could not read the book.

By now she and Bob had plenty of surrogates. Don and Evan read the manuscript at once, and Cass Canfield, chairman of the Harper's board, went over Evan's copy. Ed Guthman and John Seigenthaler prepared detailed memoranda on their reactions. Over an eight-week period Ethel Kennedy read the third copy I had left in Bob's Manhattan office; she forwarded her comments to John in Nashville. Dick Goodwin had borrowed my carbon of the original typescript, and at my request Evan had sent a Xerox to Arthur Schlesinger.

All spring their reactions were coming in. They were uniformly encouraging. Congdon and Seigenthaler were early enthusiasts. Guthman wrote: "It is a great job and I believe it will be a landmark in the history of the Kennedy era." Cass wrote me that the book was "a work of unusual distinction and great power. It will be well in demand long after you and I have disappeared from the scene." Evan told me that it was "the finest book I've read in twenty years here." Goodwin called it "a masterful achievement." Opening a six-page memorandum to Bobby, Evan, and me, Schlesinger wrote: "I think this is a remarkable and potentially a great book. The research, the feeling, the narrative power, the evocation of personality and atmosphere, much of the writing—all are superb. The text gets constantly better as the narrative takes over. The rendition of the flight back to Washington on AF-1, for example, is magnificent." Arthur expressed "deep confidence and admiration for the book," and then he wrote me directly:

It is an extraordinary job of synthesis and research and you are to be greatly congratulated on it. . . . I hope you can stop them from editing too much history out of the manuscript. . . . I know how you must feel to have the major agony over and yet still have to face a host of minor irritations. Let me know if I can help in any way to make the process less painful.

The readers' approval of the book's broad sweep did not mean that they were uncritical of it. Quite the contrary. These men were professionals. They would have been faithless to history if they had withheld their reservations. And they had plenty of them. This had been an easy book to overwrite. I had not always succeeded in resisting the temptations to embroider the obvious and to idealize the dead President. Schlesinger, for example, felt that John Kennedy was portrayed as too much of a "husband, father, the young prince and not the world leader and tough politician. . . . Worse, the narrative is too often interrupted by passages of sententious generalization." Similarly, another reader wrote that "It's almost as though Manchester had become so deeply involved in this tragic narrative that he could not resist turning it into a magic fairy tale. The marvelous Irish politician who became one of the world's great statesmen is almost deprived of his miraculous self; being seen as the child of Arthur and Guinevere [while] Black Jack Bouvier's daughter is somehow deprived of some of her hard-won stature by being born of elves in a fairy glade and dressed in . . . magic cloth of gold."

So I revised and rewrote. The analyses from Seigenthaler and Guthman received priority, for practical reasons; until they had approved the book in Bobby's name, it could not be scheduled for publication and I could not receive my third $12,000 from Harper's, a matter of some concern to me at the time. Had either John or Ed injected political considerations into the editing, I would have been quick to protest, but at this stage there was none of that. Here are a few of Guthman's comments to Evan, taken at random:

Page 10—First line. Question the use of the word . . . "ignorant." I think this should be checked. Largely unfamiliar or unacquainted might be better.

Page 71—22nd line. Question whether it is correct to say RFK personally supervised security for the Venezuelan trip. That should be checked.

Page 84—3rd line. What was Alger's role in Mrs. Johnson's spit shower? Should be explained or eliminated.

Page 457—Reference to Arlington marshals. They were deputy U.S. marshals from the District of Columbia. Check with Jim McShane.

Page 645—15th-16th lines. Is it correct that "like Wirtz, Udall had been a Johnson partisan. . . . ?" I thought Udall had wrapped up the Arizona delegation for Kennedy.

Page 686—Reference to Angel's four mighty Boeing engines. The plane is a Boeing but the engines are Pratt-Whitney.

Page 746-7—Question that inclusion of the unattributed notation in a diary about Humphrey. It seems gratuitous.

Page 1177—Wrong identification for Carmine Bellino. He is a certified public accountant.

Page 1186—Harold Reis has a title; first assistant attorney general in the office of legal counsel or else executive assistant to the attorney general.

I have re-read the part in which Caroline is told. I don't agree with you and John. I think the circumstances are understandable and I don't see how it can be omitted.

Altogether, Guthman and Seigenthaler pressed for over a hundred changes, virtually all of which improved the manuscript. Dick Goodwin recommended just three, and they, too, were adopted—the deletion of a comment about John Connally by Jackie, the cutting of a melodramatic passage at the end of the tenth chapter, and a new title. The working title had been *The Death of Lancer*, Lancer having been the Secret Service's code name for President Kennedy. Goodwin suggested I change it to *The Death of a President*. John and Ed preferred *Lancer* (so, it later developed, did Bobby) but I was convinced that Dick was right, Arthur agreed with me, and none of the others felt strongly enough to argue about it.

One Saturday afternoon in early May I was at a cocktail party in eastern Connecticut, talking to Douglass Cater, then a Special Assistant to President Johnson, when Goodwin came over and said to Cater, "Manchester has written a great book, but your boss and my ex-boss may not think so." I reminded Dick that we were working with a manuscript which was still in the process of change, but the memory of the exchange lingered because it was the first indication that I might have problems arising from my treatment of LBJ. I knew that Kennedy's successor was suspicious of my project; he and Marina Oswald, the assassin's widow, were the only two principals who had declined to be interviewed by me. I was also aware that my feelings toward him were less than reverential; other readers had proposed that I temper my criticism of him, and because I was striving for detachment I had responded to all these proposals. What I did not then know was that anxiety over Johnson's reaction would play a growing role in what had been, until then, a dispassionate editorial process.

The next indication of this came in copy of a memorandum written by Schlesinger. Arthur had been studying a copy of the manuscript which had been marked up by Evan Thomas. The Schlesinger memo was peppered with such remarks as "92–93: keep this paragraph—it consists of facts, not opinions;" "398: restore passage marked for deletion; it sums up a point;" "821–2: restore deletions. An essential part of the story;" "876: restore deleted passage at bottom of page. True and important;" and "1111: of course LBJ had more confidence in Rusk than Kennedy. Why delete?"

This was baffling to me, and for a significant reason. Evan was making changes in the text without my knowledge. Ordinarily the relationship between an editor and author is a privileged one. Now I began to realize—it was only a beginning; the full realization would take months—that Evan and I were not on that footing. Looking back, I can see three reasons why it was impossible for us to be so. I was a Little, Brown author. Harper's would be publishing no more books by me, and so as a practical matter there was less reason to weigh my judgments carefully. Secondly, Evan felt an obligation to defend Bobby, who *was* a Harper's author. In this instance that meant not offending a powerful and hypersensitive Democratic President who was well aware that the book had been written at the request of the Kennedys. Lastly, Evan could not help regarding Johnson himself as a potential author of his. Harper's was the traditional publisher of Democratic statesmen, just as Doubleday was the publisher of Republicans. Evan would have been insensitive indeed if he hadn't wanted to avoid alienating an incumbent Chief Executive who might otherwise appear one day on his list. The fact that I was slow to appreciate this is suggestive of obtuseness on my part, or the fatigue which followed a long book.

Much later, after the book was out, I was shown letters that Evan was then sending to Seigenthaler and Guthman, and I realized just how hard my editor had fought to eliminate anything which Johnson might resent. I had, for example, felt it necessary to note the hostility between Johnson and Kennedy aides during the flight back from

Dallas, and I thought it a historical fact that relations between Johnson and his Attorney General had been difficult at the new President's first Cabinet meeting. Evan took a different view. "Frankly, gentlemen," he wrote John and Ed on May 16, "I am deeply disturbed by some of this. It's in part, I guess, an ambition to make sure that Bob Kennedy is not hurt by association (an association which he cannot escape) with the book which is, in part, gratuitously and tastelessly insulting to Johnson, and for that matter, the memory of the late President Kennedy, while at the same time being a really considerable piece of work, one might almost say a great book."

After eleven weeks of studying suggestions from readers and reworking the text, I sat down with Evan in a Manhattan apartment at 36 East Thirty-sixth Street to go over the manuscript page by page, and it was then that I began to understand the depth of his feeling on this issue. He had conferred with Guthman in Los Angeles and Seigenthaler in Nashville; both had recommended early publication to Bobby, and all that remained, I thought, were editorial odds and ends. In fact, Evan and I were to remain in session for nearly 36 hours. Our first exchange was a signpost to what lay ahead. On page two of the manuscript I had described LBJ as a practitioner of political tergiversation. "What does tergiversation mean?" Evan asked. "Evasiveness, equivocation—running a broken field," I said. "That goes," he said, and struck it out with a pencil. I promptly rubbed out his pencil strokes with a gum arabic eraser. We eyed one another thoughtfully and turned back to the manuscript. Further on, using a metaphor to describe Johnsonian guile, I had written that "To him the shortest distance between two points was a tunnel." Evan was offended by the image. He said that it was a slur on the Presidency.

This sort of thing is negotiable between an editor and an author, and in fact these two points were later resolved amicably, with tergiversation going and the tunnel staying. A knottier problem was my description of the Vice Presidency as a weak office, and Johnson as frustrated in it. I had written of this sympathetically, pointing out that other Vice Presidents—and particularly strong, gifted men like LBJ— had felt thwarted by the job. An understanding of that was essential to a grasp of why Kennedy had taken his fatal trip to Texas. He went to patch up an intramural feud (Connally vs. Ralph Yarborough) within the state's Democratic party, a rift which Johnson had been unable to mend because, as Vice President, he lacked a political power base.

In expecting Johnson to end the Connally-Yarborough vendetta, I wrote, Kennedy was being unreasonable because he had never occupied

LBJ's barren office himself. I cited JFK's observation that "the three most overrated things in the world are the State of Texas, the FBI, and political wizardry of Lyndon Baines Johnson." (Evan, as I later learned, wrote Seigenthaler and Guthman that he was "especially unhappy" about this, that "I'd very much like to get this out, and if you agree, we will get it out.") I wrote that few Americans understood how unsubstantial the authority of a President's understudy is (Evan: "I don't much like the business about 'ersatz prestige' "), that Johnson pined for his role as Majority Leader of the Senate (Evan: "I don't like the lines about there being so little for Johnson to do, and his vitality being sapped") and that for all the talk about Air Force Two, which became important in the turmoil that accompanied the presidential party's return from Dallas, there really was no such aircraft—that the President had at his disposal a fleet of planes, one of which might or might not be made available to the Vice President on any given occasion, at the discretion of the White House staff. (Evan: "I don't at all like the business about Johnson having to apply to the President's Air Force aide for a plane on page 4. It's just somehow unnecessarily demeaning, as is the line earlier in the page about his phone number not attracting the slightest attention.")

There were other differences between author and editor. Evan had undertaken to rewrite the opening paragraphs of the book, using phrases which were not characteristic of me. For example, he had declared that the Johnsons planned to entertain the Kennedys at their ranch with Thanksgiving turkey "and all the fixin's," which I considered unacceptable. However, it would be wrong to suggest that we were at loggerheads during all, or most, of our session. For the most part we were dealing with the comments of Guthman and Seigenthaler, and I left New York believing that I had resolved all of their objections. I was wrong. Evan was still distressed. He was convinced that publication of the book would put Bob Kennedy in an impossible position because Bobby had authorized it; that Johnson, offended, might make things difficult for Bob at the 1968 Democratic convention. After reflection he called Bobby and said so. Bob then instructed Seigenthaler and Guthman to make a fresh, complete review of the manuscript.

At the end of June, John, Ed, and Evan met in Washington's Jefferson Hotel for what they called a "marathon editing session." On July 9 Evan flew to Nashville and Los Angeles for final checks with them. I accepted the last of their recommendations during a conference call with Evan and John on July 14. At last, after sixteen weeks of revision, we had an approved text. Speaking for Bob and Jackie, Seigenthaler declared toward the end of the call that the revised manuscript was acceptable. It could be submitted now to magazines for possible serialization, he said, and published by Harper's in January. Evan commented that he thought this verbal sanction was enough, but I, acting on Don Congdon's advice, replied that it wasn't. Bobby and I had signed a memorandum of understanding. Any modification of it, I said, should be in writing. Seigenthaler agreed; he assured me that a letter from Bob amending our agreement would be mailed to me promptly.

That was a Thursday. Until then I had scrupulously refrained from communicating with the Kennedys during the period of revision, feeling that protocol should be rigidly observed until the editorial process was complete, but that Sunday I wrote Bob and Jackie, expressing my relief that it was all over and spelling out my understanding of where we were. Seigenthaler phoned me at 1 A.M. the following morning to say that the amending letter would be delayed; Joe Kennedy had just suffered a heart attack in Hyannisport, and Bob was rushing to his side. John reaffirmed the approval of the manuscript, however, and urged me to proceed with magazine submissions. Accordingly, Don sent Thermofaxes of the text to six editorial offices later that day. Each copy bore heavily inked deletions marked "JS" and "EG" for Seigenthaler and Guthman, and each was accompanied by a letter from Don, asking editors to treat it with discretion. Bids were due at 5 P.M. July 29, 1966, eleven days later.

Each morning during the last two weeks of July I expected the mailman to bring me an envelope bearing Senator Robert F. Kennedy's frank, and day after day I was disappointed. At first I wasn't alarmed; he had always been dilatory. I would have been disturbed if I had known that Evan was urging Angie to send it to him, not me—Evan explained to her that he would keep it in his safe and use it only when he thought it "appropriate"—but mercifully I was deep in the Krupp book once more. Among other things, I was unaware of the intense maneuvering among magazine editors which Don's submission had triggered. The big moves were being made by *Life* and *Look*. Both were determined to get the book. *Life*'s editors had asked Teddy White, as an old Luce reporter, to approach the Kennedys in their behalf. *Look* sent its Washington correspondent, Warren Rogers, directly to Bobby. In a subsequent affidavit, Rogers swore that Bob told him I had volunteered to turn the proceeds from the book over to the Kennedy Library, that my only real profit would be from the serialization rights, and that "Manchester is entitled to get whatever he can from it." He added that

President Kennedy had "thought highly of Manchester" and that he, Bobby, took a "favorable" view toward *Look* acquiring the serialization rights. Bob also talked to Marquis Childs, who was later prepared to say under oath that Bobby had told him he wanted the book published in 1966, not 1968.

As the magazine submission entered its second week, the feeling grew in Manhattan that bidding was going to be high. Evan thought that about $150,000 would win it, but he wasn't in the magazine business, and this really had nothing to do with him; Harper's role was limited to publication of the book in Canada and the United States. For my part, I was growing anxious as the mailman continued to show up empty-handed. When the morning of July 29 arrived and I still hadn't heard from Bob, I telephoned Hickory Hill. He apologized, and before noon this telegram arrived from him:

SHOULD ANY INQUIRIES ARISE RE THE MANUSCRIPT OF YOUR BOOK I WOULD LIKE TO STATE THE FOLLOWING:

WHILE I HAVE NOT READ WILLIAM MANCHESTER'S AC-COUNT OF THE DEATH OF PRESIDENT KENNEDY, I KNOW OF THE PRESIDENT'S RESPECT FOR MR. MANCHESTER AS AN HISTORIAN AND A REPORTER. I UNDERSTAND OTHERS HAVE PLANS TO PUBLISH BOOKS REGARDING THE EVENTS OF NOVEMBER 22, 1963. AS THIS IS GOING TO BE THE SUBJECT MATTER OF A BOOK AND SINCE MR. MANCHESTER IN HIS RESEARCH HAD ACCESS TO MORE INFORMATION AND SOURCES THAN ANY OTHER WRITER, MEMBERS OF THE KENNEDY FAMILY WILL PLACE NO OBSTACLE IN THE WAY OF PUBLICATION OF HIS WORK.

HOWEVER, IF MR. MANCHESTER'S ACCOUNT IS PUBLISHED IN SEGMENTS OR EXCERPTS, I WOULD EXPECT THAT INCIDENTS WOULD NOT BE TAKEN OUT OF CONTEXT OR SUMMARIZED IN ANY WAY WHICH MIGHT DISTORT THE FACTS OF OR THE EVENTS RELATING TO PRESIDENT KENNEDY'S DEATH.

ROBERT F. KENNEDY

I wired Don: LONG AWAITED RFK TELEGRAM OF RELEASE HAS ARRIVED AND IS PERFECT IN EVERY RESPECT. Later in the day I learned from Angie Novello that a special delivery letter, identically worded and signed by Bobby, was on its way to Harper's. By then the magazine bids were in, and at 5:15 P.M. Don called me with the details. The top two offers were astounding. *Look* was prepared to pay $405,000 for world rights and *Life* $500,000. However, there was more to it than that. As I was learning, nothing about the publication of *The Death of a President* was going to be simple. Knowing that Jackie and Bob would be concerned about the possibility of sensationalism, I had asked for absolute control over pictures, layouts, advertising, and even the captions that accompanied the serialization. *Look* was willing to grant me that; *Life* was reluctant. Don and I discussed this awhile and then decided to give each of the top two magazines twenty-four hours to reconsider its position.

After we hung up, I returned to my typewriter. I was up to the Krupps' role in the First World War, which seemed more real to me than the conversation I had just held. To me, $50,000 was a lot of money, but $500,000 was simply preposterous. It did not remain so. After an hour of writing about Big Berthas, the 420-mm. Krupp howitzers which had pulverized Liége and Verdun, I cleaned off my desk with the pleasant realization that I had good news for my wife—that a project from which I had not expected to make much money would, under the terms of my memorandum of understanding with Bobby, make me financially independent. First, however, I had to telephone Bob.

That afternoon he had flown to Hyannisport for the weekend, and I reached him there. He was uneasy over the fact that *Life* had submitted the larger bid. "If you pick *Look* you don't have to check with me," he told me, "but if it's *Life* I want to talk about it." As things turned out, there was no contest between them. Late the following afternoon Don phoned to say that the editors of *Look* not only consented to give me editorial control; they had now raised its offer higher than *Life's*, to $665,000. I immediately called Hyannisport to tell Bob that the bidding was closed and *Look* had won. "Great!" he said; "isn't that a record?" I replied that I didn't know (actually it was), and then he said with satisfaction, "*Look* has been so nice to the family and Henry Luce has been such a bastard."

I spent Sunday, the next day, packing suitcases and strapping them in a luggage rack on the top of our Ford station wagon. We had rented a Maine camp on the Belgrade Lakes for the month of August. It would be our first vacation in four years. We planned to leave early Tuesday morning, which gave us a day to get ready. After that, I thought, I would be inaccessible until Labor Day. What I didn't know, or had forgotten, was that the Maine camp had a telephone.

Evan Thomas had been less pleased with the final text than the rest of us, and on July 18, four days after the conference call in which it was approved, he had written John and Ed that he continued to be unhappy over the treatment of Lyndon Johnson. I was unaware that on July 28, the day before the magazine bids were due, he had telegraphed Bob in an unsuccessful attempt to arrange an appointment for discussion of this. Nevertheless, I knew that his protective attitude toward LBJ was undiminished. Late in July he had sent me a note reaffirming his feeling of "responsibility since there is so much concern about any undertone of disrespect, or whatnot, for Johnson."

Disrespect, or whatnot, seemed irrelevant now that we had an approved manuscript. What I failed to realize was that the political issue was a potential threat to the entire book. Given the tremendous publicity which attended all Kennedy activities, and given the huge sum that *Look* was paying, *The Death of a President* was bound to become big news soon. President Johnson was at the crest of his power. A great many people in the Washington community were going to be extremely interested in my treatment of him. If the Kennedys, the author, Harper's, and *Look* maintained a solid front, political pressures could be successfully resisted. Should the front waver, however, those pressures could become a real menace. Evan was already wobbly. Now, for reasons which had nothing to do with politics, he was about to be joined by an important companion.

Monday afternoon, returning home from some last-minute, pre-vacation errands, I found a note to call Don. Calling him, I learned that Evan had received an anguished call from Bobby. Calling Evan, I was told the source of that anguish. Jackie, notified about the sale of serial rights to *Look*, was perturbed, apparently because the money was not going to the Kennedy Library. I was bewildered. I had, of course, been writing to her, and I had assumed in any event that since Bob was representing her, he must be keeping her informed about our progress. Now I discovered that neither was true—she had neither read my letters nor talked to him. She had returned from a Hawaiian vacation on July 28 to celebrate her thirty-seventh birthday at a party given by Bunny and Paul Mellon. She had been in Hyannisport during the *Look-Life* negotiations, but hadn't known about them until they were over. Evan sounded distraught. I gathered that Bobby was distraught, too. I decided to phone him in Hyannisport.

Instead I reached Ethel, who brought me up to date. The previous evening she and Bob had been expecting guests. Before the visitors arrived, he had crossed the Kennedy compound lawn to the President's house, to tell Jackie about the *Look* sale. He didn't return until the guests appeared, and since they were there, he couldn't talk, but Ethel knew that something was wrong. His face was strained and white.

After the company had left, he told her that Jackie was very upset about the serialization. Talking to me, Ethel said she was convinced that the storm had now passed. Jackie had driven Bob to the Hyannis airport in the morning, and they had talked in the car while awaiting the plane. Then she had spent the day with Ethel and Jean Kennedy Smith, the President's sister, who had calmed her down. I asked whether it was the $665,000 figure which had distressed her. No, Ethel answered; she had been disturbed because she hadn't understood what the *Look* serialization was all about; now that it had been explained to her, and she understood, the crisis was over. Ethel stressed that giving me permission to publish had been a family decision, that Bob had been acting as the head of the family, not as an individual—that he fully understood the significance of the telegram he had sent me and the special delivery letter to Harper's. She added that she herself had read the manuscript, which I knew, and that she thought it fine.

Yet I wasn't altogether reassured. I still wanted to talk to Bobby, who was now in Washington, so I called his secretary. Angie explained that he was in a committee meeting. She said she could pass him a note telling him of my anxiety and call me back, which she presently did. Bob had written on the back of the note, "Tell Bill I always keep my word and mean to in this case." I felt a little better, but only a little. That evening I wrote him that "the time for intermediaries has passed. Though invaluable at times, they have one weakness. The chain may lead to unintentional distortion. Therefore I suggest we adopt the following procedure. If any question arises regarding the understanding between us, let it be resolved by direct communication. I call you or you call me."

Tuesday I drove my family to Maine, and all the way to the Belgrade Lakes I wondered what had gone wrong. In the months to come, as the controversy grew, an increasing number of people would join my speculation. The obvious explanation was that Jackie must be objecting to the tone or content of my book. But during most of the ensuing uproar she hadn't even seen it. (The ultimate irony was that when she did read it, she liked it.) My first guess was that she recoiled from the idea of magazine serialization. That was right as far as it went, but it didn't reach the heart of the problem. Eventually I was to conclude that she didn't really want any book, that at most she would accept only a dull, obscure volume. ("I thought," she would tell me in September, "that it would be bound in black and put away on dark library shelves.") Three years earlier she had shuddered from the prospect of the Bishop book. I had been called in to stop Bishop. Now she was determined to stop me.

Long afterward, when I grasped this, I thought it understandable. Knowing the horror she had been through, one could only sympathize. But she was hardly being realistic. The book was now finished. I had scrupulously observed the guidelines established by Bobby, who had acted as her representative, with her consent. The manuscript had been approved and Harper's had set it in type—I was reading galleys in Maine. *Look*'s typesetters were doing the same thing, while other *Look* men were selling foreign serial rights to periodical publishers in forty-two countries. Blowing the whistle now would touch off lawsuits all over the world. Moreover, the suitors would have collected. Commitments had been made, contracts were being signed, obligations incurred. And the first commitment had been made to me, in writing, by Bobby, on her instructions. She was always distrustful of lawyers. Raising legal questions incensed her. But there was another way of putting it. At her request I had spent two and a half years researching, writing, and revising a manuscript. Surely I was now entitled to see it published.

Except on one occasion, and then only half-heartedly, the issue of outright suppression was never joined, because that level of candor was never reached. Instead, objections were raised about this or that aspect of publication, until, when all other approaches had failed, attempts were made to mutilate the text so that it would become unreadable. And all these dreary maneuvers had their origins in August 1966, when I was camped on a Maine lake and air transport was crippled by a machinists' strike.

My Maine phone rang for the first time on our second day there, Wednesday, August 3. The caller was Homer Bigart of the *New York Times*, an old friend. He had heard about the *Look* sale and was writing a story for tomorrow's paper. His piece appeared Thursday, and Friday another ring awoke me. It was Evan. He, too, had heard from Homer, and the conversation had troubled him. He had wired Bob:

HOMER BIGART OF TIMES IS ON TO BOOK AND SERIAL STORY AND HAS GATHERED MANY FACTS INCLUDING PRICE OF SALE. WE HAVE BEEN EVASIVE IN OUR REPLIES REGARDING MONEY. UNDER EXISTING TERMS WE EXPECT BOOK TO BE LARGEST SINGLE CONTRIBUTOR TO LIBRARY AND ARE DELIGHTED WITH THAT PROSPECT. IN THE ABSENCE OF ANY FURTHER DISCUSSION WE MUST ASSUME THAT ORIGINAL SIGNED AGREEMENT PREVAILS.

Bobby hadn't liked that. Since the weekend, as I later learned, he had been subjected to further reactions from his sister-in-law. Now, he had felt, Evan was needling him. He had telegraphed him a startling reply:

RE TELEGRAM WHERE YOU SAY QUOTE IN ABSENCE OF ANY IN-
STRUCTIONS SIGNED AGREEMENT PREVAILS UNQUOTE. AGREE,
AND THAT PROVIDES THAT MRS. KENNEDY AND I MUST GIVE
PERMISSION FOR PUBLICATION OF BOOK AND THAT HAS NOT
BEEN GIVEN.

Alarmed, Evan had telephoned Bob, who had said he didn't mean that, exactly; he merely thought that the author was making too much profit from magazine rights. Evan had a compromise in mind, and he had put it in writing for Angie Novello: "I am sure we can work it out so that the *Look* money goes directly to the library. . . . I will be happy to make a specific proposal and to invite an accountant nominated by Bobby Kennedy to discuss it with me should he wish." To me he now suggested that I contribute the $665,000 to the library and accept a straight royalty on the book. How, he asked, did that appeal to me? I replied that it didn't. In the first place, magazine rights were, as noted, none of Evan's affair. In the second place, Don and I had estimated—correctly, as it turned out—that book royalties would be twice as profitable as the magazine sale. The compromise would earn me twice as much money, a clear violation of the spirit of my original understanding with Bobby. I didn't spell out the third place, because I didn't want to hurt Evan needlessly. The fact was that I believed *Look* was spunkier than Harper's, and I wanted Mike Cowles, *Look's* rocklike publisher, at my side during what began to look more and more like a stormy period ahead.

That afternoon the telephone rang again, this time with a telegram for me from Evan:

SPENDING MONDAY WITH PAM TO GO OVER PASSAGES WHICH PAM
QUESTIONS. THEN SPENDING TUESDAY IN NASHVILLE WITH
SEIGENTHALER SINCE HE WANTS TO RECHECK POLITICAL PAS-
SAGES. REREADING ENTIRE MANUSCRIPT THIS WEEKEND IN
PREPARATION.

It was then that I realized that I had made a mistake in coming to this wilderness, that I should have driven to New York instead and camped in Evan's office, to restrain him. We had an approved manuscript; why was he clearing the way for further revision? "Political passages" had an ominous ring. Considering editorial directives from Pam was worse. Earlier Evan had acknowledged that Jackie's secretary was not qualified to edit a historical work. Now I reminded him in writing: "You and I agreed that once we have approval, *no* suggestion from Pam Turnure was to be even considered."

Then I called Arthur Schlesinger, who had offered his good offices should I have need of them. Bringing him up to date, I told him that I hadn't heard from Bobby since the *Look* sale, hadn't heard from Jackie since spring, and would be grateful for his advice. As it happened, Arthur was about to leave for a weekend in Hyannisport. He promised to find out what he could and call me back on Monday. He did, and like Ethel before him, he was reassuring. He had spoken to both Bob and Jackie the previous evening, he reported, and the money was not an issue with either of them. Both had been calm. To be sure, Jackie was a trifle "jittery" over the prospect of serialization, but on the whole she seemed "reconciled and tranquil."

In fact it would be a long time before any of us knew tranquillity. The story was out. Newspapermen had wind of dissension between me and the Kennedys, and they were speculating about the reason. Bigart called me that noon with an ugly report. There were rumors, he said, that Bobby was trying to suppress the book until the next election so that its appearance then could enhance his presidential prospects, and that he was having the book censored to improve his status with Johnson. The first report was never true, and the second wasn't true then. I persuaded Homer that there was no story, but it was typical of that sad summer that when Bobby heard the gossip he concluded it was an attempt by me or my publishers to blackmail him into reaffirming his endorsement of early publication.

Those were difficult days for Bob. Jackie was, a *Times* reporter put it, "raising hell." Her stature in the country was still such that a break with her would have been a political calamity for him. With good reason, he felt frustrated and resentful of the developing impasse. Jackie blamed him for it—the following month she told me that he was behaving "like a little boy who knows he's done wrong"—and on Wednesday, August 10, he tried to cut the knot. This was the one instance in which an attempt was made to quash the book altogether. He telegraphed Evan:

UNDER PRESENT CIRCUMSTANCES, WITH THE SITUATION
AS DIFFICULT AS IT IS, I FEEL THE BOOK ON PRESIDENT KEN-

NEDY'S DEATH SHOULD BE NEITHER PUBLISHED NOR SERIALIZED. AS YOU KNOW ONLY TOO WELL, THIS HAS BEEN A TRYING SITUATION FOR EVERYONE AND I UNDERSTAND THE PROBLEMS THIS HAS CAUSED YOU AND THE AUTHOR. IT JUST SEEMS TO ME THAT RATHER THAN STRUGGLING WITH THIS ANY LONGER WE SHOULD TAKE OUR CHANCES WITH JIM BISHOP.

Plainly this required a confrontation. Northeast was the only East Coast airline not on strike. My wife drove me to the Lewiston airport, where I took a Northeast flight to New York. There Evan and I chartered a plane for Washington. The two of us met Bobby and Seigenthaler in Bob's office on Capitol Hill. For three hours we conferred, fumed, shouted, and glared—and settled nothing. Bobby was at his most abrasive; at various times he threatened to take *Look* to court, insisted that I give more money to the library, and demanded that I stop the serialization, all the while assuring Evan that he wanted the book to be published. When I asked whether it was his wish that I alert *Look* to the possibilities of a lawsuit, he withdrew that threat. He said that his telegram and special delivery letter of July 29 were not meant to release the manuscript. I asked what they did mean, and he ignored the question. He charged that my publishers and I were "in too much of a hurry." Toward the end he remembered that *Look* had, at my request, granted me editorial control over the series. He importuned me to "shred and emasculate" each installment so that it would be unprintable. I replied that I couldn't do that, that it would be unethical. He chuckled. "Then give them to John," he said. Seigenthaler smiled weakly. Evan looked embarrassed. I sat very still. I remembered that Evan was entertaining John's suggestions for fresh changes in "political passages." As we broke up, Bob, now quieter, asked me to appeal to *Look* for cancellation of the series, or at least for postponement. In New York I asked Mike Cowles to delay it, and he agreed.

On August 24 Jackie summoned Cowles and his general counsel to Hyannisport, where they were confronted by her, Bobby, and her lawyer, Simond Rifkind. That meeting was also fruitless, or nearly so; the most Mike would concede was a reduction from seven installments to four.* Meanwhile, up at Belgrade Lakes, I was being inundated with demands for changes—111 from Seigenthaler and 77 from Pam. John's editing was no longer professional. It was frank distortion and resembled the scrawled comments Evan had made the previous spring—

* From his point of view, however, it was a substantial concession. He never received a word of thanks.

I was, for example, asked to rewrite my account of Johnson's first Cabinet meeting so that I would be depicting the relationship between him and Bobby as completely amicable. Pam, as she told me in a strained phone conversation, was reacting "as a woman." Whereas others had regarded the portrayal of JFK in my first submitted draft as too romantic, Pam felt that it was too earthy; e.g., that I shouldn't describe him as strolling around in his underwear before going to bed. She disliked my account of Jackie peering in a mirror, looking for wrinkles. And she had also marked great chunks of the text for the wastebasket. Here, as John Corry of the *Times* later observed, "the problem" lay in "Miss Turnure not being a professional editor or writer. Manchester had raised a structure, building scenes, creating moods, telling a story. It was simply too delicate a task to yank large sections of copy from the structure; it would have collapsed." Corry continued: "There were at least 25 areas in the book to which she had truly strong objections, and many of the objections could not be met by changing a word here and a word there. They demanded major revisions. Even more, they demanded that the author find a new orientation, a new approach to his work."

Evan, during all this, was tergiversating. His position with me was that he was receiving suggestions from John and Pam as a "courtesy" to the Kennedys, that he was making a sincere effort to "minimize the intense friction" that was developing, and that he had no doubts that we were dealing with an "approved manuscript." What I didn't know was that, at the same time, he was writing Pam and Nancy Tuckerman, another of Jackie's secretaries: "I have told Manchester that while I cannot be the last word in his editing of the largely political material that I absolutely refuse to publish the book unless he pays exact attention to Pam's wishes on this other material." These two statements were irreconcilable, of course, and before the month was out he had begun to take a harder line with me, writing of one passage that although he saw nothing objectionable in it, "Pam insists, so of course it must go." I replied that "should any letter reach me from Jackie with specific suggestions, I shall naturally reply immediately," but I couldn't submit to history being blue-penciled by a private secretary.

By mid-August the friendship and mutual trust which had bound me to most advisers of Jacqueline and Robert Kennedy was rapidly vanishing.* On August 15 a note was placed in Bobby's Washington files reporting that Pam had

---

* Though my relationships with other members of the Kennedy family were unimpaired. Two admirers of the book were Edward M. Kennedy and Eunice Kennedy Shriver.

talked with Jackie and then with Evan Thomas. Passed the message that it would be unwise for her to send anything in writing to Manchester. However, Evan was to tell Manchester emphatically that she had agreed to be interviewed by him only on the basis that she should have the right to destroy the entire transcript . . . or decide what should be edited out. Manchester knew this will be breaking his agreement with her, if he does not agree to the changes she wants.

Of course, I knew no such thing, and the notion that I did was of a piece with the fantasy that I had been "hired" to write the book. Had I known of the note I would have said so, but that would have solved nothing; looking back through the correspondence of those months, including memoranda of which I was then unaware, I realize that I had now come to be regarded as a temperamental writer who needed humoring. That was probably the explanation for a call I received August 21 from Dick Goodwin. Dick was phoning from Martha's Vineyard. He said that Jackie had talked to him twice about me, that she was distressed about the three-hour scene in Bobby's office, and that she wanted to reach me by phone and say so. I told him that I would be delighted to hear from her. The call never came.

Goodwin, however, was destined to play a key role in the controversy. In many ways his designation as a literary broker made sense to the Kennedy advisers. His Middletown home and mine were a short walk from one another. Jackie trusted him. His dedication to Bobby's ambitions for national office was absolute, and he had no love for *Look*, which had curtly rejected a piece he had written on Vietnam the previous spring. Of course, he was unfamiliar with recent developments in the struggle over the book he had titled, but other members of the Kennedy team quickly brought him up-to-date, briefing him, among other things, on their new disenchantment with me. That week Seigenthaler wrote Goodwin: "Since you are now the 'reader,' I think I should alert you to the difficulties I had in dealing with Bill Manchester. He is a great writer, but in my opinion he has very bad judgment and is extremely sensitive when faced with the prospect of editing his work."

Like so much else that was being passed back and forth, I was ignorant of that letter's existence. All I knew, from my talks with Dick in that last week of August, was that the President's widow seemed to be about to take a personal role in resolving the differences which had arisen, and I wrote Evan: "Please, for the time being, don't write any letters about the book or talk to anyone about it. I'm convinced Jackie and I can work this out."

On Thursday, September 1, the same day that *Look* took a full-page ad in the *New York Times* to announce the forthcoming serialization and print my foreword to the book, I reloaded vacation gear atop the Ford station wagon, closed the Maine camp of which I had seen so little, and headed south toward Connecticut. Goodwin having left the Vineyard that same morning, we were following the same course. That would not be true for long.

Richard Naradof Goodwin, summa cum laude graduate of Harvard Law School and a former law clerk to Felix Frankfurter, forsook a brilliant legal career to follow the star of John F. Kennedy, and since Dallas his hopes for further public service had depended upon the fortunes of Robert Kennedy. In pursuit of his goals, Goodwin's mind was his greatest asset. His appearance and his brusque manner were liabilities. Someone had described him as looking like an Italian reporter with a hangover. Jackie once told me that he always reminded her of a radical agitator shaking his fist at the sky and shouting, "Sacco and Vanzetti!" Hirsute, craggy-faced, tireless, coarse, and shrewd, Dick was a harsh figure in any setting, but he was as convinced as I was that any issues between Jackie and me could be easily settled.

He and I spent Friday morning together going over my carbon of the manuscript. He had found nothing objectionable in it in April, nor did he now. He said he shared a suspicion of mine: that overzealous go-betweens, eager to excise anything which Bobby and Jackie might conceivably regard as controversial, had marked for cutting passages that wouldn't really bother any member of the family. After a sandwich in a downtown Middletown restaurant, we phoned Jackie, who said she would set aside the following Wednesday for us. That evening I wrote her:

> Dick Goodwin and I had breakfast and lunch together today, and in between, I think, we cleared up a great many misunderstandings. I'll be on my way to the compound as soon as I've finished [a] meeting at Harper's. It is scheduled to begin at 3:30 P.M. Tuesday. I don't know when it will be over, but the instant we adjourn I'll head for the Cape, bringing with me a comb, a toothbrush, and all the fidelity and good will in the world.

The Tuesday meeting ran overlong, necessitating an overnight stay in New York. Held in Harper's Manhattan boardroom, it was attended by Evan, Cass Canfield, Don Congdon, me, and Harriet Pilpel, a lawyer representing Harper's. The conference had been called at my request; I felt a growing concern over Evan's behavior. He had written an unfortunate letter to a foreign publisher who was interested in the manuscript ("At the present time there is tremendous confusion as to whether or not the book is or is not actually released by the Kennedy family. . . ."), had given my Maine phone number to reporters, had discussed the controversy with members of the press himself, and had sent galleys to political figures who had heard that they were mentioned in the book, wanted to know what had been said about them, and demanded revisions when they found out. Don and I were grim, Cass and the lawyer propitiary, Evan subdued. Afterward I wrote Evan a confirming letter noting that we had all agreed that

> Newspapermen contacting Harper's . . . are to be told that the author will have no statements to make on this subject until the book is published. No copies of manuscripts of the book and no sets of galleys will be sent to anyone outside Harper's without written approval from the author. Any questions about first serial rights or foreign publication should be referred to the author's agent without comment.

Wednesday morning Goodwin and I breakfasted at New York's Stanhope Hotel and went over ground rules for the coming meeting on the Cape. During our Friday phone conversation Jackie had agreed that there would be no lawyers present, no other Kennedys, and, above all, "no emotionalism." Dick assured me that she was determined to be reasonable. But I wanted something more to come out of the trip, nothing less than an end, or the promise of an end, to the whole imbroglio. It would be pointless, I said, to spend a pleasant day together if we resolved nothing. We needed an answer which would be acceptable to everyone, and I believed I knew a way to find one. What bothered Jackie, as far as I could tell then, was the tremendous wave of publicity which would accompany the appearance on the newsstands of each issue in *Look*'s serialization. Mike Cowles having reduced the number of excerpts to four, he was adamantly opposed to any further shrinkage. However, there was a chance that I might be able to persuade him to run two of the installments *after* the book had been published, when they would lack any news value. *Look* would thereby lose its exclusivity for those two, and the serialization would be worth less to Mike, but I was prepared to take a substantial cut in the price he was paying me.

Dick was enthusiastic. At the very least, he said, it would be a basis for negotiation. After the events of the past month I was more skeptical. As we rode to La Guardia I had a pleasant sense of anticipation—my relationship with Jackie had always been excellent—but I cautioned Dick that we had to come back with something, that the proposal of no serialization whatever would be unacceptable to *Look* and could not, therefore, be a starting point for any productive discussion. It is my recollection that he agreed.

The *Caroline* carried us to Hyannis. It was to be my last ride on that lovely plane, and the weather was heavily handsome, as September days on the Cape can be. Jackie was waving to us as we came down the ramp. I remember that she was wearing sunglasses and a green mini-skirt; she looked stunning. In the compound we drank iced tea on the porch of President Kennedy's house. Then Dick strolled off in the direction of Squaw Island and Jackie and I changed to bathing suits. I sat on the back of a towing boat with young John on my lap while she waterskied behind—Jackie at her most acrobatic, at one point holding the tow rope with one foot and zipping along with the other foot on a single ski. After she had tired of this, I dove in, and the two of us struck out for shore. Wearing flippers, she rapidly left me far behind. Wallowing and out of breath, I momentarily wondered whether I would make it. I remember thinking: What if I drowned? Would that be good for the book or bad for the book?

Back on the porch, with the three of us seated at a luncheon table in dry clothes, I slowly realized that nothing good for the book could possibly come out of this meeting. The atmosphere was completely unrealistic. My breakfast proposal was never presented because coherent discussion was impossible. Jackie was hostile toward *Look*, bitter about Cowles, and scornful of all books on President Kennedy, including Schlesinger's. Repeatedly she expressed affection for Goodwin and me, saying "It's us against them," and, to me, "Your whole life proves you to be a man of honor." She was going to fight, she said savagely, and she was going to win: "Anybody who is against me will look like a rat unless I run off with Eddie Fisher."

Friday she had promised that there would be no emotionalism, but whenever Dick or I tried to review the facts we were answered by tears, grimaces, and whispery cries of *"Jesus Christ!"* She digressed into a long, rambling account of the President's monument in Arlington and her anguish over the fact that public awareness of the tragedy seemed undiminished. Once she said to me, "I'll say that your foreword as it appeared in the *Times* is a lie, because I'll read every word of the book.

Everybody's telling me not to read it. I'm a lot tougher than they think." I forebode pointing out that the foreword had not mentioned the fact that she had not read the book. In her present mood, it was clear, any open disagreement with her would have purposelessly ruptured the thin membrane of civility.

Twice she fled into the house to compose herself, and returned drying her eyes with Kleenex. Early in the discussion Goodwin had attempted an objective discussion of background events, but he abandoned it: these disappearances were unnerving for both him and me. During the first of them he and I silently rolled our eyes at each other. During the second I said, "I don't know what to do." He said, "I don't either. I hadn't counted on this irrationalism." After her second reappearance it was obvious that the outbursts had affected him. To Jackie's delight, he abruptly declared that in his opinion there was no approved version of the manuscript, that Bobby's telegram granting approval had been misunderstood, and that if I pointed this out to Cowles, he would have to withdraw, because his case would be too weak. If Cowles persisted in publishing, he said, I should seek an injunction. Cowles would have to sue me, and I would be backed by Jackie. She clapped her hands together elatedly and said again, "It's us against them!"

I despaired, and my despair deepened when Jackie said that she eagerly looked forward to early publication of the book by Harper's and was delighted that it had been designated a major selection of the Book-of-the-Month Club. As gently as possible I pointed to what seemed to be a basic inconsistency. How could the manuscript be approved for Harper's but unapproved for *Look*? The circumstances were entirely different, Goodwin said. *Look* published journalism; Harper's, literature. I was no lawyer, but this seemed to me to be an extraordinarily tenuous legal position. It would put me, I said, in an impossible position. I had reached a contractual agreement with *Look* based on a written authorization from Robert F. Kennedy, acting on behalf of the Kennedy family. Dick shook his head. I had no obligation to Cowles, he said: "*Look* has no feelings. They are only interested in selling magazines. Of course, I would do the same if I were a magazine editor."

At that point I decided that I had to leave. Northeast flight 772 was departing from Hyannis in twenty minutes; I asked them to drive me to the airport. Dick stayed at the wheel while Jackie accompanied me into the terminal. To my dismay I saw that at least twenty people were waiting at the airline counter, but I had forgotten who my companion was; she walked straight to the head of the line, where the clerk dropped everything else to sell me a seat. At the gate she embraced me warmly. I felt like Judas. I knew that eventually she would come to think of me that way, too. But I had to do what I had to do.

In New York the following morning I formally requested a meeting with Mike Cowles. Good faith required this; Jackie had made a proposal, and however absurd it seemed to me, I felt I owed it to her to lay it before him without comment. The publisher and his lawyer received Don Congdon and me in *Look's* offices at 488 Madison Avenue. I transmitted her request that Mike not run any installments. He reaffirmed his decision to go ahead, saying, "We'll stand pat." Then, in the flattest possible voice, I raised the possibility that I might ask a court to issue an injunction against magazine serialization. Mike held a brief, whispered conference with his attorney and then turned back to me. If that should happen, he said, he would file suit against me for "at least several hundred thousand dollars." Don volunteered that he felt such a suit would be justifiable, and we left.

Heartrending as it had been, that day of anguish on the Cape provided the controversy with a sequel of comic relief. On our way to the airport I had explained that under my contract with *Look* I would have five days, upon receipt of the galleys for each installment, to alter it. Even then Jackie must have sensed that her battle against serialization might be doomed, because she asked me if—*if*—Cowles wouldn't knuckle under, would I consider suggestions from Goodwin during those five days? I agreed, and my first act, once I was back in Middletown, was to request two sets of galleys for the *Look* installments, one for me and one for Dick.

What made this entertaining was his response, or lack of it. In Hyannisport her tears had dissolved his resolve, but in the early days of his brokerage he obviously wanted nothing to do with bowdlerizing history, and so, during each five-day period, he simply absconded. This was no small feat. Disappearing in a small college town is impossible, and since I knew his wife, Sandra, his secretaries, Barbara Satton and Tania Senff, and most of his friends, his vanishing acts required considerable ingenuity. But they were successful. He couldn't be located in Connecticut, on the Vineyard, in the Stanhope, or the Plaza, or in Washington. Sandra said she was mystified; if I turned him up, she would be appreciative if I let her know where. Like Evan, Dick was now tergiversating. It was frustrating for me, but I appreciated his dilemma. In a way I was grateful; as a consequence of it, I was doing everything possible to accommodate Jackie's wishes without, at the same time, being compelled to reject impossible demands outright.

Twice in September I was out of town during the day, conferring with Harriet Pilpel over the possibilities of libel in certain passages of the manuscript, but I was never away overnight, and I tried repeatedly to educe what new suggestions, if any, Dick had for possible improvement of my text. As each batch of galleys arrived from *Look*, I would carry the duplicate set to his office and leave it there with a covering note. The first two installments reached Middletown together. He returned them to me after more than a week had passed. His recommendations were inconsequential, affecting 568 words, but that didn't matter; they were too late. On October 7, after the third installment had come to Middletown and been returned, Mike Land, *Look*'s book editor, wrote me: "As you know, Bill, under our contract you were required to submit any changes within five days after you received the galleys. We note that Mr. Goodwin's comments on part one and part two reached us ten days after the galleys were submitted, and part three reached us twelve days after submission."

Part three had brought a sharp change. Requests for token cuts were now a thing of the past; this time I was being asked to delete 2,737 words, and when the proofs of the fourth installment were returned to me—late, like all the others—there were demands for the removal of 3,177 words. By now Goodwin was back in town, and he explained what had happened. With Goodwin's set of the *Look* galleys before them, Bobby and his political advisers had held a series of strategy sessions in his New York apartment on September 30, culminating in a dinner at Twenty-One. Jackie's intervention had given them a fresh chance to ponder the probable impact of the serialization, and a majority of them decided that Evan Thomas had a point, that some passages in the book might be used against Bob if he should run, as they all assumed he eventually would, for national office. There was the description of Johnson as a man diminished by the limitations of the Vice Presidency, there were the references to discord between LBJ and RFK, and there was the portrayal of right-wing extremists in Dallas on the eve of the assassination, a characterization which might one day lose Texas votes for Kennedy. Later Corry of the *Times* wrote: "the Senator and his advisers allowed practical politics to determine what the historical record would show. They did not raise the question of truth or falsity. . . . They wanted a truly authorized history, perhaps not an inaccurate one, but one that just omitted part of the history. Perhaps the advisers were being overzealous. Perhaps they were only capricious, but certainly they were wrong."

Nonetheless, that was the line they had decided to take. Knowing that word of their meeting would inevitably reach the press, they leaked it themselves in a fashion meant to help their man. Since Bigart's August stories, the book had become front-page news. Lyndon Johnson was bound to be interested in the details. If the President became convinced that I had treated him shabbily, and that Bobby was doing everything in his power to make me temper my criticism, Bob's stock might rise in the LBJ White House. Such was the reasoning, and such is the explanation for the accounts, widely circulated that autumn, that I had savaged the President in my manuscript. Four months before *The Death of a President* was published, *Time* was reporting that it "paints, in fact, an almost unrelieved portrait of Johnson as an unfeeling and boorish man"—that it was "seriously flawed by the fact that its partisan portrayal of Lyndon Johnson is so hostile that it almost demeans the office itself." When the book finally appeared, *Time's* reviewer recalled that "During the height of his battle with the Kennedys, it was said that Manchester had depicted Lyndon Johnson as a kind of Snopesian boor in the hours immediately after the assassination. LBJ's portrait in the book is not all that uncomplimentary." (Corry commented: "Indeed it was not; it never was. *Time* had been getting its information from the wrong people.")

Ironically, the tactics of Bobby's advisers backfired. William S. White, the syndicated columnist who was a close friend of LBJ's, wrote during the prepublication uproar that since everyone knew that the book was going to "gut Johnson," and since the Kennedys had authorized it, the attacks could have been inspired only by the Kennedys. The delay in releasing the book, which was a consequence of the controversy, merely fueled such rumors. By the time it was in the bookstores and able to speak for itself, the LBJ-RFK relationship, never warm, was chillier than ever.

The big decision reached at Twenty-One, and relayed to me by Goodwin, was not to sue. The unanimous feeling was that Bobby could not be put in the position of attempting to suppress a book, and the thought of Jackie appearing in a witness box was intolerable. Besides, *Look* might still be persuaded to yield on changes. Nobody was worried about the book. They were confident that they could handle Harper's. Evan was their man, and Cass Canfield, Evan's very gray eminence, moved in Jackie's social circle. His son Michael had been married to Jackie's sister Lee, and though the marriage had ended in divorce, Cass had retained his ties to the Kennedys.

All this time I had assumed that Harper's production schedule was rolling ahead, and that the integrity of the book manuscript was safe. Nevertheless there were continuing sources of friction between Evan and me. Despite our agreement in the Harper's boardroom he could not bring himself to turn away reporters who came to him. Jimmy Breslin of the *World-Journal Tribune* appeared in Evan's outer office with a list of questions about friction between me and the Kennedys. Evan welcomed him. When the story appeared and my agent demanded an explanation, Evan replied, "When Jimmy Breslin shows up in your office, you don't just tell him to go away, rather you do the best you can to say as little as possible, as politely as possible, blaming no one for anything."

Relations between Evan and me had now deteriorated to such a point that he proposed differences between us be adjudicated by a third party. He nominated Ed Guthman. It seemed to me that a referee would serve no purpose. The book was finished; Harper's had only to publish it. Had a mediator been necessary, however, Ed would have made an admirable choice. With the exception of Seigenthaler, no man inspired greater confidence in Bobby, and from the perspective of Los Angeles he saw clearly what was happening. He wrote me:

> I can understand your feelings very vividly, and at the same time sympathize with Jackie and Bob. This is a difficult and emotional subject for all of you, and they must come to understand the depth of emotion which you have experienced and endured in these past two and a half years, just as you must allow for behavior, which, as you put it, has been something less than the consideration which President Kennedy showed you. . . . All three of you have some strong characteristics in common—integrity and sensitivity, particularly. Your integrity and pride have been wounded, probably unnecessarily.

Ed concluded: "As we have already seen, a good-sized effort is going to be made to discredit the book, and the best way that it can be blocked is by the book and the articles speaking for themselves in their own eloquence and accuracy." That was my wish, too, but the controversy had by now acquired a life of its own, and all of us seemed powerless to stifle it. Resignedly I accepted the next development—another encounter with Bobby. On the morning of Monday, October 10, Dick Goodwin and I boarded Allegheny Airlines flight 800, from Hartford to Washington, rented an Avis car at Washington National Airport, and drove to 4700 Chain Bridge Road in McLean, Virginia, where, behind an outsize rural post box, stood the lovely old mansion known as Hickory Hill.

The meeting was conceived as a reconciliation, to erase memories of the summer firestorm in Bobby's office. After the political meeting in Twenty-One, Bob had told Goodwin that he felt contrite about the August scene in his office. He wanted to restore our relationship to an amicable basis. The ostensible reason for the truce was to be a conference on speech writing—I had done a little of that during his 1964 senatorial campaign in New York; now he was contemplating a major address on academic freedom, and wanted me to draft it—but for the most part the occasion was to be a social one. Under no circumstances, Dick told me in relaying the invitation, would we so much as mention *The Death of a President*. That was, of course, an impossible promise. We could no more have avoided the book than Moses, descending Mount Sinai with his set of tablets, could have evaded a discussion of that other approved manuscript.

Ethel welcomed us and excused herself, and the three of us walked down to the pool. The weather being unseasonably warm, Bobby decided to take a dip. Dick and I sat by the poolside, he smoking a cigar and I taking notes while our wiry host splashed and talked. Whenever an awkward question was raised, he had a disconcerting way of submerging; moments later he would reappear on the far side, blowing out his cheeks and, when he had recovered his wind, changing the subject. But that didn't happen often. Most of the time, both in the pool and sitting with us afterward over Bloody Marys, he was dignified, low-keyed, and thoughtful—the Bobby the public rarely saw, the one his friends cherished and his family knew best.

Most of the time he discussed the *Look* serialization and the political problems it might create for him, since the whole country knew that the work bore the Kennedy imprimatur. I told him I thought that aspect of the manuscript of it had been grossly exaggerated—that Johnson did not come off nearly as badly as he had been told—and I reminded him that in my foreword I would say that the author alone was answerable for the text. Beyond that I could not go. The issue of expediency had nothing to do with me; if I permitted myself to be drawn into an analysis of it, I would be lost. Lacking a pool in which to immerse myself, I took refuge in protracted silences. ("Bill," Bob said at one point with a grin, "you have the vagueness of genius.")

Since he hadn't read the book, he said, it was hard for him to assess the impact of individual passages—I thought that the understatement of the afternoon—but on the advice of his readers he was dividing proposed changes into two categories. The first were frankly political. At Twenty-One the unanimous verdict of his advisers had been that *Look*'s third installment "will injure both Johnson and me," he said, "but apparently it's factually correct and a contribution to history. I'd like you to change it, but I guess you won't." I said I couldn't. He nodded, accepting it. The second category was personal changes, matters which might be considered an intrusion on Jackie's privacy. He had to insist that I make these. I replied that I would weigh each carefully, but he had to remember that some *Look* parts had already closed, and that the entire manuscript had already been screened by his designated readers, by four subordinate editors at Harper's, by Schlesinger, and by Goodwin himself—all on the outlook for breaches of good taste. He nodded again and said softly, "I know. We haven't handled this very well."

Before leaving the pool we agreed that Goodwin would mark suggestions for political changes on the galleys with squares or rectangles; personal changes would be circled. I also told Bob that during the previous month I had checked Harper's production schedule and had established a timetable for final review of the book's page proofs. Evan would send two sets to Middletown on October 25. They would be due back in New York on November 10, which would give both of us two weeks to go through the entire text for the last time. Then we walked up to the house for dinner. I remember that meal, my last at Hickory Hill, very well. The topic of the evening was evolution. Although the children attended parochial school, their mother now learned, they were not taught to take everything in the Old Testament literally. Ethel was scandalized. Adam, Eve, Noah, the Ark—they were all real to her, and she couldn't imagine what the Church was coming to, allowing Sisters to teach such heresy. All the way home to Hartford on Eastern flight 522, Dick and I marveled at Ethel's inner certitude. In the morning I dictated sixteen "personal" changes to *Look*; the editors said they would make them if they could, and as it turned out, they could and did.

All this sounds more amiable than it really was. On the surface we were outgoing and pleasant, but the disagreements of that summer had left deep scars underneath. Newspapers and newsmagazines did not help. Several times a week "informed sources" purported to divulge information from the book, often in a way calculated to offend men and women in public life. Absurd canards were floated: that Jackie had offered me $3,000,000 to suppress the book, that Dell was paying $1,000,000 for paperback rights, that a Bobby-for-President campaign would be launched on publication day. My phone rang at all hours;

total strangers appeared at my door to discuss their theories of the assassination.

In such an atmosphere I found it impossible to write. This was a real problem, far graver than most laymen would suppose. "Writing does for H. L. Mencken what giving milk does for a cow," said Mencken, and all natural writers know what he meant. I needed to resume work on my Krupp manuscript, so I decided that after *The Death of a President* galleys had been locked up in mid-November, I would spend a month in London. I had friends in England, there was Krupp research material there; the plan seemed sensible. I reserved a cabin-class stateroom on the *Queen Mary* for Wednesday, November 16. The night before I sailed my wife and I would stay in the *Look* suite at the Berkshire Hotel. Only a handful of friends and associates knew of my plans. One of them was Evan Thomas.

It says much about the fog of suspicion which had enveloped all of us in the controversy that I said nothing of this to Goodwin, and it says more that Dick didn't tell me that he himself would spend late October and early November—when he was supposed to be reviewing the book's page proofs—at a cultural conference in Europe. Certainly there was no mention of it on the evening of October 18, when he phoned me from New York and put Bobby on the line. Bob was troubled. He wanted me to come to his Manhattan apartment and discuss drastic new revisions in the *Look* proofs. *Look,* he had heard, was sensationalizing everything. As he understood it, there was a detailed account of President and Mrs. Kennedy going to bed together. I said this was utter nonsense, that there had been no such account in any of my drafts, and that Goodwin knew it. Would I come to his apartment anyway? Bobby asked. I declined. There would, I said, be no point in it. Doors were starting to close; I had just closed one myself.

The following week I delivered a complete set of proofs for *The Death of a President* to Dick's office. Clipped to them was this note:

October 25, 1966

Dear Dick:

As promised in September, I'm enclosing a set of uncorrected galleys of the book. This is the text which was approved by Bob after four months of editing (from March 26 to July 29). I must put my final corrections in the mail to Evan on the morning of November 10, two weeks from this coming Thursday. I'll be grateful if you'll let me have your comments before then.

Faithfully,
BILL

Dick never acknowledged receipt of the galleys, but two days later I telephoned his office, and a secretary assured me that he had stopped in and picked them up. On November 10, the day before the corrected proofs were due on Evan's desk, I learned that Dick was in Italy; he was expected back later in the week. I promptly mailed my own set of corrected proofs to New York, reminding Evan of our most recent agreement—"If the author had heard nothing from Goodwin in two weeks he will write publisher and advise him to proceed with the book" —and added:

> I think we must move ahead. You and I have been at this now for seven and a half months. We have benefited from the wisdom and judgment of John Seigenthaler, Ed Guthman, Arthur Schlesinger, and others. We certainly haven't spared ourselves. Indeed, though neither of us could be called quick-tempered or irrational, we have at times tried one another's patience. Yet it has all been in a good cause: the book. No one can charge us with having been mean, or petty, or ungenerous. We have listened to all advocates, and I needn't remind you that we have put up with certain abuse which we—who never sought this task—did not deserve. But that is past. The future begins when you put down this letter. Then we can move ahead to give this country the most moving historical document of our time. Knowing that, and we do know it, the welts and bruises not only become endurable; they become insignificant.

Four days later I wrote Dick: "It's been nearly three weeks since I left the galleys for you with Barbara Satton; Harper's production schedule has come and gone, and not having heard from you I've assumed that you had no further comments or suggested changes." I added a postscript: "I tried to reach you by phone, but Tania Senff said you were in Washington."

It seemed to me that I had fulfilled all my obligations to the Kennedys and then some. I was run-down, had caught a miserable cold which I couldn't seem to shake, and felt more than ready for a restorative sea voyage. The day after leaving that last letter to Goodwin at his office, my wife and I drove to New York, left my baggage at the *Queen Mary's* pier, and registered at the Berkshire, using an assumed name to thwart snoops. Before we could ride up to suite 1704, however, a surprise awaited me in the lobby. It was Evan Thomas, bearing another set of page proofs and thirty demands for new changes from Pam and Seigenthaler.

Evan proposed that I spend the evening studying them. But that wasn't possible; my wife and I were to be guests of honor at a cocktail party, followed by dinner with the Congdons and an English friend and then a jazz concert. Moreover, fresh suggestions at this point required a review of the entire text. Evan was insistent that I review the Turnure-Seigenthaler memoranda before boarding ship, so I reluctantly agreed to sacrifice a night's sleep. After the concert I would sit up till daybreak examining the new material. I suggested we breakfast in the hotel dining room at 7:30 A.M. He said he would be there then.

It was an exhilarating evening, only slightly diminished by the prospect of the long night ahead of me. Ella Fitzgerald was the star of the concert, and her haunting voice was still running through my mind when, a few minutes after midnight, I sat down at the desk in suite 1704's living room and uncapped my fountain pen. Both of the suite's bedrooms were occupied; my wife was in one and Bob Jones, the gentle editor of *Family Circle,* a Cowles publication, was in the other. Anxious not to waken them, I worked quietly, almost stealthily, with the tools of my trade: pen, pencils, erasers, galleys, memos. I finished going over the entire book for the last time at seven o'clock exactly, showered, dressed for my voyage, and rode down to the dining room, where I handed the fruits of the night's work to Evan. Patting a dispatch case, he said he had brought me endpaper sketches and a memo from Harriet Pilpel—"Suggestions for more legal changes," he said; "You can go over them on the boat and cable me your decisions."

At that hour we were the only two breakfasters. But presently we had company. Two men entered and sat down at our table. Looking up from my menu, I saw that they were Dick Goodwin and Burke Marshall.

"Well," said Dick, with monstrous geniality, "it looks as if we'll all be sailing on the *Queen Mary.*"

Stunned and outraged, I hissed: *"What are you doing here?"*

Burke said, "Jackie must have your assurance that you will make all the changes she wants."

I didn't know what to say. I was too weary for negotiations, and I felt that this was an intolerable intrusion, but I didn't want to be rude to Burke. I liked and admired him. As a hero of the civil rights struggle, he had a special place in the Kennedy pantheon. I also knew that only a Kennedy could have persuaded him to come here under these circumstances.

"If Mike Cowles agrees to new changes, will you approve?" Burke asked. I assented, and he said, "Will you associate yourself with requests for other changes?" I looked away. It was an old story with the

Kennedy team: you made one concession and instantly you were pressed to make others. When it became clear that I wasn't going to respond, Burke said, "Do you want me to go back and tell her you won't do this for her?"

I turned to Goodwin. "You've had those proofs for nearly three weeks," I said. "Have you read them?"

He shook his head. Abruptly I stood up. I said, "I've been working all night. I'm very tired, I can't cope with this now, and I think you're trespassing beyond the borders of decency." To Evan I said, "Bring your sketches up to the suite." I walked out rapidly. He hurried behind.

In the elevator he said shakily, "I didn't betray you!"

Until then it hadn't occurred to me that I had been betrayed by anyone. Now I turned and said, "You, me, and my wife were the only people who knew you and I were going to have breakfast together— where we were going to have it, when we were going to have it."

"I didn't betray you!" he said again, very agitated.

He was still trembling when we sat on the suite's living room sofa and began going over the endpapers. We were just finishing when the doorbell rang. We stared at each other. The bell rang again, then again, and then a voice called, "Bill, are you in there?"

It was Bobby.

"Bill, I know you're in there!"

In a hoarse whisper Evan repeated once more, "I didn't betray you!"

Now Bobby was pounding on the door with his fist and shouting, "Bill, Bill, I know you're in there!"

Evan said, "You have to see him."

"The hell I do," I said. "I didn't invite him, and I have nothing to say to him. Do you really think a former Attorney General of the United States is going to break down a door?"

For a while it seemed a possibility. The noise of the hammering was appalling. My wife was cowering under her bedclothes. And Bob Jones, in the other bedroom, had a problem: he had to go to work. After greeting Evan and me—we both sat rigid and unspeaking—Jones answered the door. He said to Jones: "Ask him if he wants to see us. Just ask him that." Jones, who must have thought he was surrounded by lunatics, returned and asked me. I said I didn't, that I wanted to talk to a lawyer. Jones relayed the message and went off to his office. Presently the footsteps of the others died away and Evan left. I phoned my agent, who called a lawyer, whose advice was: "Get Manchester on that ship as soon as possible." After saying good-bye to my wife—and explaining as best I could what had been happening—I walked to Don's office.

By now a nervous reaction had begun to set in, and at the urging of one of Don's secretaries I did something I have never done before or since: I drank a tumbler of neat whiskey. I didn't feel a thing, but Don felt that he should accompany me to the *Queen Mary*. He left me at the bottom of the gangplank. We both thought I was safe there, and we were both wrong; when I reached the deck I found myself face-to-face with a CBS camera crew and Bob Trout, who wanted to ask me a few questions about the book. Sleepless and full of alcohol, it is a wonder I didn't disgrace myself. A month later, when there was a greater demand for footage of me and I was refusing to cooperate, CBS ran that sequence several times. I saw it twice, marveling that I had actually sounded coherent, even fit.

It was an illusion. In my stateroom I was seized by a paroxysm of sneezing; overnight my cold had become aggravated. Unpacking my Krupp documents, I set up my typewriter and went to the porthole for a farewell look at the Statue of Liberty. At last, *at last,* I would have a few weeks of peace.

That, too, was illusion. Trout had been aboard because he was a fellow passenger, and he had other questions for me. Then there was the ship telephone. It had been nearly fourteen years since my last voyage on the *Queen Mary,* and I didn't realize how much ship-to-shore communications had improved. Calls kept coming in from New York newspapermen and, after we reached mid-Atlantic, from British journalists. By then I was taking evasive action. I refused to come to the phone, and when the Cunard purser warned me that a delegation from the English press planned to meet me in Southampton, I persuaded him to smuggle me ashore and arrange a private car for the drive to London. I also cabled the management of my Mayfair hotel, the Connaught, instructing it to respond to all questions about me by denying that I would be a guest there. London hoteliers are skillful at protecting the privacy of their lodgers, and only two inquiries penetrated the Connaught's screen. They were, curiously, from total strangers, George Raft and the manager of London's Playboy Club, both of whom wanted to entertain me.

Writing was impracticable—I was overwrought, my cold grew steadily worse, and there were daily conferences with my British publisher's solicitor, who had special problems with *The Death of a Presi-*

dent because of English law—but I was able to organize four chapters on Krupp's use of slave labor during the Third Reich. My room looked out on Carlos Place, about halfway between Berkeley Square and Grosvenor Square. Each afternoon at 3:30 I would glance out and watch the street lamps come on, marveling at the density of the fog and wondering how the weather can get so cold in London yet not snow.

Twice I had visitors from New York. Abandoning hope of persuading me to force changes in the proofs, bowdlerizers of the text were reversing their tactics and approaching the publishers directly. On November 22, precisely three years after the assassination, Mike Land of *Look* arrived with a list of eight changes requested by Goodwin and endorsed by Mike Cowles. All were acceptable, but I was apprehensive; I remembered Bobby's plan to turn revision into a hemorrhaging of the text (to "shred and emasculate it"), and I made my agreement to the modifications provisional upon *Look's* signing an agreement promising that the magazine would not ask me to make any further alterations. After phoning New York for authorization, Mike secured *Look's* consent. Our memorandum of understanding specified: "William Manchester has examined all the suggested changes in the *Look* serialization presented to him by Mike Land today. Manchester has accepted all the suggestions and initialed all the changes, with the understanding that *Look* will present no further suggestions and that the present text, as approved by Manchester and Land, is final and subject to no further change." With that, the magazine serialization seemed to be locked up.

Eight days later, on November 30, Evan Thomas and Cass Canfield met me in the office of my British author's representative, seventy-four-year-old A. D. Peters, the Pickwickian doyen of London literary agents and a figure of massive integrity. "Peter," as the world of letters knew him, had been professionally acquainted with Cass for over forty years. Peter's Buckingham Street building, which always seemed to me to be symbolic of him, had been the home in which Samuel Pepys had kept his diary three centuries earlier. Peter had known virtually every major British writer since Galsworthy—his early clients had included Hilaire Belloc, Rebecca West, J. B. Priestly, and Evelyn Waugh, whose lifelong friend he had become—and there was little in publishing which could surprise him. He merely inclined his great head once, in a nod of acknowledgment, when Cass said they had brought a fresh set of galleys, marked up by Evan on instructions in a Goodwin memo, and a personal letter to me from Jackie, dated November 28. Peter and I read the letter together. Although she still had not read the book (here Peter arched a white eyebrow), Dick had again gone over it for her, she said, indicating changes which "all touch upon things of a personal nature that I cannot bear to be made public. There are many others, I know, but these are all of that sort and they are absolutely necessary to me and my children." She concluded: "I cannot believe that you will not do this much."

On the face of it, this was not only reasonable; it was a moving appeal which anyone would have been callous indeed to ignore. I suggested that Peter and I go over the galleys and then meet Cass and Evan that afternoon in my room at the Connaught. They departed in a swish of raincoats; it was nasty as only a raw day in London can be. Alone in Pepys' old plank-floored study, we set to work studying the key proofs. It was then that Peter discovered what the controversy was all about. On the first clipped galley a description of Lyndon Johnson as having been bored by the Vice Presidency had been marked "cut." At the next paper clip the comment that for LBJ the shortest distance between two points was "a tunnel" had been crossed out. Next the heart of my account of Johnson's first Cabinet meeting had been deleted. A little later there was an effacement of a quotation from Dwight Eisenhower portraying LBJ as confused during his first full day in office. Peter sat motionless for a long time. Then he said, "You know, this is really extraordinary."

Over the next hour we found that Goodwin had requested changes on twenty-nine galleys. Of these, sixteen could be legitimately described as personal, and I made almost all of them, together with a large number of others which, though unrequested, had seemed to me on reflection during my New York-to-Southampton voyage to be legitimate questions of legality. That left thirteen Goodwin demands which were political and therefore unacceptable. Now we were ready to talk to Evan and Cass. Before their arrival in London, Don had written Peter, "Evan has given me to understand that Harper's position is that Manchester will have approval and will have the final say regarding any of Mrs. Kennedy's requested changes. Evan also tells me Harper's position is that the present manuscript has been approved by the Senator, speaking on behalf of the family." That seemed pellucid to Peter. Under those circumstances, he couldn't see why two busy executives had found it necessary to fly to London or, for that matter, why this afternoon's meeting was essential. He was scheduled to enter a hospital for minor surgery the next day. Could he spare me?

I begged him to come along anyhow. He had only glimpsed one

passage of a Byzantine labyrinth, I said; if he remained with me he might find other surprises. In my hotel room I handed Cass the proofs he had brought me, now rolled into a cylindrical bundle and secured with heavy rubber bands. Next I typed up a two page memorandum, noting that I had made changes on pages xiii, 3, 4, 9, 10, 25, 43, 44, 45, 61, 83, 97, 99, 102, 103, 114, 117, 120, 135, 157, 164, 228, 272, 273, 291, 296, 298, 313, 328, 333, 340, 341, 343, 379, 413, 418, 419, 422, 426, 434, 445, 452, 453, 472, 476, 477, 482, 493, 498, 514, 519, 523, 527, and 614. The operative clause in the memo was modeled on the one in my agreement with Mike Land the previous week: "In the Harper's interpretation of Goodwin's memorandum he had recommended changes on 29 pages. The author has altered the text on 16 of these pages. It is understood that these constitute the final suggestions that Harper & Row will consider from any source whatsoever (barring only issues of factual accuracy or legal import), and that no further suggestions or demands will be forwarded to the author." All four of us signed it and initialed each clause. Peter gave me an owlish look—plainly he felt vindicated—and purred off in his Rolls-Royce to pack for the hospital. I accompanied Cass and Evan to Heathrow as a farewell gesture. That was a mistake. My cold was settling in my chest; I was running a fever; sweating in the airport traffic was no help. Dropping them off, I rode back to Mayfair, went straight to bed, and summoned a Harley Street physician. He told me my temperature was 104 and left me with a vial of influenza pills. I was aching, hacking, sneezing, and generally wretched when, at 9 P.M., my phone rang. It was Evan. He and Cass were at the airport hotel. One of their 707's engines had broken down in Munich; there wouldn't be another plane till morning. While Cass dozed, Evan had been reviewing my changes on the galleys. He said they were unacceptable.

"You can't understand them?" I asked, unwilling to hear what I was hearing.

"Oh, we understand them. But they're not enough."

"Evan, less than five hours ago you signed an agreement promising that you would make no more demands of me."

"We can't accept the book in this form."

"Cass signed that agreement, too, in this very room. My God, this is unbelievable!" And for a moment I did in fact suspect that I might be delirious.

"Cass associates himself with every word I'm saying. He's nodding at me right now."

"Let me talk to him."

Cass came on and confirmed everything Evan had said. Then Evan came on again.

"I won't do it," I said. "I can't. Those Johnson things—"

"They're slurs."

"They are not—they're history. Taking them out would be a falsification of history. They're bound to come out eventually. And my grandchildren would have to live with the fact that I distorted the record. Evan, I refuse."

"Then Harper won't publish the book," he said.

Suddenly suspicious, I asked, "Who have you been talking to in New York?"

"No one."

"Listen, I'm sick," I said. "I need a night's sleep. Let's meet here in the lobby at nine."

They rang off, and I phoned Peter. He was incredulous, but said he would postpone admittance to the hospital until after the morning meeting. Evan arrived alone, Cass having flown to New York on an earlier flight to meet, Evan said, other commitments. Peter snorted at that; it seemed likelier that Cass couldn't face his old friend. If so, he was wise, for Peter's scorn was awesome. Flourishing the signed memorandum in one hand and slapping the back of his other hand on the galleys, he said in his starchiest voice, "Mr. Thomas, in my entire life I have never witnessed such shocking conduct by members of what I have always looked upon as a gentlemen's profession. Harper's has been making books since 1817. It has a long and honorable career. And now two of its highest officers have cynically broken their signed pledge before the ink could scarcely dry. And all for political expediency! Or do you have another explanation?"

Evan had none, or offered none. Twice he started to speak, thought better of it, and shrugged. Then he gathered up the bulky galleys and departed wordlessly. Peter, still red-faced, entered his Rolls, leaving me his hospital phone number, and I went back to bed. Meantime Cass was landing in New York's John F. Kennedy Airport. His first act, as I later learned, was to phone Jackie and ask for a prompt meeting in the office of her lawyer. There Cass triumphantly declared, "I have applied the ultimate sanction that is in the power of the publisher to apply"—that unless I capitulated he wouldn't bring out the book. She was overjoyed. Later Goodwin, disillusioned with Cass, said bitterly that "Canfield was the hero of the hour." Arm in arm, Cass and Jackie left the office.*

The next morning, Friday, December 2, Cass and Evan, who by now were also back in New York, cabled an ultimatum to the Connaught: either I agreed to all demands for fresh changes "within 48 hours of receipt" or book publication would be stopped. At that point I threw in my hand. My flu had turned vicious, and I was becoming afflicted with that most ignoble of emotions, self-pity. Under these circumstances the exercise of good judgment was almost impossible, and on Saturday I cabled Don and his senior partner, Harold Matson, delegating my editorial authority to them:

CANFIELD THOMAS HAVE CABLED ME ARE AIRMAILING KEY PROOFS AND DEMAND FINAL AGREEMENT WITHIN FORTY-EIGHT HOURS OF RECEIPT TO RESOLVE PROBLEMS WHICH PARTLY ARISE FROM MY TOTAL DISTRUST OF EDITOR SUGGEST HAL AND DON REVIEW PROPOSED CHANGES AND LETTER FROM MRS. KENNEDY DATED NOVEMBER 28 BEARING IN MIND THAT THOSE CHANGES APPLYING TO LBJ CANNOT BE CALLED PERSONAL FOR MRS K STOP THEN SEND XEROXES TO ME WITH YOUR RECOMMENDATIONS WHICH I RESPECT AND I WILL ACT STOP PETER AGREES MANCHESTER

This was a turning point. While I had lost faith in Harper's, I trusted Don more than any man in the world, and when he phoned Monday to recommend twenty-eight changes, I accepted all but two, on pages 270 and 452, dealing with Johnson. Simultaneously, Mike Cowles was talking to Cass. They and their staffs conferred throughout Monday and Tuesday, comparing proofs, my responses as relayed by Don, and possible approaches to Jackie. Judging by the results, Mike was putting steel in Cass's backbone. By late Tuesday he had persuaded him that all legitimate objections made in Jackie's name had been met. Accordingly, both publishers wrote her on Tuesday, December 6, that they had decided to go ahead. Cass never made his letter public, but presumably he took much the same approach as Mike, who

* Canfield was quoted at about this time as saying that "Manchester must make the changes, or be without a book." How he proposed to accomplish this is unclear. By then—early December 1966—the text had been set, or was about to be set, in German, French, Italian, Spanish, Dutch, Swedish, Danish, Finnish, Norwegian, Greek, Arabic, Japanese, Portuguese, Rumanian, Yugoslavian, Chinese, Russian, Icelandic, Belgian, Turkish, Swahili, Malayalam, Tagalog, Hindi, Urdu, Braille, and, in London and throughout the Commonwealth, English.

concluded, "I realize that you may not be entirely happy about all particulars but I feel we have gone the limit to try to be fair and thoughtful of everyone's feelings and yet consistent with accuracy."

Jackie read the letters, phoned her lawyer, and told him to sue.

Marie Antoinette, of whom Jackie sometimes reminded me, is reported to have replied to her countrymen's appeal for bread by saying, *"Qu'ils mangent de la brioche,"* a remark which has been held against her ever since. It was the misfortune of both women to be misunderstood. The queen wasn't being heartless; she really thought there was plenty of cake out there in the provinces. And Jackie wasn't trying to censor the history of her husband's assassination. Others were doing that in her name, probably without her knowledge, but her position was much simpler. She just didn't want any history on that subject at *all.* She wanted it to go away. Afterward Bill Attwood, *Look's* editor-in-chief, said, "The whole affair was senseless. Jackie Kennedy could have had anything she wanted if she hadn't sued." Attwood was wrong. The only thing Jackie wanted, and the one thing she couldn't have, was no magazine series, no book; just one big blank page for November 22, 1963. Her decision to go to court was impulsive, and it was inspired, ironically, by the gallant Cass. On Friday, December 2, the day after he had announced his application of "the ultimate sanction" against me, she had been resigned to *Look's* serialization. At one o'clock that afternoon Mike Cowles had received a handwritten letter from her which said, "I have considered bringing a lawsuit to halt your printing of the book. However, to sue would only dramatize and increase the attention on the most offensive parts." As late as December 10 she inspired a Pete Lisagor story in the *Chicago Daily News* which said that although she felt I had abused her confidence and was about to reveal her most intimate thoughts to the world, she would not resort to litigation.* And the night before she made her irrevocable move, Bob Kennedy, entertaining four editors at Hickory Hill, assured them that there would be no lawsuit. The next day one of them called and asked him how he felt now. He said he was "appalled." He had a lot of company.

Cass had touched it off with his letter to her affirming his decision to stand shoulder-to-shoulder with Cowles. Feeling sold out by her closest ally, by the one publisher she had entrusted implicitly, she gave Si Rifkind his marching orders. She wanted a courtroom battle; the

---

* It is true that she had withheld nothing during our interviews. It is also true that none of that sensitive material found its way into any draft of the book. She was unaware of that then because she hadn't read it yet.

longer the casualty list, the better. She didn't care what kind of papers Si filed, she said, as long as he filed something. Of course, the law is not that haphazard. Writs, briefs, and show-cause orders had to be prepared, opposing counsel must be warned, and the appropriate affidavits and supporting documents had to be delivered to the chambers of the appointed magistrate, in this instance a sixty-five-year-old Supreme Court Justice named Saul Seymour Streit, a lifelong Democrat who had risen through party ranks as a loyal Tammany worker and who, that Hanukkah, must have been the unhappiest Jew since Job.

During all this I was literally at sea, sailing homeward on the *Queen Mary*. Apart from my persistent case of the flu, which I was treating with massive doses of antibiotics, I thought my troubles were over. This delusion vanished when I came ashore; *Look* and Harper's had been served summonses, and somewhere, it was assumed, a process-server was waiting for me. It occurred to me that he had better be a pretty good physical specimen, because he was going to have to fight his way through a lot of newspapermen. Reporters followed me everywhere; when I stopped at *Look*, three editors had to accompany me every time I used the men's room, to assure me of some degree of sequestration even there.

For me the lowest point of those precourt maneuvers came when a friend phoned me at *Look* and read me a statement which had just been issued in Jackie's name. It accused me and my publishers of disregarding "accepted standards of propriety and good faith," of violating "the dignity and privacy my children and I have striven with difficulty to retain," and of writing "a premature account of the events of November 1963 that is in part both tasteless and distorted." I was accused of "inaccurate and unfair references to other individuals"—meaning Lyndon Johnson and his aides—and was blamed for the blinding publicity the suit had triggered: "As horrible as a trial will be, it now seems clear that my only redress is to ask the courts to enforce my rights and postpone publication until the minimum limits of my family's privacy can be protected." Finally: "I am shocked that Mr. Manchester would exploit the emotional state in which I recounted my recollections to him early in 1964, and I'm equally shocked that reputable publishers would take commercial advantage of his failure to keep his word." I remembered her saying at the Cape, "Anybody who is against me will look like a rat unless I run off with Eddie Fisher." Well, she hadn't run off with Fisher, and now I was going to look like a rat.

The worst of this, the real twist of the knife, was the identification of the statement's real author as Ted Sorensen. Ted—with whom I had sat up when he was suffering through his own book on Kennedy—later confirmed this to me at a Gridiron Dinner in Washington. I had always known that politics was rough. I just hadn't thought of myself as a politician.

Luckily for my spirits, that savage attack was followed by a hilarious act of *opéra bouffe.* The reason I was hanging around *Look*'s editorial offices that afternoon, being shadowed in toilets and insulted over telephones, was that I was waiting for that summons. Ordinarily, serving a writ on a person who is not reluctant to be so approached is a straightforward matter. This case was complicated by what would become enshrined during the Nixon years in the acronym PR. Appearances were important, because the controversy was neither legal nor literary; it was political. *How* I was summoned had become a matter of concern to the other side. If I seemed to be welcoming service, they reasoned, points would be lost. Points would be gained if I appeared to be elusive—hiding, say, in Connecticut. Since the surge of publicity was turning me into a surreptitious creature anyhow, their goal seemed attainable.

When the afternoon ended without process servers inquiring after me, I made arrangements to return home in a rented Carey Cadillac. To avoid the press, now in full cry, *Look* editors led me down a maze of corridors, through another building, across an alley, down more halls and across another building to a freight-loading platform, where my hired chauffeur waited. It fooled the reporters, but it didn't fool the gumshoes employed by the other side. They had an unmarked cruiser equipped with a two-way radio, and they tailed the Cadillac all the way to Middletown. I know that because of what followed. I wasn't headed for my home, which might have been staked out. My wife and I had agreed to meet at the home of Derry D'Oench, publisher of the *Middletown Press,* for a small dinner party. Five minutes after I arrived and was sipping gratefully at a large martini, the doorbell rang. Derry went to the door, where he was confronted by two uninvited guests. Not only were they strangers; their profession was obvious to anybody who has spent time covering police courts, as Derry had. They said they wanted to see me. My host, who is familiar with the U.S. Constitution, told them to stay right where they were. He then reentered the drawing room and whispered to me that there were hawkshaws on his threshold.

Using the telephone in his library, I reached my lawyer at a Manhattan cocktail party, who then reached Rifkind at another cocktail party, who agreed that my legal firm could accept service in my behalf the following morning in its Pan-Am Building offices. Rifkind, or a member of his staff, then ordered their dicks back to New York over the two-way radio. But all this took time. And the sleuths, meanwhile, were going through hell. The D'Oench mansion is in a quiet suburban neighborhood.* It is not the sort of turf on which private eyes usually operate. For one thing, there was no place to hide the unmarked cruiser. They tried driveways, but the people who live on Phedon Parkway do not encourage the presence of unidentified automobiles, and the householders always knew about the intruders because the busies were relentlessly pursued by a pack of sixteen-year-old informers—my son John, Peter D'Oench, and their tenacious gang. Every time the flat-feet thought they had found a safe house, their lair was spotted by these merciless boys on bikes, who rang doorbells, spread the word, and then circled the cruiser, threatening the men inside with calls to—the unkindest cut of all—the Middletown police. I'm sure the beagles were glad to be recalled.

That weekend I studied the affidavits Jackie and Bobby had filed. They were almost unbelievable. Jackie—who had issued a statement that same day calling the book "tasteless and distorted"—swore that "I have never seen Manchester's manuscript. I have not approved it, nor have I authorized anyone else to approve it for me." She declared that neither *Look* nor *Harper's* had allowed her to see the proofs of the material it would use. All this was right through the looking glass. Jackie hadn't seen the manuscript or the galleys because she hadn't wanted to see them; the offers had certainly been made, and in writing. Both manuscript and galleys had been shown to her representatives, at her request. The matter of approval could be contested only if she chose to take the line that Bobby had not been representing her, an argument which could be countered by submission in court of the original memorandum of understanding between him and me, supplemented by the correspondence between the three of us since then.

If her position was specious, his was indefensible, even hazardous, exposing him to charges of perjury:

I categorically state that at no time did I ever give my approval or consent to the text of the manuscript, to any publication thereof,

---

* If Jackie's lawyer had consulted his client, she could have provided him with useful background for this caper. Mrs. D'Oench had been a classmate of Jackie's, both in boarding school and later at Vassar, and they remained good friends.

or to any time of publication; nor did I ever say or do anything from which the defendants could reasonably have believed that I did. . . . The fact is that no one who read the manuscript had authority to approve it on behalf of Mrs. Kennedy or me.

There were at least twenty witnesses who could testify that this simply was not so. "And we don't need any of them," said Mike Cowles' general counsel, who offered to resign if he lost such an open-and-shut case. "There is just no way he can walk away from that telegram and that special delivery letter to Harper's." Bob knew this, of course. Her decision to sue had confounded him. It could only add—as it did—to his reputation for being ruthless. But the political risks in an open break with his sister-in-law were ever greater. He did refuse to join her as co-plaintiff, an act which suggested some courage.

The fact, obvious from the outset, was that nobody could win this suit, in PR or any other R. The judge, a good party man who had reached his position during President Kennedy's second year in the White House, was bound to displease powerful men. Jackie would—already was—creating the very sensationalism which my project had been meant to diminish. Publications in two-score foreign countries, including the London *Sunday Times, Paris Match,* Italy's *Epoca,* and Germany's *Der Stern,* stood to lose immeasurable goodwill. And the perils threatening Mike Cowles boggled the mind. While the court was drawing up its trial calendar, Mike faced very different legal obligations to his subscribers. He was running the first excerpt from my book in the issue which would reach the newsstands January 10. It had already closed. Skipping an issue, his accountants told him, would cost between three and five million dollars. Nor did his risk stop there. All of us in the suit needed staffs of attorneys, and because the issues were momentous we had to have prestigious, which is to say expensive, legal talent. Both Jackie and Harper's had former judges. I wasn't important enough to attract a judge—several were approached, but none would take me as a client. Still, one I finally retained was illustrious. Afterward I calculated that my legal fees from three legal firms came to just under $100,000.

The trial was scheduled to open on Monday, January 16, 1967, with Robert F. Kennedy as the first witness. Meanwhile the real struggle continued to be waged in the press. Some old friends from the Kennedy years declared themselves to be on my side. In Los Angeles Ed Guthman told reporters, "History is never monkeyed around with in the book," and that any hostility between the Kennedys and Lyndon

Johnson was explained well and "with compassion." Ben Bradlee and Red Fay wrote me warm supportive letters. Evelyn Lincoln, who had been the President's private secretary, wired, REST ASSURED THAT I AM IN YOUR CORNER ALL THE WAY, and Jim Swindal wrote, "Anyone who has known you, even for a short while, would be confident that you could never 'betray a trust.' I would testify to this any time." The big guns on the other side were Pierre Salinger, who challenged me to a debate over the Canadian Broadcasting System; Si Rifkind ("I don't know about literary integrity, nor the matter of history. They don't concern me for a moment. But I believe strongly in a man keeping his word, particularly when it is in a written memorandum of understanding."); the Reverend Dr. Donald S. Harrington of New York's Community Church, who recommended that no one buy the book if it was published over Jackie's objections; and Dick Goodwin.

The problem with Goodwin was that he was in Middletown. Reporters and commentators, many of them old friends, were arriving every day to solicit statements from me, but I couldn't say anything— my lawyer told me that if I wanted my book published in the United States, I must work toward a legal settlement, which entailed avoiding the press—so they walked around the corner to Goodwin's house, where they were always received hospitably. His unfriendly comments about me were carried in local newspapers and on local television newscasts. They contributed to the general misery of those days, as did attacks from anonymous Kennedy "spokesmen." It occurred to me for the first time that there was something inherently unfair in the journalistic tradition of allowing celebrities to have privileged spokesmen. I wasn't entitled to one, and so, since I was remaining silent on the advice of counsel, the public was largely unaware of my views. Yet those of Jackie, who was swimming off Antigua, and Bobby, who was skiing in Sun Valley, filled columns every day. John Seigenthaler, Frank Mankiewicz, or Pam Turnure, each a spokesperson, would brief the press, and unattributed condemnations of me would be heard on the evening's telecast, and read in the next morning's newspaper. As one thoughtful journalist wrote afterward, friends of the Kennedys "popped up all over the place. Many of them knew reporters and magazine writers. Many of them *were* reporters and magazine writers. Manchester, *Look*, and Harper & Row were simply outnumbered."

Part of the problem, it seemed to me at the time, was that not much else was happening in the world. There were days when I prayed for some earth-shaking event which would shift the spotlight somewhere else. (Goodwin appreciated this aspect of the controversy. He asked an editor whether he had noticed how Bobby's argument with J. Edgar Hoover over FBI wiretapping had been pushed off the front pages.) The *New York Times* devoted a lead editorial to an admonishment of Jackie: "History belongs to everyone, not just to participants. . . . having made her original decision [asking that the book be written], she cannot now escape its consequences." The story was not only big in the United States; it was big everywhere. Chiang Kai-shek, apparently having nothing better to do, interested himself in rumors that copies of the unedited manuscript had found their way to Formosa, which had never joined the international copyright convention. The generalissimo let it be known that if the book had in fact reached Taipei, it would not be published there. In Hamburg, Henri Nannen, editor of *Der Stern,* announced that since any new revisions by me would be made for political reasons, he, as an old anti-Nazi, felt compelled to disregard them. Thereupon the Chairman of the Committee for Science, Culture, and Publications in the German Bundestag solemnly declared that he could find no persuasive reasons for disregarding Mrs. Kennedy's wishes.

As in any political dispute, the principals displayed certain symptoms of paranoia. Everybody was vigilant for spies from the other side, suspicious of inquisitive acquaintances, often distrustful of old associates. One evening Mike Cowles called Evan Thomas from his office. Next morning an account of the conversation appeared in a morning newspaper. Dismayed, Mike phoned Thomas and asked if he had discussed their talk with a newspaperman. Evan, shocked at the suggestion, denied it. That convinced Mike that his office was being bugged, and he called in electronic surveillance experts to check it out. No devices were found, and the newspaper story was of no consequence. It is merely indicative of a state of mind, a mild insanity which had most of us in its grip.

The eye of the storm was Middletown. At night my home, a 176-year-old farmhouse, was bathed in floodlights, with television crews standing vigil on the sidewalk. By day, reporters interviewed my children returning from school, or questioned local citizens, one of whom proudly said of me, "He put this town on the map." (One of the reasons I liked the town was that it *wasn't* on the map.) Upstairs the householder was crouched furtively over a telephone extension, whispering to his agent; downstairs his wife, who doesn't really go for this sort of thing, was functioning as a harassed press secretary. One afternoon she was dealing with an affable man from the *New York Post,* who told her that he understood I used to be a newspaperman myself, when the back door opened and in walked a Middletown cop, who disclosed that he had just been hired as a stringer for the *New York Daily News.*

If we weren't using the telephone, it rang constantly. Bigart wanted me to tell my side of the story to the press and public. Roger Mudd was calling from a phone booth on the Merritt Parkway; he'd heard that I was about to issue a statement, and had cameramen with him. Harvard wanted me to lecture there. (Yale had stolen a march on its ancient rival when Bennett Cerf told a New Haven audience that he had seen a copy of the manuscript and predicted it would "sell a million copies if it is allowed to be published, and although the Kennedys are kicking, I think it will be." Cerf found himself on the front page of the *New York Times* and in trouble with everybody's lawyers.) King Features wanted me to write three columns a week. Attleboro, Massachusetts, where I was born and from which I had escaped at an early age, wanted to hold a "Bill Manchester Day"—schools closed, kids waving tiny American flags, me riding down Main Street in an open car.* To elude the telephone sometimes I would slip away through the backyard and roam the town, but even there my status was changing. In the drugstore, in the barbershop, and at the filling station, I had always been "Mr. Manchester." Now it was "Bill" everywhere. People like to be on a first-name basis with a celebrity, which was what I had temporarily become.

What was so depressing about this was that I was being celebrated, not because people had read my book—it hadn't even been published yet—but because I was notorious, which is not the same thing as famous. During those weeks at least a dozen friends checked in with reports that at various New England parties they had met alumni of my university, each of whom had introduced himself as having been my college roommate. Like moths making for a flame, they seemed to be fleeing their own anonymity by identifying with what they conceived to be my distinction. If only they had known. I felt naked. I wanted a place to hide and didn't have any.

New York, I thought; New York's the place to go. Don wanted me there anyway to confer over pacificatory overtures from Jackie. I rode down in a Carey Cadillac and registered at the Elysée Hotel under the ludicrous nom de guerre of Jack O'Rourke. That evening, though I

---

* The apex—or nadir—of all this came some time later, when Bayer Aspirin offered me $35,000 to endorse its product on radio and television.

didn't know it, CBS-TV News ran my interview with Trout. The next morning I crossed the street for a cup of coffee in the Chock Full O'Nuts shop at the corner of Madison and Fifty-fourth. A blonde sat on the next stool, put her hand on my forearm, and said, "I want you to know I'm on your side." Where, I thought frantically, have I seen her before? The answer was, nowhere; she had seen me on the tube. Upset, I left my coffee unfinished and hurried down Madison Avenue toward my agent's office. Three times I was stopped by people coming the other way who recognized me. In great distress now, I darted into a drugstore and bought a pair of dark glasses. I was in such a state, however, that I didn't notice that the frames were studded with rhinestones, which, in those pre-unisex days, meant they were for a woman. Reemerging on the sidewalk, I was accosted by a homosexual.

I hadn't really recovered from the flu when I left London, and under these new strains I began to feel wobbly again. Repeatedly each night I coughed myself awake, the coughs reaching even deeper in my chest. Back in Middletown, I promised my family a normal Christmas. That morning I awoke with a fever, which climbed all day. When it reached 104.2, my wife called our doctor, who discovered pneumonia in my lower left lung, summoned an ambulance, and sent me to Middlesex Hospital, where I was put on the critical list. After placing me under intensive care and waiting till I slept, the doctor took an elevator to the ground floor. The elevator doors opened, and he found himself looking into television cameras from NBC, CBS, and ABC. Until then his encounters with the communications industry had been confined to reporters for the *Middletown Press*. Now he was asked to provide the networks with a full-scale medical briefing. Among the interested members of the mass audience were a skier in Sun Valley and a swimmer in Antigua, both of whom sent me get-well messages. Later a Kennedy adviser told the *New York Times*, "Christ, I thought we'd killed him."

The first member of the family to predict an out-of-town settlement was Ted Kennedy. Four days after Jackie filed suit, Ted told a television interviewer that he was "hopeful." That same day Bob called a reporter from Idaho to say substantially the same thing. The source for their optimism was their litigious sister-in-law, who had already read the 60,000 words of the *Look* installments and requested the deletion of only 1,600 words. Cowles referred the decision to me, but it was an easy one. The passages were harmless, none was political, and they confirmed my suspicion that the expurgators representing her had been far freer with their blue pencils than she would have wished. *Look* was able to stick to its press schedule and save at least three million dollars, all of it well earned.

By December 31, when I was released from the hospital—leaving through an underground tunnel that led to the adjacent nurses' home, thereby foiling reporters again—the only issue left was the book. To be sure, this time we were dealing, not with 60,000 words, but with 340,000—a 710-page book. And neither Cass nor Evan had stood quite as tall in the saddle as Mike. At that same time, we had a lot going for us. The book was less horrendous to Jackie than the serialization; book readers were more understanding, more discerning. Then there was the identity of the intermediary. The *Look* deletions had been weeded out by Dick Goodwin and Bill Attwood. Everybody on the Kennedy team liked Attwood; he had been one of them, JFK's ambassador to Guinea. But they had even greater faith in Don Congdon, who had been straightforward with all of them since the launching of the project three years earlier. Dick wound up by asking Don to be his agent. The two of them would bargain an adjective here for an adverb there, keeping score to some extent so that afterward it would be possible to say that Jackie's staunchness had forced a lot of alterations. (Once I substituted "vanished" for "disappeared"; that counted as a change.) In reality, a total of seven pages was cut, about one percent of the text. No one could be absolutely sure that this was not in vain until the plaintiff in the suit had finished her own reading of the manuscript. That happened in the small hours of January 16. Later I was told by a reliable informant that as she laid aside the final page she murmured one word: "Fascinating." Then everybody went to bed.

A few hours later Justice Streit issued a judgment and decree setting forth the terms of the settlement. There had been a few amusing maneuvers in that last week. Rifkind wanted me to promise that I would never again write about the assassination. Fine, said my lawyers; that clause would read, "William Manchester will never again write about the assassination, *nor could he.*" At that point another lawyer flashed a sign to Rifkind, and the demand was withdrawn. Another time, Jackie insisted that neither she nor any member of the Kennedy family could be thanked in the foreword of the book for their cooperation with the author. Her attorneys, going her one better, said I couldn't acknowledge the help of *anyone*. "Not even my wife?" I asked.

"Not even your wife," I was told. I dug in my heels; I was allowed to thank my wife—but no one else.

Once the papers had been signed, all the principals went into seclusion. The president of Cowles Communications had arranged for me to rent a house in Lyford Cay, near Nassau, owned by a paper company executive. It was all done secretly. Only four people knew about it, including my wife and I, who would travel under the names of "Mr. and Mrs. William Phillip Templeton." Murray Kempton rode with us to the airport, but even Murray didn't know where we were going. Our fourth day there I spotted a copy of the *New York Daily News*. The front page head was: AUTHOR IN HIDING. Expecting diversion, I opened it and read: "Author William Manchester is in seclusion in heavily guarded, exclusive Lyford Cay, a few miles from Nassau on New Providence Island, the *News* learned yesterday. He has been there since last Friday, and reportedly is a guest of one of the plush private homes near the Lyford Cay clubhouse."

That was pretty good reporting. Actually we were a hundred yards from the clubhouse, which was where I had seen the *News*. That evening my picture occupied a full page in the Nassau newspaper, and since I saw *that* paper in the kitchen of the house we were renting, I realized that we owed an explanation to the woman who ran the staff. So we called her in. "I have to tell you," I began, "that I'm not really William Phillip Templeton." She rolled her eyes and said, "Oh, you'll always be William Phillip Templeton to me." "No, really," I insisted. "Yes, really," she insisted right back. This went on for a while, until both my wife and I realized that the woman knew I was Manchester, all right, but figured my companion to be *Mrs.* William Phillip Templeton. It seemed too rich to spoil, so we left it that way.

What wasn't so funny was a 3 A.M. phone call to the Connecticut home of my family physician ten days later. He heard the staccato found on teletype machines; then a man came on and identified himself as a wire-service night editor. The voice said, "Are you Mr. Manchester's doctor?" My doctor said he was. "He just died," the voice continued. "Would you care to comment?" After a shocked pause, the physician asked, "Are you *sure?*" "Oh, yes," the man said confidently. "He died in Mexico City." "No comment," my doctor said firmly, and hung up. He had just remembered that although I hadn't told him exactly where I was going, I had said the Bahamas, not Mexico.

Doubtless such occurrences are not uncommon in the lives of permanent celebrities, and I suppose they learn to live with them. I could not. It seems to me that a writer should be less renowned than his books. I returned to Middletown trusting that the limelight would eventually recede. It did, but it took time. Obscurity was impossible as long as my name was on every newsstand. A few hours after *Look*'s first installment went on sale, 4,000 copies had been sold in Times Square alone, and twenty-four hours after United Airlines bought 1,800 copies for its planes, passengers had stolen all of them from their binders. Gallup later found that seventy million people read one of the magazines' four excerpts; fifty-four million read all four.

The book was published April 7. According to Harper's 151st annual report, it added three million dollars to the company's net sales for fiscal 1967. Over the next four years, Harper's sold 558,419 copies in bookstores; the Book-of-the-Month Club sold another 812,813. To this should be added 314,000 copies from the eleven countries for which figures were available. Paperback sales, on the other hand, were disappointing. This was a consequence of the settlement, which tightly restricted the choice of the reprint house. The result was that, at this writing, no adequate cheap edition has been issued, and the full text has never reached a mass paperback audience.

Inevitably there were political repercussions at the time of publication, though they would probably have been of far less moment had there been no controversy. John Connally, who disliked my treatment of his feud with Ralph Yarborough, said the book was "filled with editorial comment, based on unfounded rumor, distortion, and inconsistency." Governor John J. McKeithen of Louisiana said, "Kennedy is trying to destroy Johnson, and that's what Manchester's book is all about." Senator John Tower of Texas called me "just another kneejerk, ultra-liberal." A Lou Harris poll showed that sixty-nine percent of the American public had followed the controversy. As a result of it, twenty percent of the people "thought less" of Senator Robert F. Kennedy. But Jacqueline Kennedy was a bigger loser; thirty-three percent "thought less" of her.

Two periodicals which exploited the controversy were *The Realist* and *Commentary*. The first told its readers that it was publishing sections which had been edited out of the book during the negotiations which led to the settlement. The passages had never been published in the book; they were invented by *The Realist*. *Commentary* published

"Manchester Unexpurgated," an article by Edward Jay Epstein, a graduate student who had attracted Dick Goodwin's admiration with *Inquest,* a book challenging the findings of the Warren Commission. Epstein's piece is a spirited defense of those who wanted to censor *The Death of a President.* Among other things, Epstein accused me of creating "fictitious episodes for the purpose of heightening the melodrama." Three of these are cited.

"Manchester," he declared, "goes so far as to invent an encounter on the [presidential] airplane between Mrs. Kennedy and the new President. She becomes 'the first member of the presidential party to discover that Air Force One had a new commander' when she opens her bedroom door in the plane and sees Lyndon Johnson 'sprawled' across her husband's bed." Epstein commented: "That this episode is fiction we know from virtually all the other evidence. . . . Mrs. Kennedy did *not* first encounter Johnson in her bedroom." Well, the fact is that she did. The incident was described to me by Jackie during a taping session on May 4, 1964; by Marie Fehmer, Johnson's personal secretary, who was present in the aircraft's bedroom at the time, in an interview on November 6, 1964; and by Sergeant Joseph Ayres, an Air Force One steward who was standing in the corridor just outside the compartment, in an interview on September 6, 1964.

Epstein then raised the subject of Maude Shaw, nurse to the Kennedy children, telling Caroline of her father's death. Some readers found this scene too painful to be borne. Painful it certainly was, but others, Ed Guthman among them, felt that it was of historical importance, and Jackie was persuaded that this was so. Epstein, however, declared that editors tried to remove the incident because it was "tasteless" and, moreover, "appeared to be spurious." Questions of taste are individualistic and cannot be settled either way. Spuriousness is something else again. Either an account is true or false. This one is demonstrably true, having been based on interviews with Miss Shaw on April 24, 1964 and May 18, 1964, and with Janet Auchincloss, Caroline's grandmother, on May 21, 1964.

In a final footnote, Epstein charged that I misrepresented J. Edgar Hoover's demeanor toward Robert F. Kennedy after the assassination as "sphinxlike." (Epstein really said toward "the Kennedy family," but here, as elsewhere, he misquoted me.) My sources for the FBI director's conduct were a taping with Bob on May 14, 1964, and interviews with Ethel Kennedy on April 17, 1964, with Guthman on May 3, 1964, with Angela Novello on May 15, 1964, and with J. Edgar Hoover on June 4, 1964.

At one place Epstein wrote of "other such incidents" for which he was "able to find no actual evidence." That, of course, was the whole point of *The Death of a President.* Neither he nor anyone else could find all the evidence I did because they weren't in the field when I was, researching the event in the months which immediately followed it. Authorized history may be a poor idea, and certainly my experience cannot be considered a testimonial for it, but the project did have one great advantage. It permitted a trained researcher to assemble historical data when it was available—when participants were alive and, equally important, when their memories were fresh. President Eisenhower, no admirer of the Kennedys, told me in the summer after the assassination, "Something like this should have been done after Lincoln's death. Then we'd have it now." My tapes and transcribed notes constitute a permanent record of the Dallas tragedy. Their intrinsic value remains, whatever judgment future scholarship forms about the book I wrote based on them—although, as the Epstein case demonstrates, they can be used to support every statement of fact in the book.

Some of the principals in the controversy—e.g., Goodwin and Seigenthaler—I never saw again. Others, such as Guthman, Marshall, Salinger, Schlesinger, and Sorensen, were encountered in the natural course of events, and some correspondence with still others was inevitable. It was also cordial. I remembered the strife of 1966–67 with sorrow, but without bitterness. Even as I mourned the declining fortunes and eventual demise of *Look,* I rejoiced when Evan Thomas, leaving Harper's, flourished in a new editorial position elsewhere.

Amicable relations with Bob Kennedy were quickly restored, and in the spring of 1968, after he had announced for the Presidency, I was campaigning for him. Late in that season Harper's sent a check for $750,000, representing the first year's profits on *The Death of a President,* to the Kennedy Library in Boston. When Jackie learned about it, she phoned me, wrote me a profoundly moving letter, and, on June 21, issued a gracious statement to the *New York Times:* "I think it is so beautiful what Mr. Manchester did. I am glad that Senator Kennedy knew about it before he died. All the pain of the book and now this noble gesture, of such generosity, makes the circle come around and close with healing."

No acknowledgment arrived from the library. A year and a half passed. Out of curiosity I wrote to Boston, asking how much had been received from the sales of my book. Eventually this reply reached me:

JOHN FITZGERALD KENNEDY LIBRARY
Incorporated

Reply to:
260 Tremont Street
Boston, Mass. 02116

February 9, 1970

Mr. William Manchester
Center for Advanced Studies
Wesleyan University
Middletown, Connecticut 06457

Dear Mr. Manchester:
In reply to your letter of February 2nd, please be advised that the Library has received the following revenue from the sale of THE DEATH OF A PRESIDENT:

Net Sales to Dec. 31, 1967	Library Share	$ 750,000.00
" April 30, 1969	"	277,603.11
" Oct. 31, 1969	"	29,744.53
Total Paid Library		$1,057,347.64

We trust this is the information we (sic) desire.
                              Sincerely,
                              CLIFFORD J. SHAW, Treasurer

S/m

That was over five years ago. I have not heard from the library since.

Mid Campfires
Gleaming

"WAR, WHICH WAS CRUEL AND GLORIOUS, *had become cruel and sordid," wrote Winston Churchill after the Armistice in 1918. Even so, war continued for another generation to be, in the famous Clausewitzian definition, "a political instrument, a continuation of political relations, a carrying out of the same by other means." As late as 1945 it was possible for one man, with one rifle, to make a difference, however infinitesimal, in the struggle against fascism.*

The Bomb rendered Clausewitz's Vom Kriege *obsolete. In that millionth of a second over Los Alamos thirty years ago super-power warriors were forever emasculated, and the central fact about world history in the three decades since then is that statesmen have been trying, without much success, to come to terms with that frustration.*

These pages are largely concerned with war as it was. They are not meant to glorify combat, but I shall always believe that courage under fire is a virtue, and that most of the survivors emerge strengthened. A very close encounter with death alters a man. It needn't come on a battlefield. Once I spent an evening discussing this with Walter Reuther, who had been gunned down in his own kitchen. We discovered that in the most important sense our experiences had been identical. Death had invested our lives with new meaning. Each day thereafter was a gift to be cherished and, above all, to be justified. If we were to deserve the years ahead, we had to earn them, deed by deed in his case, page by page in mine.

It would be good if the whole race had been thus transformed by Hiroshima and Nagasaki. Unfortunately, the weakness of individuals for generalizing from the specific is not matched by a capacity for specification from the general. We cannot yet grasp the fact that the bell which tolled for 150,000 Japanese in the high summer of 1945 also tolled, not only for us, but for the whole concept of the autonomous nation-state, without which patriotism is meaningless. It was Toynbee who said that nationalism had become "a sour ferment" in "the old bottles of tribalism." He meant, among other things, the star-spangled mythology. And whether we like it or not, he was right.

But that wasn't always true. The wine wasn't always sour. Once loyalty to the flag was a constructive force; once phrases like "conspicuous gallantry" and "extraordinary heroism" had meaning. To argue otherwise would be chronological snobbery, the assumption that change always brings progress, and that the present is in every way an improvement over the past. It's not. The devotion inspired by the drums of yesterday deserves respect. One can only add that the highest tribute we can pay to those who marched to their beat is to make sure they never roll again.

The Spanish-American War

IN THE LAST, LILAC-SCENTED HOURS of April, 1898, Theodore Roosevelt prepared to resign as Assistant Secretary of the Navy and join the Army. As a Harvard graduate he was entitled to a commission, and since he was also something of a dude, he wired Brooks Brothers for a "blue lieutenant colonel's uniform without yellow on the collar and with leggings."

Teddy felt bully. He was convinced that "this country needs a war," and he had been trying fervently to start one—first with Britain, over Venezuela, and more recently with Spain for Cuban independence. Last month he had despaired. The President had "no more backbone than a chocolate éclair," he had growled, working off his rage by kicking a football back and forth on a vacant Washington lot. Now all that was past. A joint session of Congress, exuberantly singing, "We'll hang Butcher Weyler to a sour-apple tree," had just hoisted our battle standard. America was at war with Spain.

Why? It was unpatriotic to ask. Mute testimony to Spanish treachery lay in a glass outside T.R.'s office—a model of a sleek, white U. S. armored cruiser, her ensign at half mast. At 9:40 on the evening of February fifteenth the ship itself had blown up in Havana Harbor, killing 260 bluejackets. American naval officers hadn't been at fault; it must have been a mine. The eagle screamed for vengeance. "Nation Thrills with War Fever," cried William Randolph Hearst's New York Journal. "Everywhere over this good, fair land," William Allen White later wrote, "flags were flying." The Klondike gold rush was forgotten, and songs, gewgaws, buttons, banners—even candy drops—carried the couplet of the hour: "Remember the Maine! The hell with Spain!"

Few inquired what the Maine had been doing off Havana, although it was pertinent. Officially the ship had been making a courtesy call. In reality its visit had been the sequel to the latest in a long series of incidents over Spanish colonial policy in Cuba. For a generation the island had been torn by rebellion. Like Fidel Castro, the *insurrectos* had holed up in the rugged mountains, creeping down at night to burn cane fields or collect protection money from American owners. Other Americans in New York had freely contributed funds to the insurgents, and cargoes of arms had been smuggled in from Florida. Spanish reinforcements had been ferried across the Atlantic. Cuba was dotted with blockhouses. They weren't enough; and in 1896 Captain General Valeriano Weyler y Nicolau had taken the desperate measure of herding the sullen population into concentration camps. That hadn't worked either; the only consequences had been famine, disease and rising American indignation.

Americans were mad because they were reading the details every day. The *Journal* and Joseph Pulitzer's *World* had assigned teams of reporters to write incendiary stories, and when the truth paled they invented atrocities. Some of their accounts make grisly reading today. Dispatches described dons playing soccer with hacked-off Cuban heads, and giving their children the severed ears for toys. The cumulative impression was of a new Inquisition conducted by rapists and sadists, by "leering Latins" with "the thirst for blood inherent in the bull-fighting citizens of Spain." Something must be done, the jingo press insisted. If Washington wouldn't act, they would. One *Journal* correspondent actually broke into a Spanish jail, disguised a beautiful political prisoner as a boy, and slipped her back to New York. The country shook with cheers. The governor of Missouri suggested that the paper send five hundred reporters to set all Cuba free, and when Hearst entertained the girl at Delmonico's 120,000 people stood outside and huzzaed.

In those days New Yorkers did things like that. Much has been made of Hearst's boast that it cost him three million dollars to start the Spanish-American War; the popular assumption is that newspapers were responsible for the whole thing. They had a hand in it, but the deeper truth is that they reflected the mood of the era. It was another world, that U.S.A. of the 1890's—the heyday of the cigar-store Indian and the barbershop quartet, when men wore high-laced shoes and derbies, and women wore whalebone corsets, and no lady crossed her legs in public.

America was as sophisticated as peppermint. The popular songs of 1898 suggest its sentimentality: "On the Banks of the Wabash," "Little Annie Rooney," "Bill Bailey," "The Old Gray Mare," Paul Dresser's weepy "Take Me Back to New York Town if I'm Going to Die," and the top tune of the year, "There'll Be a Hot Time in the Old Town

Tonight." Grown men pondered the clotted piety of such tracts as *Little Susie's Prayer*. It was a time of innocence, or artlessness, of vigilant morality; and the yellow press sent knights-errant south because the public wanted a crusade.

Not all Americans were crusaders. TR wasn't one. In those days he was a bristling militarist, a member of an imperialist clique whose other leaders included Henry Cabot Lodge, John Hay, Whitelaw Reid, and Captain Alfred Thayer Mahan. When the Washington *Post* wrote that "the taste of Empire is in the mouth of the people," it was talking about these people; and the shrewdest and most energetic was the young assistant secretary with the beribboned pince-nez and the fanglike teeth. Teddy was interested in more than one Spanish colony. He was keenly aware that another insurrection was blazing six thousand miles away in the Philippine archipelago. He had quietly arranged the appointment of Commodore George Dewey, a fellow imperialist, as commander of the U.S. Asiatic Squadron, and without consulting his superior he had cabled Dewey to keep full of coal, watch the Spaniards, and, at the first stroke of war, to pounce on the Philippines.

Most of his countrymen, however, weren't interested in a land grab. They merely wanted to help bleeding Cuba. The average American, like Mr. Dooley, didn't know whether the Philippines were "islands or canned goods." Even President McKinley confessed that after the Battle of Manila Bay he had to look them up on the globe.

The President was guileless, sincere and something of a stuffed shirt. He was also sensitive to public opinion; in July 1897, he had taken the first official step toward war by warning Madrid that he would intervene if Weyler weren't curbed. Spain's premier was contemptuous, but next month he was dead, and his assassination brought to power a liberal government which sacked the butcher and granted Cuban autonomy. Then, just as the sky was brightening, the Spanish ambassador to Washington wrote a vicious attack on McKinley. It was in a private letter, but a rebel spy stole it, and Hearst printed it. Old Glory snapped angrily in the rising wind.

Meanwhile, loyalists in Havana had rioted against home rule. America's jittery consul asked for protection, and the *Maine* arrived. The mysterious blast which followed deafened the country. Madrid's frantic offers to meet every demand weren't even heard, and on April 25, 1898, the President signed the declaration of war.

He signed it in his bedroom, wearing a dressing gown. It was a fitting touch. America had been speaking loudly and carrying a frail stick. The War Department was hopelessly incompetent, and the hostilities had scarcely begun before its bungling produced a fiasco. Supplies were hurriedly dispatched to Florida, but since no one knew anything about logistics, a jam of 1000 boxcars crammed every siding from Tampa to Columbia, S.C. Vital shipments were buried in warehouses throughout the war; a two-hundred-bed hospital was lost for weeks. Frequently the equipment which seeped through was inadequate. Shoes fell apart on the first march, ponchos in the first rain. Rations were spoiled. Most extraordinary, troops were packed off to sweltering Cuba in heavy flannel uniforms and lined overcoats. Khaki, hastily ordered, wasn't ready until the onset of winter, and then it was issued to troops in the United States.

The supply snafus turned into a great scandal. Several careers were ruined, although the era itself was again mostly to blame. The McKinley years were the high noon of unbridled capitalism. Never has enterprise been freer than in the '90's. Army equipage was often inferior because contractors were unscrupulous or, in the case of rations, because the packing industry was unregulated. The Tampa embarkation docks were rented from a promoter, who paralyzed troop loading by admitting hordes of sightseers. Troop transports couldn't be required to observe convoy discipline because they were all chartered, and plans to invade Puerto Rico had to be revised because it had been discovered that privately owned cable companies were permitting orders to fall into enemy hands.

Yet even when full allowances are made, the Army looked pitiful. For one thing, there was hardly anybody in it. The total force was twenty-odd thousand men, less than the present size of the New York Police Department. Spain had nearly ten times that many in Cuba alone, all veterans. Because of the promotion bottleneck which had followed the Civil War, the American officer corps was senile; even some junior officers were white-bearded. Their maps of Cuba had been swiped from geography books, their men were trained in the mass-assault tactics of Waterloo and Gettysburg.

Uniforms had scarcely changed since Appomattox—troops still wore cerulean-blue pants, horse-collar blanket rolls, and brass belt buckles which would heliograph their movements to a tropical enemy— and firearms were hopelessly obsolete. The old Springfield rifle had the recoil of a sledgehammer. There was no modern artillery. The *New York Herald* couldn't wait for the Spaniards to "smell a little of our Yankee smokeless powder," but it was the other side that had the smokeless powder. America, after inventing it, had exported it, and our men were equipped with old black-powder ammunition which blinded them in battle and disclosed their positions.

This weakness on land could have been fatal, but as Bismarck observed, there is a special providence for drunkards, fools and the United States, and that spring providence wore the blue-and-gold of the U.S. Navy. In a war that was to be decided at sea, our fleet was three times as large as Spain's. It was strong on paper and even stronger in the water, because Spanish naval genius had vanished entirely. Their marksmanship was wretched, their ship bottoms were fouled, and they had decorated the decks of their ironclads with ornamental black-and-gold woodwork which was certain to catch fire in a modern battle. The woodwork was symbolic. It reminded them of Philip II's glorious Armada. Unhappily for them there were altogether too many such mementos around; when, at the climax of the war, they prepared to train their shore guns on our warships lying off Cuba's Santiago Bay, they discovered that five cannon were relics of the eighteenth century and a sixth bore the date 1668.

It was typical of them that they received this news with many lugubrious sighs. Back home there was some warlike spirit—Madrid had its own yellow press, which denounced *Yanquis, gringos* and *Protestantes* and published cartoons of aroused toreadors executing the Yankee hog. The military, however, felt otherwise. Its leaders hadn't wanted this war, and their attitude throughout was gloomy. Like France in 1940 and South Vietnam in 1975, they were beaten in the mind. Afterward they confessed they had known in advance that they would lose the crucial battle of Santiago Bay. To their flagship captain the first bugle note that morning was "the last echo of those which history tells us were sounded at the capture of Granada. It was a signal that four centuries of grandeur were at an end and that Spain was becoming a nation of the fourth class." He turned to his admiral and murmured, "Poor Spain!" The admiral could only nod glumly. Ever since leaving home he had been convinced that he hadn't a chance.

No such fatalism disheartened Americans. They were aggressive, confident and vehemently patriotic. In the same battle, a lieutenant aboard the *Texas* cried, "Where are our battle flags? What's a battle without battle flags?" and broke into a locker to get them while, topside, a band crashed through "The Star-Spangled Banner." Francis Scott Key's hymn was probably played more in combat in 1898 than in all the war years since. According to the *New York Times,* wounded men sang it during the battle of San Juan Hill.

It is a curious fact that in this war even the casualty tags were red, white and blue. The jingo bug had bitten everyone. At least two non-coms—a bosun's mate at Manila Bay and a sergeant at El Caney—are recorded as having rallied men by shouting "Remember the *Maine!*" Everyone wanted to be a G. A. Henty hero. One gringo boldly sailed a yacht into the waters off Cadiz; a second poked around Puerto Rico in disguise; a third crossed Cuba on foot to deliver a message to the insurgent General Calixto Garcia Íniguez, and daring missions attracted swarms of naval officers, including a young lieutenant named William F. Halsey.

We had morale, the enemy had none; that was the difference. It was not a difference of principles. Americans had gone to war shouting *Viva Cuba Libre*, but there was no real co-operation with the insurgents, either there or in the Philippines; they were used as labor troops or not at all.

This was a lily-white war. If anything, the pride of race was stronger here than among the Spaniards. Our Cuban expedition would surely have failed without the gallantry of U.S. Negro regulars, yet when the black-powder smoke drifted away they were assigned humble tasks as hospital orderlies, and Florida restaurants refused to serve them. Most Americans are unaware today that these men helped save the day at San Juan Hill.

Relations with the enemy were more cordial. Aloof from their cerulean-clad Negro comrades, our soldiers were at ease among the light-blue-and-white pin-striped uniforms of Spanish prisoners. "War as it is conducted at this end of the century is curiously civilized," wrote Richard Harding Davis, and for the socially acceptable, it was. Spanish dead were buried with full military honors; truce flags were hoisted so that opposing commanders might pay tribute to each other's valor. The American general who demanded the capitulation of Manila was escorted through the lines by a Spanish carriage, attended by liveried footmen. When a dashing American named Richmond Pearson Hobson tried to block Santiago harbor by sinking a collier at the mouth, the enemy admiral personally plucked him from the moonlit water, and when the same admiral's ship was sunk beneath him, we raced to his rescue. Several other Spanish commanders owed their lives to bluejackets. One of them, Don Antonio Eulate, captain of the cruiser *Vizcaya*, was blown overboard in battle. Waterlogged, wounded, and menaced by sharks, he was hauled aboard the *Iowa*. The *Iowa's* guard presented arms, and the ham in Don Antonio sprang to life. Straightening slowly, he unbuckled his sword belt, kissed the hilt, and offered it to Capt. Robley Evans with a charming bow. Naturally it was refused. The don then turned seaward and extended a hand toward his sinking ship. *"Adios, Vizcaya!"* he cried brokenly. At that moment the *Vizcaya,* with a superb sense of timing, vanished in a blossom of flame.

Such grandees believed that they were dealing with a fellow autocracy. To a degree they were correct. Culturally the United States was divided into rigid social castes, and the Brahmins were strong. Ambulances were reserved for officer casualties. Two cruisers were christened the *Harvard* and the *Yale.* Robber barons supported the war privately, like feudal lords. Twenty-eight of America's warships were millionaires' yachts, including J. P. Morgan's mighty *Corsair,* commanded by the former executive officer of the *Maine,* Lieutenant Commander Richard Wainwright, and Colonel Astor's yacht, which lay off Cuba and sent the colonel champagne rations. Helen Gould provided uniforms privately and made a war contribution of $100,000 to the U. S. Treasury; William K. Vanderbilt's chef served pheasant, squab, and fine wine to selected troops. Aristocracy was one of the two most vigorous institutions in the country. The other was frontier democracy, and the two were joined in the war's most celebrated regiment: Theodore Roosevelt's First U.S. Volunteer Cavalry, the Rough Riders.

Organized by Teddy and by Leonard Wood, who wore gold cuff links in combat, the Riders were a hybrid of cowboys and bluebloods. Lean, slit-eyed plainsmen with names like Cherokee Bill and Rattlesnake Pete served beside men from Boston's Somerset Club and the Knickerbocker Club of New York, crack polo players, tennis champions, steeplechase riders, Princeton linemen, Yale's finest highjumper, and a whole contingent from Teddy's Harvard, led by two ace quarterbacks. The socialites were a minority, but they saw to it that the entire regiment was outfitted with equipment unavailable to the regulars: tropical uniforms, new Krag rifles, a Colt machine gun, and a dynamite gun which was later purchased by the envious Khedive of Egypt. They also gave the unit a distinct tone, which was demonstrated during the siege of Santiago: when regimental bands were ordered to join in the national anthem, the Rough Riders played "Fair Harvard."

TR won glory as the commander of the Rough Riders, though he had already made his greatest contribution to victory when he tapped Dewey. The peppery little commodore had promptly painted his ships battle gray, and when war broke out he was impatiently awaiting ammunition from home. The day after it arrived he mounted the bridge of Captain Vernon Gridley's *Olympia* and led the Asiatic Squadron out of neutral Hong Kong. Dewey took dead aim on Subic Bay, in the island of Luzon; but Subic was empty, so he changed course for Manila. In the early hours of May first he ran the guns of Corregidor and fell on Rear Admiral Patricio Montojo's Philippine squadron.

There was never any doubt about the outcome. A British observer reported it as "a military execution, rather than a real contest." Montojo was weaker and slower, and rather than subject Manila to bombardment he had left the safety of its shore batteries for unprotected Cavite. At 5:41 A.M. Dewey said quietly, "You may fire when ready, Gridley," and the flagship's forward turret opened the ball at 5500 yards. Five times the commodore's battle line swept past in faultless formation, and when it was over all seven Spanish vessels had been destroyed. American casualties were a few scratches. The war was only a few days old, and Manila was bottled up, helpless. At home flags were waved exultantly, Dewey was acclaimed as the new Nelson, and Congress voted to buy him a fancy sword.

The White House learned about the battle from the *New York Herald*, whose Pacific correspondent was Dewey's aide. There was nothing odd about that. Newspapers took a proprietary interest in the war; reporters were often combatants. They affected tropical helmets and canvas hunting suits hung with machetes and six-shooters, and they used them. In one early brush with the enemy, when an old side-wheeler tried to land guns for the Cuban rebels, the only casualty was a newspaperman aboard the boat.

Richard Harding Davis, who had donned silk underwear to accompany the Rough Riders, joined in command decisions—actually he had more combat experience than Teddy—and after he and several other correspondents had captured a town in Puerto Rico, Stephen Crane, on orders from his literary agent, took another single-handed. Crane lost face when the *World*, bowing to protests, disowned his account of cowardice among New York volunteers, but his colleagues remained men of immense prestige. The AP served as the Navy's communications arm. Generals wooed the press, and one of them had crack troops diverted to his command by complaining to sympathetic newspapers.

Inevitably this power bred arrogance. The New York *Journal* acted as though it were a branch of the government. Hearst commanded his own private fleet, on the flagship of which he published a newspaper for the Army. Ashore, he reviewed troops on horseback—it was from him that men marching on San Juan learned they were going into battle—and later, soldiers who distinguished themselves were awarded *Journal* medals.

When Madrid sent a new flying squadron eastward to attack Dewey, Hearst assigned a reporter to bottle it up by scuttling a boat in the Suez Canal. Luckily this failed. The British would have regarded it as a very bad show. But that hadn't even been considered. Nothing, not even the national interest, deflected the yellow press from its duty to thrill subscribers. To the vexation of an American spy, the details of his mission to Puerto Rico were spread across front pages while he was still there; and despite a pledge of secrecy, the maneuvers of Rear Admiral William T. Sampson were revealed to a public which, unfortunately, included an enemy admiral named Pascual Cervera y Topete.

That betrayal came early in the war, and it was most awkward. Sampson was the Dewey of the Atlantic. He had been told to intercept Cervera, whose fleet was known to have left the Cape Verde Islands on April twenty-ninth. Had he destroyed Cervera, there would have been no need for a land campaign. He should have succeeded, for he was stronger and had guessed the Spaniard's course; but he was crippled by two circumstances, both wrought by his own civilians. To begin with, the eastern seaboard was terrified by a rumor that the enemy intended to raid American ports. Boston businessmen moved their securities to safe-deposit boxes in Worcester, real-estate men in Long Island added war clauses to leases, and Sampson, under pressure, detached part of his command to defend the coast. Next, a headline revealed that his weakened striking force was bound for Puerto Rico. Cervera read all about it at Martinique. Puerto Rico had been his destination, too, but now he headed for Cuba, and on May nineteenth he slipped past the dark green headlands of Santiago de Cuba, the isolated capital of Oriente Province.

Ten days later found him safe and snug inside the four-mile channel. In a spectacular operation, the tiny U.S. Marine Corps captured Guantánamo Bay. Stephen Crane, who had fought the Civil War vicariously in *The Red Badge of Courage*, felt "the hot hiss of the bullets trying to cut my hair." Using the bay as a coaling station, Sampson anchored six miles offshore. Blockade was the best he could do. The Santiago harbor was mined; the high ground on either side was fortified; we had no choice; we had to go ashore in strength, and Sampson asked the United States Army to take the city.

It was asking a great deal of this army, which had barely taken Tampa. One corps had been mustered for expeditionary duty, but had no plans to leave Florida. Richard Harding Davis remembered this as "the rocking-chair period of the war," when reporters lazed away the days on the veranda of the ornate Tampa Bay Hotel.

For the sweating, beflanneled troops, however, it was a struggle in sand and palmetto scrub, and to their commanding officer it was the start of a bitter personal trial. Major General William Rufus Shafter belonged in Gilbert and Sullivan. He had gout and weighed three hundred pounds. "His immense abdomen hung down, yes, actually hung down between his legs," one officer wrote home, and TR remarked bitingly that "not since the campaign of Crassus against the Parthians has there been so criminally incompetent a general as Shafter." Shafter could be shrewd, though few appreciated it. Special platforms were built so he could mount his horse, but since the animal sagged pathetically, the general rode around most of the time in a buckboard with his afflicted foot wrapped in burlap, or lay prostrate in his tent, his bullfrog jowls pulsing like bellows.

The orders he gave for embarkation were simple for him, a nightmare for everyone else. Discovering that his ships would carry only eighteen thousand of the Corps' twenty-five thousand men, he issued no new orders. Instead he merely announced that they would leave at dawn. The result was an insane scramble—a "higgledy-piggledy business," said Roosevelt, who scribbled in his diary, "No military at head. No allotment of transports. No plans."

The Rough Riders had been having a rough time anyway; they had reached Tampa by commandeering a coal train, and now, grimy and exhausted, they seized an old tramp steamer. Other regiments collapsed into chaos. Pandemonium continued through the night and was followed by senseless delays before the disorderly mass of shipping crept into the Caribbean, lights ablaze and decks rocking to the music of regimental bands. Defying every principle of naval caution, this excursion approached the misty Sierra Maestra on June twentieth.

The landing was an even greater travesty. Sampson and Shafter conferred, and fell into bilious disagreement. To the admiral, Shafter's course was obvious: he should hit the shore on both sides of the harbor and charge the fortress of Santiago Castle. The general could scarcely be blamed for declining. The British had tried precisely that maneuver in the eighteenth century, and had been massacred.

Santiago, in fact, was highly defensible at all points; for twenty miles in either direction the beach was backed by towering limestone cliffs crowned with blockhouses. Two sheltered bays were discovered, but Shafter rejected both. Instead he chose to land on Siboney and Daiquiri—open beaches east of Santiago. The Spaniards could have stopped him at the surf line. Incredibly they abandoned the bluffs and withdrew inland, and after an ineffectual bombardment the corps splashed ashore, yelping and waving campaign hats.

TR spotted his former naval aide in a passing launch and hailed him, like a taxi. Horses were less fortunate: troopers belted them overboard with blacksnake whips while buglers blew "Boots and Saddles" from the beach. Some mounts made it, but by dusk the sea was dotted with drowned bodies. One animal was later picked up swimming toward Venezuela.

Thus the cavalry division had to proceed dismounted. It retained its *élan*, however, and it was ably led by Major General "Fighting Joe" Wheeler, late of the Confederate army. Fighting Joe's appointment had been frankly political. The administration had been apprehensive about the South's reaction to the arrival of northern soldiers: troop trains had even been ordered to bypass Richmond. Joe was supposed to be a symbol of national unity. He was more. Despite his age he was a gifted commander; he still had a keen eye for terrain, and this terrain displeased him. Inland there was a well-watered plain, suitable for campsites, while the shore was a buggy trap.

The Spaniards held the one pass in the hills, at Las Guásimas. They might be reinforced at any time, so when Fighting Joe found himself in temporary command—Shafter reported that his foot was being "beastly"—he decided to break out of the beachhead. He made one error. The green Rough Riders were put in front. They marched into an ambush, were pinned down, and had to call for infantry support. Then, just as Las Guásimas was developing into a mincing machine, the obliging Spaniards withdrew again. The news of their retreat electrified old Joe. He leaped up and yelled, "We got the Yankees on the run!"

Before he could celebrate, he was sick. The plain beyond the pass might be a strategic asset, but it was no protection against malaria and the yellow fever. Illness began to spread through the dog tents the first day ashore, and doctors could do little. In 1898 fevers were generally attributed to "swamp exhalations and other noxious vapors of the soil." The mosquito was never mentioned, nor were there any typhoid inoculations; soldiers received castor oil at sick call or wore red flannel "bellybands," red being regarded as a medicinal color. As a result, disease was the more formidable enemy in Cuba. If the Spaniards could hold Santiago long enough the corps would disintegrate in the wilderness, and the one man who realized that was gross, waddling General

Shafter. He had had yellow jack once himself. It was worse than gout. He decided to rush the attack.

As soon as his foot felt like it, he held a council of war. In his judgment there were two battles to be fought, both on the same day. From his headquarters he could see the countryside; lush jungle crossed by a creek, a river, and a web of threadlike paths. This tract ended on the outskirts of the city, where the land rose abruptly in a series of stark ridges. It was on these heights that the Spaniards were preparing their big stand. Over four thousand yards of works had been dug there; in places the lines were three deep.

Shafter intended to meet this challenge head-on, but first the Army would take the spur of El Caney, six miles to the right. El Caney supported a palm-thatched fort and a church steeple full of sharp-shooters. Shafter believed its capture would protect the main attack. Six thousand men were to jump it at dawn on July first, and the moment they had carried it—they would be allowed two hours—the corps' remaining eight thousand would move on Santiago's outer ridge, the key to which was a crest with a flanking knoll. The knoll was called Kettle Hill because it was capped by a huge iron kettle, probably used for sugar refining. The taller crest, with its red-tile-roofed blockhouse, was San Juan Hill.

Such was the general's strategy. It had grave defects. He was splitting his forces—a needless risk, since El Caney lay outside the Spanish line and could have been bypassed. Nor could he himself coordinate the attack; by morning he was stricken again, this time by the heat. Further, in the principal assault, foot soldiers, backed by ineffectual artillery, were to force entrenched peaks. San Juan was within range of Admiral Sampson's guns, but Shafter had no intention of sharing honors with the Navy.

The worst botch of all was the approach march. Both pincers had to reach the front at night on a sunken jungle trail no wider than a sidewalk. Rain had left three inches of mud, and by midnight the entire corps was wedged in the swamp. The El Caney troops branched off and slept among chaparral and mangoes; the two other divisions, one of infantry and one of horseless cavalry, lurched doggedly on. "Three miles away, across the basin of mist," wrote Richard Harding Davis, "we could see the street lamps of Santiago shining over the San Juan hills. Above us, the tropical moon hung white and clear in the dark purple sky, pierced with millions of white stars."

At dawn the sun glittered tragically on a glossy Signal Corps balloon. It had been sent up to find another path to San Juan and so relieve the congestion, and it appears to have occurred to no one that if Americans could see it, so could Spanish cannoneers. Before it fell— "dying a gigantic and public death before the eyes of two armies," as Stephen Crane reported—it did discover a second route. But the enemy riflemen knew about both. Alerted, they zeroed in on the mouths of each. Our ancient field pieces opened up at 2500 yards, achieving nothing but the pinpointing of their own refuges. In forty-five minutes they were silent. The lords of military misrule had run out of their string of boners. All the enemy now faced was the courage of the individual American soldier.

It seemed insufficient. Because El Caney was proving stubborn, the San Juan drive had been halted on the edge of the jungle. Every landmark acquired a grim name: Bloody Ford, Bloody Bend, Bloody Angle, Hell's Pocket. The Seventy-first New York broke. In ten minutes a quarter of the Sixth Infantry were casualties. Messages went back, begging for orders, and shortly after noon one finally arrived— "The heights must be taken at all hazards. A retreat now would be a disastrous defeat." On the left this went to the infantry division, deployed before San Juan Hill. On the right it reached the man who had been waiting for it all his life: Lieutenant Colonel Theodore Roosevelt.

A blue polka-dot bandanna fluttering behind him, the Oyster Bay dandy mounted his horse and paraded slowly back and forth in full view of the enemy. He was brandishing a souvenir pistol from the *Maine*, rounding up troops. As cheering volunteers, regulars and the Negro cavalrymen whose survivors were later to be assigned menial hospital chores surged toward him, he wheeled on Kettle Hill and waved his hand for the charge. Then, all teeth and flashing eyeglasses, he galloped straight up the slope. Bullets singed his mount and nicked his elbow, a small stream delayed him, and forty yards from the top he encountered a fence, but leaping to the ground, he continued on foot until he and the panting ranks behind him reached the peak. They were alone; the enemy had fled. The knoll was theirs, and they were just in time to see the main assault on San Juan Hill. TR called it a "splendid view."

It was. Bully as his ride had been, the charge to his left was bullier. This was a veterans' show—red-neckerchiefed Indian fighters from the old western army scrambling upward in the sunlit, waist-high grass while the crag above crackled with Mauser fire. The hill was slippery, steep, wired; the storming troops clutched at barbs with their bare hands, sawed at the wire with bayonets.

It was not an orderly charge. There was little form to it, and not much mass. Richard Harding Davis thought the men were pitifully few: "It seemed as if someone had made an awful and terrible mistake. One's instinct was to call to them to come back." But the thin ragged line edged higher and higher, a rising ribbon of Army blue. "Yes, they were going up the hill, up the hill," wrote Stephen Crane. "It was the best moment of anybody's life." One last burst from the Spaniards, one instant when enemy riflemen were silhouetted against the bruise-blue horizon; then they were gone, and the Stars and Stripes floated over the blockhouse.

According to Shafter's calculations, Santiago should have been doomed now. It wasn't, because the Spaniards had prepared a second, stronger defense line. Teddy sprinted recklessly toward it, but after a hundred yards he hurried back. He had glanced over his shoulder and made the unsettling discovery that the Rough Riders weren't following him. Even the Ivy League had had enough. Indeed, there were doubts about whether the Army could keep the toehold it had.

That night shallow foxholes were dug in the rocky soil, and the victorious El Caney division arrived to plug gaps; but still the pessimism grew. Cuban rebels had failed to block the road to the north. A mile and a quarter away Spanish reinforcements were pouring into Santiago. Roosevelt concluded that "We are within measurable distance of a terrible military disaster." Shafter, shocked by the thousand casualties of San Juan, told Washington he was thinking of withdrawing five miles, and Sampson prepared to land for a conference—which explains why the American admiral was wearing leggings and spurs the day the Navy fought the decisive battle of the war.

It was Sunday, July first. Captain Evans had just finished his breakfast aboard the *Iowa* and was lighting a cigar when his son, a naval cadet, peered through a porthole and shouted, "Papa, the enemy's ships are coming out!" Led by the flagship *Infanta Maria Teresa*, Cervera's squadron was making its break. One by one the Spanish cruisers dropped their harbor pilots and turned westward, proceeding, said the captain of the *Texas*, "as gaily as brides to the altar." Their scarlet-and-yellow battle flags flew proudly, if despairingly.

Cervera had preferred to tarry in Santiago, but the Spanish Governor General had sternly ordered him out. U.S. sailors in the fighting tops—they still had fighting tops—spotted the move immediately. Even so, there was a chase; Sampson, anticipating a dash, had decided that the enemy could be destroyed at the harbor entrance, but his battleships took time to get under way, and presently the two fleets were sailing in parallel columns, the Spaniards near the shore and the Americans in irregular pursuit.

Both were sailing away from Sampson. Each night he had illuminated the shore with searchlights to be sure this moment didn't elude him. Now it found him off on the *New York,* approaching Shafter for their conference on the land war. To make matters worse, the command devolved upon his bitter enemy, Commodore W. S. Schley, a blustering clown whose chief contribution to victory was to turn his own ship away from the battle and bellow, "Give them hell, bullies!"

It made no difference. Bluejacket gunners were on target. The *Teresa* caught fire and turned, blazing, toward the beach. Cervera's force crumbled quickly; three hours later the last of his vessels ran aground fifty miles from Santiago. At a cost of three American casualties, Spanish sea power had been smashed. The flying squadron which was to have relieved Manila scurried back through Suez to guard the homeland. All that remained was for Sampson to dispute the laurels with Schley, which he did for the rest of his life.

Ashore, according to Lieut. John J. Pershing, "everybody drew a long breath." The Spaniards hadn't counterattacked, so instead of retreating from Santiago, Shafter besieged it. Day by day the Army extended its trenches, until the city was invested by a horseshoe of works decorated with regimental flags. Other flags—of truce—paraded back and forth between the lines. Both sides were ready to quit. The Spaniards were starving, the Americans were ill. Inept in combat, the gouty American general displayed persistent skill in negotiation, and Washington helped by promising a quick trip home for all enemy troops who surrendered unconditionally.

That did it. On July seventeenth Shafter nursed his throbbing foot into a stirrup and rode to a field outside Santiago, where the Sixth Cavalry band played "Hail Columbia." The Spanish *soldados* presented arms, and their ensign was hauled down the flagstaff over the Governor's Palace, thus ending four centuries of rule. Each side wanted the ceremony to be flawless, but it was spoiled by a New York *World* reporter. He demanded a role in the raising of the U.S. colors. Rebuffed, he strode up to Shafter, who was standing painfully in front of his troops, and punched him in the face.

So the Cuban adventure ended, as it had begun, with misconduct by the press. Today such behavior would be incredible, but it was common enough in that period, and this little war is a period piece. In each of its campaigns the same notes are dominant: American individualism, American arrogance, Spanish defeatism. The defeatism grew after Santiago's surrender. When Puerto Rico was invaded nine days later—J. P. Morgan's armed yacht led the way, flying an immense flag, and Washington learned about the landing from journalists—our officers were swamped with dinner invitations from reconciled Spanish civilians. Their army's morale wasn't much higher. The expedition, said Finley Peter Dunne, creator of Mr. Dooley, turned into a "moonlight picnic."

On Guam and Luzon there didn't seem to be any morale at all. Guam's *comandante* hadn't been told that war had been declared. Informed of it by an American cruiser, he explained ruefully that he hadn't any cannon—not, he added hastily, that he had the slightest intention of fighting; he merely wanted to fire a salute to his conquerors. In Manila, where U.S. troops had arrived, the two armies fought one of the most extraordinary engagements in history. The dons were quite willing to capitulate; they just wanted to preserve appearances. Accordingly, the Belgian consul consented to arrange a sham battle—gunfire without casualties. Once this bargain had been struck the defenders seem to have lost interest. A white banner was raised, but when Gen. Francis V. Greene galloped up and inquired whether the city had been surrendered, the Spaniards who had put it up replied languidly that they really couldn't say; all they knew was that someone had told them to hoist the flag. Later their superiors stirred themselves and called for Greene in style.

It was a good thing there hadn't been any real fighting in Manila: no one there knew it, but the war had ended the previous afternoon. Spain had prepared to throw in the towel the day the *World* man hit Shafter. Within twenty-four hours Madrid had asked Paris to intercede, and on August twelfth the French ambassador signed the peace protocol in Washington. Cuba was free; Guam and Puerto Rico were ceded to the United States, and the fate of the Philippine Islands was to be decided later. The Galahad spirit of the spring had been forgotten. McKinley's Secretary of State approached the globe in the Cabinet Room murmuring, "Let's see what we get by this."

Later that year we got the Philippines for twenty million dollars. As the President told a committee of missionaries, we meant to "uplift them and civilize them and Christianize them." The difficulty was that the Filipinos had notions of independence, and thanks to Dewey they were in a position to be difficult. After winning the battle of Manila Bay the commodore had erred grievously. He knew that Kaiser Wilhelm had been dickering for the islands, and the arrival of five German warships seemed ominous. Pacing the *Olympia*'s bridge and fingering his lucky rabbit's foot, he reached a momentous decision: Emilio

Aguinaldo, the exiled leader of the Filipino guerrillas, was to be brought back from Hong Kong as an ally. "If old Dewey had just sailed away when he smashed the Spanish fleet, what a lot of trouble he would have saved us," McKinley later complained. For Aguinaldo promptly declared himself president of a republic, and when he heard America was taking over he drew his sword. The Philippine insurrection dragged on for three bloody years, dwarfing the struggle with Spain.

Despite our military blunders we had won an easy decision in the field. Yet we had only begun to pay the price of triumph. Casualty figures were rapidly obscured by the deaths from disease, both in Cuba and in the United States, where camp sanitation was frightful. Clara Barton had hurried to Santiago, in vain. Shafter's sick list stood at four thousand. Reveille each morning was followed by the dirge of taps, echoing through hour after hour of burials until one day there were no calls at all, because the buglers were down too.

Roosevelt, now a full colonel, led a round-robin demand that the Army be moved at once, and after boarding their scraggly ships the troops were transferred to a quarantine camp at Montauk Point, on the tip of Long Island. Visiting civilians were shocked. The soldiers had left fit; now they were wasted invalids. The War Department, ever consistent, sent exercise horses for bedridden cavalrymen and, as the weather grew bleak, light duck uniforms for all.

McKinley appeared in a frock coat. "I am glad to meet you," he said to the convalescents, looking them in the eye and adding sonorously, "you have come home after two months of severe campaigning, which has embraced assault and siege and battle, so brilliant in achievement, so far-reaching in results as to command the unstinted praise of all your countrymen."

It is doubtful that even he knew how far-reaching those results were to be. Forces had been set in motion that would alter the nation's life in countless little ways. Guantánamo Bay led to a revitalized Marine Corps, bad rations to the Pure Food and Drug Laws, the pine coffins in Santiago to Major Walter Reed's identification of the yellow-fever virus. The structure on Kettle Hill turned out not to have been a kettle after all; it was the White House that TR had captured.

To America he was the Hero of San Juan Hill, despite Mr. Dooley's tart comment on his reminiscences: "I haven't time f'r to tell ye the wurruk Tiddy did in ar-rmin' an' equippin' himself, how he fed himself, how he steadied himself in battles an' encouraged himself with a few well-chosen worruds whin th' sky was darkest. . . . But if I was him I'd call th' book 'Alone in Cubia.' "

Overshadowing all these developments, however—transcending even Teddy's gubernatorial campaign in New York that autumn, with a Rough Rider bugler riding on the rear platform of his whistle-stop train—was the emergence of the United States as a world power. America the superstate was born in the fumbles and confusions of 1898. The administration had picked up vast tracts of land overseas, not all of them from Spain. Hawaii had been seized on the pretext that it was needed as a war base. From this time forward the United States was to play the role of colonial sahib, staring across the Pacific at rising Japan. The first military commandant of Manila was Major General Arthur MacArthur, whose son Douglas was then a West Point cadet.

But these legacies then belonged to the future. The great thing then was that we had won a war. The republic was exhilarated, intoxicated, ready to strut, and there was a hot time in the old town the night Dewey returned to claim his sword. Girls bought sailor hats and Dewey shirtwaists; a brand of gum was named "Dewey Chewies," and a laxative package bore his portrait and the slogan, "The 'Salt' of Salts." On Fifth Avenue the epauletted hero marched under a rococo arch on which sculptured figures represented the winged goddess Victory and the brave boys in blue.

The statues were a huge success. Unfortunately, they were only plaster.

The Great War

I N MY CHILDHOOD the statue of the lean bronze doughboy was already darkening on its marble Lest-We-Forget plinth in the square downtown, but people still sang "There's a Long, Long Trail" as they drove the family flivver in from the country Sunday evenings, and at least once a week there would be an argument down at the white clapboard Legion Hall over whether the Hindenburg Line had been broken by the Yankee Division, the Rainbow, or by the Marines.

I used to hang around the hall cadging doughnuts, and the character I remember best was a town card who had been too old to fight and couldn't have found France, let alone the Argonne, on a map of Europe. Every Memorial Day he would clown around in a mishmash of military livery: an overseas cap, a Navy blouse, sky-blue trousers and rolled puttees. He wasn't a veteran of anything—even I knew that—so he wasn't allowed in the A.E.F. parade. I wanted him to march because he looked so dashing; now I think he was truer to his time than he knew. The war he never fought, like the uniform he wore, was from first to last a hopeless muddle; but, like his uniform, the war was carried off with a flair that almost made you forget how senseless it was.

Never, not even in our war with Spain, was a conflict more fouled up. When the guns stopped, historians couldn't even decide what to call it; most were divided between the Great War and the World War. After Hitler showed his fist it was filed away as World War I, a forgotten curtain-raiser, but they were right the first time. It *was* a great war.

It was a kind of cultural binge—Lieutenant Colonel Winston S. Churchill afterward wrote, "We seemed separated from the old life by a measureless gulf"—and to the most idealistic youth the world had ever known it came as a crisis of the spirit. They had marched off to the lilt of "Tipperary" or *Die Wacht am Rhein* or "Over There," dreaming of braid and heroism. When they found that their generation was bleeding to death, with each casualty list redder than the last, the thoughtful among them fled into cynicism and despair. The composer of "Keep the Homes Fires Burning" acquired an exemption and lolled around in a silk dressing gown, burning incense; thrice-wounded young Harold Macmillan retreated into a study of Horace; Siegfried Sassoon flung his military cross into the sea and wrote bitterly,

> *Pray God that you may never know*
> *The hell where youth and laughter go.*

They were the sensitive. Most men fought stolidly. They had been bred to valor, taught fealty to the tribal deities of God or *Gott* or *Dieu*, and with numb certitude they sacrificed themselves to a civilization that was vanishing with them. They seemed marked by a sense of dedication that could only have been instinctive. In that war, said Dick Diver, touring old trenches in F. Scott Fitzgerald's *Tender Is the Night*, "You had to have a whole-souled sentimental equipment going back further than you could remember. You had to remember Christmas, and postcards of the Crown Prince and his fiancée, and little cafés in Valence and beer gardens in Unter den Linden and weddings at the *mairie*, and going to the Derby, and your grandfather's whiskers. This," he said, "was the last love battle."

That was in 1917, the penultimate year, when the lovelight was glimmering. The Central Powers—Germany, Austria-Hungary, Bulgaria, Turkey—and the Allies—England, France, Russia, Italy—seemed lost in a dark madness. On the Western Front the lines moved a few inches a day, "leaving the dead," said Dick Diver, "like a million bloody rugs." In the East, in March of that year, the tormented Russian masses revolted, and in April the United States declared war on Germany.

The Atlantic was very wide then. For three years Americans had stopped their ears against the gunfire, and some time lapsed before they understood what they were in for. On the showery morning of May 28, 1917, three score Army officers in oddly fitting mufti boarded the White Star liner *Baltic* for Europe. In London they put on their uniforms and looked even odder—they had side arms, which weren't being worn any more, and no Sam Browne belts, which were. King George V didn't criticize. He feted them royally and they crossed to Boulogne, where French greeters struggled with the name of the American leader, a rather junior general officer they wound up calling "Puerchigne."

General Pershing wasn't offended. He was quite taken with his Gallic welcome, in fact, until he reached Paris, where he was told confidentially that the Allies were at the point of collapse; the French army was in open mutiny. Pershing thus became the second American to discover that his side was about finished. The first had been Pershing's opposite number in the U.S. Navy, Admiral Sims. In London Sims had learned from Britain's Admiral Jellicoe that Germany's submarine campaign had England on her knees. Rations were tight and growing tighter. The British government was doing everything it could—draft notices were being sent to the maimed, the blind, the mad, and in some cases even the dead—but it wasn't enough. One freighter in four was going down. There was six weeks' supply of corn in the country. Jellicoe expected an Allied surrender by November 1.

All this was news to Pershing and Sims. They understood, of course, that shipping losses had to be concealed, and that Paris naturally didn't want Berlin to know that poilus were beating up generals, derailing trains and leaving trenches undefended; but they were amazed that Washington had been given no inkling. Their astonishment showed their naïveté. America's Western Front Allies weren't even confiding in each other; each was fighting its own war in jealous secrecy. Together they were defending a snakelike chain of trenches that began on the Swiss border and ended 466 miles away on the Channel, but the joint between them was very weak.

Early in the war English troops couldn't get French maps, and at one time British hospital trains, imported from England, were being charged two hundred pounds for each trip on French rails. This may seem inhospitable, but it must be remembered that France's guests were often rude. Not only was Sir Douglas Haig, the starchy British commander, openly disdainful of everything French; his India Army officers called natives "wogs" or "niggers," babbled Hindustani at them, and sometimes kicked them.

If the Entente was an uneasy one, official Allied distrust of the United States ran deeper. Americans were popular enough—they had been properly shocked by the Huns' *Schrecklichkeit* in Belgium, and some 28,000 U.S. volunteers were wearing British khaki and French horizon blue. Their government was something else again. To the belligerent eye it had been insufferably independent, permitting American trade with Germany (until the British Admiralty felt obliged to draw up a blacklist of U.S. shipping) and winking at the buffoonery of Henry Ford, who chartered a "peace ship," boarded it to the strains of "I Didn't Raise My Boy to be a Soldier," and announced that he intended "to get the boys out of the trenches by Christmas."

All Ford got was a cold and a quick trip home, but he had retained his pious air of superiority, which was also an annoying trait of his

President. As a neutral, Woodrow Wilson had damned the Teutonic and Allied power blocs alike, insisted he was "too proud to fight" and loftily suggested a "peace without victory." Even now, he was delivering sermons demanding that the world be made safe for democracy. European statesmen, who wanted only a world in which they could safely execute their secret agreements, were derisive. "My aim," said France's Clemenceau, "is to conquer."

That sort of remark made Wilson flinch. He knew a little about those agreements, and was to learn more as the revolutionary government in Russia published details. He wanted no part of them. He seemed almost bewildered by his failure to stay neutral, although actually the seed of his failure had been sown in the war's first year, and by him. The German navy had planned to counter British sea power with unrestricted submarine warfare, and on May 1, 1915, a Käpitän Leutnant Walther Schwieger prowling off the Irish coast in his U-20, had torpedoed the Cunard liner *Lusitania*. Over a thousand had drowned, a hundred of them American civilians.

In that gentler age, when war was still thought of as chivalrous, the sinking was almost unbelievable. Wilson—who hadn't known that the *Lusitania* had carried munitions—had been outraged. He had written a protest so strongly worded that his Secretary of State, William Jennings Bryan, refused to sign it. The note went to Berlin anyhow, a virtual ultimatum. Kaiser Wilhelm brooded over it and called off his subs. The meaning of the incident was clear. The American President had drawn a line. He would fight if Schwieger were let loose again.

The Kaiser was under growing pressure to take that risk. His admirals had a fleet of two hundred subs, and his top generals, von Hindenburg and Ludendorff, wanted them used. Then, early in 1917, he had a bright idea. He instructed his foreign minister to wire the Mexican government, suggesting an alliance with it in the event of war between Germany and the United States and offering Texas, New Mexico and Arizona as a bribe. If America was fighting at home, the Kaiser told his court, it couldn't take on Germany.

Unluckily for him, the British decoded the telegram; it was published throughout the United States and stirred up resentment, especially in Texas. By now the German high command was crying for action, and the Kaiser told the navy to go ahead. For the next two months the Atlantic churned with torpedo wakes. Wilson tried to dodge the inevitable by arming merchant ships, but when U-boat commanders started sinking homeward-bound American ships, he gave up, and we were in the war.

But not all the way in. Not yet. Our suspicious Allies couldn't believe we weren't after something more tangible than Wilsonian ideals, and they kept telling Washington that they could carry on in the field if we would backstop their economies. They needed money; Europe was hemorrhaging gold.

Acting on their advice, we swiftly sent bankers to write loans in London and Paris, while Congress let six weeks pass before an American army was even authorized. The first draftees wouldn't go to camp for three and a half more months, while Pershing furiously paced the red tile floors of his headquarters at Chaumont and sent back appeals for a million men. All he got that summer were marching units to show the flag to doubting Frenchmen—regular regiments like the Sixteenth Infantry, which paraded through Picpus Cemetery in Paris on July 4 as a colonel declared, in unconscious irony, "Lafayette, we are here."

What made all this peculiar was that it had happened before in this war. In 1914 the British had no intention of fighting in force. They had a big navy, lots of cash and 160,000 regulars, Kipling's original Mulvaneys, the acknowledged flower of the world's assault troops. Wearing their ribbons from the Egyptian, Burmese and South African shows, they marched to meet the Prussian Guard in flawless parade-ground formation. Unfortunately, there weren't enough of them, and there was that map problem. They went down gallantly, firing "fifteen rounds rapid" at Ypres, gone in a vision of angels at Mons. It was the last hurrah of Tommy Atkins. There weren't enough survivors even to season recruits.

The Kaiser scorned them as "contemptibles," and a generation weaned on *Soldiers Three* flocked to the colors, a million avengers on their way to death for King and Country, Kipling's own son among them. It was all very disorderly. The worst of it was that university students had been allowed to enlist as privates, which meant the pick of England's youth—the men who should have been junior officers then and civilian leaders after the war—vanished into the drifting mists of no-man's-land.

Now in 1917 the United States was being urged to follow the same fatal course. Allied generals were panicky at the thought of a big American expeditionary force. "There must be no thought of staying our hand until America puts an army in the field next year," Haig wrote anxiously in his diary June 10. There is an explanation for this remarkable attitude, and it is the key to the whole war. In that remote day of derbies, ostrich-plume bonnets and hansom cabs, civilization was in the middle of a profound transition. Culturally it remained gyved to the horsy Victorian past, yet the machine age was coming, and coming fast. Europe lay half in one period, half in the other.

Until the assassination of the Austrian archduke, on June 28, 1914, set off the chain reaction of alliances, it had not been a bad time. Churchill remembered how "the world on the verge of its catastrophe was very brilliant. Nations and empires crowned with princes and potentates rose majestically on every side, lapped in the accumulated treasures of the long peace." The flaw was that of all customs, war was the most rooted in the folklore of the past, and its traditional leaders—the princes and potentates and field marshals—were the least capable of understanding the new mechanized war they were to lead.

These fogies distrusted the A.E.F. because, among other reasons, they didn't want to share the glory—*la gloire*, the French called it. French yearning for *la gloire* was almost as great as their talent for self-hypnosis. Even as their soldiers tried to blow up their own munitions dumps and baaed like sheep to show they regarded themselves as lambs marked for slaughter, *maréchals* spoke glowingly of the natural *élan* of the poilu. They never stopped dreaming of Murat and Ney and the glint of Austerlitz moonlight on the lance heads of the emperor's cavalry. Their speech was studded with Napoleonic phrases. They plotted the *offensive à outrance,* carried out with *toujours l'audace* by gallant men singing "La Marseillaise" and crying *En avant! À la baionette!*

Of course this was for the younger men, *les jeunes Turcs.* The generals stayed out of the chilling rain, in the ballrooms of commandeered châteaux. At their age they had to take care of themselves. When the Germans sprang at Verdun in 1916, the courier who brought the news was told that "Papa" Joffre, the constable of France, was asleep behind a double-locked door and couldn't be disturbed.

England's Colonel Blimps were equally convinced that a chap could smash through that barbed wire if he had enough sand. They strode around in gleaming field boots and jingling spurs and toured the lines in Rolls-Royces, cursing bad march discipline. It was a pretty thin time for the regular service, they agreed; so many of the officer replacements weren't really gentlemen. The new fellows were sharply reminded that they should keep servants in their dugouts, that slack privates were to be struck on sight, and that before going over the top everyone must check to be sure the senior regiment was on the right. In rest camp subalterns actually were required to attend riding school and learn polo, and during the worst fighting on the Somme fussy divisional horse shows were ceremoniously held just behind the front.

The British failed on the Somme, though not for that reason; the

German generals were just as bad. *Junkers* cherished their monocles, spotless white gloves and black-and-silver saber knots. Everywhere the military cliques abused the almost ecclesiastical status they had acquired when prewar diplomacy broke down. Interlopers like Churchill, who spoke bitterly of their "pomp and power," were looked upon as cads. When the British Prime Minister questioned England's strategy, Haig said tightly, "I could not have believed that a British minister could have been so ungentlemanly." The general staffs insisted no one should have a voice in the war unless he had spent forty years in uniform, which, as Liddell Hart acidly observed, would have eliminated Alexander, Hannibal, Caesar, Cromwell, Marlborough and Napoleon.

American officers were of the same stodgy breed. Theodore Roosevelt noted that some were still too fat to mount a saddle, and others seemed to belong back at Little Big Horn. They sent white horses to France in anticipation of triumphal entries when they had slimmed down a bit; they showed their sympathy with the stale defensive tactics on the Western Front by ordering a hundred million sandbags from India, and they insisted enlisted men wear parade-ground tunics so binding that they were crippling in combat.

Doughboys complained, but by then the more fantastic anachronisms had disappeared from field uniforms. The Germans had shed the impractical spikes on their helmets; the French and British, who had had no helmets at all in 1914, were protected now. French infantrymen no longer wore scarlet trousers and blue coats, and the British had abandoned the practice of having new subalterns visit an armorer to have their swords sharpened, like Henry V, before sailing for France.

This decision wasn't made lightly. Sword sharpening had been a sentimental ceremony, like Flirtation Walk. The idea of attacking a machine gun with a saber is inconceivable today, but the generals had considered the machine gun before the war, decided it was an overrated weapon, and turned back to what they felt was real soldiering. Each year the mechanical revolution clanked out new engines of death, but the alumni of Sandhurst and *Saint-Cyr-l'École* accepted them grudgingly or not at all.

They belonged to that older generation which still called electric light "the electric" and distrusted it as newfangled. Joffre wouldn't use a telephone. Kitchener of England dismissed the tank as a "toy." Planes and submarines were deplored; poison gas, adopted reluctantly after the Germans had used it, was delicately called "the accessory." The trench mortar was rejected twice at the British War Office and finally introduced by a cabinet minister who begged the money for it from an Indian maharajah. In the gleaming châteaux this was regarded as both bad form and foolishness. The epauletted marshals placed their main reliance in masses of cavalry—as late as 1918 Pershing was cluttering up his supply lines with mountains of fodder for useless horses—and their staffs rarely visited the front, where a very different kind of war was being fought.

There, by the junk heap of no-man's-land, amid the stench of urine, feces, and decaying flesh, the great armies squatted on the Western Front year after year, living troglodytic lives in candlelit dugouts and trenches hewn from Fricourt chalk or La Bassée clay, or scooped from the porridge of swampy Flanders. They had been there since the gray tide of the German right wing—undiscovered by a hundred thousand galloping French cavalry—had made its sweep through Belgium, lapped at the breakwater of Verdun, recoiled on the Marne at the very gates of Paris, and receded to the Aisne. The efficient Prussians had tacked up propaganda signs there (*Gott strafe England; Frankreich, du bist betragen*) and settled down to teach the children German while the Allies furiously counterattacked.

The titanic struggles that followed were called battles, but although they were fought on a fantastic scale, with nearly two million men lost at Verdun and on the Somme, strategically they were only siege assaults. Every attack found the Kaiser's defenses stronger. The poilus and tommies who crawled over their parapets, lay down in front of jump-off tapes, and waited for their officers' zero-hour whistles, would face as many as ten aprons of barbed wire thick as a man's finger, backed by the pullulating Boche.

A few trenches would be taken at shocking cost—one gain of seven hundred mutilated yards cost twenty-six thousand men—and then the siege would start again. At home newspapers spoke of "hammer blows" and "the big push," but the men knew better; a soldier's *mot* had it that the war would last a hundred years, five years of fighting and ninety-five of winding up the barbed wire.

It was a weird, grimy life, unlike anything in their Victorian upbringing except, perhaps, the stories of Jules Verne. There were a few poignant reminders of prewar days—the birds that caroled over the lunar landscape each gray and watery dawn; the big yellow poplar forests behind the lines—but most sound and color on the front were unearthly. Bullets cracked and ricochets sang with an iron ring; overhead shells wabbled endlessly. There were spectacular red Very flares, saffron shrapnel puffs, snaky yellowish mists of mustard gas souring the ground. Little foliage survived here. Trees splintered to matchwood stood in silhouette against the sky. Draftees arriving from home ("The necessary supply of heroes must be maintained at all costs," said Lord Carson) were shipped up in boxcars built for *hommes* 40 or *chevaux* 8 and marched over duckboard to their new homes in the earth, where everything revolved around the trench—you had a trench knife, a trench cane, a rod-shaped trench periscope and, if you were unlucky, trench foot, trench mouth or trench fever.

Even in quiet sectors there was a steady toll of shellfire casualties—the methodical British called it "normal wastage." The survivors were those who developed quick reactions to danger. An alert youth learned to sort out the whines that threatened him, though after a few close ones, when his ears buzzed and everything turned scarlet, he also learned that the time might come when ducking would do no good. If he was a machine gunner he knew that his life expectancy in combat had been calculated at about thirty minutes, and in time he became detached toward death and casual with its appliances. He would remove cartridges at the right places in cartridge belts so that the machine gun would rap out familiar rhythms. Enemy lines would be sprayed with belt after belt from water-cooled barrels to heat the water for soup. If the Germans were known to be low on canister and improvising, the trenches would be searched eagerly after a shelling to see whether they had thrown over anything useful. Sometimes you could find handy screws, bolts, the cog wheels of a clock, or even a set of false teeth that just might fit.

After the Germans' failure to take Verdun, this had become a quiet front for their assault troops. Their communiqués customarily reported that all was quiet on the Western Front. Elsewhere there was plenty of news, however, nearly all of it good for them. Blessed with interior lines, they needed no risky amphibious operations, England's undoing at the Dardanelles. They could strike anywhere by rescheduling a few trains, and as the deadlock continued in the West they crushed a weak Eastern ally each autumn—thus releasing more troops for France.

In 1914 they mauled the Russians in East Prussia at Tannenberg, where Hindenburg and Ludendorff made their reputations. In 1915 Bulgaria joined them to knock Serbia out of the war. In 1916 Rumania, encouraged by temporary Russian gains and hungry for land, threw in her lot with the Allies, with fiasco as the result. Rumania had doubled her army during the preceding two years, but strategically she was isolated, and her officer corps strolled the streets of Bucharest, wearing rouge and propositioning each other while spies blew up a dump of nine million shells outside the city and a dozen enemy divisions, drawn from the Western Front, swarmed up the Carpathian Mountains. Just before winter snows sealed the passes the Germans broke through and Rumania quit.

The Middle East was the same story—only the camel-mounted raiding parties of a young English archaeologist named T. E. Lawrence offered a ghost of hope—and in 1917, with a succession of revolutionary governments sidestepping to the left in Russia, Germany sent a phalanx of picked divisions to reinforce Austria's Caporetto sector in Italy. On October 24 they attacked out of the Julian Alps in a thick fog. In twelve hours the defenders were on the run; by November terrified Venetians were hiding the bronze horses of St. Mark's and preparing to flee. When the Italians finally rallied they had lost 600,000 men and were back on the Piave. The most ardent disciple of *la gloire* agreed it looked like a bad war.

Nor was that the worst. In France 1917 had been a freak of horror. Both the French and British had felt bullish in the spring. Each had planned independently to make this the year of the decisive battle in the West, and each had massed its biggest battalions for a breakthrough. The French were to open with an "unlimited offensive" under their swashbuckling new constable, Robert Georges Nivelle, who had replaced the bovine Joffre. Even English generals liked Nivelle (his mother had been British), and the châteaux and horse shows thrilled to his battle cry, "One and a half million Frenchmen cannot fail."

Unfortunately the excitement, the cry and even the plan of attack reached Ludendorff. The offensive had been predicted in French newspapers and orders circulated as low as company level, which meant the Germans picked up prisoners carrying them. Nivelle knew this. He also knew von Hindenburg and Ludendorff were riposting with a strategic withdrawal called *Alberich* (after the evil dwarf of the Nibelungen legend), fouling wells and sowing booby-traps as they went. This didn't change a thing, Nivelle insisted. In fact, it ruined everything. The new Hindenburg Line was a defender's dream. It turned Nivelle's drive into a welter of slaughter. He made no real gains, and the moment he stopped, revolt spread among French troops. At the height of the mutiny fourteen out of sixteen divisions on the Champagne front were disabled. France had been virtually knocked out of the war. She had lost nearly a million men in the retreat of 1914 and now, with these new losses, she didn't have the manpower to build a new striking force.

The rest of her army huddled sullenly in the trenches, and to anoint its wounds the government named a tranquil new *maréchal,* Henri Philippe Pétain.

Now the Allies turned desperately to Haig. He responded by giving them the nightmare of Passchendaele. Attacking out of the old Ypres salient in Flanders, the British leaped toward the German submarine ports in Belgium. They never had a chance. There wasn't a flicker of surprise. A long preliminary bombardment merely destroyed the Flemish drainage system. The water, having nowhere else to go, flooded the trenches, and to make things soggier the rains were among the heaviest in thirty years. After three months in this dismal sinkhole Haig had barely taken the village of Passchendaele. His army was exhausted. In London the ambulance trains unloaded at night, smuggling casualties home out of consideration for civilian morale, and in Flanders fields the poppies grew between the crosses, row on row, that marked 150,000 fresh British graves.

The American Congress was fit to be tied. Traditionally, it blamed whatever went wrong abroad on the administration, and there was angry talk of a committee on the conduct of the war. That conduct wasn't all it might have been. America hadn't exactly sprung to arms. There was only one division in France, the First, defending six quiet miles near St. Mihiel. Pershing had wrung a pledge of twenty-four divisions by June, yet he was getting only seven hundred men a day. American unpreparedness looked bad, but the blame was divisible. The country had entered the war with 550 artillery pieces and 55 planes, 51 of them obsolete. Congress was responsible for that, and in the spring it had been as anxious as everyone else to make the A.E.F. a mere token force.

The big bottleneck was still in Europe. A million Americans were in camp now, being jabbed with paratyphoid shots, but not many were getting past Hoboken or Newport News. The Allied generals weren't balking anymore. After Nivelle, Passchendaele and Caporetto, the high commands were eager to welcome an A.E.F. "Our only hope lies in American reserves," said Sir William Robertson, Chief of Britain's Imperial General Staff, and Pétain said, "I shall wait for the Americans and the tanks." The rub was that America hadn't the ships. British bottoms were needed to send men and the fifty pounds of supplies required every day for each American soldier in France. The Admiralty, battling the recrudescent submarine attack, said none could be spared. The future remained bleak. The best Pershing could do was send the trickle of men he was getting into the forests of France to fell trees and build docks for the ships that just might come in time.

Meanwhile America was busy being American—bustling around, making sure the boys in camp were being entertained by Odd Fellows and Maccabees (and their minds kept clean by the Salvation Army), plastering the country with James Montgomery Flagg and Charles Dana Gibson posters, and organizing everything with pep, know-how and get-up-and-go.

The air was full of slogans. It was Work or Fight, Build a Bridge of Ships, and, after a food administration had been set up by Herbert Hoover, that fellow who had done such a grand job in Belgium, there was the Gospel of the Clean Plate and Food Will Win the War. Paring potatoes carelessly became unpatriotic. There were wheatless days and meatless days, and for a time, when the rumor spread that pro-German bakers were mixing ground glass with their flour, there were a few voluntary breadless days.

Never had a war been so well advertised. Hoover and Bernard Baruch were the big volunteers, but there were badges for everyone: service flags, kitchen-window posters, thrift stamps, committee buttons. The committees were endless. Mothers collected cherry pits for gas masks. Boy Scouts planted vegetable gardens. Clothing manufacturers who didn't realize what they were starting saved cloth by cutting yardage from women's clothing, and there was even a Brassiere War Service Committee. Corset manufacturers completely redesigned their product, letting out waists, and announced they had saved thousands of tons of steel for shells. Of course there were blunders. Men who had no business on these panels were appointed because they had volunteered. One who clearly knew nothing about such things recommended that corsets be further simplified by discarding the laces. "They can just as well wear them without any trimming," he said.

Everybody hated the Hun. The President might talk all he liked about fighting a government and not a people, but Americans were down on all Germans. The Kaiser, of course, was known to be insane. The goose-steppers he led were regarded as sadistic. You didn't dare admit that some of your friends were of that tainted stock. Hadn't you seen the drawings of Belgian babies skewered on Prussian bayonets? Hadn't you read Sgt. Arthur Guy Empey's *Over the Top, By An American Soldier Who Went?* It was all there in black and white.

Teutonic names were automatically suspect. If you were a Viereck or Dreiser or Mencken you really had to watch yourself. Your neighbors might hale you before a kangaroo court, splash your front door with yellow paint, or make you march in a Liberty Loan parade wearing a humiliating placard. Two men, in Illinois and Montana, were lynched, and Lutheran ministers delivered their sermons in English to prove they weren't making obscene remarks about the flag.

The German language was suspect everywhere. In several states its teaching was prohibited even in private schools. German music also was boycotted, and people who didn't know what philosophy meant could tell you all about Neitzsche, that poisonous prophet of *Der Tag*. True patriots wouldn't rest until Baltimore's German Street was renamed Redwood Street, or until a derrick had lifted the statue of Frederick the Great in Washington from its base and deposited it in a dark basement; nor would they eat sauerkraut until it was rechristened liberty cabbage.

The wave of resentment against everything German was chiefly an escape valve when we were doing so little at the front. Often it was also cruel. The loyalty of German-born professors was under constant investigation. Men who had relatives in uniform were expelled from their clubs; mothers were insulted even as their sons filed into trenches with the German-speaking Wisconsin regiment attached to the First Division.

Pershing's force grew slowly. The First was followed by the Second (Indianhead), Twenty-sixth (Yankee), and Forty-second (the Rainbow, picked National Guardsmen from twenty-six states), and in Europe a popular image of Americans was beginning to form. At first they hadn't even a nickname. The French tried Sammies, then *les amies*, and finally, after George M. Cohan's song, Yanks.

Yanks were considered very odd. They all seemed unsophisticated, wiry and very young—at this late date they were, in fact, the only youthful army in the field. Their language was like English, but different really. Lice were "seam squirrels," dice were "galloping dominoes," and everyone was "Buddy" to everyone else. They spoke their pidgin French with a peculiar twang, looked like cowboys in their broad-brimmed campaign hats, and would pay almost any price for a souvenir—a meerschaum, an iron cross, or a pair of woman's garters with *Gott mit uns* clasps.

Allied commanders thought all doughboys were pampered. Their officers never kicked or struck them, and the troops were accompanied by an amazing array of creature comforts. They had no wine, like poilus, or daily tot of rum, like tommies, but they had just about everything else. One major became a Parisian legend; he arrived with a terrier and a piano and set up a permanent billet in the Ritz. He was a banker in civilian life and therefore privileged. Even private soldiers carried $10,000 government life insurance, a preposterous figure on the Western Front. In camp they were serenaded by a gigantic army band led by Walter Damrosch, and in the field they were attended by solicitous auxiliaries with Y.M.C.A. chocolate, Knights of Columbus cigarettes and Salvation Army doughnuts.

Strangest of all, however, was American wit. Yanks joked about everything, including some things that weren't really funny. Europeans laughed politely, but were secretly baffled. The commander of the Seventy-seventh Division (New York's Own), arriving with his pitifully green draftees, lightly described them as "hardy backwoodsmen from the Bowery, Fifth Avenue and Hester Street." Doughboys turned their own homesickness into a wisecrack—"Hell, Heaven or Hoboken by Christmas." Coffins to them were "wooden kimonos," and front-line combat didn't sober them much. They kept making flippant remarks about the little streams the French called rivers; when one badly wounded man was offered a canteen he said with a faint smile, "Give it to the Ourcq. It needs it more than I do." They even bantered with rank—and about *la gloire,* of all things. General Pershing approached a private with three wound stripes on his arm. "Where did you get those?" he asked gently. The man grinned and replied, "From the quartermaster, sir."

The Yanks' image of themselves was caught in a German intelligence report on the first American prisoners: "They still regard the war from the point of view of the 'big brother' who comes to help his hardpressed brethren and is therefore welcomed everywhere." Doughboys assumed they would be popular, just as their generals expected that the American infantryman's fighting qualities would be respected.

The generals were disappointed. Yanks were more liked than feared. German officers spoke contemptuously of "American bluff" and "a rabble of amateurs." Allied observers watched the newcomers train and shook their heads. Pershing kept insisting that American "vigor and aggressive spirit" could replace "technical skill," but the Allies thought they had better ideas. Pétain suggested that American regiments be attached to French divisions as they arrived, and Haig wanted them used as replacements, fed piecemeal into the British line.

Pershing bridled. He said flatly that Americans would fight as an army or not at all, and the next thing he knew he was mired in international politics. Thereafter he had to fight both to get an army and to keep it. Clemenceau protested that his *"invincible obstination"* was threatening the entire cause; he and Lloyd George appealed to Wilson behind Pershing's back, and French and British generals kept trying to bargain with Chaumont. In the end Pershing had to compromise some, but not because he was intimidated by Pétain, Haig, Clemenceau or Lloyd George. The man who brought the first American detachments into action—and persuaded the Allies that they must have a supreme commander—was Erich Friedrich Wilhelm Ludendorff.

As German victories crowned one another through 1917 the Kaiser's general staff felt increasingly confident of victory. By early in 1918 they thought the end was in sight. The capstone was a treaty with the Russian revolutionists signed in March at Brest-Litovsk, a railway center the Germans had occupied three years before.

Overnight it was a new war. The peace in the East freed three thousand German guns and a million men—enough to give Ludendorff the whip hand on the Western Front, provided he struck before America's waxing strength eclipsed his edge. Ludendorff had designed a brilliant new attack technique, stressing stealth, surprise bombardment, gas and infiltration. He prepared a concert of thrusts in the West, and Hindenburg promised the Kaiser they would be in Paris by April 1.

Ludendorff's first blow, delivered on March 21, fell on the weak seam between the French and British armies in the Somme valley. Its immediate objective was Amiens, through which ran the only line of communications between the two Allies. After a tremendous cannonade, the Germans lunged out of a heavy fog with five times their Verdun strength. By night the line had been broken in several places. During the second day the British, weakened by Passchendaele, fell back ten miles. The bulge grew deeper each hour; Krupp cannon began shelling Paris. On the sixth day one of the railways between Amiens and the capital was cut, the starved assault troops had turned aside to pillage and the tommies held on grimly.

Ludendorff's next stroke, in April, was in Flanders. He had fog again, and again he broke through, this time on a thirty-mile front. Everything Haig had won six months before was lost. The enemy was within five miles of Hazebrouck, a vital railway junction and his goal. Then, at the critical moment, Ludendorff wavered. He couldn't decide whether or not to exploit the capture of the tallest hill in Flanders, and by the time he made up his mind the stubborn British were dug in. All he had was a second salient, which wasn't Paris.

No one doubted, however, that his masterpiece was yet to come. Marshal Foch, who in this dark hour had been made generalissimo of all the armies, called for a "foot-by-foot" defense of ground, and in

Chaumont, where files were being packed, Pershing put his troops at Foch's disposal. Curiously it was the Americans, the tyros, who picked the spot where the Germans' greatest storm would break. The Chemin des Dames ridge, north of the Aisne, was so formidable a natural stronghold that the French had manned it with five exhausted British divisions. This was the closest sector to Paris. Ludendorff's plan was to crash through and head for the capital. He knew that every reserve would be committed to the defense of the city, and when that happened he was going to wheel and drive on Haig's channel ports.

His preparations were superb. No one took seriously the American guess that Ludendorff's attack would come at Chemin des Dames because there wasn't a trace of activity from the German lines. Observation posts reported nothing, aerial photographs were a blank. Apparently there weren't even any batteries there. Actually there were nearly four thousand guns. You just couldn't see them. Moving at night and hiding in the woods by day, their horses' hoofs wrapped in rags to mute any sound, the Germans massed some fifteen crack divisions opposite the ridge.

On the morning of May 27 they sprang out of nowhere behind a tornado of gas and shrapnel. The weary British disintegrated. By dusk Ludendorff's assault columns had moved twelve miles. They crossed the Vesle River and surged on, hobnail boots thumping and gray coats swishing weirdly in the sunshine, and by the third day, when Soissons fell, they had overrun five French lines. There were no defenses after that. They were on the Marne, the tip of their salient at a place called Château Thierry. The Allied Supreme War Council met hurriedly. The marshals had agreed U.S. troops wouldn't be really dependable until 1919, but there was no one else handy, so they sent in the United States Marines.

The battle that followed has been so blurred by legend and sentiment that the truth is almost irretrievable. Despite a contemporary myth, the American troops didn't shout "Remember the Lusitania!" Nor were they the first Yanks to engage the enemy; three days earlier the First Division had taken a town elsewhere called Cantigny and beaten off seven counterattacks. The Leathernecks weren't even the first doughboys in Château Thierry—an Army machine-gun unit from the Third Division reached it first and retired slowly through the streets, covering the French retreat across the river. The Marine Corps has beatified its Fifth and Sixth regiments as the noblest of professionals; but when war was declared most of the enlisted men had been in campus blazers. The proportion of college men in the Sixth Marines was put at sixty percent. They had enlisted before the Plattsburg Plan diverted students into ninety-day Officer Training Schools, and they were American counterparts to the young English toffs who had gone off to vindicate their Kipling heroes four years before. Sergeant Alexander Woollcott of *Stars and Stripes* had heard them sing "Fair Harvard" and "Old Nassau" in camp, and now they were going into battle, and they were going to give it the old college try.

Arriving near Château Thierry after an all-night march, they were thrown across the road to Paris. Opposite them was a rolling field of summer wheat, thick with scarlet poppies, and four hundred yards beyond lay a forbidding Dante thicket of dark, tortured trees. That was Belleau Wood. The Germans had two divisions there. They were expected to break out in mass formation at any time. There wasn't any Allied line, an excited French officer told the marines, and there wouldn't be any unless they formed one. It was hard to hear him, because refugees were fleeing past with bird cages and clothing packed in rattling baby carriages. One of them shouted *"La guerre est fini!"* at the Yanks, and some truant from an American French class shouted back *"Pas fini!"* giving the sector its name.

For five days the marines held five miles of Pas Fini against the solid gray columns that came hurtling across the field. The Germans reported encountering a "shock unit." Clemenceau announced the Americans had saved Paris. That wasn't all. On June 6, in the waving wheat, the marines were fixing bayonets, preparing to storm Belleau Wood.

It took more than storming. Their first charge crumpled among the poppies, doomed by a weak barrage. The casualties were greater than those in all previous Marine Corps battles combined. Nevertheless, they reformed and tried again. By nine o'clock that night they had a toehold in the wood, and in the next three weeks they doggedly cleared the boulder-strewn, gully-laced warren of the enemy. The Germans tried a high-explosive shell bombardment, went to mustard, then withdrew. After searching the German dead for souvenirs the marines also withdrew, turning Pas Fini over to the Yankee Division.

Of the eight thousand men who had straddled the road in the crisis, only two thousand were left. More than a hundred were awarded the Distinguished Service Cross. The French renamed the wood for them. At home they were all national heroes—"OUR GALLANT MARINES DRIVE ON 2½ MILES, NOTHING STOPS THEIR RUSH," cried a New York *Times* streamer—and, in Chaumont, Pershing felt he had won a point. He had. The British Admiralty, which had discovered that convoys could cope with U-boats, was prepared to provide a bridge of ships. Camouflaged transports were ferrying 120,000 Americans a month across the Atlantic. By midsummer this had risen to 300,000. Ports worked around the clock. Boys from Montana farms and Louisiana swamplands were trudging up gangplanks endlessly and it was "Goodbye Broadway, Hello France," *We're gonna pay our debt to you,* and *Wait and pray each night for me, Till we meet again.*

Pershing had his million men now. He was taking over more and more of the Allied line—soon he would hold a fifth of it—and when the Germans tried to take advantage of Bastille Day by attacking the day after July 14 ("Sort of a frog Fourth of July," one American commander explained to his men) three divisions of doughboys counterattacked. The First and Second Divisions jumped off from a poplar forest, waded through waist-high wheat and forced the enemy to evacuate Soissons. By the beginning of August the Allies were back on the Vesle; Belleau Wood was twenty miles behind them now, and they were across the Ourcq, which the Fighting Sixty-ninth regiment—now part of the Rainbow, and redesignated the 165th Infantry, though the Irish still wore rosaries hooked through the left shoulder straps of their blouses—insisted on calling the O'Rourke.

Ludendorff's hopes were fading with the summer poppies. He had made a big thing of his July 15 drive. It had been christened the *Siegessturm,* the stroke of victory, and he had built a tall wooden tower behind the lines so the Kaiser could watch. Wilhelm perched there for six days, squinting through telescopes, trying to figure out which army was his. When he climbed down stiffly the news was all bad. This time the Germans didn't even have a bulge. Their morale was sinking fast; pitiful letters told the troops of hunger at home, and quartermasters with bare shelves were issuing commandeered women's clothing to soldiers.

Then came what Ludendorff called the "black day" of the war. On August 8 the British massed nearly five hundred tanks in front of Amiens, cracked the German line, and gained over eight miles. It was an omen. Ludendorff didn't miss it. That week he offered to quit and suggested the Kaiser ask for terms. He was put off, but a corner had been turned. Henceforth the general staff would be occupied with thoughts not of victory, but of striking a bargain and saving the army.

The Allies didn't know this. The German soldiers were fighting as stubbornly as ever, and Foch's immediate plans were to smash in all German salients, improving communications for the campaign that everyone assumed they would be fighting in 1919. One of these salients, cutting the main railroad between Paris and Nancy, had been a threat since the early days of the war. The French had lost 60,000 men trying to take it in 1915 and had called it "the hernia of St. Mihiel" ever since.

The only maps available to American officers before they entered the war had been of this sector. Pershing stalked it now. Feinting toward Belfort, he struck on September 12 with nine divisions. Despite heavy rain and bad roads—*Stars and Stripes* charged they hadn't been repaired since Joan of Arc advanced along them—success was stunning. The most hopeful appraisal had allowed two days for the attack. It took one. Entire Lehr, Saxon and Landwehr regiments were herded into prisoner pens; the defeated Germans claimed they had been preparing to withdraw anyway, but captured orders contradicted this. In St. Mihiel embarrassed doughboys were embraced by French patriarchs who toasted them with hoarded kirsch and displayed American flags copied from photographs, the stripes all black.

Elsewhere other local offensives also had gone well for the Allies. Ludendorff's spring gains had disappeared from the war maps. Germans were being pinched off all along the front, and Foch was charting an "arpeggio" of drives against the Hindenburg Line. "Everyone is to attack as soon as they can, as strong as they can, for as long as they can," he said, and "*L'édifice commence à craquer. Tout le monde à la bataille!*" Actually it was better organized than that. There was a plan, and the American army was its fulcrum. Pershing's troops held ninety-four miles on the extreme right of the Allied line. In the center were the French, with the British to their left and King Albert of Belgium on the sea, leading a combined group which included two American divisions. Much was expected on Albert's end, less from the other. Pershing was to be the Allied anchor. He had used his veteran divisions at St. Mihiel, and they needed time to reorganize. Moreover, he faced the toughest link in the Hindenburg Line, the one part the Germans could not yield and retain any hope of winning the war.

Before him lay a twenty-four mile front; in its center was the fortified alp of Montfaucon, from whose height the Imperial Crown Prince had watched the siege of Verdun in 1916. On the right were the entrenched heights of the river Meuse; on the left, the fantastic *Forêt d'Argonne*, a wild Hans Christian Andersen land of giant trees cunningly interwoven with nests of machine guns.

German strategists had prepared four defense positions behind one another in this fastness, stretching back fourteen miles and manned by double garrisons. The reason was the Sedan-Mézières railroad in their rear. It was their only line of escape to Liège and Germany. Once it was broken their army couldn't be withdrawn; it would lie at the mercy of the Allies. Foch knew how strong Ludendorff's defenses were here; that was why the chief American mission was to hold. The Yanks would join in the tattoo of attacks, but their big job was to crack the whip, with the Belgians swinging free on the other end.

It didn't appeal to Pershing. He had liked Belleau Wood better. Amassing more artillery shells than the Union army used in the entire Civil War, he rushed all available troops to the front in camions—French trucks with little wheels and no springs worth mentioning—and threw nine fresh divisions against the Germans on the misty morning of September 26. The enemy was stunned. He hadn't thought anyone would dare attack here. His forward positions were overrun, and the doughboys surged up Montfaucon and took it. There, however, the Germans' center stiffened. They retired to their third defense line, named *Kriemhilde Stellung* for the bouncing Nibelungen lady, and held. Yank dreams of orders home and Gay Paree vanished in a growing orchestra of battle. The old Sixty-ninth of New York was cut to pieces. Father Duffy was to see "Wild Bill" Donovan carried down the grim crest before Landres-St. Georges on a blanket. Donovan survived, but many in the regiment had gone forever, including Joyce Kilmer, poet laureate of the A.E.F.

Meanwhile another New York outfit was in deep trouble on the left. The battle wasn't easy for anybody, but the Seventy-seventh Division had drawn the most difficult assignment of all. They had been ordered to charge down the Argonne hogback while Pennsylvanians of the Twenty-eighth and Missourians of the Thirty-fifth outflanked the defenders. It didn't work. The Thirty-fifth was almost wiped out, but the flankers couldn't even get far enough in to establish liaison with the Seventy-seventh.

One band of hardy backwoodsmen drafted from New York's Lower East Side became celebrated as the "lost battalion" when they were surrounded and held out for six days, but in a sense the entire Seventy-seventh was lost. For two weeks its men fought their own private war in the wilderness, without contact and without artillery support, since no one could be sure just where they were. Every mile gained complicated supply problems; a company starved for four days and then returned to the rear to fetch its own corned Willy. The forest was cloaked and soaked in blinding fog. Runners, officers, command posts got lost. One patrol literally vanished Indian-file into the mist—

the men didn't return, their bodies were never found, they weren't in P.O.W. camps after the war, they are listed as missing to this day.

Then, abruptly, on October 7, the weather cleared. The trees were revealed in their October splendor—coppery, golden, purplish, deep scarlet. Even better, the spent Gothamites were reinforced by the Eighty-second Division (All-American), including a Tennessee sergeant named Alvin C. York, who captured a hundred and thirty-two prisoners and thirty-five German machine guns—the "greatest single thing," said Foch, "accomplished by any private soldier of all the armies."

Snaking from bole to bole, cleaning out ravines and machine-gun nests, the two divisions drove the enemy from the forest and joined their flanks to a new line at Grandpré, ten miles from the jump-off, on October 14. The same day, doughboys in the center of the sector took Romagne and stormed Côte Dame Marie, which Pershing regarded as the most important strongpoint in the Hindenburg Line. For the moment, however, that was that. His army was exhausted; there were more than a hundred thousand American stragglers. He was approaching the complex defenses in front of the railroad, and he had to regroup his tattered regiments before officers could shrill their whistles for a new attack.

Pershing was lining his sights on Sedan and Metz. Yet they didn't much matter now. The war maps had changed vastly since the first wave of the Seventy-seventh had disappeared into the hazy boscages. On the fourth day of that lonely struggle Hindenburg, brooding over his shrinking front, had notified Berlin that an armistice must be sought at once, and three days later he had reported in despair that there was no hope of stopping the Allied tide. The Imperial Chancellor was frantically trying to reach Wilson through Switzerland, suggesting a truce based on his proposals made nine months before. Wilson coldly referred the note to Foch. The President could read maps, too.

The war was rapidly approaching a solution in the field. There wasn't much left to bargain over. In the North Sea the antisub barrier was nearly tight. Albert was reentering his channel towns in triumph, the French were ringing their own church bells in the long-lost villages around Lille, the British were approaching Mons. Everything was slipping away from the Kaiser, including the other Central Powers. An Allied army which had been mired in Salonica since 1915 sent a spearhead of Serb mountain fighters against Bulgaria, and on September 29 the Bulgarians quit. That same day the British took Damascus;

Turkey bowed out at the end of October. Even the Italians were attacking, which meant Austria's end was near.

In the West, Pershing's advance was renewed on November 1. The enemy's last scribbly ditches caved in that afternoon, and four days later he had no front at all. Apart from stolid machine gunners, who kept their murderous barrels hot to the end, German soldiers had become a disorderly mob of refugees. They had lost heart. Reports from the fatherland were appalling. Ludendorff had been sacked, there was revolution in the streets, the fleet had mutinied when ordered off on a death-or-glory ride against the British.

In this final agony the rearguard in France, Sergeant Woollcott wrote, resembled an escaping man who "twitches a chair down behind him for his pursuers to stumble over." Each chill dawn doughboys went roaring over the top in fighting kit, driving the fleeing wraiths in field gray away from their railroad and up against the hills of Belgium and Luxemburg. It was a chase, not a battle. The galloping horses and bouncing caissons could scarcely keep up with the racing troops. Pershing told his generals to forget about flanks, light up the trucks at night, and see how far they could go—an order which touched off a frantic race for Sedan. Nobody won it, because the French were being sticky, but in the excitement the First Division forgot itself and broke all the rules of military courtesy. Vaulting out of its own sector, it crossed the boundaries of the Seventy-seventh and the Rainbow, taking Father Duffy prisoner in a hollow square and actually challenging the leader of the Rainbow on his own front line. It was an indignity no general officer could take lightly, and this one was young, proud, and named Douglas MacArthur. His protests were lost in the news of another border crossing. Kaiser Wilhelm, the Supreme War Lord, had abdicated and entered Holland as a political refugee.

Even as the First and the glowering Rainbow jointly occupied the heights opposite Sedan, the Eiffel Tower in Paris was beaming directions to German envoys, telling them which trenches to approach and where to pick up their guides. In Foch's railroad car the first of them signed his dictated terms at five o'clock on the morning of November 11. All firing was to cease six hours later; and the moment the hills were tinged with the first faint promise of morning, motorcycles spluttered up and down the American front, passing the word that the *guerre* would be *finee* at eleven sharp.

After ten o'clock the front grew noisy—everybody wanted to get in that last shot—but eyes glued to a million watches finally saw minute hands creep upright, and then there was a tremendous silence. It lasted

The Island War

PEARL HARBOR, like the *Maine,* is better remembered than the war it started. Most Americans know that the rising sun of Dai Nippon began its startling ascent in the red sky over Pearl, and at it splashed into Tokyo Bay forty-five months later after a surrender remony in which Douglas MacArthur used a lot of fountain pens. It the details between are hazy. One reason, of course, is that the untry was also busy with Hitler. Another is geography.

Men on Iwo Jima got V-mail from relatives who thought they ere still fighting in the "South Pacific." Names from the European heater were a familiar echo from schooldays, but who had heard of ap? Where was Ioribaiwa? And what was the difference between ew Britain, New Caledonia, New Guinea, New Ireland, New Geor- a and the New Hebrides?

Geography teachers, unfortunately, hadn't gone into that. Until e air age, islands like Wake, Midway and Iwo had been almost orthless, and as late as 1941 entire archipelagoes were of interest only oil and soap companies. The United States Navy started the war sing eighteenth century charts; sea battles were broken off because we idn't know where the bottom was; the first land engagement on uadalcanal was fought on the wrong river—marines thought it was e Tenaru, and discovered afterward it was the Ilu.

Most of what the public did know about the Pacific had been in- ented by movie-script writers. Even as the Japanese were pictured as blinky-eyed, buck-toothed, Gilbert and Sullivan race, so the South eas was an exotic land where lazy winds whispered in palm fronds, nd Sadie Thompsons seduced missionaries, and native girls dived for earls in fitted sarongs, like Dorothy Lamour. The girls were closer to url Ives than to Lamour, though most Pacific veterans can recollect enes of great natural beauty—the white orchids and screaming cocka-

but a moment and was followed by a deafening cheer
Generals might haggle over words, but soldiers knew t
than an Armistice. It was a surrender. It was the end
all wars, and it had come, as editorial writers every
profoundly, at the eleventh hour of the eleventh day of
month.

Yet for once the generals were right. It was to be a l
it wouldn't be peace, because more than the guerre was
were omens, for those who could read them. The belfries
ton heard calling joyously to one another across Paris
might also have been tolling for a French army broken in
to politicians like André Maginot. Something had died i
as something had been born in Russia. That very morning
victory streaked innocently over Mézières, Bolshevik troop
offensive against five thousand American soldiers who
wisely diverted to Archangel in the hope of restoring the
ment there.

The administration that had sent them was no bl
people. American voters had just defied the Spanish
polling places and discredit Woodrow Wilson, crippling
Nations and confirming the fears of Winston Church
dered, as he stood in a London window and heard
eleven, whether the world would return to international an

It would. But it would not be the same anarchy.
reached Journey's End. The door of history had shut
and potentates and plumed marshals and glittering little
—on all the elegance and fanfaronade that had marked th
secure world. The grinning doughboys stacking their an
ping cigarettes for Fritz's souvenirs might not know
Congress back home certainly didn't, and the hysteri
Times Square, the Champs Élysées and the Buckin
grounds knew it least of all, though the English had a ki
they romped over the mall with firecrackers and confett
denly darkened. It began to rain, hard. Some of the celeb
into the arms of Queen Victoria's statue, but after huddli
utes in its arms they crept down. They had found little
and less comfort. The arms had been stone cold.

toos in Guadalcanal's dense rain forests, or the smoking volcano in Bougainville's Empress Augusta Bay, or Saipan's lovely flame trees.

Unfortunately, we weren't tourists; we were fighting a war, and the more breathtaking the jungle looked, the more ferocious the combat turned out to be. Some islands were literally uninhabitable—Army engineers sent to survey the Santa Cruz group for airstrips were virtually wiped out by cerebral malaria—and battles were fought under fantastic conditions. Guadalcanal was rocked by an earthquake. Volcanic steam hissed through the rocks of Iwo. On Bougainville, bulldozers vanished in the spongy bottomless swamps, and at the height of the fighting on Peleliu the temperature was 115° in the shade. Sometimes the weather was worse than the enemy. At Cape Gloucester sixteen inches of rain fell in a single day. In November 1944, the battle for Leyte was halted by a double monsoon, and a month later a typhoon sank three American destroyers.

Like any other war, this one had its special shapes and sounds, remembered now in a kind of blurred photomontage, like childhood or yesterday's love. There was scratchy monotony on the ship PA systems (*Sweepers, man your brooms*) and sometimes high drama (*This is the captain. We are going into battle*). There were the blossoms of artillery crumps in the banyan jungles, the meatballs on Zero wings flashing under the equatorial sun, and the image of carrier pilots scrambling across a flattop deck, helmets flapping and chart boards clutched under their arms.

To a retired rifleman, however, the most poignant memory of all is that Just-Before-the-Battle-Mother feeling, in the small hours of Z-Day or A-Day or L-Day of a new operation, when you crept out of your sweaty transport bunk, toyed with your steak and eggs, watched the warships sock the shore with their fourteen-inch salvos, and then crawled down the cargo nets to the waiting Higgins boats with your pack tugging on your aching back. Peering nervously toward the purply land mass ahead, you highballed in toward Red Beach One or Green Beach Two, hoping this one would be no strain, no pain, no reefs, and knowing it would be another miserable blast furnace— wretched for infantry, yet touched, as all islands were, with a wild, unearthly splendor.

Lurid settings produced bizarre casualties. Twenty-five marines were killed at Cape Gloucester by huge falling trees; shipwrecked sailors were eaten by sharks. Japanese swimming ashore after the Battle of the Bismarck Sea were carved up by New Guinea headhunters, and others, on Guadalcanal, were eaten by their comrades. The jungle was cruel to defeated soldiers, who, as the war grew older, were usually Japanese. If they were surrounded, only ferns, snakes, crocodiles and cannibalism were left to them. Even when they had a line of escape the odds were against survival.

Surrender was out until the Son of Heaven ordered it, and even then diehards skulked in caves for years. "The Jap," as MacArthur called the enemy—the rest of us usually called Japanese "Nips"—considered it a disgrace to be taken alive. When defeat loomed officers would round up everybody for a *banzai* (hurrah) suicide charge. Men without rifles were issued clubs, men unable to walk were given hand grenades or land mines and told to blow themselves up. No one was exempted. The Saipan commander was too senile to kill himself, so an aide shot him, like an old horse; and it was on Saipan that five-year-old Japanese children formed circles and tossed grenades back and forth until they exploded.

Suicide had always been highly regarded in Japan, but to the samurai warlords last-ditch resistance also made military sense. The idea was to get a negotiated peace. "We will build a barricade across the Pacific with our bodies," said a crudely lettered sign over the Jap dead on Peleliu. The closer we came to their homeland, the more determined they became. Tokyo mobilized suicide boats, human torpedoes, and *kamikaze* suicide planes. On the eve of capitulation they were still broadcasting their final slogan: "One hundred million people die in honor!"

They also thought it rather shameful for us to surrender. Captured Allies were not kindly treated. Japs raped nurses in Hong Kong, beheaded marines captured at Makin, and left bayoneted Australian prisoners at Milne Bay with placards reading "It took them a long time to die." The result was that we also became savage. The United States Navy waged unrestricted submarine warfare; in the Admiralty Islands, Nips who preferred starvation to surrender were left in the bush and used for target practice. It was a hard war. General and flag officers were as bloodthirsty as riflemen. MacArthur told General Robert L. Eichelberger that if he didn't take Buna he needn't come back alive, and when our intelligence reported the whereabouts of Japan's great Admiral Yamamoto, we deliberately sought him out with P-38 fighter planes and killed him. That was in the early, South Pacific phase of the war, when all we had was a toehold on Guadalcanal and another in New Guinea—when the Japanese had taken a tenth of the globe in half the time they had allowed.

By late July of 1941, when Washington had courted the Pacific

war by freezing Japanese assets and cutting off their oil, their fleet had
been stronger than the combined Allied forces in the Pacific. At Pearl
Harbor they had sunk our battlewagons, and by spring they were
strong enough to shell Sydney, Australia, and reconnoiter Seattle by
air. Their ships were faster, their guns bigger, their torpedoes superior.
Their Zeros outflew anything we had, and there were many more of
them. On Guadalcanal "Condition Red," the air-raid warning, at times
became "Condition *Very* Red." An empire that hadn't been defeated
since 1592 had dealt us the most smashing blow in our history. Since
we had decided to defeat the Nazis first, there were strategists in Washington who thought it might take ten years to beat Japan.

The commanders at Pearl were given leather medals, but the real
trouble was that no one had taken Dai Nippon seriously. There had
been omens. In 1937 the American gunboat *Panay* had been deliberately bombed and sunk in the Yangtze. For years the Nips had been
building up their mandated islands. Other nations thought the
Gallipoli fiasco of 1915 proved amphibious warfare impractical. Not the
Jap; he had special landing craft in mass production. In 1941 he had
taken advantage of Vichy weakness to pour troops into French Indochina, and we thought he might trespass in Thailand, though no one
knew the corrupt Thai government would surrender to him in three
hours.

Indeed, it seemed inconceivable to us that Japan would attack at
all. Congress refused to fortify Guam; Tokyo might misunderstand.
The few planes we had on Hawaii and Luzon were lined up wing tip
to wing tip, inviting attack, while the Army and Navy took solace in
the fiction that any red-blooded American could lick any ten Orientals.
Illusions die hard. Even after the ax fell, Admiral William F. Halsey,
Jr., the Patton of the Pacific, predicted Japan would be crushed by
1943, and at home jukeboxes rasped, "Good-by mama, I'm off to
Yokohama," and "I'm gonna slap a dirty little Jap."

Actually, things were just the other way around. Starting with the
raid on Pearl, it was the Jap who slapped us. Of all our prewar errors in
the Pacific the most grievous was our conviction that the enemy wasn't
strong enough to mount more than one invasion at a time. Certainly
nobody in Washington dreamed Japan capable of simultaneous assaults
on Hong Kong, Malaya, the Philippines, Guam and Borneo, which is
precisely what happened in that month of nightmares after the raid on
Pearl. General Hideki Tojo, the new premier in Tokyo, was outblitzing
Hitler.

The first big show was in Malaya. Staging from Thailand, three big columns invaded the peninsula under an umbrella of planes from Indochina, driving the British back and back. The Jap didn't really need that much muscle, but he hoped to lure the British navy into a trap. It worked fine. Admiral Sir Tom Phillips went for the bait with the battleship *Prince of Wales* and the battle cruiser *Repulse*. His one carrier ran aground; he had lost his eyes; and on the third day of the war Jap torpedo bombers sank the *Prince of Wales* and the *Repulse*, the only two Allied capital ships west of Hawaii. Nothing could save Malaya now. Winston Churchill learned to his horror that the great guns of Singapore pointed only toward the sea.

That was the Jap's first team in Malaya, captained by General Tomoyuki Yamashita. Tojo sent Lieutenant General Masaharu Homma's second team against the Philippines, landing the first troops on Luzon December 10, the day unfortified Guam fell to the Nips. In two and a half weeks Homma was ashore at nine points, MacArthur had declared Manila an open city (it was immediately bombed), and American soldiers and Filipino scouts were retreating into Bataan peninsula. They hadn't enough troops even to hold that—the only United States regiment on Bataan, the 31st Infantry, had a front-line strength of 636 men—so they withdrew toward the island fortress of Corregidor, supported by ten obsolete planes and a few PT boats. The ranking naval officer, Admiral Tom Hart, left the day after Christmas flying his four-star flag from the biggest warship he had, the submarine *Shark*.

Hong Kong had fallen; so had Wake, after a valiant two-week stand by five hundred marines under Major James Devereux, who beat off a landing and then waited, in vain, for relief. Wake was important to us, and could have been saved. A relief expedition actually sailed from Pearl but the ships were ineptly handled and didn't get there; and after two thousand Nips swarmed ashore all the major could do was hoist a bed sheet. By New Year's Day, when Admiral Hart surfaced off Java and joined Field Marshal Wavell's Allied command, the Jap had bypassed Singapore and was headed for Java and Sumatra. Wavell looked at his war map and flew off to India, leaving the Indies, as the angry Dutch said, to their fate.

It was a bitter fate. Led by a Dutch admiral whose orders had to be painfully translated to our captains, seventeen Allied warships without air cover sailed out to stop the invasion of Java. The largest among them were two cruisers, and looming over the horizon were the pagodalike masts of seventy-four Jap ships, including four battlewagons and five carriers. In the seven-hour Battle of the Java Sea half the

Dutchman's ships went down with him; Jap planes polished off most of the rest.

Now the rising sun was blinding. Singapore had capitulated on February seventeenth ("All I want to know from you," Yamashita told Britain's General Percival, "is yes or no."), and fourteen of her Vickers naval guns were moved to an atoll in the Gilbert Islands called Tarawa. Burma followed swiftly. By the second week in March the Nips were on the road to Mandalay, which they took on May Day, sealing off China. These were big names; their loss was shocking. Less familiar, but more vital, was Rabaul, an Australian outpost in New Britain captured in January. One hundred thousand troops moved in, five airfields were paved, and Rabaul was built into an impregnable fortress, the key to a chain of strongholds in New Ireland, the Solomons and New Guinea. Jap pilots were striking at Australia; Darwin, on the north coast, had to be evacuated. In New Zealand every man under sixty-five was called up, and the country's pursuit planes were readied for combat —all nine of them. The Prime Minister of Australia warned his people to expect invasion hourly. In Washington, Ernest J. King, the new Admiral of the Fleet, was arguing against the abandonment of these two countries. "The Pacific situation is now very grave," Roosevelt cabled Churchill, and Tokyo Rose jeered, "Where are the United States Marines hiding?"

Apart from the southern Solomon Islands, Port Moresby, near the eastern tip of New Guinea, and dying Corregidor, the Jap controlled the entire Pacific west of Midway and north of the Coral Sea. He had expected at least twenty percent casualties, and he had scarcely been touched—one of his fleets had sunk five Allied battleships, a carrier, two cruisers and seven destroyers without receiving a scratch. MacArthur, evacuated to Australia, spoke brave words. King ordered Admiral Chester W. Nimitz, who had been hastily sent out in civilian clothes as the Pacific Navy's new commander, to hold the Midway-Samoa-Fijis-Brisbane line "at all costs." Yet this seemed like whistling in the dark.

At home American morale was braced with cheerful lies: that Colin Kelly had sunk the *Haruna* (he hadn't); that a naval brush in Makassar Strait was a great victory for us (it wasn't); and that the Marines on Wake had radioed, "Send us more Japs" (they certainly hadn't). Guadalcanal and nearby Tulagi were easily taken by the Japanese May third. On May seventh an amphibious force of Nips steamed into the lovely Coral Sea, intent on capturing Port Moresby and heartened by the surrender of Corregidor the day before.

The battle that followed, the first carrier-*vs.*-carrier action of the war, was a curious engagement. We were desperate; to save Australia we had to save Moresby, and two of our four Pacific flattops were sent to block the way. For the Jap, however, this was a sideshow. Yamamoto was saving his big blow for the Battle of Midway. Even so, the Nips outfought us in the air over the Coral Sea. They sank the *Lexington* and crippled the *Yorktown.* We got a light carrier. A draw, at best. Yet Moresby was saved. The pagoda masts turned back, and at Pearl it took 1400 mechanics, working around the clock, less than two days to repair the *Yorktown* in time for Midway.

Now came the crisis. To the Nips, Midway looked easy. They had twice as many ships as we had; they bulled through the water gaily singing war songs, and Jap marines, who were to land, were issued beer. Yamamoto counted on annihilating our fleet and then using Midway to jump off for Hawaii. Nimitz, however, was expecting him. U.S. cryptography experts had broken the enemy's code. Every foot of the island was crammed with troops, and every warship we could spare was at sea, including our three carriers. In the first hours of the battle it didn't seem enough, but we had two breaks: Yamamoto didn't know where our fleet was, but we had spotted him, and the Jap carrier commander had cleared his decks to recover his Midway strike, leaving him almost defenseless at the instant our planes arrived overhead.

American Devastator torpedo-bombers went in first that morning of June 4, 1942—and they were massacred by flak. Of forty-one, only six survived; none scored a hit. The pilots sacrificed themselves as surely as any *kamikaze,* and they died believing it was in vain. But they had provided the edge of victory. The Jap carriers, frantically wagging their fantails to dodge the Devastators' fish, hadn't been able to get any planes off, and the Zeros that were in the air were down low, intercepting. At that decisive moment Lieutenant Commander Clarence McClusky's two squadrons of Dauntless bombers from the *Enterprise* arrived high overhead and swooped down in seventy-degree dives. They blew three carriers apart, jumped another that afternoon and sent her down too. Four carriers were all Yamamoto had brought with him, and he had to retire; he had lost his umbrella. He sat slumped on his bridge, listlessly sipping rice broth.

Eight weeks later the United States Marines were in the Fijis, rehearsing the first American offensive of the war. They waded ashore on Tulagi and Guadalcanal August seventh and immediately wished they hadn't. The 'Canal, as it was to be known evermore, had been accurately described by former colonial residents as a "bloody, stinking hole." Supporting airfields were hurriedly hacked out of the bush in the

Fijis, New Hebrides and New Caledonia; and the campaign, christened Operation Shoestring, was launched. We had luck that first day. Only a handful of Nips were on the beach; they fled, leaving us their 3600-foot airstrip. But the second night a Jap task force from Rabaul came hissing down the Slot, the channel between the Solomons, and gave our Navy one of the worst beatings in its history. Next day our unprotected transports broke off unloading and departed. The 1st Marine Division was left with a four-day supply of ammunition, and the "Tokyo Express" started landing Nips from Rabaul—900 a night; 4500 one night.

For six months the issue was in doubt. The Jap decided to make the 'Canal a test of strength. Emperor Hirohito declared that it would be "a decisive battle." Six major naval engagements were fought around the island; sixty-five warships were sunk. To sailors the waters offshore were "Ironbottom Sound"; to marines, "Sleepless Lagoon." Each month the Jap made an all-out attempt to recapture the airstrip; he was thrown back every time, once within yards of the field. Secretary Knox prepared the public for the worst, and President Roosevelt had to intervene with the Joint Chiefs of Staff before reinforcements were sent. Convoy by convoy they came—the Americal Division, the 25th, and the 2nd Marine—until Radio Tokyo announced that it didn't want the island anyway. On the night of February 1, 1943, the last Nips pulled out, leaving 25,000 dead. For the first time in the war the Jap had gone on the defensive.

Nor was that all. The 'Canal was one of two successful campaigns waged for the defense of Australia. The other was in MacArthur's theater, New Guinea. Coral Sea hadn't discouraged the enemy there. In July 1942, he had seized a string of villages along the north shore of Papua, the New Guinea tail, and prepared to envelop Port Moresby, on the south shore, in a land-and-sea pincer. Coast watchers—British colonial officials hiding in the jungle with radios—warned us that the sea assault was headed for Milne Bay, at the tip of the peninsula; our troops got there first and threw the Nips into the sea. The land drive took off from Buna, one of the villages the Jap had seized. It was only a hundred miles to Moresby, but the Nips had to cross the awesome 13,000-foot Owen Stanleys on foot. Twenty miles from Moresby the Australians held them at Ioribaiwa and began a counteroffensive with our 32nd Division.

This ordeal, costlier in lives than the 'Canal, paid off when Eichelberger entered Buna on January 2, 1943, and the Aussies captured nearby Sanananda two weeks later. The Jap tried to reach Lae village with eight transports. On March third skip-bombing B-25's caught the convoy in the Bismarck Sea and sank all eight, plus four escorts. In the grisly aftermath seven thousand Nips were drowned or deprived of their heads by islanders. The Jap decided he didn't want Moresby.

But he had to keep Rabaul if he was going to hold the South Pacific. Rabaul was too strong to be assaulted, so we neutralized it. We began by moving into New Georgia in the summer of 1943 and pouncing at Munda. Our plans at Munda were botched. We landed too far from the field and had to attack by guesswork through thickets and over flooded rivers, against pillboxed Nips in steel vests. Still, the field fell in August, no thanks to the generals. We were moving up the Slot. Vaulting to Vella Lavella, we mopped up the Central Solomons, and on November first the 3rd Marine Division landed in Bougainville's Empress Augusta Bay. This was a giant step. If we could somehow build an airfield in this green porridge, we would be within fighter range of Rabaul.

The Jap thought it unlikely. He buffeted us by air and sea but held back his best troops, thinking we would use the bay to stage a push elsewhere. On Christmas Day we finished our big strip, "Piva Uncle," above the forks of the Piva River. The Americal and 37th divisions ringed it with a perimeter of steel, and when the Jap finally attacked with his élite 6th Division he was stopped cold. By then we had Rabaul just about surrounded. Emirau and the Green Islands had been occupied; we had taken Arawe, had occupied Cape Gloucester in New Britain, and were ashore in the Admiralties. Massive sorties from Piva Uncle were making Rabaul unlivable. The Jap evacuated his "consolation units"—Korean daughters of joy—and left the huge garrison to suffer as our bombers flew in daily overhead, unchallenged and unescorted.

So far we had only been nibbling at the edges of the enemy's position. We had spent nine months moving 250 miles in the Central Solomons, and Tokyo was 5000 miles away. World War I weapons, however, were being replaced by rockets, amphibious tractors, flame throwers that could lick around corners. We had more of everything— fifty carriers now, led by the fast *Independence* class converted from cruiser hulls. If we could somehow get closer to Japan, our submarines, which had sunk a million tons of shipping the first year of the war, could destroy the Jap's merchant marine. Soon we would even be able to reach Tokyo by air; the first B-29's, with a range of 1500 nautical miles, would be on their way shortly. The solution was to open a new

theater of war, the Central Pacific, and on November 20, 1943, the 2nd
Marine Division did that. It wasn't supposed to be easy. But no one anticipated a Tarawa.

Tarawa was the battle we nearly lost. The enemy commander
boasted that Betio, the key island in the atoll, couldn't be taken by a
million men in a hundred years. We had problems: our naval bombardment was too light, the tides betrayed us, we missed H-hour, and at the
end of the first day our beachhead was twenty feet wide. Officers stood
waist-deep in water, directing the battle by radio and praying against a
counterattack. Only the breakdown of Jap communications prevented
one. The next day we drove through and split the defenses, but we had
lost three thousand men. Next month we took Kwajalein and Eniwetok
in the Marshalls more cheaply. Yet all these battles in the Central
Pacific were short and terrible—the 4th Marine Division, bloodied on
Kwajalein, was in action only sixty-one days during the war, yet it
suffered seventy-five percent casualties.

Our strategic shift was one reason for this. New Jap tactics was the
other. The masters of the amphibious offense had braced themselves to
hold what they had. Imperial Headquarters radioed every outpost to
prepare a last-man resistance. One of them did more than that. On
Biak, an island near the head of the New Guinea bird, the Jap had ten
thousand men. Their commander, Col. Naoyuki Kuzumi, decided
dying on the beach was all very fine, but by holing up in caves his
men could prolong the slaughter of Americans. Kuzumi had made the
most murderous discovery of the island war.

Biak lay directly in the path of MacArthur's drive on the Philippines. The general, in the spring of 1944, was using a new American
tactic, the leapfrog. We had stumbled on leapfrogging in the Aleutians
while retaking Attu and Kiska, which had been seized by Yamamoto as
a diversion during the Midway operation. Lacking strength to attack
both, we bypassed Kiska—and discovered, after Attu had been stormed,
that the Jap had quietly evacuated it. MacArthur caught on. Late in
April he leaped into Hollandia, and a month later the 41st Division hit
Biak. Until now the cost of the offensive had been relatively light, but
Biak's cave defenders took a terrible toll; before the island was secured
casualty lists were approaching Tarawa's.

They might have been worse. The Jap navy, in hiding for a year,
was preparing to come out and reinforce the garrison. The ships were
already at sea, when, in mid-June, word reached Admiral Jisaburo
Ozawa that our Central Pacific drive was aiming at Saipan, Guam,
Tinian. This was a bigger threat, and bows were turned that way. The

resulting Battle of the Philippine Sea was a long-distance duel that disappointed old line-of-battle salts. Nevertheless, we won a stunning victory. Admiral Marc Mitscher's Hellcats knocked out the enemy's land-
based air power on Guam and, in eight hours of continuous fighting in
the sky, beat off four massive attacks on our fleet. It was the greatest carrier battle of the war; by the end of the following day Ozawa's air arm
had shrunk from 430 aircraft to just thirty-five, and our subs had sunk
two of his carriers, including the *Taiho,* Japan's newest and largest.
Ozawa fled and the emperor's soldiers on Saipan were cut off.

Sensible men would have hoisted a white flag. The Nips, as usual,
swore to make us pay the greatest possible price for the island. After
three thousand of them had staged the war's biggest *banzai* attack, driving GI's into the surf, we wiped them out or waited while the suicides,
including the admiral who had led the Day of Infamy raid on Pearl,
saved us the trouble. Two weeks later marines were wetting their feet
on Guam's reefs, where Navy underwater frogmen left a "Welcome
Marines!" sign. Guam was only half as expensive as Saipan, partly because the *banzai* was less effective; bottled up on Orote peninsula, the
Nips unbottled their stocks of sake and synthetic Scotch on the night
of July twenty-fifth and came staggering toward us under the light of
spluttering flares, as shells ripped their ranks.

Tinian, where the Japs had not thought our north-shore landing at
all possible, was less expensive. Yet three islands had cost 25,000 casualties. They were priceless, however. They gave us our first B-29 base,
our first grip on Jap territory. Marine General Holland ("Howlin'
Mad") Smith, the commander at Saipan, called this the decisive battle
of the Pacific war. Tokyo agreed. Premier Tojo was fired, and Americans were heartened.

MacArthur, however, had mixed feelings. Since Bataan he had
been cast in a strange role. He had become the most familiar Pacific
figure to his countrymen at home, yet he was an Army commander in
what was clearly a naval war. He had been against the invasion of the
'Canal, and these thrusts in the Central Pacific suited him even less.
Now Admiral King was suggesting we bypass the Philippines. We had
to keep faith with the Filipinos, MacArthur insisted; it was a matter of
honor. A matter of sentiment, King replied, and both appealed to
Roosevelt. On July twenty-sixth, the President arrived at Pearl to settle
things. A platoon of generals and admirals wearing dress uniforms
snapped to attention for him, executed a right face—two sad sacks
turned left—and departed, while MacArthur and Nimitz, representing
the Navy, made their cases. At the end Roosevelt said, "Well, Douglas,

you win. But I'm going to have a hell of a time with that old bear, Ernie King."

The Philippine timetable called for early landings on Peleliu, Yap and Mindanao, but Halsey made a startling suggestion. Air strikes convinced him that the enemy's air force was all through. He proposed we skip most of the preliminaries and charge right into Leyte. It was so decided, although the Peleliu operation went ahead as scheduled, with tragic consequences. Biak had become a magic word in Tokyo. It had been passed to Colonel Kunio Nagagawa, the Japanese commander on Peleliu, and like Generals Tadamichi Kuribayashi on Iwo and Mitsura Ushijima on Okinawa, he made his men moles. They burrowed in natural limestone caves linked by tunnels and cut the First Marine Division to pieces, giving us a bitter taste of what was to come. We took the island—for what it was worth.

By the time the jagged ridges north of Peleliu airfield had been cleared, four American divisions were swarming over the beach at Leyte Gulf. Less than an hour after the main landings on October 20, 1944, the 382nd Infantry had the Stars and Stripes up; four days later General Walter Krueger's 6th Army command post was ashore and Yamashita's 35th Army was marching against it. Halsey had miscalculated. The Japs still had plenty of planes. Besides, we were fighting in the wettest part of the Philippines, at the wettest time of the year, and the land we had taken was too soggy for air strips. The Jap was ferrying planes down from Japan and tripling his Leyte garrison; Krueger seemed stuck in the mud; and in Leyte Gulf the stage had been set for the greatest naval battle of all time.

Yamamoto was dead, but the Jap navy still cherished his hope for a decisive action at sea, preferably while our ships were covering a landing. This was the hour. Four separate Jap forces sailed against Halsey's powerful main fleet, which was protecting the operation, and Thomas Kinkaid's weaker group of old battleships and small carriers. The enemy admirals knew they couldn't match our new power—we had 218 warships, they had less than 100—so they hatched a brilliant plan. Leyte Gulf could be reached through two straits, San Bernardino to the north and Surigao to the south. Their center force, led by Admiral Takeo Kurita, was to head for San Bernardino while two southern forces churned into Surigao. At the same time, the fourth force, Ozawa's, was to lure Halsey away to the north. Kinkaid would be helpless. *Banzai.*

The southern prong had no luck. Admiral Jesse Oldendorf had Surigao Strait corked. Torpedoes and gunfire exterminated the first Jap column; the second turned back after firing at radar pictures which turned out to be islands. In the beginning Kurita's luck seemed bad too. Submarines destroyed two of his heavy cruisers; his largest battleship was sunk by planes. Actually these losses were a break for Kurita. Halsey, learning of them, thought him finished, and when Ozawa's decoy was sighted Halsey took off after the bait—leaving San Bernardino Strait unguarded. In the darkness of October twenty-fourth Kurita slipped through unobserved. The following dawn he sprang on Kinkaid's frail carriers.

What followed was one of the most remarkable engagements in the history of naval warfare. The carriers' only protection was their screen—destroyers and destroyer escorts, the latter being puny vessels used for antisubmarine work and manned mostly by married draftees. The destroyers counterattacked Kurita's battleships, and then their gallant little escorts steamed toward the huge Jap guns, firing their own little guns and launching torpedoes. Kurita's Goliaths milled around in confusion as the persistent Davids, some of them sinking, made dense smoke. The carriers sent up everything that could fly, and Kurita, with the mightiest Jap fleet since Midway, turned tail. The rout was complete, for Halsey was thorough in his error; he chewed up Ozawa's decoy. In the final reckoning the Jap lost three battleships, four carriers and some twenty other warships. The emperor's sea power was finished.

On Leyte the push in the mud sloshed on, with the 6th and 8th Armies pulling a drawstring around the enemy bag. GI's hit the island of Mindoro on December twelfth; three weeks later four divisions made an almost unopposed landing at Luzon's Lingayen Gulf. Bataan was attacked; then Corregidor, with a joint paratroop-amphibious assault. Yamashita lived to surrender his sword at the end of the war, when MacArthur sent Percival to receive it.

In Luzon we were, as an Army officer wryly remarked, "right back where we started." B-29's were scarring the Jap homeland, but it was still a remote fortress. Bringing it closer was the task of the other American pincer—the Central Pacific thrust that had driven from Tarawa, through the Marshalls, to Saipan. Its next target was the volcanic pile of Iwo Jima. Saipan was 1270 miles from Tokyo, just within B-29 range; Superforts had to limit bomb loads to two tons; those damaged in raids couldn't get back. If we held Iwo, 660 miles from Japan, they could carry seven tons, and Tokyo would miss raid warnings from Iwo's radar.

The Jap thought a lot of Iwo's eight square miles. We had taken some rough spots the past year, but none this rough. The Navy's seventy-four days of preinvasion bombardment scarcely jarred the enemy; he had no barracks above ground. Most of his caves were shielded by at least thirty-five feet of overhead cover. Nearly all of his weapons could reach the beach, and some were new to the war: rockets nine feet long, as big as battleship shells—marines called them "Bubbly-Wubblies," "floating ashcans" and "Screaming Mimis." The first two hours ashore were comparatively easy; then the beachhead was blanketed with mortars. Despite this, Mount Suribachi and Motoyama Airfield No. 1 were taken in the early days of the battle, and that should have been it. Everyone waited for the Nips to form a *banzai* charge and come in to be slaughtered. They didn't. They stuck to their pillboxes and ravines for twenty-six days, and when the end came in March the grim abacus showed over 20,000 marine casualties.

The abacus was grimmer for the enemy. The Japanese equivalent of "It never rains but it pours" is "When crying, stung by bee in the face." Stinging Superforts were swarming low over the homeland, beginning a methodical destruction of eighty Japanese cities, killing a hundred thousand people in a single day with the great Tokyo fire of March 9, 1945. One by one the big Jap warships were being picked out from the air. Halsey's carriers had broken into the South China Sea, cutting the enemy's oil and rice lines. The Emperor's merchant navy was a skeleton; soon the American submarine score would be over a thousand ships. Shantytowns were rising in Yokohama and Osaka, Jap civilians were racked with tuberculosis and malaria, and there was no food for their ration cards. Yet the Jap's morale showed no signs of cracking. Old men and children were being armed with bamboo spears. Come and get us, Tokyo Rose taunted.

To oblige we needed one more invasion base: Okinawa. Intelligence tried to see to it that Tokyo thought that we were after Formosa. The Jap wasn't fooled. He had been so sure we needed Okinawa that General Ushijima, the commander there, had guessed that we would land near Yontan Airfield on April first. He was right. April first was Easter Sunday; it was also April Fool's Day—and Ushijima had a surprise for us. There didn't seem to be any Nips around. We walked in standing up and examined the quaint, horseshoe-shaped burial vaults in the low hillsides. No one then guessed that it would take nearly three months to conquer the island, or that Okinawa would be the bloodiest battle of the war.

Ushijima had a hundred thousand soldiers concentrated in the southern third of the island. It was another Iwo. The burial vaults had been converted to pillboxes; caves masked heavy artillery that could be rolled in and out on railroad tracks. Ushijima expected to win, too. The Jap strategy was to wait until General Simon Bolivar Buckner's 10th Army was ashore, knock out the fleet with *kamikaze* bombers, and slaughter the soldiers and marines at leisure.

The war's final Gethsemane had a terrible magnificence. Both generals committed crack troops in the critical struggle for the hills dominated by Okinawa's Shuri Castle. Ushijima sent in picked veterans of Manchuria, and Buckner countered with the Army's 7th, 27th, 77th and 96th Divisions and the marines' 1st and 6th—in one regiment of the Sixth there were two complete All-American football teams. Even the weather caught the spirit with a three-week-long cloudburst. Offshore the Navy had 1400 ships, the largest naval force ever assembled. It was just as well Nimitz sent that many, for the "green hornets," as bluejackets called *kamikazes,* mauled the fleet. Before Ushijima disemboweled himself in his last command post—a shell had killed Buckner a few days before—the Navy had lost ten thousand men. Nearly two thousand suicide bombers had damaged more than two hundred vessels, including four flagships. Nearly two score of our ships were on the bottom of the sea.

The warlords thought they had found the weapon that would win the war. Radio Tokyo announced that the whole nation would follow the *kamikaze* example. Dead pilots were promoted two or three ranks posthumously, Jap newspapers interviewed little boys who wanted to grow up and commit suicide, and on Honshu, the main Japanese island, a million soldiers of the Emperor dug in for the American invasion. Kyushu in November, Honshu in March—that was our program unless the Son of Heaven quit, which his generals said he was not about to do. Fortunately some of the Son's advisers were civilians. Their faith in victory diminished daily. The British had recaptured Burma, the Australians Borneo; Chiang Kai-shek was attacking in China, and eight-hundred-plane Superfort raids were pounding Dai Nippon around the clock. Jap peace feelers were relayed to Washington via Bern and Moscow. Then, on August sixth, the first atomic bomb blotted out Hiroshima. In the next three days the second hit Nagasaki and Russia declared war on Japan.

Hirohito broke down in front of his cabinet, wept into his white-gloved hand, and announced that he was surrendering unconditionally. A farce followed. The Emperor recorded his first speech to his people, explaining things. Several bitter-enders sneaked into the Imperial Palace to steal the record before it could be broadcast; they failed and committed harakiri. Men knifed themselves in front of the palace, in an apology to the Throne for failing to win the war.

MacArthur staged the surrender ceremony. A white Jap plane marked with green crosses brought a delegation of enemy brass to Manila by way of Ie Shima, a little island off Okinawa ("Here the 77th Division Lost a Buddy: Ernie Pyle"), for the rehearsal. Halsey's fleet sailed into Sagami Bay, southwest of Tokyo—it was greeted by the destroyer *Hatsuzabura,* with her three five-inch guns depressed, as though bowing—and on September second Jap diplomats in top hats and claw-hammer coats boarded the *Missouri* while the *West Virginia,* sunk at Pearl and now shipshape, stood by. Everything was smooth until Allied signers came to the Japanese copy of the document. They couldn't read the characters, and four signed on the wrong lines. The Jap foreign minister protested, but he could scarcely be heard above the roar of two thousand American planes overhead. He was told it didn't matter, he could get off the ship now; and bowing like the *Hatsuzabura,* he quietly did.

Corps d'Élite

I N ONE OF THOSE FLASHES OF RECOLLECTION which illuminate early childhood, I am standing by my mother on a New England curbstone, awaiting a 1920's Memorial Day parade. From a wooded cemetery across the street comes the lilt of brassy music; it grows; there is movement among the greening trees, and the column appears, marching straight toward me, led by my father in his Marine Corps dress blues, favoring the arm that had been crippled in France.

Everyone was cheering, but I saw only him, his blouse a lyric of dark blue, red piping and gold. I don't remember what uniforms the others were wearing—they were Army, or something. The parade halted smartly at the curb and fell out; my father draped that gaudy blouse over my shoulders, and blinded by what was later called Gung ho I took off at high port, tripped, and fell into a patch of dense shrubbery.

I emerged scathed, but uncured. The fact is I never abandoned that mummery—not even on the morning twenty years later when, groggy with morphine and swaddled in unlyrical gauze, I was evacuated from a violent Pacific beach to a Hospital LST. I can denounce the Marine Corps, and I frequently have. But so can lovers quarrel, and to those who have fought in it the Corps is like the memory of an old affair, tinged with sadness and bitterness, yet with the first enchantment lingering. It is a mystique, wholly irrational; and right or wrong, a legion of men will lay down their lives for its intangible honor tomorrow. Impossible? The youngest drill instructor on Parris Island will tell you there's no such word in the Marine Corps.

For him there's no such thing as a right way and a wrong way anyhow; there's only the Marine Corps way—a liturgy as obscure as life in certain remote Tanganyikan tribes. It is select: even the model who poses for the recruiting signs outside post offices must belong. It is archaic: its attitudes have not changed perceptibly since, as the Navy's army, the Corps was the striking arm of U.S. imperialism fifty years ago. It is xenophobic: the marine is touchier than a Reising gun, and assumes as an article of faith that everyone is against him, including the military and naval might of the United States.

His code is spartan. In garrison the Marine Corps is famous for fetishistic disciplines; one celebrated commander memorized the timetables of all railroads converging on his base and withheld transfer orders until the last possible moment before train time, to keep his men on their toes. In combat the Corps takes pride in cracking the enemy's toughest nuts; Ernie Pyle was startled to find marines apologizing when their casualties were low. By a kind of inverted idealism, they sentimentalize antisentimentality; in two of their greatest battles, officers and noncoms inspired troops by insulting them: Gunnery Sergeant Dan Daly led his men into murky Belleau Wood in World War I with the hoarse cry, "Come on, you sons of bitches—do you want to live forever?" and in the desperate night on Guadalcanal's Bloody Ridge, Lieutenant Colonel "Red Mike" Edson rallied his Raiders by snarling, "The only thing the Japs got that you haven't got is guts."

In time of crisis America admires marines almost as much as they admire themselves. On Iwo Jima, James Forrestal could not see one "without experiencing a feeling of reverence." In Korea, Douglas MacArthur, a late convert, discovered that "there is not a finer fighting organization in the world." When guns are muted, however, marine popularity falls. Hecklers report that Corps rituals smack of bogus comic opera. They point out that the melody for the "Marine Hymn" was actually lifted a century ago from Offenbach's *Genevieve de Brabant.* Even the marine's military virtues become suspect. Like Tommy Atkins, the British foot soldier immortalized by Rudyard Kipling, he's the "savior of his country" when the guns begin to shoot— and its "thin red line of heroes" when the drums begin to roll—but in peacetime we serve no redcoats here.

I have actually heard tweedy Remington Raiders—chairborne critics, that is—compare marines to Nazi storm troopers, Rumania's Iron Guard, the Spanish Falange. The French Foreign Legion is a little closer. Until 1940 the Corps, like the Legion, encouraged foreign enlistments, and some of its most memorable noncoms were White Russians, Germans and Poles. But the legionnaire of legend was shanghaied to Sidi-bel-Abbes. Marines are volunteers. Moreover, I watched the Legion in Indochina in 1953; in combat it is good, but on liberty it seems undisciplined, all muscle and no head. Head is a word in the Marine Corps, though it has another meaning.

Do not think that the marine's vocabulary is limited—that he is, in the old Army jeer, a man with a size nineteen collar and a size four hat. Actually, his language is both colorful and special. His corps has no recruits, but it does enlist boots. Although the number of marines afloat is now one percent of the Corps, in shore stations the floors are still called decks, walls are bulkheads, doors are hatches. A toilet is a head, and you had better not call it anything else. Ask a buck sergeant the way to the rest room and you will meet a fixed stare, as though you mumbled something about No. 1, or mentioned your tummy.

A bar is a slopchute, a young marine is a chicken, swamps are boondocks, candy is pogey bait, rumor scuttlebutt, a deception a snow job. Every marine is "Mac" to every other marine; every soldier is a doggie and is barked at. Mac's patois is not only vivid; it is astonishingly varied. Indeed, in the Marine Corps there is no such thing as no such thing. The term for anything that defies description is gizmo.

The gizmo that spurs the marine has been defined by Hanson Baldwin, the military analyst, as "moral superiority." Others call it *"esprit de corps."* The average marine regards discussion of such matters as infra dignitatem. He irreverently corrupts the Corps motto, *Semper Fidelis,* to "Semper Fi," an expression of cloudy semantics which conveys contempt for insincere sentiment, and if you mention *"esprit de corps"* with scorn he will leer cheerily—unless you happen not to be a marine yourself, in which case you are in jeopardy. For he does consider himself unique. He may look like a doggie. Coat him with mud, as his habitat frequently does, and he is indistinguishable from one. But don't bark at him. He might bite you.

He is, in fact, inclined to be fanatical about his individuality. Officially there are no more marine gunnery sergeants, but he persists in calling five-stripers "Gunny," because the rank is unknown in the Army. He is proud of the frogged embroidery on marine officers' hats and believes, in the total absence of evidence, that the practice started on ships during the War of 1812, to identify officers to their own snipers topside in the rigging. In combat he treasures his camouflaged helmet cover because it distinguishes him from soldiers, who don't have them. To him the Army is a bland corporation, a kind of hotel chain. He bitterly watches every Department of Defense move toward unification. He is convinced that the Marine Corps attracts a different kind of recruit, and he is right.

Other branches stress security, travel, a chance to learn a trade. The ultimate Marine Corps bait is a poster with a clenched, hairy fist and the legend, "You're not good enough to be a marine!" Since the first continental marine-recruiting station opened in a Philadelphia slopchute, the Corps has been daring men to become marines. The pitch attracts candidates who are interested not in milling-machine skills or retirement thirty years hence but in status. Inevitably the net cages a few specimens who have been answering Charles Atlas ads, but if they can pass the physical they're welcome. They'll fight, too, provided they're properly motivated, and the hairy fist isn't the only psychological trick in the Corps bag. Others are unveiled at boot camp, that remarkable inoculation of gizmo that converts a gawk into a rain-cooled, Spam-fed, more or less semiautomatic flat-trajectory weapon virtually incapable of a stoppage.

Andrew Jackson, the first of several Presidents to be infuriated by marine arrogance, recommended the abolition of the Corps in his first annual message to Congress, "there being no peculiar training requisite for it." It was a curious misstatement. The training is nothing if not peculiar. The youth who accepts the fist's challenge is taken to boot camp at Parris Island or San Diego, dressed in new dungarees studded with QM tags, issued 782 gear—hardware—and shorn of all lay accouterments, including his hair. In company with some 70 other bald young men, he is introduced to a magnificent starched, hashmarked sergeant who is to be his D.I. or drill instructor. In a typical scene the D.I. strolls up, glances at the platoon and reels backward, his bird-of-prey eyes glazed in an Asiatic stare. There is a moment of stunned silence. He speaks, hollowly.

Well, he'll be a dirty bird. He'll be a sad, son of a bitch. Upstairs must be pissed off at him. He knew they were scraping the bottom of the barrel for boots, but he'll be deep-sixed if they haven't given him the barrel itself this time. These are the *saddest* sacks he's ever seen. He gives one or two orders, and is usually rewarded by the discovery of a nervous chicken who confirms his worst suspicions—a boot, told to fasten that button, timidly reaches out and fingers one of the D.I.'s, or an anxious boy snaps his rifle bolt at the wrong moment, jamming it on the D.I.'s finger with a sickening crunch. The sergeant swears mightily. Is he supposed to make *marines* out of these people? It looks impossible, but since there's no such word—he flicks his swagger stick menacingly and intones the words his platoon will hear every minute on the minute for the next three months: "You better get hot, shitheads. You better *move!*"

Thus the boot opens his career in utter disgrace. His very existence is an insult to his D.I. Nothing he does is right, and for good reason—his manners are still those of a civilian, and the stated purpose of this training is to crush them. D.I. methods have varied over the years. A generation ago, physical drill was stressed, men caught eating pogey bait were ordered to carry an oozing mass of candy around all day, and sulkers were invited to meet the sergeant after dark behind the barracks. In the early 1940's a man who dropped a rifle had to sleep on eight of them; if anybody fell out with a dirty rifle bore the D.I. would field-strip the entire piece, bury the parts in the sand, and make the guilty boot uncover them with his nose. Today the old punishments are out. A red flag flies over the parade ground on hot days, enjoining drill, and parents are invited to visit their sons, as though they were Y.M.C.A. summer campers.

Nevertheless the basic concept remains: treat the shithead with contempt, march him a hundred miles, put him through a thousand drilled acts of obedience, taunt him with the fact that he volunteered, teach him to take aim on a target 500 yards away and hit it, and then, at the last inspection, grudgingly admit that he may make a real marine someday. After that final performance, the typical boot struts off the parade ground seething with pride. His *élan*, of course, is in direct proportion to his D.I.'s scorn that first day. He has done the impossible; he has come through. The whole show has been carried out with such a flourish that even though he may suspect it's a fraud, he couldn't be prouder if he had been commissioned in the Army.

In the process he has acquired a number of illusions, all valuable. He firmly believes that in 182 years of history the Marine Corps has never failed at anything, and that upon him rests the awful responsibility of upholding the most spectacular military tradition known to man. He is convinced his own incredible achievement in surviving boot camp entitles him to an insufferable air of truculence. And he is quite sure that his dazzling superiority is a source of nagging jealousy among the Joint Chiefs, who express it in mean and devious ways.

Marine invincibility is not all myth, but neither is it entirely true. The record shows that during the War of 1812 the commandant, leader of the whole Corps, fled Washington before the British, and that his successor was cashiered for being a drunk. Marines bolted at Bull Run, though they had an excuse; many of their officers had been Southerners and were over the hill. (Later they organized a Confederate States Marine Corps, which very nearly tangled with the U.S. Marine Corps at Port Royal, South Carolina.) There was no excuse, however, in 1942, when 222 of Carlson's Raiders attacked forty-three Japanese on Makin Atoll, narrowly escaped defeat, and accidentally left behind nine men to be beheaded. Nevertheless the Corps cultivates the Atlantean legend of invincibility, on the theory that men who believe they cannot be beaten are very hard to beat. When embarrassing skeletons rattle in the closet, there is always an answer. "Surely," Major General Ben Fuller said of the Bull Run debacle, "the marines must have been among the last to run."

That marines are cocky is no news to anyone who has observed a stiff neck rising insolently from a standing blue collar. What is not generally understood is that to them attitude is a weapon. Because he was convinced that he was still a tough old bird, General Archibald Henderson, aged seventy-four, could saunter up to a Baltimore street mob's cannon in 1857 and scornfully turn the muzzle aside, giving the marines behind him a chance to overrun the gun. Because he held Spanish marksmanship in contempt, Sergeant John Quick could climb a ridge at Guantánamo Bay in the Spanish-American War, turn his broad back to enemy fire, and wigwag artillery signals to American gunboats. And "Chesty" Puller, because he was a swashbuckler, could lead the First Marines through six attacking Chinese divisions after sweeping the frozen landscape with his field glasses at Chosin and announcing loudly, "Well, we've got the enemy on our right flank, our left flank, in front of us, and behind us. They won't get away *this* time."

Modesty is a soldierly virtue only in barracks. The Marine Corps acquired its thirty-four campaign streamers elsewhere: at Tripoli, captured by Lieutenant Presley O'Bannon after a 600-mile forced march in 1805; in the Aztec halls of the Montezumas, occupied by the marines who had scaled Chapultepec during the Mexican War; in the Boxer Rebellion, where young Smedley Butler stormed the Tartar Wall in Peking with a gaudy new globe-and-fouled-anchor tattooed across his chest, and had it gouged by a Boxer sniper. During World War I the Corps' reputation was built by the troops in France who proudly advertised the apocryphal description of them attributed to a German officer's diary—*Teufelhunde,* "devil dogs"; and twenty-five years later by the grimy divisions who answered the Japanese battle cry, "Blood for the

Emperor!" with "Blood for Eleanor!" Marine éclat was won by men who strutted. They never intended the meek should inherit it.

Swagger is, in fact, handed down from one marine generation to another, like a prize recipe to be improved upon. It was a World War I officer who ignored a French withdrawal order with the curt, "Retreat, hell! We just got here." Ten years later, during the marine campaign in Nicaragua, a marine who had served in France was ordered to investigate a complaint of an uprising, and, when an indignant planter demanded, "Are you the only man they sent?" replied, "There wasn't but one uprising, was there?" I vividly remember a bearded gunnery sergeant, a Nicaragua veteran, who paused in a driving Okinawan rain and shook his fist at the leaking sky. "You up there!" he bellowed. "Knock it off!"

Scoffers may doubt that the clouds broke ten minutes later, but the fact remains that flamboyance helps marines fight. Undeniably, however, it is a file on the nerves of other services. Admirals with long memories have never forgiven two enlisted marines named Corey and Marlow who, the night before the Panama Canal opened in 1914, hoisted a tiny scarlet-and-gold marine flag to the bow of a *piragua* canoe, bluffed their way past guards, and paddled the first craft into the locks wearing dress blues. Since then the Navy has learned to be charitable, and can even smile weakly over the unofficial medal Guadalcanal veterans had struck in Melbourne after their relief, which depicts an arm with admiral's stripes dropping a hot potato into the hands of a kneeling marine, and bears the motto *Faciat Georgius*—"Let George do it."

The Army, however, is another story. Harry Truman, a former artillery captain, never became reconciled to marine attitudes. Douglas MacArthur was so affronted by those of the Corps that just before leaving Corregidor in 1942 his chief of staff omitted from his general recommendation for unit citations the Fourth Marines, who were then manning his beach defenses on the Rock. The explanation was that the marines had had their share of glory in World War I and weren't going to get any in this one.

They got a lot, but the feud between Douglas MacArthur and the Marine Corps continued through the Pacific war. It abated in Korea, when MacArthur asked a marine division to lead the Army ashore at Inchon, but by then it had amassed a lore of its own: the epithet "Dugout Doug"; the sign on the Luzon gun, "With the help of God and a few marines, MacArthur took back the Philippines"; and the savage parody which opens,

> *Mine eyes have seen MacArthur*
> *With a Bible on his knee,*
> *He is pounding out communiqués*
> *For guys like you and me,*

and ends:

> *And while possibly a rumor now,*
> *Some day 'twil be a fact*
> *That the Lord will hear a deep voice say,*
> *Move over, God, it's Mac.*

No one infected with that bitterness will ever forget it. Unquestionably it contributed to the feeling between the services which reached a climax on Saipan, when the marines' "Howlin' Mad" Smith relieved an Army commander after the Army Twenty-seventh Division had broken in front of marine howitzers, forcing the Tenth Marines (artillery) to cut the fuses of their shells to four tenths of a second and meet a *banzai* attack with point-blank fire.

After that, marines in the Pacific had no use for any Army outfit, including what was then the Air Corps. To men who took a conservative view of medals, fliers seemed like inflationists. On one island taken for its landing strip, a marine company left in garrison observed that the squadron using the field held weekly decoration ceremonies. One Saturday, when pilots and gunners fell out on one side of the strip, marines fell out on the other side wearing pith helmets and camouflaged underwear shorts. As the ranking Air Corps commander pinned Air Medals and Distinguished Flying Crosses, the marine captain went down his ranks, awarding each man a cellophane-wrapped cheroot. It was a model formation. No one smiled. The first sergeant held the cigar box.

An old sea story attributes the origin of interservice rivalry to the battle of the *Bonhomme Richard*, when John Paul Jones cried, "We have not yet begun to fight!" and a marine in the rigging allegedly muttered, "There's always some son-of-a-bitch who doesn't get the word." A more appropriate opening would be the issuing to marines, in 1798, of old uniforms from Mad Anthony Wayne's Legion—which, incidentally, had the red piping and seam stripe seen on blues today. The Corps has been an Ishmael among the services ever since, a Navy outfit using Army gear. The Army, understandably, supplies its own units first, which means that innovations are a long time reaching the marines. Inevitably this leads to friction. When the Army decided, in World War II, that combat infantrymen were entitled to a shiny badge and a ten-dollar monthly pay hike, marines, who received no badge and no raise, worked themselves into one of the great rages of the war, and in Korea's opening stages marines wearing canvas leggings fought beside Army units that had been equipped with combat boots almost a decade before.

This very argument is used by those who would lower the boom on the Marine Corps. It does nothing, they insist, which couldn't be done more humanely by the Army. Since Andrew Jackson's time there have been nine other attempts to wipe out the Marine Corps, with Presidents Theodore Roosevelt, Taft, Hoover and Truman in the assault and Congress, on each occasion, holding the Main Line of Resistance. Unquestionably some hostility can be traced to the old officer class. Fifty years ago the Marine Corps began committing the social *gaffe* of commissioning "mustangs," men up from the ranks. Its roll of heroes since reads like a roster of Mafia suspects,—"Johnny the Hard," "Hiking Hiram" Bearss, "Horrible Herman," "Old Gimlet Eye" Butler, "Dopey" Wise, "Red Mike" Edson, "Howlin' Mad" Smith, "Chesty" Puller—and its status at the Army & Navy Club has suffered as a consequence.

The public line taken by critics of the marines is that America's civilian military establishment has no place for a *corps d'élite*. Here the carpers have a case. The stock Corps answer, that it is the nation's expert on amphibious warfare, begs the question. The real issue is its concept of itself as the first team. Significantly, marines take enormous pride in the official German report on Belleau Wood, which mentioned defeat at the hands of a "shock unit." They have always relished European praise. Their Corps is an American institution, but its debt to Frederick II, the Prussian who invented military drill, and Kipling is large. It stands, today, as one of the last strongholds of nineteenth century martial chauvinism.

Skeptics are advised to visit the Corps' oldest post, at Eighth and I streets S.E., Washington, D.C., on a Friday summer evening for the weekly sunset parade. To pass through the gate is to pass into another century. Modern armies believe in utilitarian uniforms, but no man here could be mistaken for a truck driver or a Good Humor man. Each private wears tailored blues and carries an immaculate rifle; officers and noncoms flourish swords; atop the *Beau Geste* stonework of the barracks parapet, field musics in scarlet tunics sound the sad sweet notes of retreat. The gold-frogged Marine Band passes in mandarin splendor at a slow march—a formation abandoned elsewhere in America two generations ago—and as the flag floats down between two ancient cannon, the post battalion parades with fixed bayonets, looking like soldiers of the Queen leaving to deal with an insurrection in the Punjab. The band, naturally enough, plays the melody pirated from Offenbach. All hands approaching shipping-over time—when a man is thinking of re-enlisting—fumble for their ballpoint pens.

The ceremony is laconically observed by a bulldog mascot in a blue blanket and gold P.F.C. stripe who answers to the name of "Chesty." This Chesty was a gift of the British Royal Marines, Kipling's "Jollies." There have been other Jolly gifts, and all underscore the European ancestry of the United States Marines. Over 200 years ago the Royal Marines began wearing leather collars to improve their bearing on parade. They were called "boot-necks," and when the custom crossed the Atlantic their American cousins became known as "leather-necks."

Britain's most lasting contribution to the Marine Corps, however, was made by one man. In the late 1890's, when marine functions were confined to service aboard ships, and shore posts were maintained solely to supply the fleet with replacements, leather-neck strength totaled 3000 men. There was only one sergeant major in the entire Corps, and he lived in austere solitude at Eighth and I. His name was Thomas F. Hayes. He stood six feet, three inches, weighed 250 pounds, and had fought with Kitchener in the Sudan as a Color Sergeant. There was no boot camp then. A man who had been sufficiently badgered by a recruiting sergeant was issued a Krag rifle, put in the awkward squad, and drilled by the sergeant major, who also trained all fledgling officers. Thus Hayes, the very model of a regimental sergeant major, became the Corps' first D.I., and when boot camps were set up at Port Royal, South Carolina, and Mare Island, off California, on the eve of World War I, the men picked as D.I.'s were his protégés.

His legacy is evident today in sunset parades, in ornamental Marine Band baldrics, and in the custom, revived in the 1950's by a company commander at Camp Pendleton, of taking a snare drummer along on a forced march to beat out cadence. It is seen in the Corps' love of tradition and set forms, in the emphasis on the externals of soldiering which set apart the Mulvaneys of Victoria's Empire, and which give the Marine Corps its quaint color today. Hayes' influence had another aspect known to every man ever to be addressed by a gunnery sergeant in the imperative mood: the perpetuation of regimental honors. It is found in the best Army divisions—the most obvious example is the Big Red One—but in the Marine Corps it is the heart of a whole complex of values which bestow what might be called invisible rank.

There are many kinds of invisible rank in the Marine Corps: time in service, combat experience, duty status. Marines perform a variety of duties, but tradition still gives caste to the infantry soldier—one marine pilot apologetically described himself as "a rifleman who at present is flying a plane." The greatest caste goes to the men in the old-line regiments. It may surprise some to know that the Twenty-eighth Marines, whose men planted the flag on Suribachi Yama, and the Twenty-ninth Marines, who took Okinawa's Sugar Loaf Hill, lack glamour within the Corps. They were the last two regiments formed in World War II and though their men are honored, their outfits weren't around long enough to become properly encrusted with salt.

The really briny outfits are the Fourth, Fifth, and Sixth Marines— the Fourth, because it is inseparably identified with China and went down gloriously on Corregidor, and the Fifth and Sixth because they seized the Hun by the short hair and were on Guadalcanal. A chicken assigned to, say, the Fifth Marines is entitled to wear the French *four-ragère* (pogey rope) and a presidential unit citation ribbon; if he meets a high-school classmate in the Eighth Marines he invisibly outranks him, and may scorn him as a "Hollywood Marine" because the Eighth was the last marine regiment to arrive on Guadalcanal—despite the fact that both taunter and taunted weren't even born when Washing Machine Charlie, the Jap bomber of '42, flew back to Rabaul for the last time and the island was secured.

The Fifth is one of three regiments belonging to that Marine Corps within the Marine Corps, the First Division. Outsiders who have been outraged by marine pretensions will be cheered to learn that there is bickering within the Corps, and that sometimes it's pretty petty. It doesn't always involve chickens either. When the Sixth Division spanned Okinawa's Asa Kawa under fire, engineers erected a sign advertising the bridge as the longest ever built by the Marine Corps in combat. Major General Pedro A. Del Valle, commander of the adjacent First Division, heard about it, flung a plank across a gully outside his tent, and posted it as the *shortest* combat bridge built by the Corps. The curious thing is that, despite this, there are Sixth Division veterans who secretly wish they had served with Del Valle. Like all marines they are social climbers, and the First is the Corps' *haut monde*.

Like all traditionalists, marines resent change. Happily this does not apply to weapons, but it covers just about everything else: gear, uniforms, formation, terminology. In 1940, when the massive infiltration of reserves began, a tremor ran through the ranks, and there were sergeants who strode toward the nearest adjutant's office to put in letters for retirement. The tremor became seismic on that bleak winter day in 1943 when the Women's Reserve was established; that very evening, General Thomas Holcomb later recalled with awe, General Archibald Henderson's portrait toppled from a wall in the commandant's house, ricocheted off a sideboard and crashed to the floor. Females and reservists remain today. But it is significant that the Corps has brought back squad drill, that applications to D.I. school and rifle teams are encouraged by issuing successful candidates archaic campaign hats—and that there are boondock types who run around correcting everyone who calls them campaign hats because, by God, they were *field hats* in the old Corps.

The essence of marine nostalgia is in that phrase "the old Corps," which is heard every day on every post in each of the seventy-seven countries where marines are on duty. A pleasant fable has it that when the second continental marine to enlist met the first in 1775, he was greeted with the hoot, "You should've seen the *old* Corps, Mac." The old Corps, everyone agrees, isn't what it used to be. Cynics add that it never was. To some ex-marines who wear the Corps' old-school tie (there is one), it is a gilded, impossible memory of a time when every captain was a Flagg and every first soldier a Quirt, and all marines were stationed in golden Shanghai—advertising for valets in *Walla Walla,* the Fourth Marines' newspaper, guzzling Haig & Haig at ninety-five cents a fifth, and wolfing "shit on a shingle," as chipped beef on toast is elegantly known.

Nevertheless there *was* an old Corps. It existed and is definable. It was born in 1899; led by company commanders who had seen action in the Civil War, the tiny Marine Corps had just defeated a superior force with a fraction of the Army's medical casualties, and now an expedition was needed to deal with the Philippine insurrection. Congress made the obvious conclusion: Corps strength was doubled to 6000 men. Campaign hats were obtained from the Army QM, the first khaki was issued, and the old Corps marine made his twentieth century debut.

He bowed out in late 1941, when the First Marine Division

landed in North Carolina after Caribbean maneuvers and was herded into 1000 chigger-infested tents. The months bracketing that encampment saw the shelving of squad drill and the campaign hat, together with the iron kelly—the World War I steel helmet—the square field scarf, high-top dress shoes, and the '03 Springfield rifle. The whistle was blown on foreign enlistments; an expansion began in which the old-timers were lost. There were so many promotions that chevron stocks ran low, and new noncoms wore stripes on only one sleeve.

Between the Spanish-American War and Pearl Harbor, the Marine Corps had been a hard, salty outfit of seasoned troops, so small that the officers knew the names of most of the men, and so rigidly disciplined that it could always move out on an hour's notice. Almost everybody had been under fire somewhere. The old Corps fought a dozen banana campaigns in the Philippines, Cuba, Nicaragua, Haiti, Puerto Rico, Santo Domingo, Vera Cruz and China, and it survived World War I's brief expansion without losing its integrity. Of course there were changes. At the turn of the century, when marines wore spiked Kaiser helmets, privates were likely to be illiterate; during the depression there were recruiters who wouldn't look at a man unless he had a high-school diploma. But lettered or unlettered, all old Corps marines had this in common: they considered themselves professionals.

There were no Mauldins among them. They worked at soldiering, holding informal speed contests after hours, digging positions for mortar base plates, field-stripping Browning automatic rifles blindfolded. When a man made a rate he moved into another world; P.F.C.'s spoke to corporals only on business. They did not object to falling out with one foot bare for feet inspection. They took it for granted that an officer in a sparkling belt of shell cordovan would call Saturday mornings, wearing white gloves to grope for dust and carrying a half dollar to snap on taut bunks to see if it would jump back into his hand. And if a man floundered in slopchute suds Saturday night he expected, and was awarded, five days' "piss and punk"—bread and water.

It was a frugal Corps. About the only way a private could improve upon his twenty-one dollars a month was to master the '03 rifle and qualify as an expert rifleman for another five dollars, and he was docked each month for the hospital fund and the Marine Band. He achieved chic through a blend of thrift and ingenuity: campaign hats were blocked with raw sugar, shoes spit-shined with shoe polish and shaving lotion, legging eyelets polished with steel wool, leather belts saddle-soaped until they were limp.

If the Corps was careful with money, it was parsimonious with promotions. The thirty-year private wasn't unusual; a man would be acting corporal for a year before he even took his test for promotion, and if he made it, his entire company was called out in the kind of formation reserved, today, for awards of valor. The rule was, one stripe to a hash mark, and there were no slick-armed sergeants in the old Corps.

War is a great destroyer of military traditions. "It will be good when all this is over," a British general reportedly moaned to an aide as shells crashed around his command post, "and we can get back to *real* soldiering." But the hard fact is that soldiers are trained for war, and the threat of war is the only excuse for building barracks. The old Corps was more than a showpiece, because in its heyday great powers could get away with showing the flag in sulky jungle capitals. Situations are no longer taken well in hand that way, however. That kind of diplomacy died in Vietnam, and not all the ruffles and flourishes at Eighth and I can bring it back, or take the Marine Corps back to the shores of Shanghai's Soochow Creek. Today's marines divert themselves by stringing yo-yos for needy children, or parading for visiting dignitaries, or putting out brush fires. Occasionally they flex their muscles—as in the rescue of the *Mayaguez* and its crew from Cambodian pirates. But the whiff-of-the-grape way of the old Corps is as obsolete as wrap leggings.

Does all this have any meaning for the new Corps—the Fleet Marine Force, the F.M.F.? It has plenty. The making of a lady starts with her grandmother. The F.M.F.'s grandmother was not genteel, but it was everything a crack outfit should be, and it left its life, its liens and its sacred honor to its successor. To those who believe uniforms make the soldier, the bequest was lost. There was nothing smart about the faded dungarees and tattered helmet covers the F.M.F. wore in the Pacific during World War II and continues to wear today. But when word was passed to darken ship—when the cargo nets went over the side and the Higgins boats swung out from their davits—there was something in the air the old Corps would have recognized. Dan Daly might have watched aghast as eighteen-year-olds camouflaged Khe Sanh gun positions with comic books and called their despairing sergeant Daddy-O. But he would have known them, and tipped his iron kelly to them, when they held their position against all odds.

There is a seed, pride. It is planted in every man during boot training and grows to be tougher than he is. He may want it gone, but can't shuck it. He may jeer at all heroes as Gung ho. Still the thing stays inside him, and when he finds himself on the line he's got it, and it him. The dead in their wire-trussed poncho shrouds don't scare it out of him.

He can't go back—everybody around him has got the same thing; even cooks and bakers are armed when the Marine Corps goes to war, and the doctors and medical corpsmen and chaplains are Navy men. He may never have heard the Marine Band, may not even know where Tripoli is or who the Montezumas were. Still he'll jump when Daddy-O pumps an arm, because someone once told him it is better to die than to let the Marine Corps down, and he believed it then, and part of him always will.

Nobody told him he would fight for his country. He doesn't think of it that way. I once attended a Marine Corps anniversary which reached its climax in a series of toasts: to the Continental Congress which authorized the Corps on November 10, 1775; to the Phila-delphia bartender who organized the first two battalions by offering likely boots free grog; to the marines who fought at New Orleans; to the Corps' first Korean landing in 1871; to all the old battles and old regi-ments and old marines, including Captain Jimmy Bones, the old Corps ghost. Understandably, no toasts were offered to Bull Run. It was re-markable, though, I thought, that in all that beating of Marine Corps gums there was no such word as America.

But men don't fight for the flag. It's too remote; they need some-thing closer. Leather-necks have it. As in the French Foreign Legion motto, *Legio Patria Nostra*, their legion is their country. The Army has its own ways of instilling pride. Marines, however, are something apart. It is arguable that they are because they merely think they are. The effect is the same: an élite phalanx of assault troops who can be counted upon to make the most impossible assignment possible, and who ask only that the survivors be permitted to gloat. Gentlemen may deplore the exalting of such values in a nation at peace, but until peace is forever the country needs men who will fight for gewgaws and bellhop blue, and who do not ask what price glory. Ladies may protest that in violent death there can be no glory. Maybe not. But in the Ma-rine Corps there is such a word.

The Man Who Couldn't Speak
Japanese

IN THE SPRING OF 1944 the United States Marine Corps formed its last rifle regiment of World War II, the 29th Marines, in New River, North Carolina. The first of its three battalions was already overseas, having been built around ex-Raiders and parachutists who had fought on Guadalcanal, Tarawa, and Saipan. Great pains were being taken to make the other two battalions worthy of them. The troops assembling in New River were picked men. Officers and key noncoms had already been tested in battles against the enemy, and though few riflemen in the line companies had been under fire, they tended to be hulking, deep-voiced mesomorphs whose records suggested that they would perform well when they, too, hit the beach. There was, however, one small band of exceptions. These were the nineteen enlisted men comprising the intelligence section of the 29th's second battalion. All nineteen were Officer Candidate washouts. I, also a washout, led them. My rank was Corporal, acting Platoon Sergeant—Acting John.

We were, every one of us, military misfits, college students who in a fever of patriotism had rushed to the Marine Corps' Officer Candidate School at Quantico, Virginia, and had subsequently been rejected because, for various reasons, we did not conform with the established concept of how officers should look, speak, and act. Chet Przystawski of Colgate, for example, had a build like Charles Atlas but a voice like Lily Pons; when he yelled a command, the effect was that of an eerie shriek. Ace Livick of the University of Virginia had no sense of direction; at Quantico he had flunked map reading. Jerry Collins, a Yale man, was painfully shy. Stan Zoglin, a Cantab, had poor posture. Mack Yates of Ole Miss wore spectacles. Tom Jasper of Brown and I had been insubordinate. I had refused to clean a rifle on the ground that it was already clean, and I suffered the added stigma of being scrawny. I've forgotten the order Jasper disobeyed, though I knew that he too had another count against him: he admired the Japanese enormously.

Sy Ivice of Chicago christened us "the Raggedy-Ass Marines." That was about the size of it. Love had died between us and the Marine Corps. The rest of the battalion amiably addressed us as "Mac"— all enlisted marines were "Mac" to their officers and to one another— but there was a widespread awareness that we were unsuitably bookish, slack on the drill field, and generally beneath the fastidious stateside standards established in the Corps' 169-year history. If there had been such a thing as a Military Quotient, the spit-and-polish equivalent of an Intelligence Quotient, our M.Q. would have been pegged at about seventy-eight. It is fair to add that this rating would have been confined to our parade-ground performance. We were regarded as good combat prospects. All of us, I believe, had qualified on the Parris Island, South Carolina, rifle range as sharpshooters or expert riflemen. It was believed (and, as it proved, rightly so) that we would be useful in battle. Our problem, or rather the problem of our leaders, was that we lacked what the British army calls Quetta manners. We weren't properly starched and blancoed, weren't martially prepossessing—weren't, in a word, good for the 29th's image.

We were rarely given liberty, because our company commander was ashamed to let civilians see us wearing the Corps uniform. Shirt-tails out, buttons missing, fore-and-aft (overseas) caps down around our ears—these were signs that we had lost our drill-field ardor in OCS and were playing our roles of incorrigible eccentrics to the hilt. We looked like caricatures from cartoons in *The Leatherneck,* the Marine Corps equivalent of *Yank,* and the only reason our betters allowed us to stay together, setting a bad example for one another and damaging battalion élan, was a provision in the official Table of Organization for an intelligence section and our qualifications for membership in it. Between Quantico and assignment to the 29th we had all attended something called intelligence school. Theoretically we were experts in identifying enemy units by searching Jap corpses, recognizing the silhouettes of Zero fighters, reconnoitering behind the lines, etc. It was all rather vague. If we proved useless in these tasks, our commanders knew that we could always be used for odd jobs.

Meanwhile we carried out exhausting exercises in the Carolina boondocks, inflating rubber boats, getting snarled in bales of communications wire, carrying out simulated patrol missions at night.

Whenever it was Livick's turn to keep the map, we would vanish into the piney woods, subsisting on K and D rations for hours until we were found thrashing around in the bush and led back by a rescue party from the battalion's 81-millimeter platoon, our long-suffering neighbors in New River's Tent City. For the most part it was an uneventful time, however. Nothing interesting seemed likely to happen before we were shipped overseas.

Then one morning the battalion adjutant summoned me.

"Mac."

"Sir."

"You will square away to snap in a new man."

Marine Corps orders were always given this way: "You will scrub bulkheads," "You will police this area," "You will hold a field day." There was only one permissible response.

"Aye, aye, sir," I said.

"A Japanese-language interpreter," he said.

"A *what?*"

In 1944 no one in the Marine Corps spoke Japanese. Unlike the ETO, where plenty of GI's were bilingual, Americans were at a severe linguistic disadvantage in the Pacific. It was worsened by the fact that many Japs spoke English; they could eavesdrop on our combat field telephones. As a result by the third year of the war the headquarters company of each marine battalion carried on its roster a full-blooded Navaho who could communicate over radiophones in his own tongue with the Navahos in other battalions. After the outbreak of the war Washington had set up several crash courses to teach Japanese to bright young Americans, but the first graduates wouldn't emerge until the spring of 1945.

"We'll be the only outfit with its own translator," he said.

"Sir."

"Private Harold Dumas will be coming down from post headquarters at fourteen hundred."

That was too much. "He's only a *private?*"

"Knock it off!"

"Aye, aye, sir."

A noncom wasn't supposed to question higher wisdom, but clearly there was something odd here. Back in our pyramidal tent I passed the word among my people, whose astonishment matched mine. Their first reaction was that I was snowing them, but within an hour the dope was confirmed by the sergeant major, a bright little sparrow of a man named John Guard. Guard had some intriguing details, including an explanation for the translator's low rank. Until very recently—two days ago, in fact—Harold Dumas had been locked up in Portsmouth naval prison. The nature of his offense was unknown to Guard, but the sergeant major knew where Dumas was believed to have learned Japanese. He was a native of California; his neighbors had been Issei (first-generation Japanese-Americans) and Nisei (children of Issei).

The fact that the newcomer was a Californian is important to an understanding of what happened later. The Marine Corps maintained a rigid geographical segregation. Every man enlisting east of the Mississippi was sent to boot camp at Parris Island and shipped to New River after his recruit training. West of the Mississippi, boots went to the San Diego base and, once they had qualified, to nearby Camp Pendleton. Virtually none of us in Tent City knew anything about life on the West Coast. We had never seen a giant redwood, or the Grand Canyon, or Hollywood. We had never even met anyone from California until Harold Dumas arrived that afternoon at two o'clock.

He made a great entrance. He was wearing a salty barracks (visored) cap, a field scarf (necktie) so bleached that it was almost white, heavily starched khakis, and high-top dress shoes. The shoes were especially impressive. The Marine Corps had stopped issuing high-tops after Pearl Harbor, and they were therefore a great status symbol, signifying membership in the élite prewar Old Corps. Dumas was the only post-Pearl marine I ever knew who had them, but then, he was unusual in lots of ways.

Prepossessing is the word that best describes him, though it is really inadequate. The moment he strode into Tent City with his elbows swinging wide, every eye was on him. Six foot two, with a magnificent physique, he carried himself like Randolph Scott in *To the Shores of Tripoli*, the movie that had conned thousands of marines into joining up. His face was freckled, his eyes were sky-blue, his expression was wholly without guile; he was a man you trusted instinctively, whose every word you believed, for whose reputation you would fight, and whose friend you longed to be. When he removed the barracks cap, he was a towhead; and even before we had met—before that firm, manly handclasp that characterized all his greetings—he was known to us simply as "Whitey."

"The name's Dumas," he said in a rich, manly baritone, looking straight at you with an expression that, in those days before Madison Avenue had corrupted the word, could only be called sincere. Sincerity emanated from him; so did an air of achievement. Whitey was in his mid-twenties, a few years older than the rest of us, and it developed that he had used his time well. No one could call him a braggart—he was in fact conspicuously modest—but over the next few weeks particulars about his background slipped out naturally in normal conversation. He had been a newspaperman and a professional boxer. The fact that he had made money in the ring had been his undoing, accounting for his imprisonment; he had slugged a bully in a San Francisco bar, and under California law, he explained, a blow by a professional fighter was regarded as assault with a deadly weapon. If it hadn't been for his knowledge of Japanese, which he had disclosed to the authorities in Portsmouth, he would still be in the dreary exercise yard there.

"Isn't it typical of the Marine Corps to keep him a private?" Yates said scornfully. "In the Army he'd be at least a major."

The more we saw of Whitey, the more we admired him. He was everything we wanted to be. He even had a sexy wife, a Paramount starlet. After much coaxing he was persuaded to produce a picture of her, an eight-by-ten glossy print of a beaming blonde in a bathing suit; it was signed "With all my love—Laverne." Even more impressive, Whitey, unlike most of us, was a combat veteran. He had been a machine gunner in the 1st Marines during the early days on Guadalcanal. This was a matter of special interest to Sy Ivice, who had landed on the 'Canal later with the 2d Marines. Sy wanted to reminisce about those days with Whitey, but Whitey politely declined. He had lost two of his best buddies in the fire fight along the Tenaru River, he told us, and he didn't want to talk about it.

Whitey's greatest achievement, of course, was his mastery of the enemy's language, the attainment that had sprung him from Portsmouth, and it was far too valuable to be confined to my section. Shortly after we crossed the country by troop train and encamped at Linda Vista, north of San Diego, preparatory to boarding ship, our gifted ex-con attracted the attention of the 29th's commanding officer, Colonel George F. Hastings. Hastings was the kind of colorful hard-charger the Marine Corps has always valued highly. Reportedly he was a native of an Arizona town named Buzzard's Gulch. Myth had it that his middle initial stood for "Flytrap," which was absurd, but it was quite true that between the wars he had designed the Corps' standard M1A1 flytrap. Until the 29th was formed, this device had existed only on paper, but over one weekend in training he had ordered one built. It didn't work. Not a single insect ventured into it. Nobody had the courage to tell the colonel, and on a Sunday of punishing heat the first sergeants had turned everybody out to catch flies by hand and put them in the trap so that Hastings wouldn't feel crushed.

The colonel was a great, blond, buffalo of a man who always wore a bleached khaki fore-and-aft cap pushed to the back of his head. He was also the hoarsest and most redundant man I have ever known. His normal speaking voice can only be described as throaty, and he was forever saying things in it like "Here in Dixie we're in the Deep South," "Keep fit and healthy," and "Eat lots of food and plenty of it."

One sunlit morning—heavily handsome as only southern Californian weather can be—I was summoned by the sergeant major into the C.O.'s august presence. Hastings was standing beside a Lister bag in Officers' Country, slaking his thirst.

"We're going to sail aboard ship tomorrow," he barked after draining a canteen cup.

"Sir."

"The first day out I want Private Dumas to hold Japanese lessons. Just some fundamental key phrases. All officers and staff N.C.O.'s will meet on the fantail in the stern. I'm requisitioning a blackboard from ship's stores. Make sure Dumas is ready."

When I passed the word to Whitey, he gave me what we called a thousand-yard stare—a look of profound preoccupation. Then, while we were mounting the gangplank of the U.S.S. *General C. G. Morton*, lugging our seabags on our left shoulders and saluting the ship's colors as we boarded her, word was passed of our voyage's destination. We were headed for jungle maneuvers on Guadalcanal. "Oh, Christ, not that goddamned island," Ivice groaned. As Acting John I had been the first to reach the deck, and I happened to be looking at Dumas when the news reached him. He gave me a two-thousand-yard stare.

The next morning all designated hands fell out aft, with notebooks and pencils in hand. First the colonel pointed out that the blackboard was there, with lots of chalk and plenty of it, and that we were about to get some dope that would improve our efficiency and competence. Then he introduced Dumas. It was, I later thought, one of Whitey's finest hours. Arms akimbo, head high, with just the trace of a smile on that rugged face—the look of the learned teacher addressing eager neophytes—he proceeded with such assurance that one momentarily forgot he was outranked by everyone else there. Like English, he observed, Japanese was two languages, the written and the spoken. We would be chiefly concerned with the second, but it might be useful if we acquired some proficiency with the first. Turning to the blackboard he chalked with stenographic speed:

"That means 'Put your hands up, Nip!'" he said easily. "The best phonetic rendition I can give you is '*Zari sin toy fong!*'"

We wrote it down.

The next phrase was:

"'*Booki fai kiz soy?*'" said Whitey. "It means 'Do you surrender?'"

Then:

"'*Mizi pik loi ooni rak tong zin?*' 'Where are your comrades?'"

"Tong *what?*" rasped the colonel.

"Tong *zin*, sir," our instructor replied, rolling chalk between his palms. He arched his eyebrows, as though inviting another question. There was one. The adjutant asked, "What's that gizmo on the end?"

"It's called a *fy-thong*," Whitey said. "It looks like a quotation mark, or a German umlaut, but its function is very different. It makes the question imperative—almost a threat. In effect you're saying, 'Tell me where your comrades are or you're a dead Nip.'"

"Right on target," the colonel muttered, writing furiously.

Next Whitey scrawled:

"Means 'I want some water,'" he explained. "You say it '*Ruki gack keer pong tari loo-loo.*'"

Then:

"'*Moodi fang baki kim tuki dim fai?*' That's a question: 'Where is your commander?'"

A company commander raised a hand. "Why no *fy—fy* . . ."

"*Fy-thong*," Whitey prompted. He spread his hands. "I really can't explain it, sir. The imperative just doesn't exist in certain conjugations. They call it a narrow inflection. It's a weird language." He grinned. "But then, they're a peculiar people."

"Murdering shitheads," hoarsed the colonel, flexing his elbow and scribbling on.

The battalion operations officer—the BN-3—cleared his throat. He was a squat gargoyle of a man with a thick Brooklyn accent, the comic of Officers' Country. He asked, "How do you say 'I got to take a crap?'"

Into the laughter Whitey said earnestly, "That's a good question, sir. The Japanese are very sensitive about bodily functions. You have to put it just right."

He chalked:

のケ毛Υ尕 弾彼食具攵

He said: "*Song foy suki-suki kai moy-ah.*'"

The BN-3 shot back, "What about saying to a Nip girl '*Voulez-vous coucher avec moi?*'"

Colonel Hastings thought that was hilarious, and once his guffaws had sanctioned the joke, everyone joined in lustily. Everyone, that is, except Whitey. Nursing his elbows and rocking back on his heels, he gave them a small, tight enlisted-man's smile. Slowly it dawned on the rest of us that he had not understood the operations officer, that his foreign languages did not include French. There was much coughing and shuffling of feet; then the BN-3 said in the subdued voice of one whose joke had been unappreciated, "What I mean is—how do you tell a piece of gash that you want your ashes hauled?"

Now Whitey beamed. He turned to the blackboard and scrawled:

車よbろ 郜 ゑ坴 信゛ま

"How do you *say* it?" shouted the quartermaster.

"'*Naka-naka eeda kooda-sai,*'" Whitey said slowly. There was a long pause while we all made sure we had that one right. Thirty years later I can read it clearly in my yellowing notes, carefully printed in block capitals.

The colonel stood up, yawned, and prepared to shove off. He was bushed, he said, and he looked it. Doubtless this was his most intense cogitation since the invention of the flytrap. But then, we were all stretching ourselves. Although Marine Corps routine can be exhausting, it is rarely cerebral. The only man there who looked fresh was Whitey. Of course, he already knew Japanese.

The colonel was nothing if not dogged, however, and every day thereafter we assembled on the fantail for more skull sessions. By the end of the second week we were jabbering at each other with reasonable fluency, and the more enterprising platoon leaders were drilling their men in the basic idioms. Hastings, now well into his third notebook, was a bottomless source of questions ("How do you say 'Put down your weapon' and tell him to do that?") We all felt that the 29th had a distinct edge on the other twenty-eight marine regiments. Even the jaded members of my intelligence section were roused to pride—Jasper, a particularly apt pupil, marveled at the exquisite nuances of the tongue, at its Oriental precision and delicacy of phrasing—though Zoglin dampened our enthusiasm somewhat by pointing out the unlikelihood that we would ever have an opportunity to use our new skill. Japanese soldiers were notorious for their refusal to surrender. At the end of an island battle, they would sprint toward our lines in a traditional *banzai* (hurrah) suicide charge, and our people would obligingly mow them down. (*Banzai*, Whitey explained in response to a question, was spelled " 万歳 ".)

On the morning of the seventeenth day we climbed topside to find ourselves lying off the 'Canal, that lush, incredibly green, entirely repulsive island that for most of us had existed only in legend. Ivice had a lot to say about its banyan trees and kunai grass, but Whitey continued to be reticent about his recollections of it. Toward the end the journey had been a great strain for him. Of course, he had a lot on his mind. Rising in the night for a trip to the scuttlebutt or the head, I would see him lying awake on his bunk, sweating in his skivvies, preparing the next day's lecture.

Slinging our 782 gear over our field packs, we scrambled down the cargo nets thrown over the side of the *Morton,* landed in the waiting Higgins boats, and raced in them toward the shore. There we found that we were to make our training camp on the banks of a river. And there Whitey committed what seemed to be a peculiar blunder. As he looked down on the stream his eyes misted over. "Sweet Jesus," he said feelingly, picking up a corroded old cartridge case. "I never thought I'd see the Matanikau again."

Ivice looked at him in disbelief. "The *Matanikau!*" he said. "What the fuck are you talking about? This is the *Kokumbona.* The Matanikau's four miles to the east!"

Whitey hesitated and wet his lips. It was the first time any of us had seen him shook. Finally he blinked and said, "Man, I must be

Asiatic." He shrugged. "All these goddamned rivers look the same to me."

The rest of us accepted that—this tangled island bewildered us too —but Ivice said nothing. Throughout that day I caught him eyeing Whitey strangely from time to time, and the following morning, when I hitched a ride to Lunga Point on a DUKW and crossed the coconut-log bridge spanning the Matanikau I understood why. The two rivers were entirely different. Compared to the mighty Matanikau, the Kokumbona was a shallow brook. Whitey's error was inexplicable.

Ivice was the first to entertain doubts about the star of our intelligence section, and I was the second. One evening over a joe-pot I mentioned to the sergeant major that Mrs. Dumas was a movie starlet. The sparrow chirped, "There ain't no Mrs. Dumas. If there was one, there'd be an allotment for her on the books, and there ain't none. I keep the books. I *know*." Shortly thereafter I saw a pinup of Betty Grable in a slopchute near Henderson Field. I recognized the style immediately: an eight-by-ten glossy print. What Whitey had been passing off as a photograph of his wife was a publicity shot of some Hollywood aspirant. Probably he had never met her. I never learned for sure.

Bit by bit the elaborate structure he had erected so adroitly and so successfully was beginning to come unstuck. Working on the Point Cruz dock, Yates met a port battalion officer who had been an Oakland lawyer before the war and who hooted at the idea of California law defining a boxer's punch as an assault with a deadly weapon. Then a gunnery sergeant, arriving as a replacement from Pendleton, recognized Whitey and revealed the true reason he had been stripped of rank and sent to prison. While still in boot camp, it turned out, he had been arrested for impersonating an officer in downtown San Diego. Since he hadn't become a recruit until the fall of 1943, Whitey had been a civilian during the battle for the 'Canal. Ivice was confirmed; our prodigy had never seen the island before he had landed with us. There was another thing: Whitey had told us that he had been a reporter. Journalism was something I knew about—in college I had been a stringer for the Springfield *Republican*—and when I started a camp newspaper, I invited him to contribute to it. He tried; he really tried. For days he struggled with a pencil, but when the result came in, it was functionally illiterate, almost incomprehensible. If he had ever been a reporter, the paper hadn't been published in the English language.

Of course, it might have been a *Japanese* newspaper. Whitey's claim to be a linguist was the last of his status symbols, and he clung to it desperately. Looking back, I think his improvisations on the *Morton* fantail must have been one of the most heroic achievements in the history of confidence men—which, as you may have gathered by now, was Whitey's true profession. Toward the end of our tour of duty on the 'Canal he was totally discredited with us and transferred at his own request to the eighty-one-millimeter platoon, where our disregard for him was no stigma, since the eighty-one-millimeter musclemen regarded us as a bunch of eight balls anyway. Yet even then, even after we had become completely disillusioned with him, he remained a figure of wonder among us. We could scarcely believe that an impostor could be clever enough actually to *invent* a language—phonics, calligraphy, and all. It had looked like Japanese and sounded like Japanese, and during his seventeen days of lecturing on that ship Whitey had carried it all in his head, remembering every variation, every subtlety, every syntactic construction.

Whitey stayed out of jail, and in the 29th, because the one man who never lost confidence in him was Colonel Hastings. The colonel continued to believe, not because he was stupid, but because Whitey staged his greatest show—literally a command performance—for the regimental C.O. I was there, yet to this day I don't fully understand how he pulled it off. What happened was that the First Marine Division, while securing Peleliu in October of 1944, had bagged five Japanese prisoners. That sort of thing happened from time to time in the Pacific war, usually under freakish circumstances. A Jap was dazed by a shell or otherwise rendered unable to kill himself. Seized by our troops, he was physically restrained from making amends to the emperor. Five months after their capture these failed suicides were ferried to the 'Canal from the First's base on the Russell Islands. Clad in loincloths and penned behind maximum-security concertinas of barbed wire, they passively awaited the pleasure of their conquerors. But nobody with jurisdiction knew quite how to dispose of them. Then word of their presence reached the C.O. of the 29th. Hastings knew exactly what to do; he announced to their wardens that he would interrogate them through his very own interpreter, Private Harold Dumas. Whitey greeted the news with a ten-thousand-yard stare and utter silence. There was, it seemed, nothing he could say.

The POW stockade was at Koli Point, and one morning at 0800 we set out for it in a convoy, with Colonel Hastings and his private translator leading in a jeep and the rest of us trailing in a green crocodile of DUKW's, six-by trucks, and various other military vehicles. This was a big day for the colonel; he wanted every officer and staff N.C.O. to remember it. Since Whitey was riding with him, I didn't see the interpreter during the trip, and I have no way of knowing how he behaved, though I'm sure he retained his poise. Anybody who had the guts to snow his way through those classes on the *Morton* would be equal to almost any crisis; it was not crises, but day-by-day, round-the-clock testing that had led to our disenchantment with him. When I arrived at Koli, Hastings' jeep was already parked beside the huge barbed-wire coils. The colonel was outside, glaring in wrathfully. The prisoners were squatting miserably on their haunches, and Whitey, dressed in marine dungarees and a raider cap, was squatting alongside them.

Apparently an exchange of some sort was going on. Obviously the colonel thought so; his eyes darted alertly from Whitey to the Nips, and his right ear was cocked, trying to pick up a thread of sense by using the vocabulary he had learned on the voyage from San Diego. It was, of course, impossible. Whitey was adlibbing with his brilliant double-talk, which, however Oriental it sounded to us, was utterly devoid of real meaning. What the Nips were saying is a matter of conjecture, since no one there was equipped to understand them. My own belief is that they were replying to Whitey, "We only speak Japanese." All that can be said with any certainty is that the POW's and their interrogator had reached an impasse. After a long lull in the non-conversation Whitey came out with a hangdog look.

"What's happening?" the colonel asked anxiously.

"Sir, I goofed," Whitey said wretchedly.

"What? Why? How?"

With a swooping gesture Whitey swung out his right forefinger and pointed to the Marine Corps emblem printed on the left breast of his dungaree jacket. "I should never have worn this," he said in his guileless voice. "You see, sir," he explained, looking directly at Hastings, "they know what the globe-and-fouled-anchor means. They know what the Marine Corps is. They realize that the Corps is destroying their emperor and their homeland, and they just won't answer my questions."

For a long moment the colonel stared back at Whitey. Then he squared his shoulders, and his pouter-pigeon chest swelled. "Goddam right," he grated, his voice like a coarse file. He peered contemptuously into the pen and said, "Those sons of bitches are a bunch of bastards."

With that he strutted back to his jeep and soon, it developed, out of our lives—Whitey's, mine, and the 29th's. That week the battalion boarded the APA (attack transport) *George C. Clymer* for Okinawa, where the colonel left us after the first few days of battle. He was relieved of his command on Motobu peninsula after the divisional commander asked him the whereabouts of his first and third battalions and received no satisfactory reply. I happened to be there when the question was raised, and I can still see the look of utter bewilderment on Hastings' face. He had always been vague about the rest of his regiment; his heart had belonged to our second battalion; he had allowed his lieutenant colonels to run the others, and in the excitement of combat he had neglected to update his situation map. "Inexcusable!" said the general, clearly outraged. "I'm sorry. I regret it," the colonel croaked brokenly. Later I heard that he had been shunted back to the corps staff, where he was awarded the Bronze Star "for excellence in keeping records during combat."

Whitey had vanished at about the same time during a sick call. Quite apart from gunshot wounds, there was a pattern of bizarre casualties in the island battles of World War II. Some poor bastard wading toward the beach would stumble off a reef, and with eighty pounds of hardware on his back he would sink like a stone. A BAR man in Easy Company disappeared that way in the early hours of Love Day, as Okinawa's D-Day was quaintly called. Other people went rock happy— "combat fatigue," it was called. The sergeant major did; he was carried off cackling nonsense even less intelligible than that of Private Dumas. Then there was always some sad clown who, the first night on the beach, would forget that he had to stay in his hole until dawn, or "morning twilight," because the Japs were ingenious at night infiltrations. We scratched one Fox Company 60-millimeter mortarman at 2 A.M. that April 2; he was up relieving himself over a slit trench when a sentry drilled him. ("A good shot in the bull's eye," said our callous colonel the following morning, just before he was deprived of his command.) Finally, there were the back cases. Whitey became one of them.

Every salt knew that you could get surveyed if you complained long enough about chronic back pains. Back on the 'Canal I lost a Philadelphian who had enlisted at the age of twenty-eight—we called him "Pop"—and who, fed up with jungle training, used that excuse to get stateside. Whitey followed his ignoble example. To the disgust of the Gung-ho 81-millimeter mortarmen, he kept insisting that his spine was killing him, and finally the skeptical medical corpsman sighed and took him away for a check.

It was months before I learned what happened to him after that, because once the battle began in earnest, my people became extremely active. Okinawa turned out to be the bloodiest engagement of the Pacific war, eclipsing even Iwo. After it was all over, a presidential citation commended the division "for extraordinary heroism in action against enemy Japanese forces" and for "gallantry in overcoming a fanatic enemy in the face of extraordinary danger," but all I remember is mud and terror. Years later I learned from reading Samuel Eliot Morison that the 29th had sustained the heaviest casualties of any regiment in the history of the Marine Corps—2,821 out of some 3,300 riflemen. My section was cut to pieces. Once the slaughter began, we were used as runners, carrying messages between battalion staff officers, company commanders, and even platoon leaders whose walkie-talkies had conked out. It was exceptionally perilous work. We were rarely in defilade, usually exposed, and often had to spend long periods lined up in some Jap sniper's sights. I myself was hit twice. The first time was May 17 on the northern slope of Sugar Loaf Hill. It was only a flesh wound, and I jumped hospital to rejoin the battalion, but on June 5 I was decked again. That one was almost for keeps, a massive back wound from fourteen-inch rocket-mortar shrapnel. For five months I was on and off operating tables on a hospital ship, on Saipan, in Alewa Heights Naval Hospital overlooking Honolulu, in San Francisco, and finally at San Diego's naval hospital in Balboa Park.

A letter from Jasper—who survived the war to marry a Nisei—reached me in Balboa that October, filling me in on Whitey's last adventure in the 29th. I was wearing a buck sergeant's stripes by then, or rather they were sewn to the sleeves of my greens, for I was still bedridden. I have a hazy memory of church bells tolling the previous August, and my asking a chief petty officer what it meant, and his answering, "The war's over," and my saying "Oh," just "Oh." Within a few months the 29th's people began heading home. Whitey, however, was not among them. His complaint about his back hadn't deceived the mortarmen, but then, they, like us, had known him. The physicians at the regimental aid station, on an LST offshore, had been seduced by his earnest charm, though the ultimate result was not quite what he had had in mind. The docs sent him back to a Corps clearing hospital. All badges of rank having been removed before we hit the beach—Nip sharpshooters liked to pick off officers and N.C.O.'s—the hospital's medical corpsmen had no way of knowing the military status of casualties, so they usually asked them. They asked Whitey, and he repeated his boot-camp lie. He said he was a first lieutenant, reasoning that life would be more comfortable, and the chow more edible, on an officer's ward.

He was right, but there were special hazards for him there. A captain in the next bunk asked him what his job in the Marine Corps was. "Japanese-language interpreter," said Whitey. They shot the breeze for a while, and then the captain asked Whitey for a lesson. Ever obliging, our man rattled off a few phrases and jotted down some of his Oriental hieroglyphics on a slip of paper. "Very interesting," the real officer said slowly. Then he yelled: "Corpsman! Put this man under arrest!" It developed that the captain was one of the first graduates of the Japanese-language schools that had been set up after Pearl Harbor. They were arriving in the Pacific too late to do much toward winning the war, but this one had turned up at exactly the right time to nail Whitey. Our confidence man had tried to dupe one mark too many. He was shipped straight back to Portsmouth.

I never saw him again, but I heard from him once. Five years after the war, when my first stories were appearing in national magazines, I received a letter postmarked Hollywood and written in a familiar scrawl. It was on MGM stationery. God knows where he had picked it up, but he certainly hadn't acquired it legally. Letters from studio executives—for that is what it claimed to be—are typed. They are also spelled correctly and properly phrased. This one was neither. I have never seen a clearer illustration of Whitey's own aphorism that we have two languages, one we speak and one we write. He was entirely verbal; when he lectured, it was with easy assurance and an impressive vocabulary. On his pilfered MGM stationery he was another person. Gone were his casual references to conjugations, modifiers, inflections, and the imperative mood. Not since his stab at journalism on the 'Canal had he been so incoherent.

His missive ran:

Dear Bill,
     Caught your artical in this months Harpers. Real good. Always knew you had it in you.
     Look—could you give yours truely a break? Am now doing PR for Sam Goldwyn & Co and am trying to promote to stardom a real cute chick name of Boobs Slotkin. (Boobs—ha! ha! I gave her the name & when you glim her knockers youll see why.) Give me the word and I'll shoot you some pix. Some for the public and some for your private eye if you get my meaning—ha! ha!
     Sure miss the old gang on the Canal and all the good times we had. I don't hear from any of them, do you?
     Let me know about Boobs. This is a real good deal and I can put you next to her roommate whose no dog either next time your

in this neck of the woods. Brunette 37–24–30 and hot pants. A real athalete in the sack. You won't regret it believe me.

> Your old asshole buddy,
> HAROLD V. DUMAS
> Chief of Public Relations
> Metro-Goldwyn-Mayer Studios

P.S.   Dont write to me at the office as this is kind of personal. Just sent it to me care of General Delivery L.A. and it will get to me Okay.

I never replied, but I found the note strangely moving. Whitey had climbed the Parnassus of his calling, and evidently he had now slid back down all the way. He was pathetic on paper, and his assessment of the kind of material that interested *Harper's* was unbelievable. (How on earth had he even *seen* the magazine?) He had entered the shadows; for all I know, he never emerged again. It is of course quite possible that he staged a stunning caper under another name—as G. Gordon Liddy, say—yet somehow I doubt it. His big sting with us had a one-shot air about it, like the flight of an exotic bird that dazzles for a single season and is never seen again. But on the *Morton's* fantail, and outside that POW stockade at Koli Point, he had been magnificent. And to this day I feel a tingling at the base of my scalp when I think of that towheaded prisoner in his Portsmouth cell dreaming up what must have been the most imaginative con of the war, saying in that straightforward voice, "Guard, I want to speak to the C.O.," and then, "Sir, I know I deserve to be here, but my country is threatened and I want to do my share. I can really help in an unusual way, sir. You see, I speak Japanese."

Ways and Means

"WHY DO YOU ROB BANKS?" *the cops asked Willie Sutton, who replied with engaging candor, "Because that's where the money is." Where the money is often is where the power is, which is the reason for my professional interest in it. There is a driving theme in every writer's work. An author may be convinced that the central fact about man is his essential loneliness, say, or his penchant for violence, or the eternal tournament between the sexes. I see people preoccupied with the search for dominance—in politics, in war, in society, in the family—and in the struggle for money.*

I have known rich families: the Rockefellers, the Kennedys, the Krupps. Scott Fitzgerald was right; they are not like you and me. They have more clout, command greater attention, and have a far greater range of choices open to them, in everything from wardrobes to careers. They are not happier, but they have a clearer concept of the sources of happiness and unhappiness. Unlike the rest of us, they cannot blame whatever disarray there is in their personal lives on a lack of ways and means.

I have never been one of them. I am a member of the Depression generation. Those of us who reached the age of awareness between the Crash and Pearl Harbor bear what Caroline Bird has called the invisible scar. No matter how fat our bank accounts become, we buy day-old bread, have our shoes half-soled over and over, and show up at fire sales. I have no credit rating because I have never bought anything, not even an automobile, on the installment plan. I simply cannot live with debt. That does not mean that I feel powerless. Language can be a source of influence. Words have brought me a kind of potency currency cannot buy. But for most people the path to puissance runs through the teller's window. Forcing an entry, we may, if only vicariously, see where it leads. What follows is such a heist.

The Treasury Department

SOMEWHERE BENEATH THE VAST, COLONNADED PILE of Washington's off-white Treasury Building there is a cornerstone. It is a historic curio, for it was laid by Andrew Jackson, the sworn enemy of all banks, and it contains a snippet of blond hair from Jackson's secretary's baby daughter, who grew up to work for the Treasury. Unfortunately, no one can find the cornerstone. It was lost during the physical expansion of the building. The structure moved around it and over it, and all we know for sure is that it must still be down in the granite masonry—entombed, inaccessible, but nevertheless there, holding up the whole works.

In a sense the Treasury itself rests on a single plinth. Each of its "products and services," as former Secretary Robert B. Anderson called them, has a common denominator. During the Mopsy growth of nearly two centuries, the Department has acquired an extraordinary variety of functions. It has its own navy and its own diplomatic corps; it runs the most elaborate system of private eyes in the world. Its various branches employ chemists, accountants, marksmen, artists and scholars, only a fraction of whom are housed in the main Treasury Building. Yet all are bound by one tie. That tie, like the lock of hair in the lost cornerstone, is golden. It is, in fact, gold itself. It is money.

Money is the root of every Treasury bureau. Internal Revenue collects income taxes. Customs collects tariffs. The Bureau of Accounts keeps the books for the Federal Government. The Bureau of Engraving and Printing manufactures paper money on high-speed rotary presses, and the Mint strikes coins and guards the nation's bullion depositories at West Point and Fort Knox. The Treasurer of the United States, who is often confused with the Secretary of the Treasury, authorizes four hundred million checks a year. (Every day he—or, more recently, she—gets back a hundred forged endorsements.) Department economists puzzle over tax schemes, international finance and the national debt; and in the tipsy Martin-and-Coy hills of the South, airborne revenue agents hunt out the camouflaged bases of moonshiners trying to dodge the Federal liquor duty.

Actually, it may be argued, money is at the bottom of everything in the government. And indeed, at one time or another, the Treasury Department has been home to the postal service and the departments of Commerce, Labor, the Interior and the Public Health Service. One by one these were lopped off. Today most of the remaining Treasury branches have a clear relationship to mammon. One exception is the Treasury's navy, the Coast Guard. Coast Guardsmen blow up derelict ships, spot icebergs, screen seamen and investigate the weather. They haven't much to do with cash, though the service was originally established by Alexander Hamilton to foil smugglers. Similarly, the Secret Service, a Treasury branch, is best known for providing the President's bodyguards. Nabbing counterfeiters was its original assignment, however, and remains one of its greatest problems. The Service began guarding the White House after the assassination of McKinley, because Secret Servicemen were then the only house dicks on the Government payroll; J. Edgar Hoover had just been born.

T-men do not enjoy being mistaken for G-men; they have been around longer. Since the Revolution the Treasury has been responsible for the country's financial integrity. Most crime is inspired by greed, and this has always been a greedy country. It was settled by counterfeiters—colonists fleeced Indians with wampum—and it was freed by such notorious smugglers as John Hancock and Samuel Adams. Following independence, Secretary Hamilton pointed out that such goings on hurt the national credit and were therefore unpatriotic. Future scofflaws would be the prey of the Department. Other enforcement jobs arose when Congress, discovering that the power to tax is the power to destroy, created some taxes whose sole purpose was destruction. An important one was a ten percent levy on state bank notes, which paved the way for a national currency. Today gamblers, manufacturers of white phosphorous matches and owners of silencers and sawed-off shotguns must pay a special tax or risk jail. Drugs, too, are controlled by revenue stamps, which explains why the Bureau of Narcotics is under the Treasury Department instead of the Department of Justice.

Altogether the Treasury has seven different police forces. Coordination is a major job, and it hasn't always worked. In the early 1930's Secretary Ogden L. Mills called his enforcement agencies "a damned hodgepodge." Mills was mad because employees of two different agencies, stalking bootleggers in North Carolina, had opened fire on each other. Assured that no one was hurt, he added acidly that they weren't even good marksmen.

As superintendent of the nation's finances, the present Secretary ranks second to the Secretary of State in protocol, pays himself $60,000 a year and wears about twenty hats. Some are tall and silken: chief fiscal adviser to the White House, chief worrier about the debt, United States Governor of the International Monetary Fund. Other hats are scarcely more than caps: trustee of the Smithsonian Institution, honorary treasurer of the Red Cross. Theoretically he is responsible for each of the Department's 80,000-odd civilian employees—since McKinley, Congress has held the Secretary personally accountable for the safety of the President—but in practice he doesn't spend much time measuring shotgun barrels or tracking down alky stills. Such aides as the Commissioners of Narcotics and Internal Revenue are left to wreak vengeance on drug addicts and taxpayers. The Secretary concentrates instead on matters of policy from a third-floor suite which might have been conceived by the late John Marquand. Two hall signs request QUIET PLEASE. Inside is a black marble fireplace which works, a splendid view of the White House, and oil paintings of four former Secretaries.

Oil paintings hang all over the building—contributing to the Treasury's Boston-bank air. Old retainers don't shuffle around in alpaca coats and celluloid cuffs, but one feels that they should; even pinstripes and broad lapels seem impertinent here. High ceilings wear a patina of dust, wooden floors are softly rugged, corridors are lined with money-colored pilasters; office doors are slatted, like first-class staterooms on P&O steamers.

Treasury veterans savor this musty charm and recoil from change. There was an uneasy stir in 1956, when the General Services Administration decided to letter the Department's name on the building. (It didn't have a name. Since 1789 it had been called both The Treasury Department and the Department of the Treasury. Secretary George M. Humphrey, always a partisan of thrift, settled for the more economical The Treasury Department.) Some stand-patters went so far as to defend the starlings which, until recently, made walking beneath the cornices an adventure. Electrical wires now discourage the starlings, but not much has been done about the building's creaky elevators, one of which dates from 1898. Once, after an important press conference, an elevator stalled between floors, and the Secretary was rudely disturbed by screams from the caged reporters. Decorum pays dividends in the

Treasury. The sedate Dow-Jones man, who had used the stairs, beat the Associated Press by thirty minutes that day.

Under the building are huge old vaults. One of them is used by Secret Servicemen for target practice, another is linked to the White House next door by an underground passage. During World War II the Treasury basement was President Roosevelt's air-raid shelter. The Secret Service won't say whether it serves that need for President Ford, though certainly it's no longer used to store opium and precious metals. That was the original purpose of the vaults, back in the Treasury's childhood, when finance was simple, and the Secretary personally designed all Department forms, and gold was something a man could put in his pocket, not a four-letter word to affront him. Hamilton is remembered as an administrative genius, but it was a lot easier to keep the store then. The principal internal tax was on distilled spirits. Thomas Jefferson rejected even that, thus converting mountaineers to the Democratic party, and the government was entirely supported by Customs revenues.

The Customs Bureau, in fact, is older than the Department itself. It was one of the first agencies to be created under the Constitution, and as late as 1910 it brought in fifty percent of Federal income. Today it accounts for about one percent. That's still over three billion dollars, however, and because Customs men are strategically placed at ports of entry they enforce the regulations of a score of government agencies. The State Department frowns on gunrunning, but Customs men do the actual searching of baggage. They check seeds for the Department of Agriculture and parrots for Health, Education and Welfare, and at the behest of the Atomic Energy Commission they stop the transport of fissionable materials out of, or atomic bombs into, the country. Presumably they use Geiger counters, although, of course, they don't talk about it.

Last year Customs greeted over 200,000,000 people and pawed over fourteen billion dollars' worth of imports, making sure each item was correctly labeled: "Made in Japan," "Made in Ceylon," "Made in Monaco." Customs' biggest job is to administer the Tariff Act, which lists 5000 categories of dutiable goods. It takes about five years to become an expert Customs examiner. Nine laboratories help him determine classifications; they also test the purity of ores and detect hidden materials of value which may raise the duty.

The bureau is increasingly sensitive to the need for courtesy and efficiency. But even with tact, Customs is a touchy service to administer. Now and then a Customs ruling seems whimsical to importers.

Some appeal to Customs courts. Some merely gripe, as did the European lingerie manufacturer who muttered that he wouldn't be surprised to find one American appraiser classifying his bras as "meat-packing devices while another insisted on calling them jewel cases."

The smuggler, Customs' ancient antagonist, is still around. Packages can be X-rayed, but human beings are an eternal problem. Frisking every overseas arrival is impossible. It would take 50,000 inspectors to do an adequate job. Old hands have developed an uncanny knack for spotting the off-beat shipment, though: during a recent five-month period they seized a quarter of a million dollars' of contraband at John F. Kennedy International Airport in New York, which handles about forty percent of the country's imports. They are familiar with all the hoary smugglers' tricks: the false-bottomed suitcase; the bellyband under the shirt; the hollow statues and hollowed-out shoe heels, books, crutches, canes, pens, shaving-brush handles, billiard cues and golf clubs. Heroin has been found in dolls and fake hunchback humps; gems have been detected in glass eyes, in toothpaste tubes, in false teeth, in medicine-bottle cotton, in chewing gun. Swiss watch movements have been pried one by one from cargoes of gears, and with the increasing popularity among women smugglers of what are officially called the "body cavities," inspectresses have been detailed to all major ports.

Diamonds are a special problem. They are so tiny and so tempting to an amateur. An airline pilot can carry $233,000 worth in his pocket—it happened not long ago—and people who wouldn't touch narcotics see nothing wrong in sneaking a fortune in ice through a Customs shed. It looks easier than it is. The inspector has allies abroad, a network of agents reporting to the Treasury attachés in American embassies. Moreover, Customs gives informers a cut of twenty-five percent of the value of seized goods, up to $50,000. The name of the American woman who buys a glittering bracelet in Rome will be quietly registered at the American Embassy by the clerk who waited on her. It will be sent home through channels, and if she doesn't declare the bracelet when she returns, she gets the works and the Roman clerk can quit clerking.

So attractive are these moieties that the professional informer has become the bane of the professional smuggler. Naturally espionage breeds counterespionage. The bureau has never been able to pay a certain major claimant. He told his tale, it was confirmed and then, for reasons which may be ventured, he vanished.

Another big winner later went to jail. He had neglected to report his bounty on his Form 1040, and somebody had a hunch. Customs isn't the only Treasury branch that offers rewards. Internal Revenue pays up to ten percent on taxes recovered through tips. The system works admirably, though here money seems to be a secondary motive, second to envy. If a man suddenly turns into a big spender, his whole neighborhood turns green. Speculation naturally focuses on the income tax. Everyone hates to file his return. The thought that someone is welshing is unbearable, and much of the billion and a half dollars picked up each year from flouters of the tax laws may be traced to healthy suspicions.

Unhappily for the bureau, some unhealthy suspicions are directed toward its own employees. Embittered taxpayers haven't forgotten the Internal Revenue scandals of the late 1940s, when a former commissioner went to prison. Since then the bureau has been largely removed from politics. Tax returns of most Internal Revenue employees are audited periodically and until 1960 each employee was required to attach a special slip to his form, marking him for special treatment, like Jean Valjean. But distrust dies hard, and Nixon's "enemies list" rekindled it. Switchboard operators at the bureau, a few blocks up Pennsylvania Avenue from the Treasury Building, blush at the language of anonymous callers. Obscene notes arrive by mail, visitors wear dark looks. A curious result of this is that Internal Revenue is a merry place. Bureau employees seem to have taken to boisterous good humor as a protective coloration. They delight in stories about odd taxpayers— the man who inquired how he could deduct the blood he had given to a blood bank, the man who tried to pay his tax with a credit card, and the woman, in Fresno, California, who paid twenty dollars in quarters "because it said I had to pay quarterly." Let a girl appear and report that she needs a new form and Internal Revenue's day is made, and you have to stop them if you've heard the one about the address of the bureau's district director in Little Rock, Arkansas—(Capitol and Gaines streets).

Despite abuse from cranks, bureau men think highly of the average American. He is, they believe, the most scrupulous citizen in the world. It's a good thing. Although the bureau is the Department's largest—five of every eight Treasury men work there—it would be helpless without public cooperation. Only one individual tax return in twenty can be audited. If most Americans weren't honest, Washington's bills couldn't be paid. The pattern of taxation has changed mightily since 1789. The reason isn't, as some suppose, creeping socialism. There is wry irony in the location of General Sherman's bile-green equestrian statue opposite the Treasury Building. War has been hell on the taxpayer. First came luxury taxes, after the War of 1812, then an income tax, during the Civil War. That income tax expired, was revived, was declared unconstitutional and was later sanctioned in the Sixteenth Amendment. By then we had a corporation tax and World War I gave us new excise taxes. Extracting all these is the job of Internal Revenue, which harvests over ninety percent of the Federal income, about half from income-tax returns.

Internal Revenue agents are called "Mr. Whiskers." The typical Mr. Whiskers is discreet—it's a criminal offense to reveal anything from a return, even information about illegal income, without authorization —and exacts about $1,000 additional tax in his average audit. His regard for the rectitude of the American yeomanry doesn't hamper a continuing search for the unscrupulous. He likes to pore over newspapers, and his eyes shine whenever he reads of a sweepstakes winner or a home which has been looted of cash. Ritzy suburbs fascinate him; he is forever checking returns against addresses. Much of his time is spent sorting out the blizzard of W-2 forms from employers, because he is familiar with that vexing audacity known as the mass-refund racket. Mass-refund gyps file batches of fake returns, claiming overpayment of tax. Two such gangs were unearthed in San Quentin and New Mexico State Penitentiary, a discovery that gave Treasury colleagues in the Secret Service a hearty laugh until, to their own mortification, they traced a counterfeit ring to a state-prison printshop in Alabama.

Income-tax evasion has caged several celebrated American scoundrels, among them Mickey Cohen, Frank Costello, and Al Capone, whose armored car, confiscated by the Treasury, was used by the Secret Service to protect President Roosevelt during World War II. ("I hope Mr. Capone doesn't mind," Roosevelt murmured when told.) Auditors are often inadequate for these big evasion cases. Internal Revenue, like most Treasury bureaus, uses undercover men. Perhaps the most successful infiltrator was the mild-mannered agent who put Capone away; he lived his entire adult life under the name of Pat O'Rourke; his true name, Mike Malone, wasn't revealed until his death in 1960.

More than half of the Secret Service works in real secrecy. Treasury men pose as bravos, smugglers and wholesalers of counterfeit currency. Narcotics agents haggle over the price of cocaine with raffish characters with names like Gee Gim Tick and Wong Gum Hoy, and Alcohol and Tobacco Tax Division men pursue "smoker cars"—doctored automobiles, favored by modern bootleggers, which cover escapes by releasing dense clouds of oily black smoke. The naïve may think of this as amusing melodrama. In reality it is dangerous; since Repeal

moonshiners have killed more than one agent a year. It is also important. Without it the Treasury couldn't hope to ring up about 293 billion dollars annually on the national cash register.

The Treasury gives as well as receives. To know how much it may
give, it cannot wait until every taxpayer's contribution has been
tabulated. It must have some idea of where it stands from moment to
moment. Monthly revenue estimates are prepared by the Office of Tax
Analysis, which takes a keen interest in the nation's economic health,
since recession means shrinking incomes and shrinking income taxes.
Simultaneously, at the wide end of the cornucopia, the Fiscal Assistant
Secretary daily makes an educated guess as to how much the government is collecting and spending. The difference means surplus or
deficit, and is greeted by cheers or groans from the rest of the government.

The Treasury collects vast amounts of money. Customs, Internal
Revenue and employers deposit it in 11,000 private banks, and twice a
week the Fiscal Assistant Secretary calculates how much is on hand.
Bankers can lend this money without paying interest to the government, since they perform many services for the Treasury, such as
selling Savings Bonds. Since abrupt withdrawals would bruise the
economy, the Treasury calls for these funds on a percentage basis,
depending on the size of the bank. When a "call" is made, funds are
deposited in one of the twelve Federal Reserve Banks, where the Treasury keeps a deposit balance of between $450,000,000 and $550,000,000.
It is credited to the account of the Treasurer of the United States, and
checks can then be drawn upon the funds by any of the government's
2000 disbursing officers. Squaring accounts among Federal Reserve
banks is a mysterious affair involving gold certificates, the highest of
which is a $100,000 bill bearing Woodrow Wilson's portrait, and
which are not allowed in general circulation.

The Federal Reserve System, known to friends as the Fed or the
Fed'l, is not a part of the Treasury. Neither is another major fiscal
agency, the Bureau of the Budget, which is part of the President's
official household. Officially the Treasury doesn't see the budget until it
has been approved by the President. Even so, the Department has a lot
to do with preparing it, especially at the flag-officer level. (The Secretary, the two Under Secretaries and the five Assistant Secretaries are
entitled to personal flags bearing the Treasury seal, crossed anchors and
thirteen stars. The color varies with the rank. In Washington, having
your own flag is like having a key to the executive washroom.) Negotiations with the Federal Reserve tend to be more delicate. The Fed is to

the Treasury what the Bank of England is to the Exchequer: the nation's great central bank. As the watchdog of credit, it influences interest rates. Since the Department must borrow continuously to keep up with the national debt, it has a big stake in these decisions, and flag-officer approaches to the Fed are diplomatic, like those to, say, West Germany.

Debt experts have their own bureau, because theirs is the Department's greatest single chore. In Jackson's day the government owed virtually no one. Once more the change must be chalked up to wars; each victory has left the Treasury holding a bigger bag. The Treasury's arrears are massive, but only because the government is massive. Private indebtedness has been growing far more rapidly. Since 1945 corporate debt has more than tripled and consumer debt has increased over ten times, while Federal obligations have increased by almost twenty percent. The national debt needn't terrify us, though managing it does take some doing.

Treasury securities are divided into two groups: marketable and nonmarketable. The largest group of nonmarketable securities are Savings Bonds—formerly called Defense Bonds and War Bonds—and while all of these—over $50,000,000—could be cashed in at once, it's not likely. The real problem lies in marketable debt.

During World War II the Fed pegged the market for government securities, buying Treasury bonds at low Depression rates. Late in the Truman administration there was a row. Cheap money was causing inflation, so the Fed decided to quit bailing out the Treasury. The government was forced to pay higher interest rates, and the cost of servicing the debt rose. Since the early 1960's the Treasury and the Fed have been working together on a new tack: high rates for short-term loans, to discourage the flow of hot money from the United States, and low rates for long-term loans. Negotiations between the giants are conducted in the ionosphere of economics. The smallest detail becomes incredibly technical.

Fiscal sophistication is the most awesome aspect of the Department. Primitive tribes barter or swap precious metals, but in the Treasury Building, the home of the big money, there are only ledgers and digits. Government securities worth billions are bought and sold in the bond market. The bigger the man, the more intangible is the wealth with which he deals. Former Treasury Secretary C. Douglas Dillon was born rich; in private life he was an investment banker. Yet he confessed that the first time he looked closely at a dollar bill was when his own signature, as Secretary of the Treasury, began to appear on currency.

And a dollar, when you come right down to it, is only a symbol. Any bill—even a $100,000 note—has an intrinsic worth of less than a cent, its manufacturing cost. Money is faith, scraps of paper.

The scraps serve their purpose, though they cause certain practical problems. Paper can be lost, mislaid or damaged. It happens all the time, and the Treasury is sympathetic. There are some two and a half billion Savings Bonds records. A fifth of them represent outstanding securities. More than a million substitute bonds have been issued by the Bureau of Public Debt. If a widow believes her husband held some bonds, a letter will bring confirmation or denial. Similarly, the Treasurer of the United States handles a thousand lost-check claims a day. Even mutilated currency can be replaced, provided it is recognizable. Specialists in the office of the Treasurer of the United States, puzzling over charred fragments of currency, can spot redeemable paper where an untrained eye would see only ash. The rule is, face value for three-fifths of a note, half that for two-to-three-fifths. Many a man has cooled the embers of a blackened cash box and wound up with a roll of bills. One found a fortune moldering in his father's grave. A refugee from Nazis hid $33,000 in greenbacks in a tree in Germany. It was soggy pulp after the war, but the Treasury paid off.

The Department's valuable publications are turned out in the Bureau of Engraving and Printing. The bureau does all sorts of job printing for the government—bonds, checks, officers' commissions, citations, White House invitations, liquor stamps and 23,000,000,000 United States postage stamps a year, to which it affixes a million pounds of stickum. Most of the presswork, of course, is paper money. The bureau makes $30,000,000 a day. Not many people have seen its ornate gold certificates, since you have to be a Federal Reserve Bank to spend one, but everyone knows its popular line of green goods. They come in three distinctive, eye-catching, easy-to-use models: silver certificates, United States notes and Federal Reserve notes. They are distinguished, respectively, by their blue, red and green seals and serial numbers. Some bills with yellow seals and serial numbers are still in circulation; every now and then one drifts back to the Treasury. They were designed for the invasion of North Africa in 1942. If the Germans had captured our paymasters, the special notes would have been declared illegal tender.

Experience has taught the Treasury to be suspicious, and this prudence is most conspicuous in the bureau's pressrooms. Visitors are blinded by the sight of so much cash. Greenbacks stand imperiously in million-dollar stacks, and though nothing larger than a $100 bill has been printed since 1945, there are plenty of serviceable old $1000,

$5000 and $10,000 notes around. Tidy girls patrol the halls carrying natty purses which, upon being opened, are discovered to contain .38 caliber pistols. Despite these precautions there are slip-ups now and then. A few years ago a $58-a-week bureau handyman outwitted security and made off with two wrapped "bricks" of twenties worth $160,000. He was collared quickly. "It's stupid to steal new money. The serial numbers can be traced so quickly. But I won't say it couldn't happen again," an official said recently, resting his elbow on a bale of 232,000 silver certificates.

Each year 600,000 tourists parade through the shop. In the spring the tide becomes a flood—9000 visitors a day, mostly schoolchildren, all of whom are escorted in groups of twenty-five by guides. Employees report that nine out of ten children ask slyly where they can get samples. The joke has become an occupational bore. To the bureau, making money is just a job, like making doorknobs. It does have its trade secrets, however, and some of them are top secret. One is the formula for that chrome-green dye, of which 4,000,000 pounds are manufactured annually. Another is the identity of the animals whose hides are used to size the paper. The threaded paper itself is such a sensitive topic that you can be jailed for making any paper—even blank paper—with red and blue cotton fibers in it. The Treasury's supply comes from a heavily guarded mill in Massachusetts. Each sheet is impregnated with resin and can take over two thousand double foldings in the same crease without tearing. Eventually money does become soiled and worn, of course. Filthy lucre is destroyed—Federal Reserve notes are cut in half, shipped to Washington on separate days and burned—and crisp new tender, after undergoing twelve countings, is issued through the Fed's banks. At any moment about thirty billion dollars is in circulation, five billion of it ready for the incinerator.

If men like former Secretary Dillon don't ogle greenbacks, plenty of others do. The Treasury maintains a steady correspondence with people who are fascinated by folding money. Certain questions recur. Isn't the flag on the back of the ten-dollar bill upside down? (No.) What's happened to the White House on the back of the twenty? (The Truman balcony has been added.) Is the automobile on the ten a Ford? (It's a composite.) The superstitious think they see the figures "172" in the Lincoln Memorial shrubbery on the five, and, in the scrollwork, the Pope.

A more sensible criticism of our currency came from the late W. A. Dwiggins, the type designer, who complained that the intricate vignettes, tracery and ornamentation in the engravings were bad art.

Bureau engravers weren't offended. They don't try for art. The purpose of their fancy doodles is to thwart counterfeiters, and they passed their greatest test in World War II, when Germany decided to ruin Allied economies by flooding them with bad bills. The Nazis raised hob in England—pound notes had to be completely redesigned—but they quit trying to duplicate American money. "It was too good for us," Hermann Göring said.

Carpers never mention the vulnerable Treasury seal, which is reproduced on the face of every bill. The Latin legend is an abbreviation of *Thesauri Americae Septentrionalis Sigillum,* "The Seal of the Treasury of North America"—an obvious error. The dots on the shield are the heraldic way of depicting gold, although United States currency hasn't been convertible for over forty years. Nevertheless, all Federal Reserve notes must be backed by twenty-five percent gold (the other seventy-five percent is commercial paper).

Watching the bullion in the granite sepulcher of Fort Knox, and the mints and assay offices of Denver, San Francisco, Philadelphia, and New York, is the responsibility of the Bureau of the Mint. As long as gold is taken seriously, the Mint lavishes care upon it. Each vault door bears a double seal; two men, each with a different dial combination, are necessary to open it. Every mote of gold dust is cherished. Tender instruments move ingots, to prevent abrasion; when the San Francisco mint was abandoned, the building was torn apart and $175,000 in gold sweepings was recovered.

Silver, which is no longer sold by the Treasury and which is being withdrawn as backing for part of our paper money, has its own mausoleum at West Point. Because silver circulates, some vanishes each year. Reno and Las Vegas tourists keep silver dollars as souvenirs, and even the normal wear and tear on a half dollar, quarter or dime may diminish its size by as much as six percent.

Coinage, like the printing of greenbacks, is a tidy, businesslike operation. Some tricks of the trade are ancient: rims of silver coins are receded to discourage trimming, a fraud that goes back to Roman days. Other practices are triumphs of automation, thus permitting the mints in Philadelphia and Denver to churn out twelve million coins a day with one fourth of the old work force. Most of the Mint's shimmering cascade goes to thirty-seven steady clients—the twelve banks of the Fed, their twenty-four branches and the Treasurer of the United States. The bureau also strikes military medals and a medallion for each President (copies of all thirty-four are available at $3.00 apiece), and since 1937 it has produced coins for over thirty foreign countries.

Minters watch the American economy carefully, for money itself is as responsive to the law of supply and demand as the things money buys. If times are hard, there is less coinage. In addition, the small-change market varies seasonally, reaching a peak just before Christmas. It is different in different places. The Mint keeps tabs on how many people are attending movies in Chicago, whether new vending machines are being installed in Texas, which towns on the West Coast are adopting sales taxes or installing parking meters, where cash-and-carry chains are expanding. A single nationwide boxtop-and-a-coin campaign may bring sixty million pennies into a Midwestern town. One month recently a cigarette tax rise required the dispatch of thirty Mint trucks to New Jersey, each truck carrying fifteen tons—$43,000—in pennies.

Despite its vigilance, the bureau is occasionally surprised by sudden demands for coins, and certain regional quirks have never been explained. New York accumulates half dollars. Boston spends them. Tellers in Baltimore never seem to have enough five-cent pieces. The explanation dawned on a high official of the Mint over one weekend. He was standing in front of a Maryland one-armed bandit at the time, and had just finished feeding it his fiftieth nickel.

The Mint has, at one time or another, made half-cent, two-cent, three-cent and twenty-cent pieces. In 1943, when copper was scarce, it produced a zinc-coated steel penny, and in recent years it has reduced the silver content of dimes, quarters, half-dollars, and cartwheels. Designs aren't altered often, though. Congress, to whom the Constitution gave the coining power, prohibits changes in a new coin for twenty-five years. Sometimes congressmen become interested in details; they were responsible for the Washington quarter. As a rule, however, the Mint does the designing. Once the Secretary has approved its decision, production is routine. Silver, alloy, bronze, and cupro-nickel bars are rolled flat. Blanking machines stamp out disks. Presses imprint letters and images, automatic scales reject defective pieces, machines tally the final result and the bright merchandise is poured into buckets and packaged in canvas bags.

After a decade or two the coins return, dull and defaced, in other bags. These beat-up pieces are counted and the sums charged to the Federal Reserve. Then the bags are held over fires. Flames eat away the canvas bottoms and the tired shekels tumble down to be melted and molded into fresh ingots. A cashier in the Philadelphia mint once decided to extract a profit from this final step. Wearing a coat with a hidden pocket in the tail, he would stand over counted bags of half dollars and scoop up a few each day. The fires couldn't inform on him, but

Mint men are paid in new money, and fellow employees, observing his old change, became suspicious. Arraigned and confronted with his hoard of battered fifty-cent pieces, he betrayed an imperfect understanding of numismatic theory. "I wouldn't steal from the Mint," he said. "That's Fed money."

The cashier wasn't stupid. After his hitch in the pen he went into legitimate business and cleaned up. It is one of the marvels of the annals of Treasury crime that sane men, intelligent men, even shrewd men talk themselves into elaborate con games and wind up by conning themselves. "One great error," said the first Secretary of the Treasury, "is that we suppose mankind more honest than they are." Another is to suppose that dishonest men are cleverer than we are. The present Treasury Building owes its existence to two brothers who became enmeshed in a scheme to defraud the Department. Reflecting that they might be caught, they decided to destroy the Treasury's records on March 31, 1833. Owing to an oversight they burned not only the incriminating papers but the entire structure as well. The blaze attracted the eye of Andy Jackson next door in the White House, and he started an investigation which brought them to the dock.

Most counterfeiters are bumblers, especially minters of false coin. In 1957 a design engineer examined a nickel and concluded that Mint work wasn't so hot. He felt sure he could do better. He struck some dies and posing as an owner of vending machines he deposited $5000 in phony five-cent pieces in a number of banks. Newspaper stories soon disclosed that the jig was up. He tossed his equipment in a river, but the Navy retrieved it, and off he went to jail. Such men baffle the Treasury. Clearly no one can get rich making bad pennies (though some have tried). Among the Treasury's most treasured souvenirs is a trove of counterfeit half dollars containing more silver than the real thing. Every time the manufacturer passed one, he went deeper into the red.

Counterfeit paper—alias "the queer," alias "the curly"—is a graver matter. Lately, indeed, it has become cause for some alarm. There is no chance that the Department will face anything like the crisis of 1863, when six thousand kinds of curly were being pushed and a third of all American money was bogus, but during the 1960s more than $60,000 in green poison was being extracted from the financial blood stream each month. The Secret Service thinks technological advances are a major reason for this. In the old days you had to be a master engraver to make a money plate, and the Service kept a file of all engravers who were bad hats. Improved photographic techniques have changed all that.

The new counterfeiter is the minor printshop employee or the hobbyist with a do-it-yourself press. One putterer was a publisher of school yearbooks whose hellbox yielded developed negatives and plates for American bills, Canadian currency and American Telephone and Telegraph Company stock certificates. His name was actually George Humphrey.

George Humphrey was a clumsy crook. His curly was crude. But then, most curly is. It's a rare counterfeit note that slips past bank tellers and reaches the Fed. Nearly all homemade currency could be spotted by laymen if laymen would take an interest in it. People know very little about their currency, and much of what they think they know is false; for example, the widespread belief that any note with red and blue fibers in it must be good. Of all the safeguards against counterfeiting, this one is the most easily evaded. Anyone with cigarette paper, two spools of thread and an egg beater can whip up a reasonable facsimile—crumple the rolled results in coffee and few can tell the difference—and a really cautious counterfeiter can always turn out a peroxide job, bleaching a dollar bill and reprinting it as a ten or a twenty. In inspecting a doubtful bill the best places to look are the points of the Treasury seal and the background of the portrait. It takes a real pro to get those points sharp, to keep that background from running together. But the public rarely gives greenbacks a second glance. Often it doesn't give them a first glance; a South Carolina filling-station attendant once accepted a five-dollar play-money note which his little daughter later spotted in the cash register. This is why the Treasury prohibits reproduction of currency patterns in any form. Recently the Secret Service printed a flyer picturing a bogus note. An Alabama newspaper published the picture without permission, and the next day someone clipped it from the paper and tried to pass the clipping for a genuine note.

Picked field agents form the Secret Service's White House Detail, which means that it would be hard to shove any counterfeit money at Gerald Ford. In fact, it is difficult to shove anything at any member of the first family unless the Treasury approves. Even flowers thrown during parades are caught by smiling agents, who are well aware that a bouquet might blow them up. The agent in charge is in absolute charge. Theoretically he may order the President around, though as Mike Reilly, head of the Detail in Franklin Roosevelt's time, said, "Every White House Secret Service boss knows that if he orders the President of the United States to do *anything* the agent will very shortly be giving the bank teller at No People, South Dakota, a lecture on how to tell a counterfeit two-dollar bill from a true one."

The Kennedy assassination demonstrated that the President's body-guards are fallible, but they take their assignments very seriously. All agents are crack shots, skilled boxers, experts in jujitsu. Before the President takes a stroll they scout the route; when he walks they are in front of him, behind him, on the other side of the street and in cars cruising by. They lurk near his office during the day, and should the White House catch fire at night, Detail men would lead the family out. Every package addressed to 1600 Pennsylvania Avenue is X-rayed; each year the Service studies over 18,000 ill-tempered letters addressed to the President.

Perhaps detailing Treasury men to guard duty isn't so odd as it seems. The Department, after all, is a protective organization. Everyone in it is protecting something. The Comptroller of the Currency shields depositors by examining national banks. Messrs. Whiskers watch over the Federal pocketbook. Customs men safeguard tariff revenues and turn back unwelcome cargoes. Narcotics agents protect us from heroin and cocaine. The Office of Tax Analysis and the Tax Legislative Counsel defend the tax base by submitting reports to the Congressional tax committees on some 300 tax proposals during each Congress. The Office of International Tax Affairs ferrets out tax havens in Panama, Liberia, Liechtenstein and the Bahamas.

Each Secretary does it in his own way. The difference isn't always political: Former Secretary Henry H. Fowler thinks that "the Treasury is changed less by administrations than by events," and he cites the gold outflow, an event calling for specific measures, regardless of party. Yet Secretaries do assign priorities, and private creeds have a lot to do with the assignments. President Washington's financial minister, no matter who was chosen, would have had to face the problem of public credit, but because he believed in a strong governing class, Alexander Hamilton's solution feathered the nests of various Cabots, Higginsons and Lowells. Andrew W. Mellon reduced income taxes for the rich and spent an extraordinary amount of time fussing over his own tax forms. Albert Gallatin considered it his first duty to pay off the national debt. John W. Snyder wanted low debt costs, even though that meant rising prices. Henry Morgenthau, Jr.'s number one priority went to a plan for reducing Nazi Germany to a farm state, while George Humphrey (no relation to the counterfeiter) was convinced that business would prosper if the Secretary oozed confidence, that prosperity would balance the budget and that a balanced budget would bring stability.

As money has become more complex, it has also become more international—international in a sense never anticipated by Nathan

Rothschild. Financially the West is one world. Europe is safe only if greenbacks are sound—"Trust in the dollar," says a Treasury official, "is the cement that binds the grand alliance together." The present Secretary, William E. Simon, understands this, and his career suggests that of all his Federal duties—principal money maker, Coast Guard boss, foremost administrator of America's Rube Goldberg tax laws, head bodyguard of the Fords—the one which he, his Government, and his Department take most seriously is that of defender of the capitalist faith.

The Great Bank Holiday

IT IS OVER TWO-SCORE YEARS NOW since panic closed America's banks—since that improbable month when Norman Vincent Peale denounced capitalists, John D. Rockefeller ran out of dimes, Macy's announced that demanding cash from its customers would be unpatriotic, and what were then known as step-ins were solemnly accepted as legal tender in Madison Square Garden.

Even then it had an air of fantasy, and was quickly forgotten, just as it had been unforeseen during the lame-duck winter of 1932–33 which led to it. And yet there had been omens of the panic. There was, for example, the jigsaw-puzzle craze, which reached its crest at the very moment America was plunging into the terminal trough of the Depression. During that winter some 6,000,000 puzzles were sold, and in retrospect the significance of the vogue seems painfully clear. It was a time of searching for elusive answers in politics and economics. The jigsaw turned out puzzles a man at least could solve.

In Detroit the weekend of February 11–12 newsstands enjoyed a heavy sale of 500-piece (Lincoln) puzzles. They were tough to do. Thousands of automotive workers were still frowning over card tables Monday night as their children, huddled by radios, hoarded the currency of the young—Ralston box tops, Ovaltine seals, Rice Krispies labels, Tastyeast wrappers. None of the puzzle workers, of course, suspected that very soon American parents would be reduced to even stranger exchange. But the time was at hand, and for Detroit it was the very next day, St. Valentine's Day, 1933.

President Hoover was singing his swan song over the networks at ten o'clock that evening before the Republican National Committee. Among those not listening was the Democratic governor of Michigan, William A. Comstock. It was nothing personal. At three o'clock that af-

ternoon he had received an urgent telephone request to join a conference of bankers in downtown Detroit, and he had been there ever
since. Detroit's Union Guardian Trust Company was in straits. If it
failed it probably would take every other bank in the city with it, and
the bankers were asking Comstock to declare a banking moratorium
throughout Michigan. At midnight he agreed, drove to the state capital
at Lansing, and issued a proclamation closing the state's 550 banks. He
called it a holiday.

The idea was not new. For more than a year the nation's harassed
business community had been begging for breathers, and in two states,
Nevada and Louisiana, it actually had been given them. Nevada, however, had a population of only 91,000, and Louisiana's moratorium
covered just one weekend. Michigan, on the other hand, was the heart
of the automotive industry. Its citizens, moreover, were depleted of cash
after the long weekend, and unprepared for Comstock's valentine. The
proclamation was too late for the regular editions of the morning
papers; extras greeted workers arriving downtown with the news that
they were cut off with whatever cash they had in their pockets. In some
cases this was almost nothing, but there was no hysteria, no gathering
in front of the closed banks. The general mood was casual, even gay.
After all, it *was* a holiday.

To be sure, it was awkward. Many of the newsboys peddling the
extras were obliged to sell on credit. Those who did collect coins found
themselves hailed by cruising merchants waving bills and pleading for
change. A few storekeepers, unable to locate silver, had to close their
stores; those who sought relief in Windsor, Ontario, were coldly told
their checks would be accepted "subject to collection," and under the
phony holiday air there was a feeling of uneasiness about the value of
what currency there was. The Dow Chemical Company of Midland
began coining magnesium into "Dow-metal Money," with an arbitrary
value of twenty cents—the first of a series of substitutes which were to
plague the economy for a month.

Still, there were reassuring signs. Merchants talked of organizing a
change bureau. Milk companies promised to continue deliveries. Before
noon a shipment of gold estimated at $20,000,000 was flown from Fed-
eral Reserve coffers in Chicago, and that night another $5,000,000 ar-
rived from Washington to meet money orders and Postal Savings
withdrawals. Surely, everyone said, the bronze doors would yawn wide
the next day. Wags told other wags the story of the man who had to
call his wife, couldn't cash a bill, and borrowed a nickel from an apple
seller on Woodward Avenue.

But the doors didn't yawn. Later in the week they were held slightly ajar—depositors could withdraw five percent of their accounts. It wasn't enough even to meet local payrolls. Detroit's Colonial Department Store, frankly resorting to barter, offered dresses for salted Saginaw herring, suits for livestock, assorted merchandise for eggs and honey. By the following week jokes were discarded. The holiday had been extended.

Michigan's plight had been aggravated by plunging real-estate values, but the Depression was nationwide. Since the crash of 1929 more than 5500 American banks had failed, and the public, understandably, was edgy. It responded by hoarding. Gold was vanishing from vaults at the rate of $20,000,000 a day, and depositors who couldn't get metal were taking paper, so that the government was called upon to expand its currency at the very time the gold on which it was based was disappearing.

Bank panics are always suicidal. In 1933, however, the situation had been complicated by three years of deflation. Even the soundest institutions held securities which had fallen to a fraction of their former value. The nation's 18,569 banks had about $6,000,000,000 in cash to meet $41,000,000,000 in deposits, and bankers who were forced to sell mortgages or securities to raise cash would suffer heavy losses. President Hoover was trying everything he could think of to turn the tide— R.F.C. loans to banks, debtor relief, higher duties on Japanese sneakers and Czech rubbers—but nothing seemed to work.

Now Michigan had fallen. Abruptly the daily outflow of gold from the rest of the country's banks jumped to $37,000,000; currency withdrawals to $122,000,000. Banks everywhere were swarming with wild-eyed depositors taking out cash—in the Bronx a young mother rented her baby, at twenty-five cents a trip, to women who used it to claim preference at the head of bank lines—and the week of February 20 in Maryland the Baltimore Trust Company paid out $13,000,000, nearly half of it on Friday. Late Friday night Governor Albert C. Ritchie declared a three-day holiday for the state's 200 banks. The second state had collapsed.

Responsible men were making a painfully self-conscious effort to keep their heads. The Detroit *News* commented, "It is an experience we shall have to look back upon, and no doubt grin over," and the Baltimore *Sun* said cheerily, "Life . . . will be filled with pleasant and unpleasant things as it was before. And it will have the additional advantage that everybody will have something to talk about." The president of the Baltimore Association of Commerce saw no reason why business should not continue as usual; the Bureau of Internal Revenue issued a stern reminder that income taxes were due in two weeks.

Nothing from Hyde Park dispelled the illusion of unreality. Indeed, the pixie mood of the press seemed superbly matched by President-elect Roosevelt's selection of a man to be Secretary of the Treasury, a puckish little railway-equipment manufacturer who wore a gray toupee, loved puns, collected five-dollar gold pieces, and spent his leisure time composing on a guitar. A week later, when the new administration took office, the country was to know another William H. Woodin—hard-driving, ingenious—but on the eve of office his most striking achievement, so far as the public was concerned, was the composition of a song for children:

> *Let us be like bluebirds,*
> *Happy all day long,*
> *Forgetting all our troubles in*
> *A sunny song.*

In Indianapolis and Akron that Sunday, February twenty-sixth, banks followed Michigan's lead in announcing that withdrawals would be limited to five percent of balances. During the night institutions in a dozen other Ohio cities fell into line, and on Monday—as flames gutted the Berlin Reichstag and Japanese troops marched into a Manchurian blizzard—the number grew to one hundred. Across the river from Cincinnati, five Covington, Kentucky, banks adopted similar restrictions. Monday evening Governor Gifford Pinchot of Pennsylvania signed a bill permitting individual institutions to close at will, and Thomas W. Lamont informed Hyde Park that in the view of J. P. Morgan, "the emergency could not be greater."

It could be, and soon was. By Wednesday, frantic governors had declared bank holidays in seventeen states. Pinchot acted so hurriedly he had to watch the inauguration five days later with only ninety-five cents in his pocket. Governor Allen of Louisiana, on the other hand, openly withdrew his expense money for Washington and then entrained, leaving behind his dictated proclamation closing all banks.

It was on Wednesday, March first, that the President-elect—who, Arthur Krock reported, was being asked by responsible men to assume power *now*—drove to his Manhattan home at 49 East Sixty-fifth Street and went into conference with Woodin. They did not emerge until Thursday afternoon, when, preceded by the screaming sirens of twenty motorcycles, they raced down Fifth Avenue and turned west toward the river. During the morning a light snow had sifted over the city. New Yorkers stood silently in it, staring at the cavalcade. Outside Radio City Music Hall, a cardboard King Kong, enjoying his first Manhattan run, leered toothily. In the Hudson the French Line steamer *Paris* lay quietly at berth, her cargo space reserved—though no one in the party knew it yet—for $9,000,000 in fleeing gold. On the other side of the river a special B.&O. train was waiting, and all that afternoon, talking now with Woodin of banks, now with Farley of religion, Franklin Roosevelt thundered through a cold fog, toward Washington.

It was sleeting when they reached Union Station. In the presidential suite of the Mayflower Hotel a sheaf of telegrams awaited Roosevelt: banks were closed, or closing, in twenty-one states and the District of Columbia, and Federal Reserve figures showed the week's gold loss to be $226,000,000. He was scarcely unpacked when Woodin drew him aside. Secretary of the Treasury Ogden Mills and Eugene Meyer, of the Federal Reserve Board, had telephoned to suggest a proclamation closing all banks. President Hoover felt less drastic action, under the Trading-with-the-Enemy Act of 1917, would do. Roosevelt's approval was solicited, but he, still declining to act until he had the authority, refused to advise anyone. Fair skies had been forecast for Saturday's inauguration, but now the barometer was falling.

The last page of the *New York Times* of Friday, March third, carried an ad depicting "John Doe" and "Jane Doe" acclaiming the "Good Work" of the Bowery Savings Bank. Presumably its purpose was to hearten depositors. It failed. By noon long lines of New Yorkers had formed opposite Grand Central Station and were filing into the world's largest private savings bank, demanding cash. By 3 P.M. the Bowery closed its doors, with a huge crowd still unpaid. At that same hour Governor Henry Horner of Illinois sat in the Federal Reserve Bank of Chicago, plucking nervously at his mustache, reading figures which showed that Chicago banks had paid out $350,000,000 in two weeks. After seventeen days in the hinterland, the storm was hammering at the nation's two financial strongholds.

That morning Miss Catherine Shea, a messenger for the Treasury Department, had brought Herbert Hoover his last $500 pay check. He had received it with a semblance of cheer; reports reaching him before noon suggested that the panic was lessening. After lunch, however, it became clear that this was only an illusion. Minnesota and Kansas were gone, North Carolina and Virginia were going. Hoover, too exhausted for the traditional inauguration eve dinner with the President-elect, received Roosevelt formally at 4 P.M. They parted at dusk. An hour later Governor Horner, who had given up all hope of attending the inauguration, flung himself across a bed in Chicago's Congress hotel. His bankers remained in session.

In Washington the National Symphony Orchestra had scheduled as its first number that evening a composition by the incoming Secretary of the Treasury. Woodin had reserved a box, but wasn't in it. He was in the Presidential Suite with Roosevelt, Raymond Moley, Cordell Hull and Jesse Jones, debating the wisdom of a nationwide bank moratorium, while in the White House the same question engaged Hoover, Mills and Meyer. Hoover called Roosevelt twice, to compare notes. Thomas Lamont, who was at the New York Reserve Bank with sixteen other bankers, telephoned the Mayflower. Daniel Ellis Woodhull, president of the American Banknote Company, was with them and was prepared to print scrip, but the bankers didn't feel this was necessary; they were sure they could stay open.

At 1 A.M. Roosevelt suggested to Hoover that they turn in and get some sleep. They did. And as they slept, their advisers decided everything for them.

Moley, stepping from the elevator into the Mayflower lobby, found Woodin waiting for him. "This thing is very bad," Woodin said wearily. "Will you come over to the Treasury with me? We'll see if we can give those fellows a hand."

At the Treasury were Mills and Meyer, back from the White House, A. A. Ballantine, Mills' Under Secretary, and F. G. Awalt, his Acting Comptroller. Before them lay the latest bleak Federal Reserve figures. During the last two days, $500,000,000 had been drained from the nation's banks. They were convinced that the New York bankers did not understand the immensity of the disaster, and must be protected. Governor Herbert Lehman, who had canceled his trip to the inauguration at 11 P.M., awaited the decision of the Lamont group. Mills and Woodin agreed that regardless of what the bankers decided Lehman must be persuaded to close New York's banks, and that Horner must also declare a moratorium for Illinois.

At 1:45 A.M. Horner's hotel telephone jangled—his groggy bankers were ready to capitulate. He taxied to meet them, and together they held a telephone conference with Lehman and the Treasury. At 2 A.M. he proclaimed his holiday. The sixteen New York bankers, meanwhile, piled into five limousines and drove to Lehman's home, where arguments continued. Moley, spent, fell asleep in Mills' office. Finally, at 4:20 A.M., the governor of New York reached his decision.

Woodin shook Moley. "It's all right, Ray. Let's go now. Lehman's agreed."

Hoover was told at 6 A.M. "We are at the end of our string," he said. "There is nothing more we can do."

On Saturday, March 4—the day Franklin Roosevelt took office and Howard Scott, technocrat, was formally declared bankrupt—inauguration visitors in Washington found this notice posted over hotel counters:

MEMBERS FIND IT NECESSARY THAT, DUE TO UNSETTLED BANK-
ING CONDITIONS THROUGHOUT THE COUNTRY, CHECKS ON OUT-
OF-TOWN BANKS CANNOT BE ACCEPTED.
The Washington Hotel Association

The financial heart of the country had ceased to beat. Banking in every state was wholly or partly suspended. Flags flew in Wall Street, honoring the inauguration, but the Stock Exchange was closed indefinitely, and so, for the first time in eighty-five years, was the Chicago Board of Trade. By 10 A.M. Woodhull's presses were roaring, turning out $250,000,000 in scrip for the New York Clearing House.

Arthur Krock compared the atmosphere in Washington to "that which might be found in a beleaguered capital in wartime." The sky was the color of slate. Money worries had kept half the anticipated crowd at home; Vice President Garner wore a borrowed muffler; Woodin, unable to reach his seat, perched on a railing with a cameraman; and during his address Roosevelt, uncovered and coatless, braced himself in the chill wind.

"President Hoover, Mr. Chief Justice, my friends . . ."

He was flaying the money-changers, gone from the temple. Later it occurred to some that his speech had political implications, but actually it was mild abuse that weekend—Norman Vincent Peale, no revolutionary, demanded from his Fifth Avenue pulpit the following morning that the bankers and corporation heads get down on their knees before God and confess their sins. The fact is that the Treasury, at least, had never been freer of politics. Awalt, the Republican Acting Comptroller, was working on under the Democrats, his uncut hair hanging over his ears. Ballantine, the G.O.P. Undersecretary of the Treasury, was drafting Roosevelt's first fireside chat on the banks. And Mills' invocation of the Trading-with-the-Enemy Act, originally written for Hoover, was issued by Roosevelt Sunday night.

His cigarette holder atilt, the new President declared the next four days a holiday for all banks and empowered Woodin to make exceptions. An embargo was declared on the export of gold—the *Paris* sailed without her precious cargo. Congress was being called into special session on Thursday, when emergency legislation would be ready. Meanwhile the people of the United States would have to manage without money-changers.

How was it done? A great deal depended on who you were—and where you were. As a rule, the farther a man was from home, the greater was his plight. If you were in Havana, you found that Cuba had declared its own holiday. In Cairo you were offered seventeen piasters to the dollar—the previous day's rate had been twenty-eight— and in Montreal your dollar dropped thirty-five cents in value overnight. Traveling salesmen had to hitchhike—one, in New York, hawked his shoe samples in a hotel lobby to earn his fare home. Ten New Yorkers stranded in Chicago were sent home in a bus by their hotel.

In Reno that week, fewer than a half-dozen court cases were filed each day; women had court costs and fees, but lacked funds for train tickets. Miami was in an uproar—the American Express Company declared a fifty-dollar limit on the cashing of its checks there Monday as 5000 tanned visitors lined up. Pasadena's exclusive Huntington Hotel printed scrip for stranded millionaires; among those seen in the lobby queue were Edward Bausch, of Bausch and Lomb; Sir Montagu Allan; and Prince Erik of Denmark. In Washington, Cordell Hull's first official chore was to deal with enraged diplomats, who argued that their money was entitled to diplomatic immunity from sequestration. He held them off—their plight was no worse than that of many an American alone in a strange city where his credit meant nothing. In New York a drunken Hawaiian entertainer killed his partner for accepting a check. As Prince Mike Romanoff, the noted impostor, noted piously, "A great many people's checks are now as good as a great many others."

At home Americans struggled along with varying success, depending upon the length of local holidays. Detroit, in its fourth week of moratorium, was suffering. Two thirds of the city's 1400 laborers had been unable to raise anything on their pay checks, and several fainted on the job from hunger before emergency food cards were issued. Merchants estimated their business at 60 to 70 percent below normal, restaurant cash registers were crammed with signed lunch checks, and doctors, unable to get gasoline, had to restrict their calls. In Springfield, Massachusetts, on the other hand, a newspaper survey showed that the average citizen had $18.23 cash—in trousers, purses, teapots and baby banks—when the city's banks closed on Inauguration Day.

In such communities the problem was not cash, but change. Many a man was walking the streets with a full wallet, unable to buy cigarettes, ride a bus, or use a pay telephone, because no one would break his bills. As early as Saturday, March 4, New York suburbanites began redeeming their commutation tickets to obtain silver. That night a crowd flourishing $100, $500 and even $1000 bills formed in Pennsylvania Station—buying tickets to Newark so that they could get change.

Automats were invaded by women in mink who got twenty nickels change for dollar bills and left without eating anything, subways by men in homburgs who had never ridden a subway and didn't intend to start now. Clerks, watching their stocks of coins shrink, became wary. On Lexington Avenue a man with a fifty-dollar bill tried to buy $3.52 in shaving supplies; he was advised to grow a beard. The Commodore Hotel turned away a changeless man with a $30,000 certified check. Hotel managers sent bellhops to churches to exchange bills for silver. Churches, however, were having their own difficulties; even the devout were close-fisted that March 5. One Methodist minister in New York advised his congregation to keep its silver; another solicited an offering of IOU's.

As the week wore on the shortage of change became crippling. On Monday storekeepers in Elgin, Illinois, learned that a sixteen-year-old boy had saved 11,357 pennies toward his college education, and within an hour they had his home surrounded. There weren't many such caches, however; by Wednesday even the eleemosynary Mr. Rockefeller had run out of dimes and had to give his caddie a whole buck. About the only people with fluid currency were the Alaskans, who were using gold dust, and bootleggers.

Credit, indeed, was the only solution to the holiday, as smart retailers had realized at the beginning. "If I try to get all my cash I shall certainly make matters worse," declared Jesse Isidor Straus, president of R. H. Macy & Co., which normally dealt only in hard money. "Use your charge account at Lord & Taylor!" "Use your credit!" cried newspaper ads. "Do not declare a moratorium on your appetite," advertised the Hollywood Cabaret Restaurant. In Texas, pharmacists accepted IOU's for prescriptions. Gimbel's extended credit to patrons of its restaurant, and taxi dancers in Manhattan's Roseland Dance Hall accepted IOU's—from men who could produce bankbooks.

Harry Staton, manager of the Herald Tribune Syndicate, was in California when the banks closed there. They kept on closing ahead of him, but he returned to New York on ten dollars, signing his name all the way. When he visited a gambling casino, the manager agreed to give him chips on credit, but warned that he would be paid in chips if he won. In Florida, two race tracks folded. More significant to the economy were the steel industry, whose orders hit a new low; the real-estate business, which was paralyzed; and the automotive industry, some of whose plants were forced to close. Barbershops and railroads reported sharp declines. Hollywood was near ruin—box-office receipts dropped forty-five percent, and every studio shut down. King Kong went into his second week at Radio City, but he was snarling at empty houses.

Where credit failed, people fell back on barter or improvised scrip. During the first week of the new administration, stamps, phone slugs, Canadian dollars, Mexican pesos and street-car tickets were used for currency. Mormons in Salt Lake City designed a paper money that could be used locally. The Greenwich Village Mutual Exchange issued $1000 in tokens to member businesses. In Princeton the *Princetonian* printed twenty-five-cent scrip notes for students, to be redeemed when the banks reopened. A Wisconsin wrestler signed a contract to perform for a can of tomatoes and a peck of potatoes; an Ashtabula newspaper offered free ads in exchange for produce; and a New York state senator arrived in Albany with twelve dozen eggs and a side of pork to see him through the week.

The most spectacular experiment in barter was conducted by the New York *Daily News*, which was sponsoring the semifinals of the Golden Gloves tournament in Madison Square Garden. The price of seats was fifty cents, but any article worth that amount was accepted as admission, provided the five-cent amusement tax was paid. An appraiser was engaged, who inspected, during the evening, frankfurters, mattresses, hats, shoes, overcoats, fish, noodles, nightgowns, steaks, spark plugs, cameras, sweaters, canned goods, sacks of potatoes, golf knickers, mechanics' tools and foot balm. A boy presented his *New Testament*, a girl her step-ins. The items most frequently offered were jigsaw puzzles.

Nearly everyone assumed the holiday would end with the formal adoption of scrip—local currencies, managed by states, cities and individual firms. Atlanta, Richmond, Mattituck, L.I., and Knoxville, of all places, were already on the stuff; before the week of March 6 was out Nashville would have $1,000,000 in circulation; Philadelphia, $8,000,000. The Louisville *Courier-Journal* was paying its employees in private scrip. More than a hundred communities were having notes printed, including Chicago, Boston, Providence, New Haven, Detroit and New York. Governor Lehman had appointed Al Smith chairman of an Emergency Certificate Corporation, and tellers' cages were being constructed in the New York Clearing House to distribute rainbow-colored bills ranging in value from one dollar to fifty dollars. Woodhull's Bronx plant now employed 2500. In Nutley, New Jersey, a safety-paper company which had been working three days a week for months went on three shifts, turning out six tons of scrip for Wisconsin and Tennessee.

To Secretary of the Treasury Woodin, however, the thought of state and municipal currencies and company certificates floating around the country was appalling, and at breakfast on Tuesday, March 7, he told Moley that he had been up half the night, brooding over alternatives. Scrip wasn't needed, he had decided. "We can issue currency against the sound assets of the banks," he said. "It won't frighten people. It won't look like stage money. It'll be money that looks like money." There was nothing to lose. After all, he said publicly, "We're on the bottom. We're not going any lower."

Working endlessly in his Carlton Hotel suite with Carter Glass, Woodin met Thursday's legislative deadline. As congressmen filed into the special session the finished bill was handed to the clerk—"My name's Bill, and I'm finished, too," Woodin muttered—and was read aloud. Few representatives heard it above the hubbub. They had no copies of their own. There had been no time to print them. Even the copy given the clerk bore last-minute changes scribbled in pencil. In thirty-eight minutes they whooped it through while Eleanor Roosevelt sat knitting in the gallery like a benign Madame Defarge, counting votes. Then they crowded into the Senate chamber to hear Glass explain just what it was they had done.

The little Virginian backed it, though he acknowledged there were parts which shocked him. It was, in fact, a shocking measure, ratifying all acts "heretofore *or hereinafter* taken" by the President and the Secretary of the Treasury. It provided prison terms for hoarders, "conservators" rather than receivers for weak banks—a euphemistic triumph almost as great as "holiday"—and authorized the issuance of $2,000,000,000 in new currency based on bank assets. At 8:36 P.M. a rumpled Roosevelt signed it in the White House library, surrounded by unpacked books and pictures from Hyde Park. That evening the Bureau of Engraving and Printing recruited 375 new workers. The official printing presses of the United States finally were going into action.

All that night and the next the lights of the Bureau twinkled across the Tidal Basin. There was no time to engrave new dies—plates bearing the imprint "Series of 1929" were pressed into service. There wasn't even an opportunity to acquire facsimile signatures of two officials from each of the twelve Federal Reserve banks; signatures were taken from files in the district and sent by messenger to the American Type Foundry in Jersey City, where logotypes were cut. Early Saturday morning planes began taking off from Washington bearing bales of cash. The first were delivered to New York's Federal Reserve bank shortly before noon. Transfer to member banks began immediately.

The real trick was prying open the rigid fists of hoarders, who in one week had taken fifteen percent of the nation's currency out of circulation. Even a bewitched Congress couldn't make the penal clauses apply to hoarding that already had taken place, and so the government turned to the spur of publicity. On Wednesday, March eighth, the Federal Reserve Board announced that its banks would prepare lists of persons who had withdrawn gold since February first and who failed to bring it back by March thirteenth, the following Monday. Newspapers had scarcely appeared with this announcement before bank switchboards were jammed. Anonymous callers wanted to know what would be done with the names, what it was all about. The replies were ominously vague. Callers were told only that if they had gold and wanted to return it, the banks would open for them, and newspapermen would be kept out of lobbies.

In the next few hours thousands of mattresses were torn open, cans dug up, hidden boxes brought forth. Banks everywhere reported long queues, reminiscent of the preceding week's panic but comprised this time of men and women carrying Gladstones and briefcases. In Cleveland $300,000 was deposited that day; in Minneapolis, $182,000. Thursday, the day Woodin's bill was cheered through Congress, Cleveland took in $500,000, Philadelphia $700,000, Richmond $163,000. The real flood of double eagles, however, was in New York, which, despite a fifty-six-mile gale—which tore loose the stitching in a woman's petticoat and sent a sheaf of gold certificates scudding across Sixth Avenue—banked $30,000,000 that day. One man brought in $700,000; one firm, whose identity remains a secret, delivered $6,000,000 in bullion to the Federal Reserve Bank.

Encouraged, the bank extended its order on Friday, asking for reports covering withdrawals of the past two years. The widened hunt brought bigger game; the nation's gold supply rose dramatically. By 9:30 A.M., when the Federal Reserve Bank of New York opened, there was a line of 1000 people, their pockets and luggage sagging with gold. An hour later, the crowd had grown to 1500. Filing through the grilled gates, the depositors filled out deposit slips, presented the same bags and rolled paper stacks they had withdrawn, and waited while the money was counted. When the bank closed at 5 P.M., two hours late, 4000 people had passed in and out.

The flow continued, uninterrupted, on Saturday, enhanced in Wilmington by a twenty-year collection of gold pieces turned in by Irenée du Pont. By that night, Federal Reserve banks had recovered $300,000,000 in gold and gold certificates, enough to support $750,000,000 additional circulation. Even before the planes took off with new bank notes, Woodin had permitted individual savings banks to dole out ten dollars to each depositor. Business began to stir, and not all the money was spent for necessities. In Boston Saturday afternoon a *Herald* reporter found several hundred women crowded around five counters in a bargain basement, buying jigsaw puzzles.

Roosevelt extended the national moratorium while the Treasury separated strong banks from the weak. After the passage of Thursday's bill Woodin invited applications for permission to reopen; actual openings would start Monday. It was the next week that killed Woodin—he was under a doctor's care before it was over, and in his grave the following year. Yet despite his heroic effort, the staggering task of examining 18,000 institutions would have been impossible without the technical knowledge of the Republicans, who stayed at their desks. Awalt, in the first few days, returned home only to shower and change his clothes; James Douglas, who had been assistant secretary under Mills, served as the contact man with the twelve Federal Reserve Banks, forty state banking departments, and clearinghouses everywhere. In the whirlwind tempers were short, but did not follow party lines. "We were," Moley later recalled, "just a bunch of men trying to save the banking system."

In New York on Monday, all but nine national banks were allowed to reopen; in Philadelphia, all but six. At the end of the week 13,500—seventy-five percent—of the country's banks were back in business, and the sweet notes of gongs again were heard in stock exchanges. Price rises on the Chicago Board of Trade strained at the legal limit, and in New York stocks jumped fifteen percent. We have John T. Flynn's word for it that the New York ticker clicked off the message, "Happy Days Are Here Again."

Of course they weren't really. One dollar in every ten was tied up in frozen deposits on March fourteenth—when the Bureau of Internal Revenue finally agreed to give income-tax payers sixteen days grace—

and as late as October the government still was trying to reorganize 376 banks. But the panic had been ended without currency chaos or nationalization of the banks. Undoubtedly the medicine had been strong; the inflationary movement, once started, was irresistible; in April America left the gold standard. The months that followed saw an entirely new concept of the economy developed in the NRA, AAA, CCC, the Federal Securities Act, the Stock Exchange Act, and, in 1935, the Public Utility Holding Company Act. The power of the bankers had been irrevocably broken.

It was in Roanoke, Virginia, that J. P. Morgan was discovered during the holiday on his annual automobile trip south. He was shy as ever, and declined comment on the Depression. He did, however, remark that he was glad the morning's fog was lifting.

"I like to read the signs along the road," he said.

Slumlord

A MAN I SHALL CALL Dan Marner, a typical metropolitan slum landlord, once had a friend. He was a real friend, not just another useful contact in the local Bureau of Buildings or land-record office, and before he and Dan broke up over a roofing contract he gave him a Christmas present. It was a game of Monopoly.

Dan never used it. He studied the rules carefully and then shelved it. For several years it has lain in a ledger case beside his scarred desk, gathering office dust. "It was those 'Community Chest' cards you got to pick," said the estranged friend later. "Dan Marner couldn't bring himself to give anything to charity, even in a game."

Dan himself explains that the game sounds foolish. To him it probably does: In Monopoly, the winning player usually must acquire the most expensive properties on the board—"Park Avenue" and the "Boardwalk." Dan knows that real estate doesn't work that way. In the twenty years he has been working the shabby side of his city's map, he hasn't had to pay the "Community Chest" or "Go to Jail" once, and he has been a consistent winner. On paper, indeed, he is a millionaire, the title owner of 327 deeds. Each month he grosses $6,000 from rents and auxiliary sources. His expenses are comparatively small—his three sons act as office and field assistants, slum tax assessments are low, and Dan never repairs houses voluntarily.

At seventy-two, Dan is a dour, bespectacled man, wise in the ways of the drab districts that dot every metropolis on the eastern seaboard—districts built before World War I, paved with Victorian cobblestones, and peppered today with pawnshops, cut-rate drugstores, and warped doors bearing the crudely chalked names of tenants. The increase of traffic in the interiors of cities long ago sent the original householders to suburbs on the perimeter. Into the vacuum they left, men like Dan moved—first as managers, later as landlords.

Dan's headquarters is in a dingy office building on the edge of the slum. There his tenants—some black, some white—bring their weekly money and wait in line while his sons stamp their rent books, which are small and black and resemble bankbooks. Some tenants send money orders, but none mail cash. Long ago they learned that since there is no record of a cash mailing, they have no recourse if Dan tells them their envelopes have been lost in the mails. Like many professional slum landlords, he has a reputation for sharp practice. The office building, which he shares with several competitors, is known in the trade as "the Den of the Forty Thieves."

Dan's reputation doesn't affect his business, and so it doesn't bother him. Within obvious limits, he is candid, and he will open his records to the outsider who guarantees him anonymity. They reveal that his typical house was built about sixty-five years ago, is on the outskirts of the downtown area in his city, is overcrowded, lacks plumbing, has no central heating, and frequently lacks heating equipment altogether. Dan rents it for $56 a month. It costs the occupant $18 more for utilities, which means that the typical tenant spends a quarter of his income on housing characterized by defective wiring, blind rooms, an outside toilet, a leaking roof, and massive rat infestation.

Unless he is goaded by the law, Dan pockets the two percent depreciation allowed him under the Federal tax laws and mends nothing. Suggestions that he should do otherwise baffle him. To Dan, his career is not merely defensible; it is admirable.

"What I did," he says, peering over his steel-rimmed glasses at the files of paying tenants, "any of them could do."

That is a difficult argument to answer, because it is literally true. Like most of the other Forty Thieves, Dan is a product of the slum. His rise is a kind of twisted Horatio Alger story. Tubercular as a youth, he left school in the seventh grade, married early, and was earning $18 a week in a canning factory when the Depression threw him on relief. In 1934, after two years on the dole, he rented a vacant house, agreeing to clean it for the first two weeks' rent. He swiped a rusty bedspring from a junkyard, set it up on four soapboxes, and advertised a room for rent. Saving his coins and assembling other makeshift beds, he converted the vacant building into a profitable flophouse.

The owner of the house, an elderly woman who had inherited money and moved to a suburb, admired Dan's ingenuity. She owned five occupied buildings in the same block. Times were hard, the occupants were in arrears, and she appointed Dan her rent collector. He was so persistent at extorting money from his neighbors that one, in exasperation, slugged him. The story made the papers. The public may have disapproved of Dan's methods, but other absentee property owners decided he was just the man they needed. He became the busy manager of several estates, charging, under standard practice, a five percent commission on the rents he collected.

Actually he charged much more, if those who knew him then are to be believed. According to them, Dan, knowing that absentee landlords rarely visit their properties, extracted money from them for repairs he never made. At the same time, it is contended, he jacked up rents on his own authority and kept the difference. Dan admits none of this. But it is a matter of record that in two years he had saved enough to buy his first house, a dilapidated two-story building offered by the city in a tax sale.

The following year he bought his second house in a low-income white neighborhood. Dan moved a black family in and took advantage of the neighbors' panic to buy four more homes in the same block at bargain prices. He had to mortgage everything he had to do it, but today the street is a respectable black district, a faithful producer of weekly money orders. He has acted as a "blockbuster" on several occasions since, serving as an incidental agent of desegregation.

Dan goes into debt frequently. Every cent he makes is invested in new property. In courthouse circles he has a reputation for not being able to answer a judgment without selling a house. If a house becomes burdensome, he usually finds it profitable to have the mortgage foreclosed. He will keep it until he has cleared his investment and then cut off payments to the building-and-loan association. Occasionally the auctioneer will fail to meet his expectations, and he will be obliged to pay the association a small deficiency decree, but as a rule he finds foreclosure cheaper than a broker's commission.

All other things being equal, Dan prefers black tenants to white. Blacks, confined to the slum by social pressures, are of all types. White families can live elsewhere, however, and those he gets are inclined to be irresponsible. There is one exception to this: the handicapped of all races are sound risks. Late in the 1930's, for example, Dan took in a veteran of the Argonne, a chronic victim of combat shock. The man, unmarried, received $125 a month from the Veterans Administration. He regularly turned his check over to Dan, who saw to it he was supplied with coffee and beans from the corner grocery until his death, which Dan deeply regretted.

Exploiting the handicapped may seem beneath a millionaire, but Dan doesn't look at it that way. "Life is dog eat dog," he says, shrugging and spreading his hands. "It's survival of the fittest." His fortune has been built from stacks of small change, and no device is too petty for him. If a Department of Highways inspector insists he repair one of his sidewalks—a twenty-five-dollar job—Dan dutifully takes out a Bureau of Buildings permit, indicating that he intends to do the work. The permit costs one dollar and gives him thirty days' grace. By then the inspector is looking over another neighborhood. When he returns next year and finds the walk worse, Dan will explain that he has been unable to find a contractor. He will take out another permit as evidence of his good faith. He is prepared to go on from permit to permit, always promising and never performing, to avoid paying that $25.

On the other hand, he knows all his rights. Since Dan's days as a rent collector, the city has established a small-claims court, and he is one of its steadiest customers. In theory, the court is for taxpayers who cannot afford to press extensive suits. Actually, two-thirds of its docket entries are rent cases, with the city acting as agent for complaining landlords. If the tenant falls into arrears, Dan drops into the court, fills out a slip, and pays a one-dollar fee. A policeman then serves a summons on the tenant. Most occupants of slum homes are terrified of authority. Frequently the lax tenant will borrow the cash that day and rush to Dan, who will also recover the one-dollar summons charge from him.

Dan's big property gains were made during World War II. On the eve of Pearl Harbor, he was worth about $100,000. He held title to thirty-four houses, acquired at public tax sales, from out-of-town heirs unfamiliar with local values, or from hard-pressed owners needing quick cash. Each month, his records show, he was grossing between $850 and $900 in rentals, and he was branching out. He had become a professional bondsman, pledging his property as collateral. His eldest son hung around police stations soliciting business. Dan always made certain his bonds were secured by chattel mortgages, and he always demanded the maximum legal interest—ten percent in Federal court, five in local courts. Each year he met a score of bonds and took in upward of two thousand dollars in bail fees. He had plenty of free capital —too much, indeed, to suit him. "I was uneasy," he says. "I figured someone would find out and make an excuse to sue me for something."

Unfortunately, investment opportunities were limited. The specter of competition was rearing its head: other landlords were bidding against Dan at auctions, and the market was tight. He wanted to pioneer a new field by buying a block of Victorian mansions on the slum fringe and converting them into apartments, but the zoning statute prohibited it. Then, at the appropriate time, the Japs attacked. War industry boomed, and the city was invaded by Southerners who wanted to work but had no place to live. Dan took a plunge. He bought the block, went to the zoning-appeals board, and explained he would house the war workers if the board would overlook the law. It worked: His peculiar contribution to the war effort was accepted.

"I didn't get the Army-Navy 'E'," he recalls, "but I got a precedent, and in 1946 I got rid of all those hillbillies by moving one black family in."

Dan's one serious challenge has come from the local Health Department. Late in the war the department set up a housing bureau, and under its leadership a team of inspectors invaded the slum, looking for infractions of the law. In one fourteen-block area, with 791 properties, they found 13,589 health, building, fire, and electrical violations. Notices were issued ordering repairs, and the team moved on, checking off kerosene space heaters, outdoor hoppers, exposed wiring, and sagging walls. A week later they struck the first of Dan's blocks.

The campaign was a real threat to him. Structural repairs are expensive—mending his houses properly would have taken more money than he had, or so he now says. He began by protesting that his property rights were being invaded, but the inspectors had strong public support. Protest failing, Dan quietly told each of his tenants he could buy the house he was renting with no down payment. The terms were farcical; Dan retained the deeds, and he was permitted to cancel the contract if one weekly payment was one day late. Most occupants fell for the "buy-instead-of-rent" gimmick, however, until Dan started forwarding Health Department notices to them. Ownership, he piously explained, implies responsibility.

The department argued that Dan was still the landlord, and a legal battle opened to determine where ownership really lay. Meanwhile, Dan had opened a contracting sideline. He outfitted a man in neat white coveralls, with the word INSPECTOR embroidered over the left breast pocket, and sent him out to trail bona fide Health Department inspectors. After the Health Department men had gone, Dan's "inspector" would call and ask the bewildered tenant if he might look at the house. Usually he was admitted without question.

Inside, he would explain that this or that had to be done. When the frightened occupant, thinking of himself as the house's owner, asked where repairmen might be found, the "inspector" said he had friends who did work at cut-rate prices. The prices were, of course, inflated, for Dan extracted a referral fee from the plumbers and roofers he sent out. Under this ingenious arrangement, the repairs were not only made; Dan made a profit on them. According to one report, Dan's "inspector" dismantled a furnace one bitterly cold day, left, and returned the following day with an installment-sale furnace contract. The shivering householder signed.

The courts decided that Dan, as deed holder, was legally responsible. Since then he has been erecting cardboard partitions and installing inferior wiring—doing the work, in short, but in the worst possible fashion. The Health Department keeps after him, and he has paid a few ten-dollar fines for failure to comply with its notices. But he is still the winner. Ten years after its ambitious opening, the department's campaign is hopelessly bogged down in detail. By fighting it every step of the way, Dan is defeating it.

Outside the Health Department and a few civic organizations interested in slum clearance, there is little local interest in Dan. The business community is almost wholly indifferent. Some of its members, one suspects, secretly admire him. They think of him as a shrewd trader, a self-made man, an individualist who is defying bureaucracy and managing to get away with it.

Dan is all those, and more. He is a symbol of the spreading rot in metropolitan areas, and his story has as many implications for economists as for moralists. Since 1935, when Dan bought his first house, the assessed value of his properties has dropped twenty-seven percent, meaning his municipality gets nearly $8,000 less in taxes from them each year. The city is spending forty-five percent of its income in the slums and getting six percent of its taxes there.

The forty-five percent is spent in many ways. The neighborhood Dan converted to apartments during the war now leads the city in juvenile delinquency, with twenty cases per thousand population annually. About one-third of the city's inhabitants live in the slums, but they account for eighty-three percent of its syphilis and seventy-one percent of its tuberculosis—one of Dan's blocks has five active TB cases today. The cost of slums in petty thefts, bastardy cases, and social parasites is incalculable, but census figures show that eighty-one percent of the welfare cases are concentrated there.

Dan's admirers may not know it, but they all contribute to his loot through the relief rolls. A home-owner with an assessment of $10,000 pays the equivalent of three weeks' rent each year in taxes. Through their unfortunate tenants, Dan and his colleagues get a big slice of this.

Such implications have no interest whatever for Dan. His outlook is expressed in a few catch phrases: dog eat dog, tooth and claw, survival of the fittest. He came up the hard way, and he argues anyone else can do it, though if pressed he will modestly admit that stamina, brains, and what he calls "realism" are necessary for success.

The Founding Grandfather

FIFTY-SIX FLOORS ABOVE Manhattan's Rockefeller Center, William Couper's bust of America's first billionaire gazes out stonily on the private offices of his four surviving grandsons. Those who knew him in his later years find the likeness striking, for at the end of his life John Davison Rockefeller (1839–1937) had a remarkably graven look. He is remembered as a wrinkled, bony nonagenarian who distributed 20,000 dimes to strangers—he started with nickels but found them too heavy—and spent his last days among the black parishioners of the Union Baptist Church in Ormond Beach, Fla., chanting prayers and reedily affirming in his quavering tenor that when the roll was called up yonder, he'd be there.

Like so much else in his extraordinary career, this final tableau is deceptive. All his life John D. deftly masked his real self from an inquisitive public. Leafing through an album of photographs of him is like reviewing the disguises of a celebrated character actor. His use of his hair is illustrative. When side whiskers were the fashion, John D. wore them. After they went out and long mustaches came in, he went to the barber, and when shorter mustaches became the vogue he went again, always emerging the image of the average businessman.

This protean performance became impossible after a series of illnesses brought on by anxiety over the government's determination to disassemble his beloved Standard Oil Trust. All his hair fell out, including his eyebrows. To his horror, his bald head glittered like a knob of buffed marble. He wore a skullcap for a while, and then he acquired a wardrobe of wigs, one for church, another for golf and a third for street wear. By then there wasn't much point in pretending he was average anyway, so he lived on into great old age wearing the quaint frock coat and plug hat of Victorian bankers.

Inasmuch as his lifetime spanned three generations and the industrialization of a continent, he had time to play a great many roles. Americans over fifty recall him as the wraithlike citizen of Ormond Beach who was mortified by the local garden club's decision to disqualify him from its annual flower show after the ladies discovered that his butler had arranged his blossoms—logical to the end, John D. argued that the butler was an extension of himself—but at the height of his powers he had been anything but vulnerable. Throughout the last third of the nineteenth century, he was a powerfully built, rawboned titan with hypnotic eyes who was, in his own words, "all business," and who strode purposefully over the mustard-colored carpets at 26 Broadway, Standard Oil's great keep, swapping refineries, railroads and mountain ranges glittering with iron ore.

His refusal to abandon cherished objectives reminded James Ford Rhodes of Napoleon and Bertrand Russell of Bismarck, and his passion for facts was much like that of a fictional character, the industrialist Thomas Gradgrind in Dickens's *Hard Times*. Indeed, throughout John D.'s life Dickensian names cropped up in his retinue with extraordinary frequency. They included his ruthless successor as president of Standard Oil (Archbold), the former Baptist clergyman who opened his fortune to a host of charities (Gates), a labor-baiting monopolist (Welborn), the pompous homopath who enjoyed issuing bulletins about his health at the turn of the century (Biggar), a night nurse (Sly) and the physician who checked him a few days before his death and thought he looked just fine (Merryday). A clergyman who matched John D. stroke for stroke on the golf course was a Bustard.

One character in his life that the tycoon never resembled was his father, William A. (Big Bill) Rockefeller, a celebrated mountebank who roamed the frontier playing a violin on his hip, selling elixir by the bottle and advertising himself at county fairs as a "botanic physician" or "herbal doctor." Big Bill was a cancer quack. He was also a rake. Between hawking fake nostrums and hoodwinking credulous rubes, he spent a lot of time in strange beds, and on one of his infrequent visits to his family in the upstate New York town of Richford, he was indicted by a Cayuga County grand jury on charges of ravishing a working girl. After that, his appearances in his home became even rarer. His most famous son evokes a rare pity when it is recalled that, as a lonesome child, he played by the road in a homemade suit and waited, month after poignant month, for a glimpse of his absent father.

Big Bill was spectacular when he did come—an immaculately dressed giant with a Stonewall Jackson beard who galloped up behind sleek new horses, never with less than a thousand dollars in his pocket.

It would be wrong to picture him as generous, however. To a neighbor he boasted that he cheated his sons "to make 'em sharp." He loaned little John D. five-dollar gold pieces at ten percent interest. That seems hard, but few parental lessons have been better learned. At the age of seven the boy was filling a blue china dish on the family mantel with coppers earned from digging potatoes, managing a turkey flock, and—an omen—buying candy by the pound and selling it to his brothers and sisters by the piece.

At thirteen he was lending $50 at compound interest. At fourteen he was a boarder in Cleveland, a city to which he had moved in order to attend Central High, where Mark Hanna, a fellow student, later recalled that John D. was "sane in every way but one—he was money-mad." To a classmate, the future billionaire confided that the thought of his father supporting him gave him a "cold chill." After a three-month bookkeeping course he went to work for a produce commission merchant, where, he later said, he fell in love with "all the method and system of the office."

He liked everything about it—the smell of the ledgers, the feel of the high desk, the sunlight slanting across his blotter—and after he had opened his own produce commission office at the age of nineteen, he began working later each evening. At one point he wrote in his private journal that he had "covenanted" with himself not to be seen at his books after 10 P.M. for thirty days. Later he wrote under this, "Don't make any more such covenants." His mother, a chanter of proverbs, had taught him that "willful waste makes woeful want," and he was nagged by the fear that he might squander precious hours.

One day in 1863 he glanced out the window and observed a kerosene scow floating by on the muddy water of the Cuyahoga River. He was making good money selling salt and mess pork to the Union Army, but the war wouldn't last forever, and he reasoned correctly that after it, the moving frontier would leave Cleveland produce behind. Therefore, he invested in a small refinery. By the end of the year he was donning hip boots and toiling in the slime of Pennsylvania's oil regions.

Allan Nevins once called the Rockefeller fortune a historical accident. Certainly John D. looked out his window at the right time. As a child in Richford he had read by candlelight. The only oil business then had been run by the whalers of New England. Petroleum was something that ruined salt wells, or was sold by peddlers like Big Bill to relieve aching joints. Then, while John D. was still in Central High, a Dartmouth professor had found a way to refine it, and the month after the young commission merchant's twentieth birthday, the first oil well was sunk near Titusville, Pennsylvania. Gasoline was merely an annoying by-product in the eighteen-sixties, but even so, the possibilities were exciting: kerosene for illumination, paint bases, industrial lubricants.

At the time of John D.'s arrival on the scene the petroleum market was being drowned by overproduction. The price of oil hovered just above that of water. Willful waste was making woeful want, the oil industry needed organizing to curb the cutthroat price war among rival drillers, and nobody could organize like John D. He wasted nothing. Meal stops were short on the trains of those days, so when he traveled he would leap off, cram his cheeks with food, and methodically masticate all the way to the next station. ("I always had a good big mouth," he later explained gravely.) Blotting his signature took valuable energy, so he hired a man to stand by his desk, blotter in hand. Concluding that he needed more rest, he moved a couch into the office and addressed colleagues from his pad.

In his new enterprises little economies mounted. Forty drops of solder were being used to seal each five-gallon can of kerosene; he experimented, found that 39 drops would do as well and rejoiced in the saving. Barrels cost other refiners $2.50 apiece; John D. made them for 96 cents each. Presently he had his own wagons, lighters, warehouses and railroad tank cars. By 1869 his refinery was the largest in Cleveland, and he was learning that the bigger he became, the more efficient he became. To him the lesson was plain: He would achieve the ultimate in efficiency if he became the only oil man in the world.

John D. wasn't much interested in oil production, in the frowzy oil regions he scornfully called "mining camps." He was after the refineries, which J. A. Hobson, the English economist, has compared to the highway "narrows" that medieval barons seized to tax passing commerce. Control the refineries, seize the narrows, and John D. would dominate the industry. His weapon for reducing competition was similar to what is called today the quantity discount—the more a customer buys, the greater his markdown. His capacity had reached 1,500 barrels a day. Many of his rivals were refining only a barrel or two. He was in a position to drive them to the wall by demanding lower transportation costs than they could get, and that was what he did. First he demanded, and received, a rebate of 15 cents a barrel from the Lake Shore and Southern Michigan Railroad. The principle established, he incorporated the Standard Oil Company of Ohio with $1 million on Jan. 10, 1870.

His rebates grew higher and higher; at one point competing

refineries were paying transportation charges five times those of Standard Oil. Even more vicious were his "drawbacks"—fixed rates that the railroads paid him for every barrel of rival oil they carried. They didn't haggle. He was managing their traffic, guaranteeing them huge daily shipments and absorbing all their credit risks. After the panic of 1873, he began absorbing competitors right and left, and in 1882, when he organized the Standard Oil Trust, altering the meaning of a word whose definition had been benign, he had 14,000 miles of pipeline webbed under U.S. soil and controlled 95 percent of the country's refining capacity.

The Standard was now the largest and richest company in the world. Its undisputed commander was John D. He knew his refineries down to the last pipe and vat. No by-product escaped him—Vaseline, chewing gum, paraffin, whatever—and if a political campaign was shaping up, he was prepared to fuel the torchlights, even though, as in 1884, the first minority party to assemble was dedicated to putting him in jail. "Rockefeller," said John Archbold, who served for many years as his chief lieutenant, "always sees a little farther than the rest of us—and then he sees around the corner."

It was part of John D.'s genius that he could persuade almost anyone to join him. Archbold was one convert. Another was Roger Sherman, a heroic enemy of monopoly in the courts who switched to become a Standard attorney. A third was Cettie Spelman, who became John D.'s wife. Cettie had been a dedicated Congregationalist, and her graduation essay at Central High had been "I Can Paddle My Own Canoe," but when she married him she quietly followed him into the Baptist Church.

Part of the trouble with fighting him was that you never knew where he was. All important messages were in code—Baltimore was "Droplet," refiners were "douters," the Standard itself was "Doxy." Shadowy men came and went by his front door; shadowy companies used his back door as a mailing address. For a long time the public didn't realize how powerful he was because he kept insisting he was battling firms that he secretly owned outright. John T. Flynn cites the case of a last-ditch Cleveland refiner going to Peru for oil and finding that all available wells had been bought by a company that was a subsidiary of a corporation owned by the Anglo-American Oil Company of England—which belonged to John D.

By then Standard Oil was operating in each of the world's twenty-four time zones. John D.'s six-hooped, bright blue barrels of Royal Daylight or Atlantic Red kerosene were being borne by elephants in India, by camels on the Sahara, by coolies in Asia. From Manchuria to the sacred fires of Baku on the Caspian, drillers knew that they need only reach the nearest Standard pipeline to get a certificate at least as good as gold. Foreign governments discovered what the vanquished refiners of Cleveland could have told them: there was no stopping John D. They built tariff walls; Standard men climbed them. Sinaean mandarins, at the urging of local vegetable oil guilds, made the use of Standard fuel a capital offense, and their peasants secretly bartered rice and chickens for Royal Daylight to light the lamps of China.

And that was only the beginning. Peering around the corner and into the future, John D. saw the dawning age of the internal combustion engine. He quietly ordered the development of gasoline and machine oils. When Gottlieb Daimler unveiled his automobile on March 4, 1887, Standard Oil was ready. The sequel astonished the world. Unhampered by income taxes, the Rockefeller fortune, which had been $40 million the year the trust was founded, had quintupled by 1896. Despite gifts to charities, it more than quadrupled again by the eve of World War I. "Who," John D. wondered at the end of his life, "would ever have thought that it would grow to such a size?"

Even today the extent of his wealth boggles the mind. Nobody has ever been richer than John D. at his peak. Only the old pendragon himself, who had a balance sheet struck to the penny at the end of each day, knew exactly how much he had, and he was among the most discreet men in the history of commerce. It is known, however, that in 1913 his assets were worth over $900 million, and one dollar then was worth six today. At one point his fortune was growing at the rate of $100 a minute, which amounts to over $50 million a year. The precise extent of his heirs' wealth is unknown even to them, because of interlocking trusts, jointly held estates, fluctuating securities markets and stocks that have been accumulating capital gains and compound interest for the better part of a century. However, the late Stewart Alsop estimated that the family's combined wealth in the nineteen-seventies may run as high as $10 billion.

For as long as they can remember, opulence has been a central fact of the Rockefellers' life. John D., Jr., the tycoon's only son, said that from his birth big money "was there, like air or food or any other element." Bobo Rockefeller, the first wife of one of Nelson's younger brothers, the late Winthrop Rockefeller, who served three years as Governor of Arkansas, once observed that if you belong to the family, "you can almost feel the prices rise when you walk into a store." During one of Nelson's campaign autographing sessions in New York, an eager young man actually thrust a blank check toward his wiggling pen, and when the Rev. Frederick T. Gates, John D.'s chief almsgiver, once suggested to him that he ought to try to make more friends on golf courses, the old man replied drily, "I have made experiments, and nearly always the result is the same. Along about the ninth hole out comes some proposition, charitable or financial."

Greedy strangers were the least of the hardships his wealth brought him. From the day Standard Oil emerged as a stifler of competition, John D. was a target of ferocious press attacks. Editorial writers denounced him as the "Anaconda" and the "New Moloch." Cartoonists depicted him as an octopus with pipelines for tentacles and dollar signs for eyes. For children he replaced the bogeyman; "Rockefeller will get you if you don't watch out," their mothers told them. He was accused of fleecing his friends and dynamiting rival refineries, and attacking him was smart politics.

John D.'s daughter-in-law gave birth to a son, John D. 3d, but his grandfather couldn't see him because the Attorney General of Missouri was harrying the old man up and down the roads around New York brandishing a subpoena. When Cettie died, John D. couldn't bury her for four months because process servers were preparing to waylay him at the grave; the body had to be kept in a friend's mausoleum while the Governor of Ohio straightened things out.

The pattern of harassment had become clear in 1890, when the Sherman Antitrust Act became law. Two years later the Attorney General of Ohio announced that John D.'s trust violated the charter of the Standard Oil Company of Ohio. The trust was safe for a while—the New Jersey Holding Company Act rescued it before the bailiffs closed in—but then two calamities doomed it. An assassin made Theodore Roosevelt President, and Mark Hanna, who had been the Standard's best friend in Washington, died. TR attacked all "malefactors of great wealth," and everyone knew precisely which malefactor he had in mind.

John D. was golfing when a messenger brought him word that Judge Kenesaw Mountain Landis, with a thump of his gavel, had fined the Standard $29,240,000 for shipping carloads at secret rates. He paused briefly, turned to his companions on the tee, and said, "Well, shall we go on, gentlemen?" Four years later, on May 15, 1911, the U.S. Supreme Court ordered the trust dissolved within six months. The monopoly was split into 33 giant companies. John D. formally quit as president, and by 1924 he wasn't even a stockholder in the key firm,

Jersey Standard, though to this day his heirs get unsolicited advice on how to run Exxon, its corporate descendant.

The titan's attitude toward his critics never changed. To him they were all "spoiled children." "We must be patient," he told his son, and again, "Let the world wag." Furtive by temperament, he fought extradition and dodged process servers, while telling his Sunday school class with a straight face, "The kind of man I like is one that lives for his fellows—the one that lives in the open." He believed a strong man should "get all the money he honestly can" and extend charity to the poor. When hecklers gathered outside his door he mounted a bike and pedaled off to play golf.

Early in the eighteen-eighties he had moved to Manhattan. Thereafter most of his middle years were spent within a triangle bounded by the roll-top desks at 26 Broadway, his brownstone house at 4 West 54th Street, and the Baptist Church on Fifth Avenue, though he would venture forth on special occasions—to meet the trains of new men from Cleveland, for example, introducing them to guides who would show them to available houses, and always taking his leave with a cheery, "God bless you, and God bless Standard Oil." Winters he would have the side yard of his home flooded, and there, not far from the Rockefeller Center skating rink of today, he would methodically circle the ice each morning before work, with skates clamped to his patent-leather boots, his silk hat jammed over his pate and his frock coat sailing sedately behind. He also liked buggy racing. From time to time he would don a yellow duster and goggles, summon his carriage and pair, and trot over to Seventh Avenue looking for competition. He would go all out when he got it, winning, on one occasion, by hotrodding to safety at the last split-second and passing so closely by a heavy dray loaded with scrap iron that he scraped its hubcaps.

Everything John D. did was strategic, even at home. Taking the family swimming, he wore a straw hat in the water to ward off the sun. On iceskating expeditions he issued his son a long narrow board to be carried under the arm in case the ice broke. He liked blindman's buff, and he played as he worked, for keeps, trying to trick children with complicated feints and lightning thrusts and huzzaing when he succeeded. Success in everything was important to him; when John D., Jr. became manager of the Brown football team, his loyal father attended a game between Brown and the Carlisle Indians in New York. The old man may have come out of duty, but once he was there his powerful competitive instincts were aroused. He was out of the stands before the game was over, prancing along the sidelines in his beaver and cheering the team wildly. (Brown won, 24 to 12.)

His opinions on everything of importance had been formed in childhood, and they never changed. More than any other man he underwrote modern medical science, yet when he himself was ill he relied on medicasters or smoked mullein leaves in a clay pipe. A true loner, he never needed outside stimulus—he said he never experienced a craving for tea, coffee or "for anything." His most extravagant comment was "Pshaw!" He reserved it for extraordinary situations, such as when he was accosted by an enemy of the Standard, or had triumphed in a bitter pipeline war. He absolutely refused to deal with anyone who tried to hurry him, and he declined to honor his membership in the New York Stock Exchange by appearing on the floor because he despised the turmoil there.

Because the popular press regarded him as an ogre, there was little suggestion in it that he was human, let alone virile. Yet his family knew him as a man of considerable physical courage. One evening the house burglar-alarm rang and a frightened maid cried that there was a prowler in one of the upstairs bedrooms. John D. called for his revolver and, without waiting for it, dashed to the back door to intercept the intruder, who escaped him by sliding down a pillar. On another occasion, the dynast insisted on driving his son to Grand Central Station at a time when anarchists were threatening to kill him. John D., Jr., thought it would be prudent to take a bodyguard along, but his father wouldn't hear of it. "I can take care of myself," he said, adding, in a Nick Carter riposte, "If any man were foolish enough to attack me, it would go hard with him."

His privacy became increasingly important to him. If his son wanted to communicate with him, he had to write him a letter, even though they worked in the same building. Later, when the younger Rockefeller visited his father, he was required to stay in a nearby hotel. After acquiring his 4,180-acre estate at Pocantico Hills in Westchester County, John D. built a mighty iron fence around it. John D., Jr., who worked with the architects, was lucky his father would settle for the fence; the old man had wanted to ring the estate with barbed wire. Yet there was no arrogance in him. He wanted to be known as "Neighbor John," and always addressed his grandsons warmly as "Brother."

To the annoyance of the family, he declined to replace clothes until they became shiny, and when his son presented him with a fancy fur coat, he wore it a couple of times, sent it to storage, and finally gave it back. He never mentioned his great wealth at home. There he remained merely the attentive father, obviously well-to-do but still a man of plain tastes. One of his favorite dishes was bread and milk, and he liked to keep a paper bag of apples on the sill outside his bedroom window and eat one each night at bedtime.

The world does not remember him as a wit, but his grandsons do. With mournful gestures and a piteous voice he would start a tragic tale, turning at the end to a grotesquerie. They heard the same jokes again and again and always laughed, especially if there was a guest present who was deceived by the solemn opening. His humor was anything but sophisticated. A typical story described a visitor's call at an insane asylum, where he met an inmate who complained that he had been unjustly confined. In John D.'s tag line the inmate concluded, "If you can't get me out, bring me a piece of dry toast. I'm a poached egg." Nelson recalls how one of his brothers, forgetting where he had heard this one, retold it to John D., winding up, "Bring me a piece of toast. I'm a poached egg."

After a grave silence his grandfather looked up.

"*Dry* toast, Brother," murmured the old man, who liked to get things right.

"What do the figures show?" he used to ask his grandsons. "It's the figures that count." Nelson still marvels at his astonishing grasp of detail—how, rousing from a nap, John D. would beckon him over to his Morris chair and ask searching questions about Rockefeller Center, for which Nelson, then fresh out of Dartmouth, was leasing office space. In his prime he had always been able to pinpoint the exact location of Standard tankers on distant seas, and in his eighties he would exasperate golfing partners by interrupting the game to search painstakingly for lost balls. He just liked to know where things were.

His approach to golf was typical of him. He took up the game at the turn of the century, after his doctor told him that he needed more recreation. Golf was then relatively new in this country. One of the few players John D. knew was Cettie, who was getting to be pretty good. He decided that he would get to be better on the sly. According to Joe Mitchell, the pro who tutored him, he proceeded with the same methods he had employed in tackling the oil industry: secrecy, cunning and resourcefulness.

Rubbers and an umbrella were strapped to his caddie, in case it rained. Then a watch was maintained by other youths, who would call out if Cettie drew near, whereupon John D. would vanish into a clump of bushes until she had passed. Alone once more, he would hammer croquet wickets over his feet to keep them in position while a boy, hired to stand opposite him, kept repeating, "Hold your head down! Hold your head down!" Next the old man chalked the face of his club, swung back, and uncoiled. If the ball's mark was in the center of the club he would cry, "See, see! Method, method!" If it wasn't, he would bow his head and mutter, "Shame, shame, shame." Finally, he hired a photographer to make a series of pictures of his stroke. Studying them, he developed fair distance. Ready at last, he strolled up to Cettie one day when she was squaring away on her first tee and remarked casually that it looked like a nice game; he might try it. To her astonishment he belted the ball 160 yards.

Until he discovered golf, the Baptist Church had provided his chief social life. As a young bookkeeper he had always rung the Sunday bell at Cleveland's Erie Street Baptist Mission. At seventeen he was a trustee of the church, sweeping its floors and washing its windows in his spare time; at nineteen he saved it from a $2,000 mortgage; for thirty years he was a Sunday school superintendent, and when his wife was in childbed he brought foolscap to church, took notes during the sermons, and repreached them to her at home.

During the week, life for the Rockefellers revolved around the morning Bible readings (with a penny fine for those who were late), the Friday evening prayer meeting, lantern slides shown by visiting missionaries and sessions at which the head of the household would lead the others in chanting: "Five cents a glass, does anyone think/That is really the price of a drink?"

To this day, a bottle of liquor is the one thing you cannot buy in Rockefeller Center, though the family's puritan discipline has relaxed a great deal since the days when ministers came and went in the West 54th Street home, and the rosewood sliding doors separating rooms on the first floor were thrown open to accommodate rapt congregations who sat erect on massive furniture between the dark red brocaded walls while speakers discussed charities, missions and the evils of booze, or led the group in prayer so solemn that, John D., Jr. noted in an essay written at the age of eleven, even the dog "would lie down under a chair and be very quiet until the exercises were over."

On trips John D. always took a minister along to preach at way stations and lead the family in rollicking hymns as their private train thundered across the country. At home Cettie served cold meals Sundays because it was a sin to cook then. Much as John D. loved ice skating, he wouldn't skate on the Sabbath or even direct workmen to flood his yard until 12:01 Monday morning. It is worth noting that Nelson taught Sunday school through four years at Dartmouth and took his first oath as Governor of New York on Cettie's old Bible.

On those rare occasions when reporters managed to corner John D., they would ask him to comment on Luke xviii, 25: "For it is easier for a camel to go through a needle's eye, than for a rich man to enter into the kingdom of God." He would quote the Scriptures back—"Seest thou a man diligent in his business? He shall stand before kings"—or simply say of his career: "I was right. I knew it as a matter of conscience. It was right between me and my God." Still, reconciling his piety and his great wealth wasn't that easy, and his determination to find another way is the explanation for his extraordinary philanthropies.

He had begun to tithe as a boy. While still a poor bookkeeper he bought a cheap ledger to record his contributions one by one ("Method, method!") and the ledger, which is extant, reveals that his first gift to the poor, wrung from his slender hoard during a winter when he himself was too poor to afford an overcoat was, symbolically, a dime. At the same time, he began contributing to the Underground Railroad. Belief in racial equality was a thread that ran through his entire life. It is significant that at the end of his life, he was the only white parishioner in a Negro church. Nelson points out that Spelman College in Atlanta, founded by John D. in 1881, was almost unique: "It's marvelous now to think of Grandfather giving money to a college for black women when higher education for *either* blacks *or* women was unheard of."

For the most part he gave as he earned, secretly. He liked to sit in church and scan the congregation for needy brethren; before leaving he would furtively press cash into deserving hands. They had to be deserving. He had to be sure that the money would do some good. His idea of bad charity was the annual dinner given for tramps by Cleveland's Five Points House of Industry. He did not want handouts, but results. As long as his largess was limited to the church, he could be sure he was getting them, but checking up became harder as his bounty grew. In 1891 he took the plunge into what Gates called wholesale philanthropy by establishing a big Baptist university in Chicago. Its grateful students sang: "John D. Rockefeller, wonderful man is he/Gives all his spare change to the U. of C."

"The good Lord gave me the money," he said, "and how could I withhold it from the University of Chicago?" That was always his attitude. He called his fortune "God's gold," and once he refused to get out of his car at the dedication of a project he had endowed because, he said, he hadn't had much to do with it; he had just given the money.

Altogether he donated $600 million to various causes, and John D., Jr., dispensed another $400 million, which comes to an even billion.

One of the difficulties in appraising John D.'s personality is that he often comes through as a caricature of himself. There is an explanation for this. Essentially a loner, he was hounded, decade after decade, by journalists and politicians who believed that the public had a right to know more about a man possessed of such power than this man was willing to divulge. They had a point, but he was never willing to concede it. Hence his camouflages, disguises and masquerades, John D.'s approach to public relations was, quite simply, to ignore the public.

Nevertheless, he had two Achilles' heels: his piety and his love of his family. Like many another industrialist, he longed to see his son succeed him in the corridors of power. But John D., Jr., Nelson's father, was cut from a different bolt of cloth. Deeply troubled by the arrogance of his father's lieutenants and sympathetic to the nascent labor movement, the son decided that he wanted a different career. He felt that he could best honor the Christian principles his father had taught him by devoting his life to almsgiving. And John D., always the shrewdest member of the family, understood and approved.

John D.'s influence on John D., Jr.'s, children is more diffuse, largely because the age gap is so great. The oldest of the titan's grandsons, John D. 3d, was five years old when the Supreme Court broke up the Standard Oil Trust. Nelson was born on his grandfather's sixty-ninth birthday. Understandably, their memories of him are hazy. But they are all firmly convinced that their civic activities are a contemporary expression of his Baptist faith. Like the sons of Joseph P. Kennedy, they were told early that they must justify their wealth by public service. The difference is that Rockefeller wealth is much greater than that of the Kennedys, and Rockefeller eleemosynary activities are consequently far more conspicuous.

The family's philanthropies include the Rockefeller Institute for Medical Research, five national parks, Colonial Williamsburg and countless other endowments whose beneficiaries are often unaware of where the money came from. Sociologists pore over the Lynds' "Middletown," birth control advocates over the work of Margaret Sanger and physicists over the studies of Fermi and Oppenheimer, unaware that Rockefeller money was behind each. Few librarians know of Rockefeller gifts to bibliothecae in Geneva and Tokyo, let alone the Library of Congress, and hardly any prostitutes are aware that John D., Jr., established the laboratory of social hygiene at the New York State Reformatory for Women.

At the end of his life the titan was baffled by the Depression. In 1894 he had stopped a panic with a European draft for 10 million dollars. After the 1929 crash, he placed a dramatic bid for a million shares of Jersey Standard at $50, tried to buck up confidence by saying that he and his son were buying common stocks, and gave $2 million for emergency relief in New York. It wasn't enough. In 1932 all he could say was, "God's in His heaven, all's right with the world."

Five years later, he died in Florida at the age of ninety-seven, hoarsely whispering to his valet, "Raise me up a little bit." The sexton of the Union Baptist Church tolled its steeple bell and posted the twenty-third Psalm, a favorite of John D.'s. For five minutes petroleum workers around the world stood in silent tribute to his memory. Everywhere his dimes had been saved and were treasured; one admirer, a ferry tender in Nyack, N.Y., proudly exhibited four of them to passengers. Bales of unsolicited flowers preceded mourners to the Cleveland cemetery where the family laird was buried between his mother and his wife, and John D., Jr., led his five sons in decorating nearby graves with overflow blossoms.

Yet the image of the New Moloch was not dead. Even as the old man lay in state, squads of state troopers were stalking intruders in the seventy miles of private roads behind the iron fence in Pocantico Hills, and after the family had left Cleveland, two cemetery guards, alert for cranks, began a three-month vigil. The Rockefellers had learned long ago that they could never escape the legend of their wealth.

John D. accepted that, but all his life he was curiously indifferent to the symbols of his affluence. Once when his securities filled a whole suite of safe-deposit rooms, a secretary begged him to come and see them. He went, poked a couple of drawers, and excused himself. He was always more drawn by the rituals of business than by its rewards.

Yet he was always moved by the highlights of his career. Even in old age, a glimpse of the building in which he first went to work as a bookkeeper could bring him to his feet, quivering with emotion. The anniversaries of his first job and his first partnership were red-letter days for him. When they rolled around he always ordered the flag at Pocantico Hills unfurled, to snap over his estate like a festive pennant. It is still hoisted on those days. Yet nobody notices it now. Today the Pocantico flag flies all the time.

Americana

Q. If you find so much that is unworthy of reverence in the United
States, then why do you live here?
A. Why do men go to zoos?

*Thus the catechism of H. L. Mencken, who nevertheless loved
American libertarianism with a passion that was as intense as it was
concealed. He said to me, "Be sure to tell 'em I've always been a patriot"—typical Menckenian mockery, but it is significant that his national identity was never far from his thoughts. He was aggressively un-
American, which made him a nonconformist and thus a true
American. In the case of Luella Mundel, described in these pages, President George Hand of Fairmont State College was asked in court for
his definition of an American. He replied that it was "the right to be
different." Mencken was certainly different. Yet he could quote the Bill
of Rights from memory. He believed in civil rights to the last limits of
the endurable. He was a genuine patriot.*

"Behind every great civilization," Christopher Dawson wrote in
The Dynamics of World History, *"there is a vision." In the United
States it is the vision of an open society. But there is more to a nation
than its psyche. In this country there are America's institutions, her incredible vitality, her cultural pluralism, and the stunning panorama of
her natural beauty, which, at present anyhow, still exists. Being more
of a continent than a nation, the United States offers a breathtaking variety of countrysides. As a New Englander, I feel a special affection for
my own corner of the land, but I've seen the rest of it, and I exult in
the Grand Canyon and the Mississippi, the dogwoods of Georgia and
the giant redwoods of California, the vastness of Texas and the broken
sod of Illinois.*

There is much that is mean in the United States, much that is ugly, and some that is shameful. The violence that runs through the American character is a national disgrace, and we shall never cleanse ourselves until we acknowledge it. What is chiefly interesting to me about the millions of words which have been published in denunciation of America, however, is that most of them have come from the pens of Americans. The United States has had plenty of critics abroad, particularly since her emergence as a superpower. But the sharpest prose, damning everything from the banalities of our small-town life and the wretched conditions in the ghettos to the CIA, has been written by citizens of the United States. The Momuses of Europe, Asia, Africa, and Latin America find the material for their polemics in our books. It was true in the days of Mencken. It is true in the days of Norman Mailer and Gore Vidal. The day it ceases to be true will be the day America betrays what Lincoln called "the last, best hope of earth."

You will not find much contempt for the republic's frailties in these pages, but the fact remains that I am free to condemn an evil President, scorn the national anthem, and take to the streets in demonstrations against a wicked American war. I have done all of these things, and the certainty that I can continue to do them is, for me, a source of great national pride.

Q. If you find so much that is unworthy of reverence in the United States, then why do you live here?

A. Where else is there so much freedom?

The Tribal American

ENCKEN ONCE FOUND a Maryland undertaker who had been in-
itiated eighteen times. "When he robes himself to plant a
fellow joiner he weighs three hundred pounds and sparkles
and flashes like the mouth of hell itself," Mencken reported. "He is entitled to wear seven swords, all jeweled, and to hang his watch chain
with the golden busts of nine wild animals, all with precious stones for
eyes. Put beside this lowly washer of the dead, Pershing newly polished
would seem almost like a Trappist."

Grotesque? No: merely a sublime example of a national quirk.
Alexis de Tocqueville called Americans the greatest joiners in the
world, but in his day the urge to join was simply a yen. Since then it
has become a lust. There are about a hundred million members of
leagues, councils, societies and clubs in the United States. Fraternal orders alone have some twenty million initiates, whose We feeling is
suggested by the names of their chapters—Temples, Shrines, Bethels,
Dens, Nests, Hives, Parlors, Tabernacles, Wigwams (Improved Order
of Red Men), Groves (United Ancient Order of Druids), Forests (Tall
Cedars of Lebanon), Pup Tents (Military Order of the Cootie) and
Aeries (Fraternal Order of Eagles).

Nor are swords and gilt busts extraordinary. You have only to see a
Knight of Columbus in his sash, baldric and plumed hat, or the
Supreme Queen of the Daughters of the Nile giving the year's password to sister queens in majestic gold coronets, to realize that America
is the shrine and aerie of mummery. In pomp and spangles, in cryptic
raps and knuckle-twisting grips, in arcana and palladia and abracadabra
our mystic brotherhoods are unmatched. "It's just like a Maori war
dance," John Marquand's sociologist says of a club outing in *Point of
No Return*, but he's wrong; the Maori doesn't live who could hold a
Masonic candle to the sunbursts of tribal America.

Even the Mau Mau couldn't touch them. A shiver of anticipation
ran through America's 125,000 lodges in the early 1950's, when it was
rumored that members of this Kenyan patriotic fraternity had devised a
blood-curdling new ritual. It turned out the bush was only bush league.
The initiation was warmed-over voodoo. The blood oath was on the
Tom Sawyer level; the post-ceremonial beer drinking was a crude parody of some of our magnificent initiation banquets. When it came to
mumbo jumbo, Mau Mau wasn't even in the same class with Hoo Hoo,
the American lumberman's fraternity, whose devotion to the black cat
and its sacred nine lives is so great that the lodge convenes only in the
ninth month, has nine officers, and charges new members exactly $9.99.

Joining wasn't invented in the United States. The Masons and the
Odd Fellows, our two largest orders, began as guilds in medieval
Europe. Daniel Defoe mentions the Odd Fellows; Freemasonry goes
back to the tenth century, and the Ancient Order of Hibernians is said
to have been traced to the eviction of a sixteenth-century Irish widow
named Molly Maguire. Africa's Egbo society has long had a complex
ladder of rites up which an ambitious warrior may advance, becoming,
in time, a sort of thirty-second-degree Egbo, and since Plato first observed Athenian lodges the institution has turned up in Borneo, among
the Plains Indians, and in northern Alaska, where Eskimo males still
withdraw to a separate hut they call the *kozge*.

It is in the United States, however, that the joiner has found his
palatinate. Scarcely anyone is immune. Mencken mocked the undertaker, but he himself was a faithful member of Baltimore's Saturday
Night Club. Marquand thought his fictitious sociologist ridiculous, but
when real sociologists invaded his hometown of Newburyport, Massachusetts (pop. 14,000), they found 357 formal associations and several
thousand cliques. Henry David Thoreau hated organized society so
much he preferred jail. Yet he is venerated today by the Thoreau Society, with a membership of about six hundred and fifty.

Some Americans join everything in sight. When the Attorney
General's List of Subversive Organizations was published, during the
Truman Administration, a Baltimore reporter discovered that he
belonged to eleven of them. He wasn't a Red. He just wanted to Belong. Inquiries have been addressed to at least one lodge that doesn't
even exist—the Knights of the Burning Pestle, after the title character
in a comedy written by Beaumont and Fletcher in 1613. Many years
ago a wag founded the Society for the Prevention of Calling Sleeping-
Car Porters George, specifying that only men named George need

apply. The S.P.C.S.P.G. was supposed to be a joke, but look who agreed to serve as officers: Senator George of Georgia, George M. Cohan, George Cardinal Mundelein, and, as Sergeant at Arms, George Herman Ruth. Franklin D. Roosevelt was always pledging something; he became a Mason, an Elk, an Odd Fellow, and a member of the AHEPA, a Greek-American society. John F. Kennedy was a Knight of Columbus and an Eagle—Aerie No. 1445. Chief Justice Earl Warren was an Odd Fellow, an Eagle and a Rotarian. Gerald Ford is a member of Phi Delta Phi, a Deke, and a Mason.

At first glance Rotary may seem out of place here. Like Kiwanis, the Lions, Civitan, Gyro and Cosmopolitan, it is a lunch club for businessmen eager to meet on the level and part on the square, and the only drums it beats are the tom-toms of service. Its boosters don't wear fancy pajamas or carry jeweled scepters, or prance around under glamorous banners. Their leaders aren't called Sapient Screechers or Great Incohonees, and the closest thing they have to a ritual is an occasional rule that a man late to lunch must wear his hat or sing a solo during the meal.

The tribes of backslap, in short, don't appear to be tribes at all. Yet each has its slogans, badges, high signs, oaths—tokens of what a philosopher described as "the umbilical cord that unites man with his fellow man in a primitive tribal society." One band of hustlers actually calls itself the Tribe of Yessir. Candidates answer a series of questions known collectively as the Tribal Pledge. (Q.: "Do you further pledge yourself not only to admit, but positively insist that —— is a real good town, full of good fellows, and that all the world is bright and sunny and getting brighter and sunnier constantly?" A.: "Yes, sir!") The service clubs, like other orders, exert a powerful influence over the dress, manners and beliefs of their votaries, and if they lack mystery, so, increasingly, do the classic brotherhoods; the Eagles have abolished their secret password, and Masonic liturgy is no longer the dark mystery it once was.

Here some understanding of tribal evolution is useful. Freemasonry, the first great American order, reached its zenith during the Revolution. The Boston Tea Party was a lark of Boston's St. Andrew's Lodge. The Redcoat alarm was spread by Paul Revere, Right Worshipful Grand Master of Massachusetts. Washington, Franklin, Patrick Henry, Tom Paine and John Paul Jones were ardent Masons, and so were most of the Signers of both the Declaration of Independence and the Constitution.

Masonic dominance continued until 1826, when it suffered a staggering blow; a Royal Arch Mason named William Morgan published everything he knew about the order. Morgan vanished—according to a shaft still standing in Old Batavia Cemetery, midway between Rochester and Buffalo, New York, he was murdered—and for a while all societies, including Phi Beta Kappa, had a thin time. In 1832 feeling against the Masons was so strong that an Anti-Masonic party was formed. It carried only one state, Vermont, but the order was badly shaken.

There was a growing demand for new lodges, however, and since Masons knew the ropes they founded or wrote rituals for a glittering array of brotherhoods, including the Knights of Pythias, the Ancient Order of United Workmen, the Modern Woodmen of America, the Grange, and the Noble and Holy Order of the Knights of Labor, America's first real union. Freemasonry itself began to undergo a kind of cellular division—today there are fifty orders allied to the original rites.

Still other Masons were establishing college fraternities, whose ceremonies borrowed heavily from Masonic rubrics, or joining such Victorian curiosities as the Supreme Mechanical Order of the Sun, the Prudent Patricians of Pompeii, the Improved Order of Heptasophs, and the Red, White and Blue Lodge (three degrees; the top men were bluebloods). Meanwhile actors and writers had created the Loyal Order of Moose and the Benevolent and Protective Order of Elks. The stampede was on. By the 1890's there were so many societies in the land that William McKinley, campaigning from his front porch, could address an endless procession of marching clans.

Later the more absurd lodges died of embarrassment. Yet wherever one fell, a dozen sprang up. As de Tocqueville had predicted, Americans were forming associations of every sort, "religious, moral, serious, futile, general or restricted, enormous or diminutive." They are still forming them. Today Freemasonry is stronger than ever—one out of every twelve American men belongs—and the National Fraternal Congress reports that the rest of the brotherhoods are booming too.

There have been some changes. Among the newer organizations, for example, the American weakness for what John Quincy Adams called "childish pageantry" seems to be diminishing somewhat. As America grows more urbane its tribes are becoming smoother, quieter, broader in the tie and longer in the coif. There is less emphasis on hieroglyphics, more on social skills.

But this is only a difference in packaging. Here and there lapel pins have replaced robes, that's all. The motives of tribesmen haven't changed a jot. "Man is a gregarious animal," I was told by the secretary-treasurer of the Fraternal Congress, "and he still seeks the company of other men and women." Behind the pink geniality of the luncheoneer's meeting, behind the cigars inserted in the elliptical faces, lies the same feeling of security that members of the Mafia, a nonservice club, acquire from those they call *gli amici*, the brethren. The first Rotarian, Paul P. Harris, put it peppily: "Here's the foundation of success, the practicalized, sterilized, scientized, vitalized, idealized foundation of your success, my success, the world's success—acquaintance, the dynamics and harmonics of Rotary."

Joiners do join for various reasons, of course. This woman acquires prestige from the Junior League, that one from the National Secretaries Association. A realtor discovers that all the big men in town are Shriners, a grocery clerk gets a thrill out of being High Priest on lodge night, a henpecked husband yearns for the distinction of the thirty-second-degree Freemasonry, or of the Knights of Columbus fourth degree or the seventh degree of the Grange. At bottom, however, every member is drawn by the dynamics and harmonics of acquaintance, and this craving for herd warmth binds all American voluntary associations, from the pals of the Exchange Club to the sheeted creeps of the Ku Klux Klan; from Vogue, the high-school sorority, to the Minute Women manning the watchtowers of the republic.

The need for group stimuli is no respecter of class lines. Once the lodge was regarded as a sort of non-U country club, but a recent study revealed that the typical joiner is a middle-aged college graduate with either a profession or an executive position. The report should have surprised no one. Our tribes have always attracted eminent people, and not all of them have been Americans. George Washington brought Lafayette into Freemasonry at Valley Forge, and Benjamin Franklin taught Voltaire the Masonic grip. Florence Nightingale followed the gleam of the Eastern Star (Masonic women); a Speaker of the House wrote a degree for the Rebekahs (Odd Fellows' women). All Catholic archbishops wear the breastplates of the Knights of Columbus, and virtually every United States Senator belongs to something. It's good politics, of course, but as a rule public men make solemn brothers. During the Revolution, when a British military lodge lost its Masonic paraphernalia in battle, Washington returned it with a guard of honor. A mayor of New York said that he felt the fraternal spirit whenever he came into a room full of chairs, and FDR had the White House closed to visitors while he took three Pythian degrees.

Among less eminent members lodge loyalty may transcend every other tie. Let the klaxon wind and the faithful drop everything. A Lions convention attracts thirty-five thousand roaring beasts. Fifty thousand stamp collectors assembled in New York not long ago, and there have been cases of boosters who, told that the Local attendance record was in jeopardy, insisted on being carried to meetings on litters. James J. Davis wouldn't serve as Harding's Secretary of Labor until he had been assured that his duties wouldn't interfere with his Moose work. When Admiral Peary reached the North Pole he planted the American flag and then, right under it, the standard of Delta Kappa Epsilon. "Next to God," said an Episcopalian bishop, "I love dear old Psi U."

Sophisticates may jeer, but the joiner jeers right back. Dedicated tribesmen are likely to look upon nontribesmen as outcasts. College Greeks call nonfraternity men Barbs or Culls. To Red Men all beyond the glow of the Council Fire are Palefaces; to Klansmen non-Klansmen are Aliens. A German sociologist concluded that the American who isn't a member of any club at all is "a sort of pariah," and an American Legion commander looked forward to the day "when any man eligible to become a member of the Legion, who does not belong, will be looked upon with suspicion, and justly so, by the community where he lives." Everybody should join, the compulsive joiner argues, because everybody can.

That's not strictly true. Most groups are selective—that's the point of the thing. Freemasonry picks its men; so do Boy Scout troops. The discriminatory character of high-school societies has inspired half the states to pass restrictive laws, which are widely flouted by junior joiners. One of the initiation props of the Independent Order of Odd Fellows is Moses' rod, "to smite the high, thick walls of prejudice which shut away man from his fellows"; nevertheless the order itself shuts away black fellows. That is the significance of the name—it became independent of the Grand Lodge of England after the two had disagreed about racial barriers in America. *La Société des Quarante Hommes et Huit Chevaux,* the fun-loving affiliate of the American Legion, similarly excludes black veterans. Virtually all fraternal orders are segregated. An exception is the Knights of Columbus, but a Supreme Knight once admitted to me that local lodges are free to use the racial blackball.

Still, if one hall won't give you the password, you can always shop around. Individual tribes may be exclusive, but the system itself is inclusive. Somewhere there's a crowd that wants you. If you dislike "going through the chairs" of Odd Fellowship, or find the thirty-two steps of the Masons' Scottish Rite tedious, there are the quick, painless single-degree orders: the Moose, the Elks, the Eagles. And the mystic brotherhoods are only the beginning. We have national organizations for euthanasia enthusiasts, simpler spellers, astrologists, soap sculptors, truant officers, twins, trailer owners, shut-ins, homing-pigeon racers, baby-sitters, autograph collectors, parachutists, left-handed golfers, and short men, whose motto is, "We Shall Undercome."

There are Golden Age clubs for senior citizens and, for people who want to Take Off Pounds Sensibly, TOPS. Sundry societies study African violets, tropical fish or internal secretions. Men (women) born in California may belong to the Sons (Daughters) of the Golden West, and people who think that historians have libeled Aaron Burr are welcome at the Aaron Burr Association, whose President General happens to be a man named Burr.

Drunks can join Alcoholics Anonymous. Drug addicts are eligible for Narcotics Anonymous. Associations await ex-Rhodes Scholars, ex-FBI men, ex-airline hostesses and ex-rural letter carriers; others entice the Friends of Children's Museums and the Defenders of Furbearers. Godmothers have a League, grandmothers a Federation, women who have christened ships a Society.

Our tribal press alone is staggering. Men who have become heads of companies before the age of forty are Young Presidents and read *Enterprise*. Cheerleaders get *The Megaphones*; amputees *The Amp*; members of the National Puzzlers' League *The Enigma*. The Society for the Preservation and Encouragement of Barbershop Quartet Singing in America puts out *The Harmonizer*, and its female auxiliary, the Sweet Adelines, issues *Pitch Pipe*.

Any common enthusiasm is sufficient reason to form a clan. Once the vows are taken the enthusiasm may wane, but the fellowship has a life of its own. After all, Freemasons haven't built a cathedral in centuries. Mah Jongg belongs to the 1920's, but the Mah Jongg League has an enrollment of 150,000. Nearly a century has passed since the Knights of Pythias had any connection with civil servants, though it was started by them, and most Elks and Moose have forgotten their artistic origins. Sometimes an association doesn't appear until long after the event it commemorates—the Blizzard Club, honoring the blow of '88, wasn't founded until 1940—though here we get into something else: the tribal reverence for the past which one historian of American organizations calls ancestor worship.

The seed for American ancestor worship was sown in 1783, when George Washington's officers established the Society of the Cincinnati and decided that membership should descend to their children accord-

ing to the English law of primogeniture. Washington was appalled by
the hereditary provision, but the Cincinnati has flourished ever since.
Moreover, the society's refusal to broaden its qualifications led to the
Sons of the Revolution, which led to the D.A.R., which led to all sorts
of extraordinary things.

The National Society of the Colonial Dames wasn't satisfied with
tracing its members' pedigrees back to independence. To be a bona fide
Dame, you had to have a forefather in the colonies by 1750. Having
made the D.A.R. look tacky, the Dames in turn were upstaged by the
Descendants of Colonial Governors Prior to 1750, the Colonial Lords
of Manors in America, the Jamestowne Society (for people whose fore-
bears lived in Jamestowne before 1700), and the Mayflower Descendants.

The Mayflower should have been the end, but it wasn't. The
Baronial Order of Runnemede was founded for those who had an ancestor on a certain English meadow between Windsor and Staines on
June 15, 1215, and the Order of Three Crusades "traces genealogy of
persons descended from a participant in one of the first three crusades."

It was fated that someone should remember the Crusades. They
are ancient and, more important, they were martial. Military snobbery
is one of the great spawners of American tribes. Any war will do—there
are associations named for every campaign, including the Boxer Rebellion (Imperial Order of the Dragon) and the Archangel Expedition of
1918–1919 (Polar Bears)—though the two world wars have proved to be
the most fertile. Quite apart from the big veterans' organizations, we
have the Seabee Veterans, American Ex-Prisoners of War, the Military
Order of the Purple Heart, the Legion of Valor, for holders of high
decorations; the Retreads, who wore the uniform in both wars; and the
Fighter Aces, whose members have shot down five enemy planes.

Old soldiers are clannish everywhere, of course; one thing that sets
America apart is the remarkable number of organizations for survivors
of the home front. Tribes sound assembly for War Dads, discharged
WAC's, former nurses, even for conscientious objectors. Our women
have established a kind of Valkyrie whose adjuncts include the Moms
of America; the Gold Star Wives; two separate associations of Gold Star
Mothers; Cosmo, for war brides; and the Lady Bugs, who beckon to relatives of men who have served abroad.

Most commemorative societies erect a plaque now and then and let
it go at that. There are exceptions. The United Daughters of the Confederacy try to shame the descendants of Sherman's soldiers into sending their loot back to Georgia. The D.A.R. has taken stands on every-

thing from the United Nations and the Supreme Court to fluoridation, and one of its chapters once urged that women raped by the enemy in wartime be declared wounded in action.

Essentially, the difference between plaques and lobbying is of no consequence. The point is that every organization must have *some* purpose, must be about *something*. Goals may be quite vague. The Kiwanian motto is "We Build." Lions growl, "We Serve." League of Women Voter units study problems. Other leagues get down to cases. The National Sling Shot Association promotes "the sport of sling shooting," the National Association of Gagwriters "the production of laughs," the American Sunbathing Association "the advancement of nudism"; and 300,000 white-ribboned women of the W.C.T.U. have sworn eternal hostility to every form of bottled tragedy. Yet all these come down to the same thing. Each tribe needs a totem.

Certain aims are common. Most societies are vehemently American. In the 1950's a cluster of I'm-a-better-American-than-you-are tribes sprang up—Birchers, Christian Crusaders, Circuit Riders, Liberty Lobbyists, National Indignation Rallies. They offered nothing new to the social anthropologist. You can't be an Elk and be, or ever have been, a Communist. The pledge of allegiance is mandatory at meetings of clubmen and brethren, including Klansmen, and sometimes it is accompanied by inspirational lyrics ("Lift up thine eyes! The flag passes by!"). An Eagle Haus in free Berlin helps escapees from the East, and Odd Fellows receive reports from underground lodges behind the Curtain. Anyone under the impression that the men of the Shrine are just a bunch of fezzed clowns was set straight when the Past Imperial Potentate served notice on the Kremlin that "the eight hundred thousand Shriners of North America, each having placed his trust in God and standing foursquare for God, for Country and *our* Flag, shall stand like a mighty phalanx, opposing this scourge from Hell until their arms shall strike no longer and their tongues shall speak no more, defiantly saying to the hordes of Communism, 'Thou shalt not pass!'"

"Foursquare for God!" could be an interfraternal motto. In the brotherhoods piety is even more important than patriotism. It is rarely a sectarian reverence, but candidates must be prepared to testify that they believe in a Supreme Being, or, if they want to be Improved Red Men, in the Great Spirit. A Bible lies beside the flag in Eagle initiations, on an embroidered cloth in Knights of Pythias ceremonies, under crossed swords during sessions of the Scottish Rite's Supreme Council. The mighty Grange devotes its fifth degree to the lessons of faith. Lions remind you that Jesus was the Lion of the Tribe of Judah, and several fraternal names have had Biblical origins—Job's Daughters (Job 42:15), for example, and the Neighbors of the Modern Woodmen of America (Proverbs 27:10). There was a time when Odd Fellows really believed that Odd Fellowship was builded upon the Rock of Peter, an illusion which understandably irritated theologians.

Clerics have been peeved at other societies too. Jurisdictional disputes were inevitable; with their regalia, ceremonies and teachings the brotherhoods often serve as informal sects. Their power has waxed as the power of the church has waned—it has waxed, indeed, for that very reason. In attempting to make the glory of the Lord shine round about the brethren, some ritualists have treated Scripture as a lodge tract and usurped the sacraments of the church. They have never baptized babies or performed marriages, but they have been in there at the end with their own cemeteries, burial rites, epitaphs, funeral chants. ("There is gloom upon each feature, there is sadness in each eye, as the lengthy train of brothers passes slowly, sadly by.")

Once fraternal intrusions inspired wrath in the pulpit—Pope Leo XIII attacked Freemasonry as a "foul plague," and one minister asked the women of his congregation, "Do you want your husbands and sons to be brought up under the influence of a ball-loving fraternity?" Today the cloth is more or less reconciled. The Vatican is on the best of terms with the Catholic Knights of Columbus, and many a clergyman has become a joiner himself.

The humanistic character of associations is their most admirable aspect. They are tribes, but they are benign tribes. The solace they offer their members doesn't stop with the ritual. Funerals became important to them in the first place because frequently it was the lodge that was paying the undertaker. The understanding was that you paid a dollar whenever a brother died, and when you died, the rest of the brothers would pay to bury you. This chain-letter principle started a century ago with the Ancient Order of United Workmen, whose leader was felicitously named Father Upchurch. The concept evolved into cheap life insurance and is the core of such orders as the Knights of Columbus, the Vikings, the Maccabees, the Royal Arcanum and the Ancient Order of Hibernians. Some members don't want it, but ten million Americans know a good thing, and they are covered by a four-teen-billion-dollar bursary.

In a sense this is another dimension of the search for group protection which led the joiner to join in the first place. "You can spend a lifetime in Odd Fellowship," the Odd Fellows say, and you can; there are sixty-four homes for men of the three links (Friendship, Love, Truth) who are old or down on their luck. Moosehaven, Florida; the Elks estate at Bedford, Virginia; the Pythian homes—all are sanctuaries where elderly brothers await the last thump of the gavel.

Tribes have always worked this way. Men take care of others so that one day others will take care of them. In America, however, the light of collective benevolence takes on a brighter radiance. Dear as security is to the joiner, the happiness of children is even dearer, and so we find the Eagles providing college scholarships for the children of brothers killed in war, and the Moose running an entire city, Mooseheart, Illinois, in which it has raised more than five thousand orphans of the order.

Childhood has a special significance for brethren. At least one American fellowship was founded by men who just wanted to relive the boyhood excitement of Halloween. Later that lodge turned into the Invisible Empire of the Ku Klux Klan, but elsewhere sentiment still rears its violin-shaped head. Whenever Moose are gathered at 9 P.M., they are expected to "stand with arms folded and heads bowed . . . and remember our children at Mooseheart," and it was a Moose who said, "No man stands so tall or so straight as when he stoops to lift a child." The Knights of Columbus specialize in "boyology"; the Shriners call their seventeen hospitals for crippled children "temples of baby smiles."

But tribesmen give far more than bathos, and no order confines its gifts to members of its own tribe. Nationally they build clinics, contribute to Boys Town, and run marbles tournaments and soap-box derbies, while local lodges provide eyeglasses for myopic students, subsidize Boy Scout troops, buy watches for playground supervisors, show movies at Christmas, and hide Easter eggs and give the finders prizes.

The joiner's generosity isn't confined to youth. If orphans need help, so do all who are homeless and friendless and sick. To true brothers and doers every call for help is a call to the clan. Some Samaritans specialize. The Tall Cedars of Lebanon fight muscular dystrophy, the Veiled Prophets of the Enchanted Realm (also called the Grotto) help victims of cerebral palsy. The Lions concentrate on the blind and, being businessmen, keep an annual audit of their good deeds, of which there are over 500,000 every year.

Other associations aren't so tidy, but charity is habitual with them; it's one of the ways you can spot an American tribe. High-school sororities contribute to the Community Chest. The D.A.R. publishes a civic manual for immigrants. In emergencies the Legion is an arm of the

Red Cross. Every day in every way clubs are beautifying communities, visiting the sick, giving blood, holding rummage sales to help poor farms in the county or working in other ways to insure domestic tranquillity and promote the general welfare. Even the KKK, plodding its lonely road, passes the wool hat for churches.

It's a lucky thing our tribes are eleemosynary, because if they ever took another tack they'd be hard to stop. They have vitality, men in power, and immense wealth—some ten billions in assets, including the land under Yankee Stadium, which belongs to the Knights of Columbus. Quiet as they are, they have altered American life in countless ways. "Under God" was added to the pledge of allegiance at the insistence of the Knights. The D.A.R. started teacher oaths, the Lions introduced white canes for blind men. Clubwomen started juvenile courts. Until recently the Legion of Decency had a lot to say about the movies you see, and if "The Star-Spangled Banner" is played in public, you will rise, because Colonial Dames spread the word that sitting was disrespectful. Authors cowed by the Daughters of the Confederacy call the Civil War the War Between the States. Newspapers attentive to the S.P.C.A. run pictures of lost dogs, and Rotary was responsible for Chicago's first public comfort station.

The Grange gave us rural free delivery and Cabinet rank for the Secretary of Agriculture. The Eagles screamed for the Social Security Act, and Brother Roosevelt, in signing it, acknowledged the fact by presenting the pen to the order. Lately, balding Eagles have been trying to outlaw employer discrimination against older men. They are working through fraternal lobbies, which is the way most tribes get things done—or rather, the way they get things done now. During the War Between the States the Knights of the Golden Circle tried to seize Indianapolis Arsenal, and in 1866 fifteen hundred Fenians actually invaded Canada with a hazy plan for liberating Ireland.

Another Irish order, the Hibernians, was blamed for the Molly Maguire murders in Pennsylvania. The connection was denied, though the Mollies were all members of that Ancient Order and used its passwords. In the end the leaders of the Mollies were caught by Pinkertons and hanged. The captain of the Pinkertons had an odd fate. To obtain evidence he had posed as a member of the society and adopted its customs, which included the drinking of tremendous draughts of cheap liquor. Unhappily, he was allergic to bad whiskey. After the trial all his hair fell out.

Today the chief Hibernian activity is marching in St. Patrick's Day parades—a grand sight and one of our great tribal feasts, ranking with Mother's Day (another Eagle first) and fraternal conventions. All conventions are tribal, and all tribes have conventions. The pressure to convene is irresistible. Each year ten million Americans head for twenty thousand blowouts, where they don celluloid badges, subsist on a diet remarkably like that of Federal penitentiaries, and consume enough setups to harrow the ghost of the hairless Pinkerton. Chicago, with as many as twenty-seven conclaves on a single day, is the convention capital of the country, but clans can assemble anywhere. Lawyers have convened in London, Rotary met in Tokyo one year, and several festive clans have sailed off on Caribbean liners.

Cruises are out for most tribes, not because of the expense but because there isn't a vessel afloat that could meet the delegates' requirements. Every occasion has its special demands. Veterinarians must have cages for animals. Bowlers want miles of alleys. Dining-car stewards look for vast kitchens to serve them elaborate meals, and the hairy-chested orders need arenas for he-man-sized blasts.

Parades alone may last seven hours—a Shriner march engages over a hundred bands, twenty-five thousand Nobles and assorted troops of horses, camels and jackasses. One ball for Lions and their lionesses filled Madison Square Garden and two hotels; one clan hired a new cement mixer to shake up the tossed salad. Even if a ship had the resources, the problem of nomenclature would remain. Conventions are rarely called conventions. They are Camporees, Jamborees, Encampments or Wrecks, and the trembling ground beneath each becomes an Oriental Kingdom, a Realm or a Desert. How could the Red Men hold a Hunting Ground on a boat deck?

Some tribes are pallid. They park their wives in hotel rooms, huddle demurely and listen to speakers over closed-circuit television. No firecrackers for them, no nonstop busts, no cocked hats or flashing satin pants. They never get drunk and chase drum majorettes down corridors, never derail streetcars or steal a traffic cop's revolver. The memories they carry home are a montage of ashtrays, water pitchers and aspirins. Obviously these dull bands lack the true joiner spirit. The business of tribal America is more likely to be non-business, at least when the faithful assemble. It is slapstick, showmanship, and Barnum burlesque, and it reaches its gala, confetti-sprinkled summit in the annual jousts of the show-off orders.

These are the lodges for joiners with tired blood. They have been created out of older associations; candidates must belong to the parent order first. The idea is that men need to let off steam after the strain of fraternal duties. Some brethren are elevated by the ruffles and flourishes of marching units—the drum corps of the Grand Aerie, say, or the Knights of Columbus Zouaves, or Odd Fellowship's Patriarchs Militant, whose dashing uniforms are approved by Congress, and whose general is entitled to wear five stars in a circle, like a General of the Army.

Other brothers prefer Keystone Cop buffoonery. For them there are the playground organizations, where a man can take pratfalls without tarnishing the sacred name of the true fraternity. A Knight of Pythias on a toot is a Knight of Khorassan. A Legionnaire dons a light-blue hat and is transformed into a member of the Forty and Eight. The Ancient Mystic Order of Samaritans is the rumpus room of Odd Fellows, and Master (Third Degree) Masons are eligible for the Grotto and the Tall Cedars. The most spectacular playground of all, the Ancient Arabic Order of the Nobles of the Mystic Shrine, is for the Masonic elect, and even this has foaled its own society-within-a-society, the Royal Order of Jesters, whose motto is "Mirth is king."

Shriners are kings of mirth. If Legionnaires fire live ammunition in a hotel lobby, the Nobles go one up by populating other lobbies with exotic animals. If Georgia Elks try to buy souvenirs with Confederate money, members of the Ancient Arabic Order appear wearing twenty-dollar bills as eyeshades and riding horses fitted with horn-rimmed spectacles. They are past masters of the boutonniere that lights up, the exploding cigar, the paper bag of water dropped from the second-story window, and the misplaced men's room sign. A bearded Noble in a passing taxi removes his fez—he is a chimpanzee. Male bellies throb like bellows in a fleshy hula—it is the faithful from the Honolulu Oasis, performing for the Imperial Potentate and his Divan. And when the Pote arrives for his Enthronement, an electric carpet gives him a fiendish shock.

Shocks are also designed for feminine pedestrians. To convening funnymen, every skirt is a challenge: somehow its hem must be lifted. Buzzer sticks, jets of air and sprays of freezing ethyl chloride usually inspire satisfactory leaps, and if these don't work, a bunch of fellows can always form a circle around a woman and make her leap over their interlocked arms.

Convention cities are tolerant toward these raffish digressions. No one believes they mean a thing. Yet it is just possible that they mean more than all the bells, books and candles in all the rituals in the land. A key to any tribal society is its regulation of sex. Primitive sects lock up virgins and regard matrimonial decisions as a privilege of the men's lodge. American tribes don't work that way, and the joiner sallying forth to pinch a leg may be a creature of atavistic instinct, grimly avenging all his lost rights.

He has lost more than authority; he has lost its very symbol. The lodge is no longer his domain. In its heyday, American Freemasonry was as virile as the Eskimo's *kozge*. Morgan, the squealer, said that the order forbade the initiation of "an atheist, irreligious libertine, idiot, madman, hermaphrodite"—or, last on the list—"woman." After his disappearance, the wives of Masons began to rebel against this sexism. Morgan had disclosed that no brother was permitted to violate another brother's women, and it was argued, with some logic, that the only way to make assurance doubly sure was to give the ladies the Masonic sign of distress.

They never got it, but they formed the Eastern Star anyway. This celestial body now has three million followers. Womenfolk of other Master Masons may join the Amaranth or the Golden Chain or, if their husbands are Shriners, the Daughters of the Nile. A rib of the Improved Order of Red Men is the Degree of Pocahontas; Maccabees are married to Ladies of the Maccabees; women of the Moose gather under the spreading antlers.

Some men continue to be sour about mixed societies. After nearly seventy years the Cincinnati refuses to affiliate with the Daughters of the Cincinnati, and the Knights of Columbus remain aloof from the chesty tribettes of Ladies of Columbus and Columbiettes. But these holding actions are as futile as the struggles of a black widow spider's mate. Experience suggests that while the world may little note nor long remember the high jinks of the Forty and Eights, it will be listening to their ladies for some time after the last legionnaire has blown his last spitball at his last spree.

In the past, women concentrated on church work and left fraternities to men, but in the 1960's the *American Journal of Sociology* noted that the higher a wife's social position, the more tribal activity was expected of her. Masculine stubbornness has merely swelled the rolls of such organizations as the National Association of Women Lawyers and the League for a Woman for President. Undoubtedly the monasticism of Rotary is responsible for Soroptimists and Pilot International, the businesswomen's booster clubs, which European men regard with glazed horror.

Pilot International for grown girls, Key International for female teenagers—so the web spreads, and the men of the tribe have less and

less they can call their own. The Key clubs suggest a further devalua-
tion of the coin of male status. Children's singing acts no longer satisfy
children; they want lodges of their own. It is now possible for them to
start associational activity in grade school. They become Little
Leaguers, Cubs, Brownies, Future Teachers of America. In the
brotherhoods boys belong to De Molay, the Junior Knights, the Junior
Odd Fellows; their sisters are Rainbow Girls, Sunshine Girls, Job's
Daughters or Theta Rhos.

If they don't have memberships of their own, they just tag along
with Dad. Atlantic City hotels employ masses of baby-sitters, because
entire families arrive for conventions, and a recent Lions get-together in
Chicago staged a rock-'n'-roll dance for six thousand. The Lions had
brought their prides.

This togetherness is having a zany effect on the orders. On the one
hand, most of them note a decline in attendance at meetings. The old
masculine haunt, with its starred mirror, glass chandelier and shabby
card tables, is suffering. Red Men offer engraved tomahawks to encourage recruiting; some societies are electing local officers by mail. On the
other hand, social membership is rising. Lodges with Bingo, slot machines and rathskellers aren't worried about backsliding, and those with
ballrooms and swimming pools—attractions for the whole family—report
that knighthood is in flower.

Observing all this, what would the tribesman of another land
think? We can picture him ceremoniously slitting the throat of a white
cock in Malaya, or enjoying an old-time circumcision rite in Samoa, or
squatting solemnly with his fellow studs in the Naga Hills to touch a
tiger's tooth and munch a bit of his ancestors' bones. We can imagine
him turning to examine American pageantry, and we can predict some
of his reactions. He would understand Dekes whacking pledges with
inch-thick paddles. He wouldn't understand the Klan vision of ghostly
riders in the sky, but he would be impressed by it, and the cabala of the
Kickapoos and the Lu Lus and the Bagmen of Bagdad would send him
groveling in the village dust, convinced that he was in the power of superior sorcerers.

But suppose he then glanced up and beheld the ladies of the Marine Corps League Auxiliary cakewalking by in dress-blue uniforms?
Suppose the ranks parted to reveal an Elks' mixed bar and bar-b-q, and
suppose this was followed by a glimpse of family bowling night at a co-
tribal lodge, with all the Nobles, Queens, Princes and Daughters
cavorting together in unisex pants suits?

What could the overseas brother possibly infer? Would he regard it as a hex, a hoax or the greatest marvel of all? The answer is as obscure and inscrutable as *omertà*, the Black Hand's terrible oath of secrecy. We can't even speculate. The cultural castration of the American male doesn't bear thinking about. To invoke the motto of the now defunct Get There America Benefit Association: "Mum's the Word."

The New York Times

MOST NEWSPAPERMEN SECRETLY ADMIRE *The Front Page,* and in one of the lines they cherish a Chicago police reporter growls, "I was on a New York paper once—the *Times.* You might as well work in a bank." Laymen may think this churlish. The *Times,* after all, is our one pukka newspaper. But that is precisely the problem. Its awesome majesty is disquieting to raffish members of the sodality, whose attitude toward their craft was eloquently expressed in a filthy Korean press hut by Homer Bigart, when he plucked a louse from his person and declared, "Let's face it, gentlemen. This is a low profession."

The *Times* disagrees. In its editorial chambers a few dark steps from the wanton glare of Times Square, journalism is upper church and pinstriped. It has never been otherwise. Henry J. Raymond, starting his straight news sheet ten years before the Civil War, set out to please "the best portion of our citizens." Adolph S. Ochs, the former Chattanooga typesetter who snatched it from its creditors in 1896, rejoiced that reading it was "a stamp of respectability." Today circulation posters recommend it to "rising executives," and even Consulting Editor Ted Bernstein, a crusader against flat prose, says the paper "does not entertain; it informs." That means no Zsa Zsa, no Love Nests Bared —and, as the small son of any subscriber can tell you, no funnies.

It also means an *éclat* which is the envy of the bawdiest tabloid. Virtually every President since McKinley has started his day with the *Times.* An Eisenhower train passing through Grand Central Station paused while Secret Service men picked up armloads of first editions, and Winston Churchill, out of touch for a few days, cabled for back copies. It was to the *Times* that Charles Lindbergh turned when he wanted photographs of his kidnaped baby distributed, in the *Times* that official Washington has read important state documents from the

British White Paper of 1914 to the Pentagon Papers. People in the know either tell *Times* men or, as often, find out from them. The late Anne O'Hare McCormick once asked a diplomat if he could add anything to an account in the paper. "Good heavens, no, Anne," he said. "Where do you think we're getting our information?" And when Sputnik I was successfully launched, Russian missile experts meeting in their Washington embassy heard about it from the *Times* reporter who was covering them.

One reason people confide in the *Times* is its prestige—its men have won over two-score Pulitzer prizes—and another is its integrity. The *Times* is devoted to news. Its editors often chuck anywhere from eight to forty columns of advertisements for a good yarn. But if they think an article will damage the public interest, they scrap it. Among the stories they have suppressed over the years are an exclusive interview with Kaiser Wilhelm, a New York scandal which would have shaken municipal credit, and the imminent failure of a city bank— though the paper had $17,000 on deposit there and lost it when the doors closed. Other newspapers were delighted to print tart notes from Harry Truman; Editor Charles Merz acknowledged receiving several "lively letters" from him, but none was published. He wouldn't have dreamed of needlessly embarrassing the White House. The Presidency, after all, is a national institution, like the *Times*.

Like the Presidency, the paper has had to pay the price of eminence. It bears the traditional scars of journalism—Winston Churchill's American grandfather, an early stockholder, for example, defended the office with a primitive machine gun during the draft riots of 1863, and a recent letter to the editor bore the piquant address, "Left-Wing Department, Un-American Fluoridation Director." Being the *Times*, however, it has acquired enemies more august than plug-uglies and crackpots. As a world newspaper it has been threatened by potentates, dictators, and offended governments, including its own. James "Scotty" Reston attracted the professional interest of the FBI after he was slipped the Dumbarton Oaks documents, and twice *Times* men have been haled before Senate committees—in 1915, on the charge that they had been bought by British gold, and in 1956 when Senator Eastland hunted Reds on the staff. More recently, of course, it was on the receiving end of the Nixon administration's big guns. Under fire the *Times* is serene. Its attitude toward traducers is reflected in a note Arthur Hays Sulzberger, Ochs' son-in-law and the publisher between 1935 and 1961, wrote to himself before testifying at a hearing. "Keep calm," it read. "Smile; don't be smart."

Even *Times* gentility is an inviting target. Hecklers dub the paper The Old Gray Lady, The Good Gray *Times* and, meanest of all, The National Biscuit Company. Those taunts don't come from the rabble, who rarely see it; Harrison Salisbury, covering juvenile gangs for the *Times,* became known to them as "the man from the *News,*" because that was the only daily the cats read. The paper's critics are literate, but titillated by the reluctance with which the *Times* yields to the times. It was twenty years old before it carried a headline wider than one column; once it ran six years without a byline. In 1945 it was still spelling "Dunkirk" "Dunkerque" because the newsroom atlas said so. "Eisenhower" and "Rockefeller" were cast in narrower type to squeeze them into manageable headline space. The world might call them "Ike" and "Rocky," but *Times* men dasn't.

New Yorkers are proud of the paper's starch. When the late Meyer "Mike" Berger quoted someone as saying that the racketeer "Dutch" Schultz was a "pushover for a blonde," Dutch was outraged. "What kind of language is that to use in the *New York Times?*" he protested. Old subscribers would take satisfaction in knowing that as late as 1937 the chief editorial writer worked in a frock coat, striped trousers, and wing collar, that Merz wrote his editorials in longhand, and that he and Sulzberger occasionally composed Double-Crostics, though once they lost an answer and had a terrible time solving it. Now and then, however, *Times* conservatism gets a bit thick. It is all very well to outlaw such newly created words as "percentagewise" and "finalize," but too often fidelity to style ends in what Bernstein acidly calls "deadheads"—"Symposium Scheduled," "Institute to Open," or, disastrously, "Flies to Receive Nobel Prize." Sometimes the determination to be correct has ended in outright fiasco, as when the paper insisted that an ad featuring a futuristic line drawing of a nude be enhanced by a futuristic bra, or when Sulzberger, lunching with an eminent Latin American, decided it would be gracious to say something in Spanish. Unfortunately, as Arthur Krock later recalled, the publisher had memorized the wrong phrase, and at the door he murmured a dulcet farewell which, translated, meant, "Wipe your face, you dirty pig, your snout is greasy."

It is easy to exaggerate this sort of thing. Tweakers of the *Times* do. They rejoice in the music critic who wrote learnedly of the "diapasonic profundities" of a howling Times Square mob. They relish telling how Brooks Atkinson was sent to Asia as a war correspondent and cabled back a review of a Chinese *Hamlet,* and how Judge William D. Evans, the late chief of the obituary desk, discovered he was the second-oldest living alumnus of Yale and began eagerly polishing up the ranking man's obit. A composite picture of priggish men in black alpaca, wiggling quill pens emerges. It is entertaining. It diverts other reporters, bored with the mediocrity of their own papers. The image, of course, is entirely false, not just because the alpaca has a scarlet lining, which it sometimes has—at his death the seraphic Henry J. Raymond was being blackmailed by a fancy woman, and the composing room tacks up as many bawdy pinups as the *News*—but because, for all its occasional turgidity, the *Times* remains the world's greatest newspaper.

It has, indeed, no rival. In its role as historian of the present it is a journalistic miracle, bringing readers in some twelve thousand American communities a faithful record of each day's events. Since the *Times'* two-week beat on Sherman's March to the Sea, it has published a remarkable number of exclusives, among them accounts of the Battle of Port Arthur, the sinking of the *Titanic*, the Versailles Treaty, Einstein's Theory of Relativity, the formation of the UN, the Marshall Plan, the Truman-MacArthur talks on Wake, and Stilwell's break with Chiang—a Brooks Atkinson triumph, after *Hamlet*.

But now and then the *Times* has had to hang its head. It thought the Teapot Dome scandal a red herring, thought Hitler washed up in 1932. Hanson Baldwin had just finished impressing readers with the might of Nasser's new army when Israel annihilated it in the Hundred Hour War. Yet no paper hates being beaten more than the *Times*, and none is readier to remake at the ring of a teletype bell. The emulous instinct even infects the Sunday Departments—the Magazine has its own bureaus in Washington, London and Paris, and on Saturday nights *The Week in Review* closes fifteen minutes after the news section.

Competition, however, is naturally strongest on the daily paper. In a newsroom filing cabinet is the home telephone number of just about everyone in the country a reporter might want to rouse at edition time. At three o'clock each morning, when the Late City Postscript nears the end of its run, a red light flashes in the bedrock cave thirty-four feet below street level where the massive presses are anchored. They rev down, sigh to a stop, and fifty thousand copies are held until the last possible moment—just in case. In one year about twenty major stories broke after trains had left for Washington with the first edition. Daily circulation in the District is only twelve thousand, but each time the managing editor ordered the copies that had gone by train scrapped and the replate flown south by chartered plane. Even in other cities the *Times* asks no quarter.

Save for explosive stories that are taken to the *Times* by canny officials because they know it will handle them properly, most *Times* exclusives are trophies of individual initiative. Admiral Peary, off for the Arctic, and Lindbergh and Amelia Earhart, flying the Atlantic, were under contract to the paper before they left the country. Herbert L. Matthews found Fidel Castro in the wild Sierra Maestra because he grew tired of writing editorials and flew down to learn what was really what. And Carr Van Anda, the *Times'* great managing editor of a generation ago, seized on the Theory of Relativity because he was one of the few men in the country who could understand it. V. A., as he was called, was a mathematical prodigy. Once, after reading a report on an Einstein lecture, he phoned Princeton and corrected an equation. Another time he was studying photographs of hieroglyphics from King Tut's tomb and discovered an ancient forgery, which scholarship later confirmed. "Only the *Times*," said Mike Berger, "could have scored a scoop on a story three thousand years old."

The incomparable V. A. did all this at his desk—not even the *Times* could have had a witness at the forgery—but most of the paper's historic accounts have come from reporters who were there. *Times* men were at Harpers Ferry and Gettysburg, at Los Alamos for the first atomic bomb, on Cape Canaveral for the moon shot; and a foreign correspondent went down with the *Andrea Doria*. Assignments take men to the ends of the earth—once a reporter left for the North Pole as another started for the South Pole—and you never know where you may bump into one. Southerners discovered *Times* correspondents were living in scores of communities in the South, watching their reaction to integration; Jehovah's Witnesses wading to their baptisms off Orchard Beach were accompanied by a *Times* photographer in a bathing suit; treasure seekers working in eighty feet of water off the coast of Scotland noticed a London Bureau man gravely peering through the window of his diving helmet. In New Jersey a *Herald Tribune* promotion man thrust a copy of his paper at a random passerby and was about to snap him for a poster when he realized he was focusing on a *Times* reporter.

The ubiquity of *Times* men is scarcely surprising. Nearly a thousand are in the news department alone. In the block-long city room the news editor looks distantly across the endless desks. The city editor summons his men over a P. A. system; the managing editor keeps opera glasses in his desk and sometimes squints around like a huge bird watcher. The *Times* has eighteen regional offices in the United States, including the Washington bureau on K Street, which has more reporters than most metropolitan dailies, and the sun never sets on its thirty-one foreign outposts. The paper, an editor explains, makes a point of being represented in every important capital. Just keeping its reporters' names straight is a problem; the composing room maintains a byline bank, 160 names cast in metal.

None, however, is a cipher. With so much talent there is little room for panjandrums. Everybody has got to do his share of slogging. Homer Bigart was greeted with routine local assignments when he moved uptown from the *Herald Tribune,* and when Clifton Daniel, Harry Truman's son-in-law, was being groomed for a Moscow assignment, he was packed off to a Russian class like any tyro. After twenty-one years of lofty journalism he studied next to Columbia undergraduates and pored over books nights. Daniel wound up with a B-plus. He was, he said, gratified that the managing editor didn't cut his allowance. Even the *Times* copy boys are college graduates. They write editorials on the sly, and sometimes see them printed. On a typical evening the newsroom garrison will include a dozen former war correspondents and ex-bureau chiefs, though until his death the star was Mike Berger, who made his name as a local reporter. To the city he was a second O. Henry, a Manhattan legend.

When I was a correspondent in New Delhi, the *Times* man there was Bob Trumbull, whose air-conditioned suite always seemed to me to be crowded with emissaries of the Prime Minister, maharajas bearing gifts, turbaned bearers, and whiskey wallahs in splendid robes. Trumbull's position in India roughly corresponded to that of the American ambassador, and no wonder; he knew more about the country; and his influence, there and in America, was at least as great. His important dispatches were read by everyone who saw the diplomatic pouch from Delhi and were delivered to an international *Who's Who* of subscribers: premiers in Africa, scientists in Europe, explorers in lonely outstations near the slab of Antarctic ice Admiral Byrd christened Adolph S. Ochs Glacier.

The only catch was that his stories had to be significant; otherwise they were likely to be spiked. Plenty of worldly correspondents and prize winners fail to make even the *Times* first edition, just because there are so many of them. Everyone cheerily admits that the paper is overstaffed. It is set up for the big story—the New England hurricane of 1938, when thirty-five reporters were used, or the pre-election surveys, which take a score of men. Other times idle hands play pinochle, or congratulate the nearest copy boy on his latest editorial, or write B matter—background material, to be used if and when.

B matter sounds dull, yet it is one secret of the *Times'* greatness. When momentous events break, there is usually something in what is called the "Deepfreeze," ready to be thawed and run. Often it needn't even be thawed. There are over a thousand advance obits on hand, and those of the President and Vice President are kept in type on the composing-room floor, ready for the make-up man's mallet. When the Supreme Court ruled against school segregation in 1954 it was background copy, pecked out on lazy evenings, that provided one of those monumental examples of complete *Times* coverage, with fifty-five columns of charts and side stories on every aspect of the decision.

It wasn't meant for subway poring. Like all such issues it was for the record, to be filed by librarians in rag-paper editions and listed in the *Times* index. The only man who seriously expected readers to wade through every edition was Ochs, who vetoed a News of the Week in Review during his reign on the ground that it would encourage readers to be slackers. He was being unjust. No man, devoting all his waking hours to the paper, could finish every story. Each day a million words— twice as many as in *Gone With the Wind*—come into the newsroom from the local staff, and by cable, transocean wireless telephone, and thirteen news services. This vast total is reduced by five copy desks to 150,000 words. Three tote boards, similar to those used by race tracks, keep track of the avalanche until it reaches the great battery of web presses. There, hard by a sign reading "Don't Waste Newsprint," it is metamorphosed into issues which, on a Sunday, may weigh five pounds and run over five hundred pages. Even summarizing it is a staggering task, as announcers for WQXR, the *Times* radio station, discovered during a newspaper strike in the late 1950's. Several went hoarse and required throat sprays.

Among the most heroic examples of the *Times* dedication to the record was its publication of the secret Yalta text. One March morning in 1955 Reston called New York and said he had it.

"But," he added, "I must have it back tomorrow. It can't go to New York." On his desk lay an 834-page document bound in two thick volumes—a historic beat but a somewhat dismaying one. The paper was unconfounded. For twenty hours twelve telegraph lines relayed copy from K Street, eighty-four linotypes hummed and clacked, and the next day the document was spread across thirty-two pages of the *Times*. When the cross-indexers in the third-floor morgue finished scissoring it up, it went into 2400 folders. Inch for column inch, that morning's paper was as bright as the works of Bede, but nobody could call it frivolous, and Carr Van Anda, who thought of his men as "the keepers of St. Peter's daily ledger," would have hefted it with pleasure.

Those who regard the public as a low beast may wonder how the *Times* can make any money carrying its interminable speeches, treaties, and papal encyclicals. Actually it does show a profit. There are many reasons for the *Times'* affluence, including shrewd investments in Canadian paper mills, but the biggest is that some people—not all, not even a majority, but enough—want to know what's really happening in the world. Telling them is good journalism and good business. Other publishers thought young Ochs was being droll when he started printing his daily "Arrival of Buyers." He was being smart. Merchants might chuckle over "The Yellow Kid," but if they wanted to stay solvent they had to buy the *Times*.

That principle remains the backbone of the paper. Today it prints over thirty percent of the advertising that is carried in New York newspapers. At 10:30 each evening queues form at newsstands all over New York, waiting for the first edition. They may not give a hang about the distinguished foreign correspondence, but they do want to be among the first to see the new classified ads in the back.

Among that Stygian mass of classified linage are boxes of statistics, each vital to some trade or interest. If you're an insurance underwriter, you want to know where yesterday's fires were. If you're in the hardware business, you turn to Naval Stores. Even if you're none of these, but are just fed up with talk about the local weather, there's a list of temperatures elsewhere, and to a surprising number of people that is the most important record in the paper.

To some people the thoroughness of the *Times* will always be an enigma. Anastas Mikoyan shook his head over it. *Pravda*, he said, does the same thing in four pages. It doesn't, of course. No other paper does. All tell you some of the news, but only the *Times* tries to give you the works. To the sophisticated reader, or the engineer interested in the specifications of the old Third Avenue El—or the scion curious to know whether his grandmother was on Ward McAllister's original list of the Four Hundred (it was less than three hundred, the files reveal)—the front of the *Times* will remain as indispensable as the charts and tables elsewhere are to others. Essentially the paper is one huge potpourri of fact, with something for everybody. All its myriad departments have in common are the requisites that they be respectable and significant.

Even these requirements are elastic. Ochs said of his Hall-Mills murder coverage that it would have been smut in a tabloid, but "if the *Times* publishes it, it's sociology." *Times* readers being what they are, the most unlikely feature may have educational value. Ochs fought crossword puzzles with a ferocity suggesting they were barely above the level of girlie magazines. The *Times* started running them in World War II, and readers, who will go to great lengths for solutions, learn a lot from them. One morning an eight-letter word was defined as "Leader of the Leathernecks." By noon the Marine Corps office on Broadway was swamped by hundreds of calls, asking help. The duty sergeant, who had assumed that everybody knew his boss was General Shepherd, was patient with them, though what he said privately wasn't fit to print.

Crossword puzzles may have smacked of harlotry to some fundamentalist readers, but true votaries know that custom cannot stale the paper's infinite piety. It is said that Queen Victoria never looked for a chair before sitting; she knew one would be there. *Times* men lock up their forms with the same regal confidence. Their professional world is secure, if a bit insular. In a skit marking the installation of a *Times* man as president of the National Press Club, the outgoing president played the part of the *Times* managing editor. He wore a tuxedo. When a performer asked whether the paper's managing editor always did that, he replied distantly, "Doesn't everyone?"

At Mike Berger's audience with Pope Pius XII Mike spoke more solemnly for the *Times* tradition of journalistic eminence. The Pontiff thanked him for stories he had written on Catholic missionaries and then blessed him. Mike's response was instinctive. He said, "God bless you, too, sir."

A Slight Case of McCarthyism

HERE ARE NO COAL MINES IN Fairmont, West Virginia, but bituminous fields surround the city, and every day long lines of coal cars move ponderously along the B&O tracks by the Monongahela River, throwing clouds of soot up the hill, staining the garish business district a deeper and deeper gray. The businessmen don't much mind: the miners support them, and slate falls, drift-mining, and C.I.O. politics have long been the pivots of street-corner conversation—provided one excepts the early 1950's, when they were dropped for the more compelling issues of Communism and godlessness.

There were no avowed Communists in Fairmont, either, as the most ardent Legionnaire would quickly admit. "We don't allow them here," he would tell you with that deep, easy laugh boosters translated into a town slogan, "Fairmont is Friendly." But as the laughter died the Legionnaire would draw you aside and explain, with many winks, nudges, and knowing nods, that Fairmont did have its problem citizens, or, to use his word, its "crackpots." "Same as any other place," he would add defensively. But Fairmont was doing something about its crackpots. Fairmont, he would say, jerking his thumb toward the west end of town—"Fairmont knows when it's had enough."

Westward, past a mile of sore-eyed frame houses pitched awkwardly on steep sloping hills, lay Fairmont State College, too remote to give the city a collegiate atmosphere, too close to be unobserved. Since its founding in 1865, the school had alternately been Fairmont's pride and its sorrow—its pride, as the state's first private normal school; its sorrow, as a state teachers' college which legislatures of the eighteen-seventies refused to support; its pride, under Joe Rosier; its sorrow, under George Hand.

Rosier, until his retirement in 1945, was considerably more to the community than a college president. He was an ardent Methodist, a conspicuous Rotarian, and a political ally of Fairmont's first citizen, seventy-seven-year-old Senator Matthew Mansfield Neely, the dean of West Virginia politics. When Neely temporarily exchanged his senatorial seat for the gubernatorial chair in 1941, he chose Rosier to complete his term in Washington, a signal honor, surely, for a mere educator. No one was happy to see Senator Joe quit Fairmont State two years after his return to College Hill, unless it was Hand, who shocked Fairmont, upon his appointment, by retiring Rosier's closest cronies. But even so, the town reflected, there was little cause for worry. Neely, as governor, had been provident enough to name a Fairmont woman to the State Board of Education, and everyone knew Thelma Loudin would keep a sharp eye on Hand.

In the beginning, the handsome new president and the dark, regal board member were on excellent terms. They were members of the same church—these things were important in Fairmont—and from her observation post as organist at Central Methodist, Mrs. Loudin heard splendid reports of Hand's attendance at First Methodist. Hand was a model of rectitude, industrious in behalf of civic causes, and the town was settling down when he and Mrs. Loudin began to quarrel over administrative detail. Fairmont again turned a critical eye westward, noted that Hand had brought a suspicious number of outsiders to the faculty, and grimly awaited the fireworks. They came during the Christmas season of 1951, and they were so spectacular all Marion County will probably remember the name of Mundel when Rosier Stadium is black with soot.

Dr. Luella Raab Mundel, a frail, bespectacled, somewhat nervous Iowan in her late thirties, came to Fairmont in September 1949 as chairman of the department of art, bringing with her a Ph.D. from Iowa State University and a sheaf of teaching references from other institutions. Dr. Hand passed these along to H. K. Baer, the neat, busy secretary of the Board of Education, and the appointment was approved at a meeting which Mrs. Loudin attended. The new teacher's salary was $3,700 a year. Her position was subject to three years of probation, although no one told her that. Neither was she told that all Fairmont faculty contracts are subject to annual review by the board. She assumed, quite wrongly as it turned out, that her previous experience entitled her to the prospect of tenure.

Her colleagues knew her, during that first autumn, as abrupt, independent, and, in private conversation, somewhat embittered over the memory of a three-year-old divorce. She shocked one devout teacher, who told of seeing a vision, by replying tartly, "Some people who hallucinate just hear voices." On another occasion, while arguing for an across-the-board raise at a faculty meeting, she said casually, "I guess I'm a Socialist." Her conduct before her classes was thought wholly competent, however, and on the first anniversary of her hiring, the board, upon Dr. Hand's recommendation, voted her a $200 raise. Until then she had been something of a recluse, but now she began to emerge into faculty life. She made friends in the community, designed color schemes for the new $400,000 library, and became more hospitable to invitations. In the spring of 1950, she had declined Dr. Hand's suggestion that she attend an American Legion "Americanism seminar" in downtown Fairmont—she thought politics dull, and hadn't even bothered to vote in 1948—but when the seminar was repeated the following March and her new friends advanced the same suggestion, she accepted.

The meeting was held in the Fairmont Hotel. The hundred or so Fairmonters attending were addressed by several imported ex-Communists. Question periods followed the individual talks, and during these Dr. Mundel was conspicuously active. She rose to ask one man his proof that Owen Lattimore was a Communist, to demand of another how he could tell a Communist when he saw one, and to express her resentment at the implication that college faculties were heavily stocked with Reds. She said she thought the identification of liberals with Communism particularly unfortunate, since that was precisely what the Communists wanted.

At one point during the evening, portly Harold D. Jones, the college librarian, directed Dr. Mundel's attention across the aisle, to her left, identifying a woman sitting there as Mrs. Thelma Brand Loudin.

Later Mrs. Loudin vigorously denied that she was at the seminar, but two months later, at the annual budget meeting of the Board of Education in Charleston, she suggested Dr. Mundel's name be dropped from the faculty roll. Dr. Hand asked why. "Well," he was told, "let's say she's a poor security risk."

Dr. Hand asked, and was granted, an opportunity to investigate this charge. That evening, meeting Mrs. Loudin in Charleston's Daniel Boone Hotel, he learned she felt she could not vote for the Fairmont State budget as long as it bore the name of Luella Mundel.

Informed of all this, the art chairman suggested the president check with the FBI. He did: the FBI reported nothing against her. Meanwhile, Mrs. Loudin had called upon him to explain that by "poor security risk" she really meant "poor teacher." To evaluate this new charge, he interviewed faculty members and art students. Ten of Dr. Mundel's colleagues split eight to two in her favor. The nine art majors all liked her.

At the same time, the college president learned that a subordinate of Dr. Mundel's, an artist who had preceded her in the department but had been prevented from assuming the chairmanship by a lack of advanced degrees, was telling friends he had been "guaranteed" his boss would be fired. The day after the initiation of the campus investigation, this man had sent Mrs. Loudin a letter, attacking his superior. Subsequently, Mrs. Loudin turned the letter over to the Fairmont *West Virginian,* in whose columns it was published.

On June 30, the art chairman's contract expired. Dr. Hand assured her the board couldn't help seeing things her way, and she continued into the summer session on a temporary basis. Nevertheless, she began to worry. Her weight dropped to ninety-five pounds, she could not sleep, and she found people obviously were avoiding her. At the end of six weeks of summer teaching, she asked to be relieved.

Meanwhile the board had met to consider Dr. Hand's report. He told of his inquiries and recommended that she be retained, that her pay be raised, and that her subordinate be dismissed for unethical conduct against her. Mrs. Loudin informed him that she did not think "an atheist" should be permitted to teach on a college faculty, and he was asked to leave the room while the vote was cast. He was reversed on all counts. Five days later, on Bastille Day, Dr. Mundel read in the Fairmont *Times* a board announcement of her dismissal "for the good of the college."

That afternoon Fairmont State's psychology professor, a wry, aging collegian named Spaulding Rogers, called on Mrs. Loudin in behalf of the local chapter of the American Association of University Professors. He was, he said, a one-man fact-finding committee, and the fact he wanted to find was—what was Mrs. Loudin's attitude toward faculty participation in a pro-Mundel petition? Such a petition existed, he explained, and several of his colleagues contemplated signing it. They were, however, wary of the board's reaction. Could Mrs. Loudin guess what it might be? Mrs. Loudin could. She observed that anyone who questioned the board "would do well to move along and move while the moving was good."

Dr. Rogers, who shortly thereafter sold his farm in Fairmont and moved to Hollins College, Virginia, made notes of Mrs. Loudin's comments, but at the end of the interview she and her husband, a Fairmont department store manager, relieved him of these and destroyed them. Afterward he did, however, remember that she made this comment: "I am a theist, Dr. Rogers, and would expect to stand judgment if I condoned its opposite."

At about the same time, Mrs. Katherine Roberts, a county grammar school teacher who had taken art courses at the college, called on Mrs. Loudin and said she thought Dr. Mundel was being treated shabbily. She was informed that the dismissed art teacher was a member of a faculty clique which had become dangerous because of "certain opinions" its members held. Mrs. Loudin asked the visitor to tell her with whom she had discussed the matter. "I refused," Mrs. Roberts later recalled. "She said, 'It doesn't matter, we have the names'—and she started to name names."

July melted into August; Dr. Mundel was out of a job; she looked for another. But none of the half-dozen teaching agencies she wrote offered the slightest hope, and she reached the conclusion that unless she could clear her name in Fairmont, her chances elsewhere would be slim. She appealed to the board for a hearing. Her request was supported by a petition signed by about a hundred and twenty-five Fairmont students, by the leaders of the local AAUP and the American Civil Liberties Union chapters, and by the two organizations accrediting Fairmont State, the North Central Association of Colleges and Secondary Schools and the American Association of Colleges for Teacher Education.

The board met on September 5, grilled Dr. Hand on his failure to suppress Dr. Mundel's supporters at the college, and decided not to grant her a hearing.

On September 27 she filed suit for $100,000, charging Mrs. Loudin with slander. Her attorneys were whimsical old Tusca Morris, of Fairmont, and Horace S. Meldahl, West Virginia correspondent for the American Civil Liberties Union. Mrs. Loudin was represented by Senator Neely and the Senator's son, Alfred.

The case came to bar before Judge J. Harper Meredith on the bitter day of December 19, 1951.

The Marion County courthouse, a Corinthian mass of gray Cleveland sandstone crowned by a domed clock-tower and a copper statue of Justice, dominates downtown Fairmont. It was built at the turn of the century after a savage row between city dwellers and county taxpayers, who resented the cost, and the first case to be tried in the barnlike second-floor courtroom was heard in late November 1900.

The defendant was the board of regents of West Virginia University. The plaintiff was Matthew Mansfield Neely.

That was eight years before he was elected Fairmont's first Democratic mayor, thirteen years before his first term in Congress, twenty-three before he went to the Senate. He was then a young veteran of the Spanish-American War, a brilliant campus orator who had just been expelled from the university for his role in a now obscure student prank. (The Senator later said he had defied a Yankee college president by singing "Dixie"; Morris, a fellow student, recalled that some cadavers were involved.) Neely asked for a writ of mandamus compelling the regents to take him back, and, as usual, he won.

Now, a half-century later, in a courtroom crammed with townspeople and students, he rose and stalked the all-male jury—a chunky, jut-jawed figure in a double-breasted suit and blue suede shoes, crouching over the jury box, delivering his opening statement in phrases redolent of the days of William Jennings Bryan.

For over an hour he paced before the awestruck twelve, delivering a thundering defense of the Board of Education's right "to purge its school of teachers it believes incompetent, atheists, Communists, horse thieves, murderers, or just too ignorant to teach children." He called for "teachers without any high-falutin ideas about not being able to prove there is a God"—teachers who would not corrupt the minds of students "in the sunny morning of life" by "making kindling wood out of their little hopes"—"teachers who believe in the old-fashioned American way our forefathers handed down from the time the barefooted soldiers of Washington stained the snows of Valley Forge with their precious blood."

"I'm for them," he vowed, "A to Z. I'm not for teachers tainted with foreign isms."

He indignantly attacked critics of the American Legion—of "those boys in the first world war" who "left their last best hope on the altar of their country" and "fought to the death in the Argonne Forest and the Belleau Wood, with death and barbed wire around them, where exploding shells and campfires gleamed."

Luella Mundel, he declared, was a woman who would "tear down the man of Galilee from the Cross"—a woman who "boasted of painting pictures which arouse sexual desires in men." The Senator said he stood foursquare against any school which "tolerates Communism, atheism, or any other godless philosophy in its halls" and wound up with a plea to the jurors to "burn incense on the altar of almighty God, asserting the right of every American to sing such songs of gladness as

'Jesus, Lover of My Soul' and 'My Country, 'Tis of Thee.'" He illustrated by reciting the choruses of these in a quavering voice.

"If that's reactionary," he cried, "make the most of it!"

Meldahl, himself a Legionnaire, protested he couldn't make anything of it at all, except perhaps an attempt to prejudice the jury. The Senator objected: he didn't know how they tried cases where Mr. Meldahl came from, but this was Fairmont, West Virginia. Meldahl came from Charleston, West Virginia.

The outsider began his parade of witnesses with Dr. Hand. His client was absent. She, shaken by Neely's references to her art, was in the women's lounge, weeping inconsolably. She therefore missed a further development of this theme in the Senator's cross-examination of the college president. Dr. Hand, it turned out, had admitted to the board at one of its meetings that he thought his art chairman sometimes used poor judgment. Under Neely's skillful probing, he first confessed this meant the use of "crude language"; then, squirming under the frozen stare of a thousand eyes, he reluctantly specified this.

The specifications were highly damaging. In their entirety they were not: Dr. Mundel had merely repeated to the Hands a locker-room joke Dr. Rogers had made about one of her abstract paintings, which Jones, the librarian, had purchased. But the whole story—the fact that a psychologist had taken an earthy dig at modern art, and the artist had been amused—did not come out until the following day, when Meldahl got another crack at his witness. The gist of Dr. Hand's answers, under Neely's careful questioning, was that Dr. Mundel had given Jones one of her pictures and told him it would "make him masturbate."

The impact of this on the spectators was electrifying. For a long moment they huddled in stunned silence; then a woman in the rear of the courtroom jumped up, clutching a scarf and galoshes, and darted out, throwing quick, frightened looks behind her. That night a knot of Fairmont men gathered before a magazine store two blocks from the courthouse, telling one another they "sure would like to see that picture." The display window behind them was choked with such books as *The Loves of a Harlot, Passion C.O.D., Free Lovers, The Affairs of a Mistress,* and *Women of the Night* ("No Matter How Hard She Tried She Couldn't Be Good").

The following morning Meldahl appeared carrying masked examples of his client's painting, specimens of extreme cubism, scarcely comprehensible to the untrained eye. When he removed the masking, everyone enjoyed a disappointed laugh—everyone, that is, except the jurymen. At Senator Neely's insistence, the pictures were not immediately entered as evidence, and the frustrated twelve craned their necks over the jury box, unsuccessfully trying to peep. The only frame within their line of vision was still covered with newspaper, a page from the New York *Herald Tribune* bearing a photograph of nine Long Island drum majorettes, legs rampant.

Later, when Dr. Mundel was on the stand, Neely seized one of the paintings and thrust it at the jury, asking her if her work consisted of "teaching pupils to draw pictures like THIS thing." The jurors then passed a pleasant ten minutes twisting the frame at various angles and nudging one another. The Senator also attempted to elicit from the witness an opinion on "what color excites the sexual faculty or passions." She answered dryly she did not know, but thought the matter proper study for a psychologist.

Beyond certain veiled references to the "propaganda" of the American Civil Liberties Union, the only nonprofessional organization to which Dr. Mundel belonged, Senator Neely did not attack her patriotism, and except for her retirement to the women's lounge that first day, she held her own very well, until he led her down the dark and tortuous lanes of theology. Until then she sat erect in her slack woolen suit —not so poised as Thelma Loudin, who smiled supreme confidence at her husband and counsel, but certainly composed—and answered all questions in her terse, starchy Iowan accent. No, she had never been a Communist, a fellow-traveler, or a Russian sympathizer. No, she was not an atheist.

This last inspired a torrent of senatorial questions: What was her attitude toward the Supreme Being and the Creator of the universe? Had she ever admitted there was a God? Just what was an accurate statement of her religion?

She survived the first such session with the help of Noah Webster. Webster, she pointed out, defines God as something man worships, and she worshipped truth. If the Senator preferred, he could call her God a belief in the order of the universe. The Senator preferred no such thing: he didn't want to degrade Him and himself by expressing a scintilla of doubt in His almighty existence. What did the witness mean? What about those old Aztecs, praying to the sun and stars, and the Japs, prostrating themselves before Buddha? Did she mean to stand on her oath and say whatever man worships is God? She did. If they deify it, she said, it's God to them. Of atheists, she observed that Webster defines them as denying the existence of a Supreme Being, and she did not do that. Dr. Mundel rather thought she was an agnostic.

Long after judge, jury, and principals had left that afternoon, spectators stood in the darkened courtroom, arguing obscure ecclesiastical points. The following morning Mr. Loudin toiled behind his wife with an armload of Biblical encyclopedias, closely followed by an eager mob carrying lunch boxes. They were disappointed: Dr. Mundel was at home, ill, and Meldahl proceeded to examine a half-dozen of her former students on her teaching competence. His most spectacular motion that day was his least successful. He proposed to enter in evidence excerpts from the U.S. Constitution, certain sections of the West Virginia Code, and a passage from the Supreme Court decision in the famous West Virginia flag salute case. Neely protested this was unprecedented, and Judge Meredith agreed. The motion was denied.

Article 3, section 11 of the state constitution provides that "no religious or political test oath shall be required as a prerequisite or qualification to vote, serve as a juror, sue, plead, appeal, or pursue any profession or employment." Section 15 of the same article specifies that "no man shall be compelled to frequent or support any religious worship, place, or ministry whatsoever . . . but all men shall be free to profess, and, by argument, to maintain their opinion in matters of religion; and the same shall, in no wise, affect, diminish, or enlarge their civil capacities." After Meldahl's attempt to read this into the record, a courthouse regular was found on one of the elevated porticoes outside the building, leaning against a fluted column, overcome with laughter. "Read the code to Neely?" he choked. "He wrote the damned thing!"

The Supreme Court decision, which the Senator did not write, said, among other things, that "if there is any fixed star in our constitution constellation, it is that no official, high or petty, can prescribe what shall be orthodox in politics, nationalism, religion, or other matters of opinion, or force citizens to confess by word or act their faith therein. If there are any circumstances which permit an exception, they do not now occur to us."

On December 27, when the court reconvened after a Christmas recess, Meldahl lost another round, this time a move to inform the jury on tenure regulations of Fairmont State's accrediting organizations, and Dr. Mundel, pale and shaky, remounted the stand. Neely crouched over the counsel's table. Upon her last appearance, he recalled, she had testified she worshiped truth. He now asked her to define truth. She told him she could not: that truth was relative to the information on hand at a certain time. Once people accepted the premise that the world was flat; now they knew better. "I suppose," she said, "I am a relativist."

The Senator did not care what she supposed—he wanted to know what it was she worshipped. Her answer, she said, indicated a principle that she worshipped. "Does that mean you have two Gods, truth and principle?" Neely snapped. She asked him to rephrase this. "What I am asking you to do," he asked her, "is distinguish between your God truth and your God principle." There was no answer; she sat in one corner of the witness box, as far from him as she could get, with her chin in her hand, looking directly downward. The stenographer read the record back to her and the court asked if her answers were as read. Still she did not reply. "Do you understand what the Senator is trying to get at?" asked the judge. The answer was barely audible: "Not very well."

"Did you—" asked Neely, "Did you—"

Dr. Mundel turned to the bench. "You must excuse me," she said. "I am ill."

Before she reached the rear door she was crying violently, and her sobs, coming from the corridor by the judge's chambers, echoed in the vast courtroom. The Senator told the court that although he had the greatest sympathy for the sick, he felt his questions were merely embarrassing to one who "doesn't want all the truth to come out." He said he considered it a duty "to my client and my country" to make the cross-examination "pitiless and as thorough as possible."

Dr. Mundel was sent home under sedation. That night, in the square, shingled home where she roomed, she threatened suicide. She told her doctor she was broke, had no way of earning a living, and had nothing to live for. She said she had eaten nothing for several days and asked him to commit her to a mental hospital, where she would be fed. Eric Barnitz, a young sociology instructor, and his wife stayed with her through the evening. On one occasion she ran into her bedroom and tried to lock the door. Another time she announced she was going to slash her wrists, ran into the kitchen, and grabbed a carving knife. Mrs. Barnitz disarmed her. She told the couple she was "caught in a trap," saw no way out, and had "no reputation left, and no profession."

"May God have mercy on her," said Neely, when all this came out in court the following morning. "No one has pity for her as much as I have."

He declined, however, to accept Meldahl's suggestion that the defense proceed with its case pending the plaintiff's recovery. The Senator said his obligations to his client were clearly defined, and he declined to cross the line binding them "by the diameter of a single diminutive hair." He reaffirmed his duty to protect "parents and teachers and little ones from godless and unAmerican philosophies."

Meldahl accused Neely of "browbeating" his witness. "That's a barefaced lie!" Neely shouted, waving a fist. "If you're a man you'll come outside and say that! You're a filthy, lousy liar when you say it!" Judge Meredith made a soft, pawing motion with his hand, much like a football referee's signal for unnecessary roughness, and the Senator quieted down. Later, however, when Meldahl offered to shake his hand, he refused the gesture.

The trial was at an impasse: Dr. Mundel was her own last witness, and nothing further could be done without her. The issue was resolved by taking a deposition in her home, with the necessary officials present. The transcript of this was to be read in court the following Monday, New Year's Day, but the jury never heard it, for on Sunday the case blew up.

The demolisher was Fairmont's Episcopalian minister, the Reverend F. Graham Luckenbill, an Episcopalian clergyman with a reputation for independence. Mr. Luckenbill, addressing his congregation from his lectern, described the trial as a "farce" comparable to "all the bad traits of the Inquisition and the Crucifixion." As long as a teacher in a state institution makes no attempt to teach his religious or political beliefs, the minister argued, those beliefs are his own and should not be considered by his superiors. Actually, he suggested, when Dr. Mundel said she worshipped truth she was considerably closer to God than Senator Neely, since God is Truth.

The clergyman's statements were carried in Monday's Fairmont *Times*, and the Senator strode into court that morning brandishing a copy of the paper. He demanded a mistrial and got it, over Meldahl's strenuous objections. Judge Meredith ruled the minister's comments "improper" and, because of his influence in the community, prejudicial. There was some talk of haling Mr. Luckenbill into court on a contempt citation. Nothing came of it, but the Fairmont Ministerial Association, representing twenty-four local clergymen, issued a statement disassociating themselves from him and denouncing the trying of court cases in the pulpit. The association president, pastor of the Central Christian Church, explained that Mr. Luckenbill did not belong to the organization. Membership, he said, is reserved to those clergymen "who desire to co-operate."

For one reason or another—lack of news enterprise being one reason, the holidays another—the metropolitan press was poorly represented in Fairmont Christmas week, and that pleased no one there. Dr. Mundel's supporters were hopeful of finding an audience in urban communities, and a reporter for the Fairmont *West Virginian,* which supported Mrs. Loudin in its news columns, expressed chagrin at not seeing representatives of "the *New Republic,* the *Daily Worker,* and the rest of the New York papers." The Associated Press dealt by telephone with a highly reliable reporter on the Fairmont *Times,* but it dispatched no staff men to the scene, and its editors sent out a wire photo of the defendant bearing the name of the plaintiff. The *Columns,* the college's student paper, carried nothing during the trial. "Our paper," it explained in a post-trial editorial, "is distributed each week among most if not all high schools in the state. Our purpose in doing this is to advertise Fairmont State as a suitable school where high-school students may continue their education. We feel that if emphasis were placed on any conflict, of any nature, our purpose in distributing this paper among high schools would be hindered."

The accounts which did appear were eagerly read in Fairmont, however, and Senator Neely, in a sharp allusion to Dr. Hand, deplored the "disgraceful publicity" which had "probably wrecked" the college. It certainly wrecked Dr. Hand locally. Although he had friends well placed in the state, the Board of Education dismissed him on March 27. Six members of the faculty then resigned in protest. Adlai Stevenson found a place for the former president at Southern Illinois University. The six protesters drifted off to other campuses. Dr. Mundel remained in Fairmont, hoping for a favorable resolution of her suit.

The city continued to be in a state of trauma. Mr. Luckenbill's telephone was still ringing constantly when Senator Neely gave the local newspapers a copy of the deposition taken in Dr. Mundel's home. In it, outraged defenders of Mrs. Loudin read that although the art teacher thought the local school too small to represent all shades of opinion, she did believe that "one good Communist on a large university faculty might be very useful to the student body." She went on to explain that his ideas could easily be discredited by the other professors. She declined, under the Senator's continued questioning, to recommend Earl Browder as a desirable addition to the faculty of Fairmont State College.

Her mail was heavy all spring. Support, some of it financial, came from various university professors, lecturers, lawyers, and editors, and from two Unitarian ministers, two Catholics, and a Christian Scientist. She also received three shipments of religious tracts, an anonymous card from a sex crank, and a card informing her that "God has allowed you to live long enough. Now He is about to destroy you."

The second trial opened on July 7, 1952, with Mrs. Loudin's defense bolstered by a $2,500 contribution from the treasury of the local Legion post. She firmly denied every charge against her, and her colleagues on the education board paraded to the stand to support the thesis that Dr. Hand had been responsible for the whole mess. It turned out that she had little need of their support, for the judge ruled that her statements as a board member were privileged, unless, of course, they had been malicious. In his closing address Senator Neely, who referred to the plaintiff as "Mrs. P. H. D. Mundel," said the question was whether schools should be operated by men and women of good will or by "agnostics, Socialists, and screwballs." The jury deliberated less than two hours and then announced for the defendant.

On the Sunday after the trial two of Dr. Mundel's supporters hurriedly summoned police to her apartment. She had not answered their urgent knocking, and a strong odor was seeping into the hall. Forcing an entrance, the policemen found her in a gas-filled bathroom; the window was tightly shut and the door calked. No charges were brought then, but after a night with friends she was accused of attacking her hostess with a letter opener. This time she was held in the Fairmont jail on charges of lunacy and assault, under constant supervision, until her sister arrived to take her home to Iowa. She went along quietly.

In Defense of Snobs

I DISCOVERED MY SNOBBERY the way most people learn grave truths about themselves these days, from an expert. I was discussing prison conditions with a sociologist, who agreed with me that they were bad and then went on to suggest extraordinary remedies. The first step, he said, was to change nomenclature; instead of *penitentiaries, guards,* and *convicts,* we must speak of *penal hospitals, psychiatric aides,* and *social patients.*

"Then we can establish outpatient clinics," he continued, "and give these sick people treatment. Remember, we're dealing with the emotionally underprivileged. Basically they're no worse than the rest of us."

I spent several years covering police courts for newspapers, and, remembering a certain ax murderer in Baltimore, I said, "They're worse than I am."

A sharp exchange followed. The sociologist looked more and more upset. He had always known me as a liberal; a supporter of foreign aid, birth control and equality at the lunch counter. Now, clearly, I was sick. What was worse, I had a social disease.

"I'm afraid you're a snob," he said diagnostically.

I knew the word "snob" had evolved much during the past generation, but this was the first time I had heard it used in what is becoming its ultimate sense: to describe someone who regards himself better than anyone—literally *any*one—else. I hope no one will confuse me with a Ku Kluxer when I say that I'll have to get off here and walk back. I've passed my stop. I'm willing to grant that men often preen themselves for absurd reasons, but they're not *my* kind of snob. I don't see why the fact that some standards are idiotic means there oughtn't to be any standards at all, and I refuse to slink away because I didn't hear Caryl Chessman's bell tolling for me.

I refuse, in a word, to become an egalitarian. I am aware that I'm being unfashionable. In his classic work on snobs and snob worship, Thomas Carlyle observes that every age reverences its "gilt Popinjays" and "soot-smeared Mumbojumbos." The current totem is this curious theory of equality. Of course, scarcely anyone calls it egalitarianism. Most egalitarians prefer to think of themselves as lower-case democrats. "We're terribly democratic," they say, and they are, they're terribly democratic, though, of course, they don't mean it that way. One of the conveniences of egalitaria is that if you denounce all precepts, you yourself needn't conform to any. You needn't, for example, use words properly. Someday I'm going to shove an egalitarian nose in *The Oxford English Dictionary*, whispering all the while in an egalitarian ear that democracy is a political concept, a form of government; that only in the last generation has it acquired its present significance. I doubt, however, that I shall be as successful as the managing editor of a large metropolitan newspaper, who appointed an assistant city editor and then found himself confronted by an office petition requesting him to change the appointment. "We've voted," the chairman of the petition committee explained brightly. "We're against Smith. We want Jones." The editor, a Democrat at the polls but a snob elsewhere, turned on his heel. "I believe in democracy," he snapped, "but this newspaper is not one."

If popular usage is undoing the concept of democracy, that of snobbery is already undone. William Makepeace Thackeray would be appalled to see the ruin of it. It was he who popularized the word, in whose changing definitions one can read a lot of social history, some of it splendid, some dismaying. In 1830, when Thackeray was a Cambridge undergraduate, a snob was a member of the community who wasn't connected with the university—in short, a townie. Nobs were better than snobs, and that was that. Then Thackeray observed that certain members of the lower classes were getting uppity. Writing in *Punch,* he broadened the term to include them, giving it an interpretation almost precisely opposite its meaning today.

Thackeray didn't live to see his word and his world turned upside down. After his death, contempt for the dirty shirt was succeeded by contempt for the stuffed shirt. In England nobs were transformed into tax fugitives, in the United States *Town and Country* chronicled the blurring of class lines, and in Webster a snob became a man with an extravagant notion of his own worth. A dart once aimed *down* was now fired *up*. It was, in fact, becoming bad form to have any notion of worth at all. If you acquired a light, you cast about quickly for a bushel. As early as 1916 Yale athletes were observed wearing their letter sweaters inside out; today letter sweaters are rarely seen anywhere. Nor are Legion of Honor ribbons seen, nor Phi Beta Kappa keys, nor any of the bijoux of distinction in which people once took pride. In their place is a strange, false humility, sometimes ludicrous, sometimes moving. The most striking example of it I have ever seen occurred in the Summer of 1945, when a group of veterans of Iwo Jima and Okinawa were decorated by the U.S. Marine Corps, an organization of insufferable snobs devoted to democracy. As the ceremony broke up, men unpinned their medals and thrust them in their pockets and shuffled off, as though in shame.

Preposterous? Of course. Yet it made a hideous kind of sense. Today a great war, a Depression, another great war, Vietnam, and Watergate have destroyed respect for the image of authority. It has become awkward to admit that you have the conn—awkward even to acknowledge achievements, since superiority of any kind is suspect. Thus everyone tries to look as much as possible like everyone else, and thus all distinctions which once separated man from man have become unsavory. Instead of football captains we have co-captains, or revolving captaincies which change with each game; instead of judges we have referees; instead of a chief executive we have a team; instead of a general-in-chief we have a chairman of the joint chiefs; and in lieu of graceful manners we have the cult of informality, which, in a way that eludes me, is regarded as a democratic virtue—as though Mirabeau and Tom Paine would have smiled benignly on jeans and come-as-you-are barbecues and, most frightful of all, the aggressive use of nicknames.

The decline of formal address deserves special mention. It becomes increasingly difficult to find out to whom you're talking. Everyone you meet is plain Pete, or Al, or Jane, or Jill. A President of the United States is Ike or Gerry. The Secretary of State is simply Henry the K. We know these men from their pictures, but what happens when you drop down a ledge or two? Confusion happens, that's what. A dazzling Washington hostess I know holds parties around her swimming pool at which guests, clad in bathing suits, are introduced to strangers by coy diminutives. Once she led me to two elderly Englishmen dozing in the sun. "Billy," she said, "This is Denny and Bobby." Exit the hostess, into water. After a reticent, fumbling conversation I discovered that Denny was an eminent political scientist from Thackeray's university, and Bobby had been an Air Vice-Marshal of the R.A.F. during the Battle of Britain. ("You *have* heard of the Battle of Britain, haven't you?" he asked wistfully.)

After such an affair men mutter to their wives—or, in this deliciously casual age, to the wives they happen to have in tow—"Who was that bearded Cuban? You don't suppose. . . ." No real harm done, though in public this custom, or absence of custom, can be highly embarrassing. When my first book was published I appeared in an hour-long radio program at the invitation of Mary Margaret McBride. There was another writer present, a gray, shaggily handsome man to whom she presented me moments before the broadcast. "Here's Bob," she told me. I was about to inquire further when I found we were on the air. I hadn't his other name, so I called him by that one for the first ten minutes; then the mistress of ceremonies informed the audience and me that this Bob had been awarded *four* Pulitzer prizes. He was Robert Sherwood. I writhed for the rest of the hour. I had no way to greet him. I could hardly start using his surname, yet Bob now stuck in my throat; at the age of twenty-eight I wasn't his equal, and if Miss McBride did not realize that, Billy keenly did.

Nominal equality has become a fetish in modern offices. Once an employee was expected to sir his boss. Now he's not even allowed to mister him. Here and there a thin red line of snobs fights a gallant rearguard action (when Roy Howard ordered New York *World-Telegram* reporters to call him Roy, A. J. Liebling cited his record on the paper and concluded, "Now may I please call you Mr. Howard?"), but they are hopelessly outnumbered by dense squares of jovial executives who, during coffee breaks and at company parties, stridently insist that nobody rise, let's not stand on ceremony, feel free, and remember, we're all Joes here. One Joe may have absolute power over the other Joe's career. One may be the pile-driving force behind the firm; the other may be a forelock-tugging serf. Still they speak as brothers, and if Big Joe has an order to deliver he prefaces it with some such groveling remark as, "Just let me give you my thinking on this," or, "This is off the top of my head," or, "Probably I don't know what I'm talking about." Is this democracy? I think it's hypocrisy.

In any event, snobbery is dead.

Or is it?

Twenty-five years ago Russell Lynes picked up Thackeray's fallen pen and pricked what he called The New Snobbism. Like his predecessor, he recognized that the essence of snobbery is ego manipulation. Every honest snob will cheerfully acknowledge that. Lynes went on to say that since nearly every ego needs some titillation, we are all snobs of one sort or another. He listed some of the chief categories he had found: social snobs, intellectual snobs, regional snobs, moral snobs, sen-

sual snobs, physical snobs and occupational snobs. We've all encountered varieties of these. In any group there are people who are proud of
the schools they attended, or the clubs which have admitted them, or
the books they have read, or the fact that they go to Florida every winter, or stay physically fit (or don't), or can replace a faucet washer (or
can't), or have a taste for fine wines (or can't tell one from another).
Frequently the reason for a man's vanity is as fatuous as that of Aesop's
fly, who sat on the axle of a chariot and marveled at the dust he raised,
but often it is entirely justified: Omar Bradley *is* a famous soldier,
Mayor Daley *is* a gifted politician. Anyhow, pride is here to stay; no
vigorous society can do without it. The Russians tried to abolish distinctions in the twenties; by the thirties they had brought back fashion
shows, hand-kissing, saluting, and full-dress clothes—for banquets on
the anniversary of the Revolution.

Today's American effort is more determined, which brings us to
Lynes' final category—the reverse snob, or anti-snob snob. I have already introduced him as the egalitarian. He is the pious worshiper of
the Divine Average, the man who adopts what Robert Frost described
as a "tenderer-than-thou" attitude toward social problems. Sometimes
he is as transparently bogus as the late Diego Rivera, who used to dress
carefully in a khaki shirt and greasy corduroys before being driven in a
limousine to rallies of Mexican workers. Other times he is pitifully sincere, like the president of the teachers' federation who warned his colleagues several years ago that they were "in danger of considering
themselves as just a little bit better" than the rank and file of laborers.
At all times, however, he is bent on downstaging the rest of us, carrying himself with an air of craven modesty and reproaching with cow
eyes everyone who holds himself erect. He is, as Lynes suggested, the
worst sort of snob, and he behaves in execrable taste.

No well-bred snob, for example, would dream of sneering openly
at those who lack what he prizes. It would violate his sense of decency
to imply that there's something wrong about a house furnished with
Grand Rapids imitations, say, or to let on that it's a bit shaming to have
been born outside Virginia (or Boston, or Charleston). I may give low
marks to the man who prefers C. S. Forester to E. M. Forster, thinks
Jackie Gleason funnier than Alec Guinness, enjoys Atlantic City more
than Watch Hill, and orders a Scarlett O'Hara when martinis are available. I shouldn't tell him that to his face, though; that would be shabby
of me. The egalitarian has fewer scruples. He attacks religious snobs in
the religious press, cultural snobs in parent-teacher journals ("What
Can We Do About Snobbery?" "Don't Raise a Snob!"), and intellectual

snobs on the floor of the Senate. Evidence cannot stand against him: if genetic research turns up new evidence of inherited characteristics, then the geneticists are anti-democratic impostors. No national priority deflects him: on the eve of Hitler's invasion of Poland, the superegalitarian J. B. Priestly actually charged in the London *News Chronicle* that the greatest threat to Great Britain was snobbery. And to simplify his argument, the enemy of standards has completely corrupted Thackeray's meaning. Margaret Kennedy tells the story of a Welsh woman who learned that a neighbor's daughter was about to be married, although not pregnant. She exclaimed, "There's snob for you!"

Against such tumidity the proper snob, a courteous chap, is almost helpless. "Snobbery," wrote Dixon Wecter, "may be regarded as a form of self-protection against the social consequences of democracy." Its critics notwithstanding, it is essentially defensive, and it seems to me that it grows more defensive each year. In the last generation a George Bernard Shaw could assert that England's snobs were actually her greatest strength; a Virginia Woolf could defiantly proclaim her artistic superiority; a José Ortega y Gasset could observe that the average citizen is "incapable of receiving the sacrament of art, blind and deaf to pure beauty." Today, either because of the bitterness of the assault or because the other-directed virus has infected even us, we snobs are more diffident, more anxious not to appear gross. And so the virtue of our time has become what Bertrand Russell ironically called "the superior virtue of the oppressed." And so the gray tide of mediocrity rises higher and higher. Of mediocrity—and of worse.

The greatest egalitarian gains were made in the years immediately after World War II. It was in 1946 that the Army's Doolittle Board, goaded by wartime egalitarians like William Mauldin, stripped rank of its privileges. Indeed, it was a novel about the Army, James Jones' *From Here to Eternity*, which most clearly expressed the reverse values of the new egalitaria. The measure of a man's worth was in inverse proportion to his pay grade, education and civility. Anyone with a commission was an outcast. Women were similarly graded. The essence of purity was the prostitute. The faithful wife was a fallen sister.

A subtler specimen of egalitarian literature is *The Man in the Gray Flannel Suit*. Sloan Wilson's seraphim aren't dope fiends and hookers, but like Jones, Nelson Algren, and Tennessee Williams he stands on his hands to look at the world. His protagonist is a man who wants to make more money. He leaves an easy berth for a job with a higher salary and discovers his new employer expects him to work. His reaction is moral outrage. He concedes that the employer is dedicated, but cannot admire him, because the old man is industrious and diligent —in approved cant, he is a driven neurotic. The employer is apologetic, as villains are in all sophisticated melodramas; he can only plead for understanding. "Atlas," wrote Carlyle, "the hero of old has had to cramp himself into strange places: the world knows not well at any time what to do with him, so foreign is his aspect in the world!"

In supporting this twaddle, the passionate egalitarian tirelessly generalizes from the specific. He had this second john, see, and the creep couldn't even read a map. (Leaders are incompetent.) Talk about swinging from both sides of the plate—Charles Dickens kept a mistress. (Moralists are phonies.) A junior exec in the front office just fired a man for wearing Bermudas. (Bosses are blackguards.) But this is cheating. The issue is not whether rules are broken. It is whether we ought to have any rules at all. Snobbery's quarrel with the anti-snob isn't that he's affronted by snobs who blot their copybooks, for he's not; he exults in them; they support his argument. This argument, and the real issue, is that every homo Sap is like every other homo Sap—that the differences between us are infinitesimal, and may be put down to external influence. If evil is done, society is to blame. If evil is redressed, society is triumphant. It naturally follows that anyone who believes this, and is honestly convinced that we are all children of the same gravid earth bitch, must regard any pretension as a bugbear and any authority as a fee-faw-fum.

As illogical as a superstition, this notion also has a superstition's power. It would be hard to find an American citadel free of its spell. Certainly the home isn't. The dictatorial father of Freud's time is virtually extinct. Once he roamed the land in vast herds, snorting virile snorts and refreshing himself in austere men's clubs walled with fumed oak, before thundering home to preside over his cave. In the 1970's he exists as a flaccid parody of his grandfather, a comic figure on television programs whose cretin blunders are deftly corrected by his amused family. The teen-ager who wants to get married while in high school does so, because, as a mother explained to me, "Kids are people and have a right to make up their own minds." Her husband was unreconciled, but he recognized that he was a low, atavistic creature, and he merely looked uncomfortable when she added airily, "We believe in democracy at home."

"Democracy at home." Is this the last slogan of egalitaria? It is more than a slogan. It is a course of study in grade schools. Snobs suffered one of their first routs in public education; they have no friends among the jitney messiahs of bread-and-circuses curricula. The number of classrooms which vote on what they are to be taught is small, but pupils are polled on nearly everything else, including the personality of the teacher, the value of her instruction, and the real-life meaning of a course: "How many think Lincoln was well-adjusted? Hands, please." Popular sovereignty extends to the intellectual coin of the realm, the language which, according to egalitarian dialectic, should be determined by a kind of continuing voice vote. If sufficient people say, "I feel badly," or "It is me," then grammatical snobs are confounded; the error is accepted. "That's what we mean by usage," an Ed. D. blandly explained to me, though he twitched when I asked whether he would endorse the usage of the Massachusetts legislator who said, "Teachers is cheap."

Democracy at home: teachers is cheap. There is a rough justice in this equation, in which, please note, there is no allowance for the variable factor of ability. Young intellectual snobs must be suckled on the thin broth of the insipid mean; to give them a richer diet would, in the glib cliché, be undemocratic. It is not undemocratic, of course, to provide special schools for retarded children; they are below the general level and must be brought up to it. Thus we see again the topsy-turvy dogma—the same twisted thinking which corrupted Franklin D. Roosevelt's "The poorest are no longer necessarily the most ignorant part of society" to mean "The commoner the man, the wiser he." Gifted children ("double-domes") are distrusted. The dull and delinquent ("underprivileged," "sick," "victims of society") belong to a privileged caste. We must look down on those above us, up to those beneath us. So sacred is this doublethink that we rarely challenge it, though sometimes it is carried to a Tartuffian extreme and we see a glimmer in the night. The last time I visited the Barnum and Bailey sideshow, the barker interrupted his spiel to deliver a brief sermon. He just wanted us to know that these fine tattooed, misshapen and deformed people on the stage were folks, same as you and me. Why, you'd be glad to have any of them in your home, he said. Sure, they were interesting. But— and his voice dropped to a tactful whisper—they weren't *freaks*.

Meanwhile, what of the snob? Prayer seems to be all that he has left. Every institution in the republic, from the Army to the pulpit, is at his throat. Here and there a country club holds out like a Beau Geste fort in the Sahara, but to the thoroughbred snob these odious allies are worse than none at all. Apparently he is a doomed species, destined to die without heirs. Yet we are left with a paradox. Why do the anti-snobs persist in railing against snobbism's tattered remnant? Why can't they leave us with our illusions of superiority, which they are so sure are spurious? There are two excellent reasons. The first is that they aren't at all sure. Deep in every egalitarian breast there is a gnawing suspicion that he is inferior and, since the suspicion is fully justified, it won't be still. The second reason is that they desperately need us. They are what they are because we are what we are. They, like all snobs, must look down on someone. To satisfy this human craving they have created their own inverted pecking order, with us at the bottom of the pyramid. Neglect us, and they would lose their illusions; forget us entirely, and each of them would be obliged to recognize the clod in his shaving mirror.

Shall we then scorch the earth, recant, disperse? No, that's not our way. Like that grand old snob Homer, who urged warriors into battle by reminding them of their heroic lineages, we must hold fast and trust that victory may yet ride at our stirrups. It won't be easy. Belonging to an élite has never been easy, and we may as well face it; these are the times that try snobs' souls. There are endless snubs ahead from Joes who think they are better than we are because their manners are worse, their pasts shadier, their brainpans smaller. Decorated veterans will be insulted by soldiers with unimpeachable records of cowardice. Hi-fi women will be cut dead by the arrogantly unchaste. Offspring will deride us because they are dependent upon us, and unlettered graduates of Teachers College, Columbia, will leer when we don't talk like they think we should. Still we must keep our noses high, even when the press traduces us:

"The real triumph of democracy will not be recorded until every man jack American practices equality in his daily rubs against the coat sleeves of his fellows."

Every man jack?

And: "Call no man democratic who forgets that his barber, cook and errand boy are made of the same human clay as himself."

My barber? *My* cook? *My* errand boy?

And, from a wartime patriot: "Many an elevator's boy's life is made intolerable by the little Hitler who is his elevator starter; he wonders how much good will be accomplished by getting rid of the big Hitler if the little Schicklgrubers still [sic] persist."

It is dark in the Führerbunker tonight. Outside, the egalitarian legions press harder and harder, led by AWOL privates and nursed by Florence Nightingales on leave from call-girl clienteles. We can no longer see properly. An athletic snob is doing push-ups, a travel snob fingers lovingly the thick visa inserts in his passport, a music snob rewinds his gramophone and replaces a Bach with a Bartók, but the rest of us are at loose ends. Directly across from me an F.F.V. representative has put aside her stars-and-bars embroidery. Beside her a Harvard man (Porcellian Club) has abandoned his translation of *Ajax*. Others were reading Rilke; were reading Wilbur; were hanging Braque canvases; were rearranging Biedermeier furniture. Now they are sitting idle on the bunker floor in an arc—rather a cramped arc, since no one wants to be on the left. Yet none of us is bored. We are carrying on bravely in the spirit of Tommy Carlyle, Billy Thackeray, Bobby Frost, Bert Russell, Georgie Shaw, Ginger Woolf, Evvy Waugh and Josy Gasset. Russ Lynes started the conversation, and now everyone has joined it.

We're bragging.

Public Men

IN JANUARY 1953 I crossed the Atlantic on the Queen Mary. My stateroom was next to Winston Churchill's suite, and I covered the Prime Minister's voyage for Reuters. Each day at sea I saw him alone briefly, but my most vivid memory of the trip was a public episode. The evening before we docked in Southampton, first-class passengers were shown a documentary film about the first half of the twentieth century in England. The climax was the Battle of Britain. At the height of it, the sound track carried dubbings of Churchill's voice delivering his famous speeches of that year. And as the unforgettable rhetoric rolled through the first-class theater, Churchill, who was in the audience, rose and walked out on himself.

Why did he do it? There are several possibilities. Conceivably he was moved. Perhaps he was bored; he had, after all, heard all this before. He may have wanted to use the toilet, to light a cigar, to finish that last inch of brandy in the bottle he had nearly consumed at dinner. Or maybe—and I think this is the likeliest explanation—he may have known that no one who was there would ever forget it.

Churchill was wholly the public man. We never conversed. He addressed me as though I were a one-man House of Commons. If he had a different manner in private, I never saw it. Nehru was like that; so was U Nu of Burma; so, I'm told, was Franklin Roosevelt. Most political figures, however, divest themselves of their public manner when away from the limelight. Eisenhower could be crisp and sometimes even cold. John Kennedy was an adroit conversationalist; Bob Kennedy a tender father; Nixon profane and paranoid.

Entourages become familiar with the switch in the demeanor of most statesmen when they withdraw from their constituents. Sometimes the leader is more impressive behind closed doors (Eisenhower

*was), sometimes he is less striking (Nixon was). The octaval shift is es-
sential to their renewal and regeneration. If this suggests that there is
something of the charlatan in each of them, let the implication stand.
That is the way they are because that is the way they must be if they
are to survive emotionally. I think we should be tolerant of a little
fakery in our politicians. We must also reconcile ourselves to a certain
amount of misbehavior in their private lives. The man who has nothing
in his closet may not have anything in the attic, either. If constituencies
cannot accept that, we may be cursed with leadership by the bland.*

*And that isn't good enough. Without imaginative politicians,
democracy will collapse. Periodically Americans display open contempt
for politics. This has been especially true since Watergate. It is wrong,
it is dangerous—precisely that attitude destroyed the Weimar Republic
—and it is unjust. For over a quarter century I have been a professional observer of public men. Some have been stupid, some weak, a
few venal. They have not been typical, however. Characteristically the
public man is ambitious and sensitive. He has a social conscience. He is
shrewd and a believer in expediency, but he is capable of nobility. The
extent to which that capacity is realized depends upon the press and
the voters.*

*There is an old Zen allegory: "I am a mirror. Whoever looks at
me looks at himself. Whatever he sees in me, good or bad, reflects him."
It is the same with politicians. If you condemn them all, you condemn
yourself. Honor the best, and the likeness in the looking-glass will improve. Even a mirror, metaphorically speaking, needs self-esteem. And
no one is prouder than good public men.*

Adlai in Defeat

ADLAI EWING STEVENSON lost the Presidency on November 4, 1952, while winning 27,314,992 votes, more than any previous winner except FDR in 1936. One of those Stevenson votes had been cast by me. My heart went with it, which hardly made me unique, since he was among the best-loved losers in the history of American politics. When he conceded, saying he was too old to cry, I was but one of millions who wept for him. That week I sent him a copy of my first book. Back came a surprisingly prompt acknowledgment from him, which confirmed my lack of confidence in the judgment of the electorate, and in January, still heartsick, I flew off to Asia as a foreign correspondent for the Baltimore *Sun*.

Abroad I continued, at long-distance, what had developed into a Hildy Johnson–Walter Burns relationship with Neil H. Swanson, the *Sun's* executive editor. He was forever sending me service messeages like:

PROCEED LAHOREWARD SOONEST COVER QUADIANI RIOT ETDENY OR CONFIRM AP FACTWISE SWANSON

UPFOLLOW FULLEST DULLES STEPTAKING INSURE SEVENTH-FLEET READINESS EVENT COMMIE UPRISING RANGOON ACKNOWLEDGE SWANSON

YOUR STORIES UNARRIVED RENEGOTIATIONS CUMMOSADEQ STOP FLASH RUSSENVOY FACTS TIMELIER FULLER WITH VIGOR DETAILS COLOR ACCURACY WIT ETBALTIMORE ANGLE WHENEVER POSSIBLE REGARDS SWANSON

Usually I filed these in the nearest wastebasket or, more mischievously, mailed them to Russell Baker, now a New York *Times* columnist and then the *Sun*'s one-man London bureau. Russ couldn't retaliate, for although I had his Fleet Street address, he never knew where I was. I was always on the move, living out of a musette bag. Swanson caught up with me only once, when I was staying at the Semiramis Hotel in Cairo. My bedside telephone rang. "Swanson here," shouted a voice from the other side of the world, sounding as though it were being relayed through a wind tunnel. "The Russian legation in Tel Aviv has just been bombed. How fast can you get there and cover it?"

To appreciate the peril this put me in, you must remember that Egypt and Israel were still in a state of war. In Cairo the new Naguib-Nasser junta was suspicious of all foreigners. They shadowed correspondents and eavesdropped on their telephone conversations. I knew they were listening to all of mine, because just the day before, John Gunther, who was in the same hotel, researching *Inside Africa*, had phoned me in my room to suggest that we have a drink, and the man bugging his line got into a jurisdictional dispute with the man on mine. They broke into our conversation, arguing aloud in Arabic. Eventually they completely drowned us out. (We never did have the drink.) Had I so much as acknowledged Tel Aviv as a contemplated destination in my exchange with Swanson, the authorities would have jailed me within an hour. I took the only sensible course.

"I'm sorry, you have the wrong number," I yelled back, and hung up on the executive editor of the *Sun*.

The following day I cabled an explanation from Cyprus and flew on to Tel Aviv, where I actually entered the razed Soviet embassy on Rothschild Boulevard by pretending to be a member of an Israeli delegation which had come to apologize for the incident. That story ended the furious rockets from Baltimore (BADLY BEATEN TIMES SPLASHING FRONTWARD UNRUSSIAN DEMONSTRATION HAIFA), and I heard virtually nothing from the home office until, having completed a tour of southern India, I was settling in at the Cecil Hotel in Old Delhi and preparing to research a series on Benares. Then I received instructions which more than compensated for all the abrasive messages of the previous month:

UNPROCEED BENARESWARD MEET STEVENSON CALCUTTA INTER-
VIEW FREQUENTLY USING YOUR DISCRETION AM AIRMAILING
DETAILS DEHIS SCHEDULE SWANSON

I didn't need the schedule. I had been following Stevenson's current tour of the world by reading the cables in the New Delhi office of

Bob Trumbull, Indian correspondent for the New York *Times*. While traveling, Stevenson was writing about his trip for *Look* magazine. Thus far he had, in a period of six weeks, visited Hawaii, Okazaki, Tokyo, Formosa, Okinawa, Hong Kong, Manila, Singapore, Saigon, Hanoi (then in French hands), Jakarta, and Kuala Lumpur, and before landing at Calcutta's Dum Dum airport on April 28 he would have stopped in Bangkok and Rangoon also. Along the way he had been interviewed four times, had held three press conferences, and had spoken to the Japan-America Society, attended four state dinners, observed the training of ROK troops, visited the front lines above Seoul, which were being shelled at the time; inspected a U.S. warship in the Sea of Japan, reviewed Chinese Nationalist regiments on Taiwan, and—in what seemed to me to be an unnecessary indignity—had been notified that the Gagwriters Association of America had voted him its annual award.

In Malaya he had nearly been killed when his helicopter caught fire and crashed in a jungle clearing. He had been formally received by, among others, Japanese Premier Yoshida, Emperor Hirohito, General Mark Clark, Chiang Kai-Shek, Premier Quirino of the Philippines, President Sukarno and Premier Min Notewidigdo of Indonesia, and Premier Pibul Songgram of Thailand. Everywhere he had been greeted by cheering throngs. His eloquence during the presidential campaign had delighted vast numbers of English-speaking people in other countries. It had been said that he could have been elected Prime Minister of any country in Europe that year, and educated Asians admired him, too. As a result, he was experiencing the kind of receptions given to the winners, not the losers, of presidential elections.

Looking back on the dispatches of those days—my own and those of other correspondents along the way—I wince at the Cold War rhetoric which crept into Stevenson's speeches and at the eagerness with which we quoted him. He warned the Japanese against being "lulled to sleep" by hopes for a favorable change in Soviet foreign policy because Stalin had died, praised the achievements of Chiang's Formosa regime as "the most important historical accomplishment of many years if not many centuries in the Far East," expressed pleasure in Malaya's suppression of Communist guerrillas, said in Saigon that the blame for the Vietnamese war lay in Moscow, warned the Thais that "I do not see any evidence of sincerity or peaceful intentions in the Communists' activities in Southeast Asia," said he was "alarmed by the Communist invasion of a new state—Laos," and repeatedly doubted that the Communists really wanted to end hostilities in Korea. But that was how all public men in the West talked in those years. It is easy to condemn them, but it is also chronological chauvinism. Stevenson erred, which means he was human. One might add that it was the very dimensions of his humanity which set him apart from most of his contemporaries.

On Tuesday, April 28, 1953, I arrived at Dum Dum less than an hour after he had landed there from Rangoon, and within another hour I was in Calcutta's Great Eastern Hotel, looking for him. It was hot work. The Great Eastern, a rambling, rococo, white wooden relic of the Raj, was an insane jumble of dead-end corridors and roller-coaster flights of stairs; a trip from the lobby to the nearest men's room took on the proportions of an expedition. I had thought the great pre-monsoon heat would keep Stevenson in his suite long enough for me to get there, but I reckoned without his relentless schedule. By the time I had registered with the local police as an alien, he was off to interview the Chief Minister of West Bengal, and most of his party—William Blair, Jr., his law partner; Barry Bingham, publisher of the Louisville *Courier-Journal*; and Dr. Walter Johnson, chairman of the history department at the University of Chicago—had accompanied him. The only one still in the Great Eastern was Bill Attwood, then the young foreign editor of *Look* and a colleague of mine. I walked in on Attwood.

He was stripped and prostrate on his bed near the room's air-conditioning machine. We exchanged hellos, and he wearily motioned me to the place of privilege, by the machine.

"This is brutal," he said faintly.

I agreed that it was pretty awful.

"I don't mean just the heat," he said. "This whole trip—it's impossible. I'm a reporter. I like to get to a town, make my appointments, see people, check everything. But everyone's got to see *him*, all the officials. Everybody wants to hear *him* talk."

Bill explained that *Look* was paying $60,000 for the Stevenson series, together with the group's expenses, in the hope of adding thousands of his admirers to its circulation lists. The hitch was that the articles had to be turned out en route, which meant that Stevenson, a slow and painstaking writer, had to produce a piece every two weeks. The one exception was the next article, which Attwood was to write on Stevenson. Apart from that, Stevenson wouldn't stand for any ghosting. "I could do them like that," Attwood said, snapping his moist fingers. "It's my trade. But no; I write a first draft and he rewrites my draft, and it's murder for both of us. Stevenson's punchy. He's been getting about three hours' sleep at night, and it's killing him. Wait till you see him."

I said I couldn't, hardly, and he told me that the rest of the party would soon be back from the Chief Minister's. I decided to wait in the hotel's air-conditioned dining room. Providentially, Stevenson had just returned with the same thought, and as I entered I found him with the others at a little table near the bar. It was dry Tuesday, Calcutta's concession to Gandhi's enthusiasm for prohibitionism, and so the group was just sitting there in wilted cord suits, panting, perspiring, and waiting for lunch. Blair was crew-cutted and equine, Bingham was dapper and handsome, and Johnson, who had been the founder of the Draft-Stevenson movement in Chicago, had the crinkly face of a puckish boy.

Of course, my chief interest was in Stevenson. This is what I saw:

A bald, slumped man in his early fifties with spectacles perched on the end of his rather hawkish nose, poring over a thick sheaf of mail. He was conspicuously pallid. His head was cocked, in that way he had, and though he was unsmiling now, obviously he had laughed a lot in his life; parenthetical lines of humor ran from midpoint on the sides of his nose to the ends of his full-lipped mouth. Despite his critics, he was no more egg-headed than the rest of us, but his torso was egg-shaped; I guessed, correctly, that he was worried about his weight and that he was, in fact, a worrier by habit—his brow had those telltale furrows. The hair he had was dark and silky. It suggested virility.

One had the instant impression that he wasn't comprehending much of the content in the letters he was dropping, one by one, into his lap. His pudgy hands moved in slow motion, his shoulders sagged, his eyes were lusterless, the lids were puffy with fatigue. Attwood was right. He was exhausted. My first thought was that it was just as well the bar was closed. One gimlet, or even a shandy, and this man would be Out.

I greeted Blair, and he introduced me to the others, beginning with their leader: "Governor, this is Mr. Manchester." The Governor looked up dully. Under the circumstances it would have been cruel to remind him of our correspondence; doubtless he had received bales of letters like mine. I chatted with the others while he returned to his somnambulant movements with the mail. Attwood appeared, having just filed his copy at the cable office, and I was invited to lunch with them. We were about to rise when a wizened Indian in a dhoti ran up. "Mr. Stevenson?" he asked. Stevenson gave his head a defensive, if-you-insist nod. The man reached down, wrung his hand, and fled without another word. The Governor watched him go with astonishment. "Gosh, I didn't think I'd get off that easily," he said, thrusting his letters into his suit pocket. His voice lacked that dramatic, reedy quality which had marked it during the campaign. It was slurred, almost drugged by weariness.

On our way to the table I asked whether encounters of that sort were common, and Blair said they sure were. "We were in the interior of Cambodia, looking at a temple, when we heard a female shriek, 'Adleee!' We looked around, and here came this woman in a mother hubbard, carrying a camera and running across a field." "Just an American tourist gal," Stevenson explained. "She said, 'I've only got one shot left,'" Blair went on. "'I was saving it for a water buffalo, but I'd rather take you.'" "It was a most engaging experience," Stevenson said, reaching for his chair and managing a low chuckle. "We changed it to Manila for the purposes of the article," Attwood said. Bingham said, "We arrived in the Philippines the same day as Miss Universe. There was a wind, and it blew her skirts up to her neck, and she was wearing striped pants. The crowd broke right through the police lines. They weren't interested in us. Stevenson just hollered, 'I'm not Miss Universe,' and there wasn't any trouble."

I had more or less assumed that the Governor would retire to his suite after lunch for a long nap, but his agenda didn't allow it. Hardly had we bolted chicken sandwiches when Calcutta's U.S. Consul General arrived to drive us to the headquarters of the Damodar Valley Corporation, Northeast India's TVA. There I witnessed what was to become a familiar spectacle: Stevenson trying to act as a journalist and being defeated by his celebrity. We sat in a semi-circle of chairs around the desk of the corporation's chairman. The Governor produced a little notebook and an automatic pencil. He was poised for the reply to his first question when the door opened and an Indian darted in, hand outstretched. That happened seven times. We were just beginning to study a wall map of the project when it was time to go. Stevenson cleared his throat. "Well," he said, "that's quite a little dam you're building up there, it seems to me." An eighth Indian bounded in and thrust an enormous package of printed Damodar matter at him. He shrank away. "I'll take it," Johnson said easily. "In a couple of months you'll be writing about this, and you'll want it."

The next call was at the official home of H. C. Mookergee, Governor of West Bengal, who presented Stevenson with a cardboard cutout of an Indian saint. There was a gap in the schedule then, and Stevenson could have returned to the Great Eastern, but he said he was determined to do *some* reporting. He asked me where he might get a glimpse of a seamier side of Calcutta, and at my suggestion we headed for Howrah railroad station, on the far side of the Hooghly River, one of the mouths of the Ganges. The station, the most unsavory sight in the city, had become a camping ground for hundreds of Hindu refugees from East Pakistan, and as we entered they were everywhere we looked, cooking, sleeping, and nursing babies on the concrete floor. Stevenson moved slowly through the human wreckage, a short bowed figure half obscured by the guttering flambeaux of makeshift stoves, carefully lifting his polished loafers over the litter of arms and legs of men shuddering on the rack of famine; of frail little children with distended bellies; of the sick and diseased and helpless. The smell of smoke was almost overpowering, and under it there was a sharper, human odor. "Can't something be done about this?" the Governor asked an Indian official. The man explained that homes had been found for many of them in nearby Orissa, but they kept returning to the station, insisting that they wanted to live in Bengal. "Well, it seems they could do *something*," the Governor said, his face puckering in a frown. "Look at that old man! He doesn't look like he's ever going to move. And look at *that!*" Toward the end of an immense corridor—it is the very enormity of Indian interiors which strikes visitors from the West; all rooms, halls, and foyers are outsized—a dozen naked little boys were huddling together. He said heavily: "That would make a picture, wouldn't it? The Boys Club of Calcutta."

The Howrah station is all the slumming most Calcutta visitors can take in one day, but Stevenson had seemed more at home there than in the Damodar office. I was beginning to observe in him a quality I had seen in other politicians—Churchill, Naguib, U Nu, Nehru—who seemed to gain strength from tours of public places, as though they could actually draw vitality from the masses they, or other politicians, sought to represent. When we returned to the Great Eastern he said to me, "Let's see a little more of India," and headed down a swarming sidewalk.

We edged past two cows blocking the way and turned down a street named Waterloo, toward a square called Chowringi. Here and there turbaned men in loincloths were sleeping on the pavement. Most of those on their feet seemed to be beggars who thrust clawlike hands at us as we passed. Stevenson appeared to be looking for something. Farther down the street, opposite the stall, he found it: a Communist bookstall. "Let's see what they've got," he said, stepping up briskly. The racks carried such titles as *The Life of J. Stalin, New China Forges Ahead, American Shadow Over India,* and as he inspected these a lean young Indian clerk, taking him for a potential customer, held one out to him: *Why is the Korean War Being Dragged Out?* Stevenson, who after all had been asking for it, recoiled, flushing. "Isn't that shocking?" he spluttered. "Look at that stuff! Marx! Stalin! He tried to sell me that stuff!" He was indignant, I was indignant; we were a couple of touchy Cold Warriors.

We turned down a side street, past a funeral parlor which advertised that it was open twenty-four hours a day, past a horribly twisted youth who pawed us in a gesture of supplication, past sweating, teeming gangs of women towing little children who were weeping in the bitter heat, and Stevenson was silent all the way back to the hotel. Unlawfully, the Great Eastern served us drinks in his suite, but the Governor's martinis didn't do much for his spirits. In the dining room the others in the group turned to their food with zest, but Stevenson didn't eat his. He toyed with it for a while and then put his spoon aside. "I'd enjoy this more if I hadn't seen all those starving people," he said finally. "It's the children, the little children, that get me." The rest of us looked down guiltily at our empty plates.

I became accepted as a temporary member of the party until Stevenson left India two and a half weeks later. There were no other applicants—few American correspondents lived in Asia then—and the Governor had a special reason for wanting me by his side. After a quick courtesy call on Shiekh Abdullah in Kashmir, and another on Nehru, he was going to tour South India. He needed a reliable guide and decided that I qualified. Meanwhile the rest of the group around him was shrinking. Attwood felt ill, and Johnson wanted to pursue some inquiries in the Punjab. Therefore just four of us—Stevenson, Blair, Bingham, and I—took off in shirtsleeves for an extended journey to Nagpur, Hyderabad, Madras, Bangalore, Trivandrum, the Malabar Coast, Cochin, Mangalore, Bombay, and then New Delhi—about 17,000 miles, most of it by plane, but some by car and once, across a river, by raft.

The patterns which I had first seen in Calcutta continued. There was just no way for Stevenson to escape his fame. Seen from Springfield, Illinois, our caravansaries in the southern tip of India were literally on the other side of the globe, yet privacy eluded him even there. Autograph hunters hid in shrubbery and ambushed him at airports, even at zoos. Villagers dissatisfied with their conditions presented him with petitions. Dark youths lined streets to stare as his car passed. Local panjandrums turned out bands to honor him by tooting western tunes. (The favorites were "Swanee River," "Marching through Georgia," and, though it had no relevance for him that month, "Happy

Birthday to You," which was always played as though it were a John Philip Sousa air, with martial brasses and all the percussions clanging.) Americans who had worked for his election at home, and were now employed here in consulates or on aid projects, lurked outside his hotel rooms. I was in no position to criticize them—in a sense, I was a lurker myself—but toward the end of the first week I began to appreciate his frustration.

Aboard planes, Stevenson and Blair had worked out an effective defense against curious fellow passengers. The Governor would take a window seat and plant his briefcase beside him. Blair would sit directly across the aisle, so that, if an intruder bothered Stevenson, they could ostentatiously peer around him at each other until he was made to feel very much in the way. Nevertheless, there were a few presumptuous admirers who stayed anyway.

At Nehru's direction the government did what it could to help. Mostly unknown to Stevenson, agents of India's Criminal Investigation Department accompanied us everywhere. Twice we swam on a magnificent beach of white sand studded with coconut trees in Travancore-Cochin; watching us were three CID inspectors and twelve of their men, all disguised as fishermen. When we drove seventy miles to an industrial exhibition at Quilon, the route was patroled by bomb experts. (Stevenson heard about that afterward. He said miserably, "Gosh, you don't realize the trouble you make.") In all this unwanted hoopla, I remember just one comic incident. The landing field at Mangalore was new. It had been formed by shearing off the top of a mountain. As we entered our glide pattern, we saw a huge mob staring up at us, and Stevenson moaned. But when we taxied up to the terminal, the crowd was melting away. We inquired and were told that the engineers had built a very short runway; a pilot who put his wheels down a few feet from one end would just stop a few feet from the other end. The people had come, not to see a celebrity, but in anticipation of a possible crash. Stevenson was delighted.

The local press was a special problem, arising from the veneration which they, like intellectuals everywhere, felt toward him. (John Foster Dulles visited India the following month and was virtually ignored.) Being human, they often brought their wives and children just to touch him, or be touched by him, and it all added to the congestion. An example was R. Satakopan, a husky, amiable Indian and a friend of mine. When he was not serving as correspondent for the Associated Press, Satakopan was a professional photographer. Stevenson had rebelled at the suggestion that he be trailed around the world by *Look* cameramen, so Attwood was hiring local men in each country. In India it was Satakopan, who, at three successive stops, introduced the Governor to his elder brother, his younger brother, and a college classmate, and photographed each of them at the Governor's side.

Normally Stevenson was adroit at fielding reporters' questions, but his *Look* contract had put him in a bind. It specified that he could not anticipate his magazine material in newspaper interviews. Therefore he was obliged to be very general with journalists and, now and then, a trifle inane. He told one in Nagpur that he had "enormous respect" for the Indian people, that he was hopeful that relations between America and India would become "better and better and better," and that he thought a third world war was "very far away." At a Malabar ferry he told a journalist in a jibba and dhoti that he was impressed with the government's five-year plan, and thought the rice fields very pretty. A Hyderabad newspaperman learned that the Governor was interested in the granite formations around the airport, and that in Stevenson's opinion the day was a pretty hot one.

Under the circumstances he could hardly be expected to put in a stunning performance as a reporter himself, and he didn't. After a while he stopped trying. His notebook appeared less and less frequently. "God, I envy you newspaper guys, the way you get everything down," he said to me in Quilon, gazing out the car window as a scene of coir carriers, Mobilgas stations, mayflower trees, and Communist flags swept by. "I haven't taken a note for two days. I get too interested in people." That was half of it. The other half was their abiding interest in him. He was incapable of tuning them out, of growing a thick skin and rejecting the more outrageous trespasses on his privacy. Three times during one evening in the guest house of Trivandrum's rajpramukh he tried to cope with a long-distance call from California. Apparently someone wanted him to sign up for a speaking engagement there. The operators couldn't clear the line. All he heard was static. There was no possibility that he could accept any such invitation—his schedule would be full when he got home, too—yet he wouldn't let anyone else handle it for him. I remember the rest of us sitting around the dining table, admiring a white elephant standing just outside in the warm moonbright night, while down the hall Stevenson was bellowing hoarsely into the phone, trying in vain to make himself understood.

Often with him one had the feeling that he would never come to terms with his immense popularity. Evidence of it, which appeared daily, merely bewildered him. Once on a verandah overlooking the Indian Ocean Blair appeared with news that Stevenson's book of campaign addresses was on the *Herald Tribune*'s best-seller list. I predicted that it would stay there a long time. Stevenson gave me a look of disbelief. "You really think so?" he asked. "After all, they're just speeches." Several days later I was seated directly across from him at a state dinner given by the Governor of Bombay. En route I had learned that the photographer who had taken a picture of Stevenson's shoe with a hole in it had just been awarded a Pulitzer Prize. I told him over soup. He didn't believe me. Turning to Shri Shantilal Shah, who was seated at his right, he said, "Mr. Manchester is ribbing me." "Ribbing?" repeated the Indian, clearly baffled. "Teasing," said Stevenson. "Ah!" sighed Shantilal.

It had happened, just the same. In defeat he had become a world figure, with all that that implied—the eminence, the ceaseless scrutiny, the adoration of liberals everywhere, and the vexations of being a great celebrity. What he needed was an entourage, a shift of Secret Service agents, or at the very least a personal servant to deal with the trivia and the nuisances besetting him. I particularly recall one sultry evening at the Connemara Hotel in Madras. At Stevenson's request, I had brought to his room an irascible old English colonial administrator with an exceptional knowledge of South Indian politics and absolute mastery of all the local languages. For nearly two hours the Englishman rattled on, prodded now and then by a question from Stevenson. The night thickened around us with no slackening of the heat—there were no air-conditioned rooms in the Connemara then—and from time to time a bearer, aware that Stevenson would be there only one night and eager to be tipped now, would come in and fuss needlessly with the furniture. At length the Briton and I departed. Stevenson thanked us, a damp, pudgy figure waddling slightly as he stripped to his undershorts. We three debated the value of mosquito netting, which was available but which would block any night breezes that might spring up. "You don't need a net if your punkahs are on," the Englishman said, pointing to two big-bladed ceiling fans overhead. "They blow the bugs away." "That so?" said Stevenson, and we left him struggling with the fan controls.

His struggles, I learned the next morning, had been only partially successful. When we met in the lobby at 6:30 A.M. I asked him how he had slept. "I didn't," he said hollowly. "The fan over the bed didn't work, so I crawled up on the sofa, under the one that did. Four bearers kept running in and out, telling me they wouldn't be here in the morning, so I finally gave them ten rupees. It was the smallest I had. They went away and then the bugs started to bite. They didn't bite me on the side where the fan was, but they got me on the leeward. I tried to fetch one of the bearers to help me with the bed fan. They'd all disappeared with the rupees. I ran up and down the halls looking for them, but they weren't around. So I went back and got bitten. God, what a night."

He should have complained to the manager—Nixon would have put the man on his enemies list—but Stevenson didn't want to offend anyone, not even the autograph seekers. Gandhi had solved that problem by charging five rupees, $1.20, for each signature. Stevenson couldn't do it. Even nervy salesmen could badger him. He was about to enter a car at one point when a frail Indian boy, having slipped through the C.I.D. screen somehow, stepped out from behind a post and handed him a package wrapped in newspaper. "What's this?" asked Stevenson, surprised. The boy gestured, suggesting that he open it, and he did. Inside was a cheap mirror in a brass frame. "Twenty-one rupees," the boy said. The Governor looked troubled. "Gosh, I'd like to," he said earnestly, "but you know, I'd have to carry it halfway around the world. I don't have any room. In my baggage." The boy wobbled his head sorrowfully. "You understand," Stevenson said to him and turned to Blair. "You think he understands?" he asked him. "Do you?" he said to me. We spread our hands. "Thanks very much," he said, carefully rewrapping the mirror and handing it back, "but I just can't." We slid into the waiting DeSoto. "He looked so hurt," the Governor said worriedly. "I can never tell whether they understand or not." He muttered defensively, "I just don't have the room."

The Cages of Bombay outraged him. These were two blocks of two-story buildings faced with iron bars. Each room, or cell, contained a naked prostitute who conveyed with spirited pantomime the nature of the services she was prepared to perform. The purpose of the iron bars was to keep non-paying customers out, not to imprison the harlots. This was carefully explained to Stevenson. He was also told that the custom had persisted for centuries—that girls born into that caste enter the Cages with the onset of puberty while their brothers become pimps. It made no difference to him. The spectacle was an offense to his sense of human dignity, and unlike most tourists he left seething. I was proud of him for that.

In other ways he could be disconcertingly banal, even Babbitty. It was easy to shrug at the one occasion when he himself became an autograph seeker—a traveler doesn't often have the chance to acquire the signature of a man with a name like Chakravarti Rajagopalachari, Chief Minister of Madras—or to pass over Stevenson's purchase for himself of a native costume in a bazaar. Less understandable was his jeer when an Indian presented one member of our party with a garland and a bouquet of flowers ("Now he can work for the State Department!") or his remark when he was told that he would meet a team of executives from the Tata steelworks in Bombay: "My God, it will be good to get the viewpoint of some hard-headed businessmen."

"Say, there's a nice-looking gal," he said in Nilokheri, beckoning to a little child. An Indian bystander volunteered that it was a boy. "His hair's long, though," Stevenson said. "He's a Sikh," the man explained; "Sikhs grow their hair long." "Back home we call them New Dealers," Stevenson said, and I briefly felt betrayed. One evening after we had watched a performance of masked kathakali dancers, Stevenson mounted the stage and posed with them for Satakopan. He did it with a broad grin and many stage whispers—"They'll never believe this in Chicago"; "Maybe they'll let me into the union"; "Careful, these fellows have been dancing overtime"—and when Satakopan had put his camera away, the Governor tried to execute a clumsy little Buffalo shuffle and stumbled badly.

That wasn't the Adlai Stevenson I had worshipped six months earlier, but of course that Adlai never existed. Had he beaten Eisenhower, those who were bitterest at his defeat would have been the first to be disillusioned with his administration. His eloquence had blinded them—us—to the fact that in many ways he was a middle-aged, conservative Princetonian with the limitations, prejudices, and, yes, the petty conceits of his generation and social class. He had "AES" embroidered on his shirt pockets. He ate too much and blamed his excess weight on his glands. He complained to me, "I think India's got to realize what Communism is. I think they've got to stop treating it as something that will go away if they just stop talking about it." In his only visit to a USIA library he made just one comment—an expression of scorn because he found a three-volume Martindale-Hubbell Law Directory on the shelves. (It had been a gift.) He was painfully eager to be one of the boys; at the beach he joined the fishermen tugging a canoe up on the sand, and none of us who knew had the heart to tell him that they were the C.I.D. men detailed to guard him. "Just like Rehoboth!" he merrily called to me as we battled the surf, and I felt sure he would have cried, "Just like Jones Beach!" if I had been from the *Times* or "Just like the Cape!" had I been from Boston. Perfectly acceptable, but also very ordinary, and in November he had seemed absolutely extraordinary. I was nagged by feelings of disenchantment.

And yet . . .

He made it all happen again in Trivandrum, where what had started out as the most distressing incident of the trip turned into its one triumph. The evening before we flew down there Blair received a telegram from Harold Otwell, the USIS librarian there, saying that he had "taken the liberty" of arranging a full schedule of interviews, a press conference, and a public meeting where Stevenson was to speak for an hour. "'Taken the liberty,'" Blair repeated and groaned. Bingham said, "That hasn't happened any other place we've been. It's inexcusable." It really was; Trivandrum was supposed to be a holiday. Attempts to reach Otwell by phone were unsuccessful, so Blair sent a wire canceling everything and reaffirmed the revocation when the librarian met our plane the next morning.

Then Stevenson started to worry. Travancore-Cochin was the most heavily Communist state in the country, ironically because American missionaries had taught the natives to read, making them vulnerable to subversive tracts. The Communist Party of India would exploit the hard feelings which would inevitably follow a total wipeout of the announced schedule. Then there would be all those hurt feelings, all those disappointed people. That, I think, counted more heavily with him than the prospect of losing a small round in the Cold War. In any event, he ended by compromising. There would be a sprinkling of interviews, a ceremonial call on local officials, and a "civic reception" that evening, at which he would say a few pro forma words.

It turned out to be quite a reception. The affair was held in a large floodlit square bordered on three sides by two-story office buildings and on the fourth by an alley. In the middle of the square was a long table, obviously the head, equipped with a microphone and loudspeakers. Scattered about were little tables for four; invited guests sat there. The bulk of the throng—and it was vast—was perched in the windows of the office buildings, on their roofs, atop and behind wooden barriers; anywhere human beings would fit. In the dark a reliable estimate of the crowd was impossible, but it was upward of 10,000. When I saw it, I warned Stevenson that the situation might become awkward for him. Obviously a lot of planning had gone into this. And there were no members of Nehru's Congress Party present. The Trivandrum government was Socialist. This was going to be a Socialist show first to last, which meant it might also carry heavy anti-American overtones.

It did. Stevenson was introduced by Trivandrum's Socialist mayor, Balakrishnan Nair, whose remarks were laced with references to India's distaste for "global power conflicts." He had a lot to say about American involvement in Korea, most of it uncomplimentary; there was even a suggestion that China's germ-warfare charges ought to be investigated by a neutral nation. Twenty years later, after the horrors in Vietnam, Nair's comments do not sound incendiary, but they were strong political medicine at the time. The leader of the United States' majority party could not let them go unanswered, and the mayor's flattering references to Stevenson merely made his guest's task more difficult.

Nair sat down. Stevenson rose. And for the first time since the previous autumn I heard the dramatic, reedy lilt in his voice.

I have been deeply moved by the mayor's speech. My only regret is that I did not make that speech in the United States during the last election.

You have welcomed me, sir, in the name of the common people. May I say that in America, we consider the Democratic party the party of the common people, and I am therefore glad to offer you all honorary membership in the Democratic Party of the United States.

As a boy in northern Michigan I spent many pleasant hours on a sailboat named the Malabar. Now, in coming to the Malabar coast of India, the coast Christopher Columbus may have been seeking when he found my own country, I am fulfilling the ambition of a lifetime.

And what have I found here? I have found one of the most luxurious and exotic fragments of the entire globe. I have found a country rising again to make its contribution to enlightenment in the hearts of men. I have talked to your speaker and your Chief Minister, and I know of the difficulties you face.

My own country struggled and fought for freedom from Great Britain with no aid from any source. We had, of course, the vast resources of an unconquered continent.

With confidence in your destiny, with the vigor and determination I know rests in the hearts of your people, I know your country will be all you expect it to be.

I appreciate the message of the mayor's speech. Peace is the great unfinished business of our generation.

But in the United States we believe there is something even more precious than peace—freedom. We would rather perish as a people than see liberty diminished. The determination of men to forge their own future is not, we think, peculiarly American. It is Indian. It is Korean. It is European. It is Asian. It is found wherever the children of God lift their faces to His sun in prayer and hope. It is universal. It is the yearning to be forever free.

We have much to learn from you. We hope we can contribute

to your magnificent efforts. We trust that while we may disagree on much, we may do so with civility and mutual regard for each other's honor. We further trust that together we may grasp the larger hope of a brighter, more abundant future—provided always that neither relinquishes for a moment our precious independence, nor suffers silently while the independence of mankind is in jeopardy anywhere.

I am sorry I could not speak at greater length. If anything, it is you who should speak to me, for I came to listen, not to talk. And here I am, talking. But that's characteristic of politicians the world over. I thank you, Mr. Mayor, and I wish you all Godspeed.

He got a tremendous hand. Then, after a religious play by some masked performers, we departed, Stevenson and Blair in one car and Bingham and I in another. Back at our quarters Blair said to me, "That was some crowd in the streets. Leaving, we had to turn on the light in the car, so they could see the Governor. It was like old times." He turned to Stevenson. "Remember during the campaign, when the people would shout, 'Turn on the light, Adlai, or we won't vote for you?'" "Sure," said Stevenson, chuckling. "And we did—and they didn't."

The next day I asked Bingham whether he thought Stevenson would run for President again. "I don't know," he said. "It wouldn't be pushed on him another time. It's hard for him to make big decisions, you know. There's some talk about him becoming president of Harvard, but they've just had a president very much involved in public affairs, and I don't know whether they want another right now. Also, he isn't a graduate of Harvard. They've never had a president who wasn't a graduate." He thought a moment. "He'd make a wonderful cabinet member, if we ever have another Democratic President."

Late that afternoon—we were at the beach, toweling after a dip—I told Stevenson that after the election Gerald W. Johnson of Baltimore had said there were five reasons why Stevenson had lost: five stars. The Governor said he didn't think that was quite right. He thought there were five reasons, all right, but those weren't the ones. "Judging from the letters we got, I'd say that twenty years of Democratic administrations and Trumanism were the big things. The hostility toward Truman was really vicious at the end.. Korea, corruption—what was generally called the mess in Washington—were the others. Ike's popularity and military background I would put last. Indeed, the fact that I was unknown, and spoke well, and came upon them unknown probably helped me." At lunch in Cochin the subject of a second presidential campaign arose again. Blair said to the Governor,

"You're still getting a lot of mail urging you to run next time. For God's sake, don't discourage them." Stevenson grinned wickedly. He said, "I'll answer them with a regurgitive exclamation."

I left the party when we landed at New Delhi's Willingdon Air Station. There was never any doubt about the crowd there; we knew it would be big. When the airline ramp was rolled up to the plane door, a beefy American was standing on the top step. "I'm Charles Stone, Consul General here," he said, pumping Stevenson's hand. "Get out of the way, Stone!" someone shouted, and as he stepped aside a battery of flashbulbs exploded. Stevenson was surrounded before he reached the ground, and I saw his bald head, still red from the Malabar sun, bobbing erratically in a crush of expatriate Americans, reporters, and Indian admirers.

I shouldered my way toward the baggage, to make sure my kit was separated from the others' luggage, and found that a member of the embassy staff had everything organized. He also had in hand a copy of Stevenson's itinerary between Delhi and the end of his journey fourteen weeks later in New York. It included stops in Karachi, Lahore, Rawalpindi, Riyadh, Cairo, Luxor, Beirut, Jerusalem, Tel Aviv, Ankara, Istanbul, Belgrade, Dubrovnik, Athens, Rome, Venice, Vienna, West Berlin, East Berlin, Bonn, Paris, Nice, and London. He was expected to ride a camel around the pyramids. He was going to tour the Negev Desert, lay the cornerstone of an Israeli dairy barn, and address the Israel-America Friendship League. In Turkey he was slated to pay a formal call on Mrs. India Edwards and attend a benefit for the American Bristol Hospital. He would confer with Tito, be received by the Pope, visit the headquarters of SHAPE, discuss the European situation with President Auriol of France, lunch with Prime Minister Winston Churchill, and be presented to Queen Elizabeth II.

As I waited for a cab to take me home to Old Delhi I glimpsed him over many heads. His back was against a wall; he was facing the capital's press corps like a quarry at bay, which in a way he was. "Will you run in 'fifty-six?" a reporter shouted. "I don't know, and if I did, I wouldn't tell you!" Stevenson cried, desperately feigning cheeriness. I didn't try to hear the rest. By now I knew all the questions and, pretty much, what the answers were going to be. I only wondered whether, here and elsewhere, this weary, lonely, sensitive, articulate, and complex man would ever get to ask many questions of his own.

Walter Reuther

O NCE WALTER REUTHER ACTUALLY TOOK A HOLIDAY. The afternoon he left he was in his Solidarity House office in Detroit, grimly trying to cram a few more statistical abstracts in his briefcase, when an assistant looked in and said, what the hell, Walter, why not live it up a little? Take a *real* vacation. The earnest advocate of more leisure time for everybody else was startled. He recoiled, protesting he'd be bored, but agreed to shelve the reports and take instead a telescopic fishing rod his older daughter had given him. A few days later he sent a note back.

"I caught five fish on Monday, seven fish on Tuesday, and six fish today," it read, "and I'm going to catch all the fish in the lake before the end of the week."

"Every one was the big one for Walter," a friend recalled long afterward. "Everything was for keeps. He even went after trout with all twenty guns roaring."

In their later years Walter's wife, May, gave up the thought of vacations. She knew her husband would be delighted to plan one down to the last detail, but she also knew something would come up at the last minute, and that even if they did make it he'd find some challenge —a lake of fish to be caught or, as in Northern Michigan's Spider Lake years ago, a forest in need of clearing. He had gone there with some relatives, "and as soon as we reached the cottage," one of them remembered later, "Walter spotted some little trees nearby. He thought they didn't look right there, so while everybody else headed for the lake, he marched into the brush with a hatchet."

That was in the late 1930's, when he was just the leader of a United Automobile Workers local on Detroit's West Side. Between 1946 and May 9, 1970, when he and May were killed in the crash of a private plane, Walter, or the redhead, as he was known to the million members of the U.A.W., was president of the union, and in 1952 he succeeded the late Philip Murray as chief of the Congress of Industrial Organizations, which he and the American Federation of Labor's George Meany welded into the A.F.L.-C.I.O. in 1955. The redhead couldn't vanish into a thicket after that. He was too busy, for one thing, and for another, his bodyguards wouldn't let him.

Walter needed protection because he was so controversial. Hardly anybody in public life was more controversial, and few outside the Pentagon were more scarred by their careers. When he was ten, in Wheeling, West Virginia, he had molten glass spilled on his nose and right eye by a workman in a neighborhood factory operating without safety precautions. During Walter's trade apprenticeship in his teens a huge die fell on his foot, and the first joint of his big toe was amputated. Twice during the labor battles of the 1930's he was beaten by thugs; in 1948 he was shot down in his own kitchen, and his right arm was almost blown off. He saved it after a long convalescence by constant exercise, building a modern house with his own hands; but he was maimed for life.

Walter's powers of recovery were remarkable, perhaps because of his extraordinary drive or because, as his mother Anna believed, he had "always had good blood." His enemies, however, also reached him through his family. He was painfully aware that other Reuthers suffered for him. Anna could remember driving at breakneck speed from Wheeling to Detroit, to sit by her son's hospital bed, wondering whether he would live. A year later she repeated her race—bravoes had shot out the right eye of Walter's brother Victor, the U.A.W.'s dark, intellectual educational director. The following Christmas some ill-wisher sent the union a package containing thirty-nine sticks of dynamite. After that Walter, May and their two daughters, Linda and Lisa, lived behind a ten-foot fence patrolled by guards and German shepherds.

The statute of limitations ran out on the shootings, with no sign of a conviction. In looking for motives the police had an embarrassment of riches. So many people had it in for Walter: embittered employers, Communists, the Ku Klux Klan, the numbers racketeers he swept out of the factories, sullen union rivals. The name of Reuther attracted lightning like a Franklin rod. Throwing it into a conversation was like tossing up a baseball bat on a sandlot; people chose up sides over it. Most critics didn't want to see Walter actually assassinated, but plenty would have liked to see fate lean on him a little, and few of them wept when he died. To Jimmy Hoffa he was an antagonist far more deadly than all anti-Hoffa industrialists combined; to John L. Lewis, "a pseudo-intellectual nitwit"; to George Romney of American Motors, "the most dangerous man in Detroit."

In 1958 Republican candidates across the country ran eagerly, if unsuccessfully, against Walter, and twice Presidents ran afoul of Reuther haters. Franklin Roosevelt, greeting him as a member of a labor delegation, extended his hand and said grandly, "Ah, here's our engineer!" Another labor leader, unaware of the Veblenesque meaning of the term, as a social planner, muttered balefully, "Walter's no engineer, he's only a tool-and-die maker." When Dwight Eisenhower invited him to a stag dinner with a group of businessmen, the evening turned into a verbal free-for-all, with Walter against the field. Ike may have understood how the field felt. Walter stepped on him once, hard. The President was telling a group how he knew labor's problems; he had been pushed around as a boy, working twelve hours a day. Walter broke in. "General," he said, "you should have joined the union."

Walter's difficulty, in the opinion of Rabbi Morris Adler of Detroit, was that "some people never forgive a man with a new idea." Certainly the redhead crackled with new ideas. Days he scribbled them on thick pads; nights he sprang from bed to jot them down. He was forever hatching some new scheme to break up racial segregation, or cow company negotiators, or enlarge the union's role in what management felt was its own business. His goal was a "mixed economy"—an American version of England's Labour Party program. This enraged one end of the political spectrum but enchanted the other. When he spoke at the University of California he set an attendance record which was broken only once (by Kinsey), and elsewhere Reuther votaries included Chester Bowles, Aneurin Bevan, Jawaharlal Nehru and Eleanor Roosevelt, who thought he might even be qualified for the White House. His appeal to women was immense. During the U.A.W. presidential balloting in 1948, the sixty feminine delegates voted for him almost as a bloc. Women of strong liberal bent often swooned over him. They felt, as one of them said incoherently, that he had "a stranglehold over the wave of the future."

The lady should be excused. She was only aping her idol. Walter once described a company negotiator as "a man with a calculating machine for a heart, pumping ice water," and another time he charged that Jimmy Hoffa, Dave Beck and Joe McCarthy were reactionaries "in bed together, hand in glove." Anybody who used as many words as he did was bound to be tripped now and then by a stray metaphor. He could talk endlessly, on anything; Murray Kempton of the New York *Post* called him the only man who could reminisce about the future. If you mentioned milk to him he would cite figures, in buckets, on the comparative yield of Guernseys, Holsteins and Jerseys. If you admired the bird feeder in his backyard you would be lectured on the migratory habits of rare Michigan birds. "Ask Walter the time," said Spencer McCulloch of the St. Louis *Post-Dispatch,* "and he tells you how to make a watch."

Only rarely was his talk small talk. Usually it was grist for his one mill—the need for "dynamic relationships" and "an economy of abundance"; labor's right to a "bigger piece of a bigger pie," and so forth. It could confuse strangers, particularly when he got into statistics, and yet there was a simple melody to it. Walter was different from other men because his appetites were different. In ideas he found the exhilaration others got from cronies, liquor or tobacco, none of which appealed to him. As a youth, cycling through Germany with Victor, he downed a stein of beer on an empty stomach; after that his drinking was largely confined to Anna's homemade grape and dandelion wines.

One of his first acts as U.A.W. sovereign was to turn thumbs down on late poker sessions at union meetings, and though he took a few puffs on a cigar when he came to power, as a gag, he didn't much like it. Once Linda Reuther and a teenaged girl friend asked permission to smoke. Their mothers said they could when Linda's father did, so Linda, her friend and Walter sat down and lit up. After a few drags the girls put their butts aside and just stared, fascinated by the spectacle of Walter awkwardly trying to cope with a cigarette.

The men who used to win big in poker growled that he wore "a neon lining on his hair shirt." But it wasn't hair to him. In his youth he was an ardent member of the Wheeling Y.M.C.A., and late in life he still enjoyed the innocent pleasures of his youth. In his early days he was picked as basketball center over his brother Roy, an inch taller and a star, because he had more bounce. He always had it. Lunching in Mory's, in New Haven, with a group of Yale students late in the 1950s, he sat beneath a fifty-year-old gallery of Eli football captains. The resemblance between him and the hale men on the wall was striking, and afterward, when he breasted the campus air with his pouter-pigeon chest, he looked like an aging, somewhat elfin Frank Merriwell, back for a day of nostalgia under the elms.

After a block the boys in the blue blazers fell behind, breathing hard. Nobody, not even Harry Truman, could outhike Walter. Sometimes he was on the streets past midnight, always hatless, and once in his early fifties he tramped seven miles into town with a young friend after a meeting outside Denver. At the end they saw *The Bridge on the*

River Kwai. The friend just had to sit down. Walter, however, was up next morning for his usual hup-hup calisthenics. Exercise, like talking, was a release for him, and like his abstinence it was a reflection of his Horatio Alger attitudes. They baffled other labor leaders. Hoffa thought him a prig and a patsy. R. J. Thomas, who was Walter's chief rival for the U.A.W. presidency, was taken aback when the redhead offered to shake hands before the vote. He declined, and Walter actually said, "Tommy, if you're not big enough to lose, you're not big enough to win." Tommy then lost.

None of Walter's copybook virtues unsettled the labor fraternity more than his devotion to thrift. Most union bosses, having achieved power, assume they're entitled to a few perks. They draw pay as high as $75,000 a year, convene in exclusive resorts, and take up golf. Walter was as frugal as they come. He had a running argument with his subordinates, who couldn't get more money till he did; his salary was $22,000, and he cut it five percent in the 1958 recession. On the road he was a straight ten-percent tipper and carried a little memo book to itemize expenses. Every big A.F.L.-C.I.O. powwow in Miami or Puerto Rico was a crisis of the spirit for him. In Florida he shared a bedroom with an assistant and took off the instant business was finished. George Meany, a cheerier sort, had to trick him into agreeing to a winter meeting in Puerto Rico. Walter was wretched there. His only happy moment was when he joined a local picket line and ate from the strikers' kettle. During their stay May found a souvenir, a four-dollar Puerto Rican salad bowl, but Walter made her take it back. He told her tersely he'd make her a better one at home.

At home, May, a handsome former teacher with abundant, almost botanical red hair, did her own housework and cooking. In the late 1950's the Reuthers traded in a Rambler for a Plymouth; May drove it. They were amiable hosts; although most guests were offered tea, or something from the fruit dish that always sat in the living room, there was liquor for those who asked. Cleaning out his suite after a Chicago meeting, Walter discovered two bottles which the management had provided for other union delegates. One was full; the other had three fingers left. "Is this good whiskey?" he asked Jack Conway, his administrative assistant. Conway told him it was the best. "I'll split it with you," said Walter, handing him the three fingers and carefully packing the fifth for May's cupboard. It was one of the few times he ended being one up on a convention hotel. Usually he was defeated, as in Pittsburgh, when, avoiding reporters with questions over whether he would succeed the late Philip Murray as C.I.O. president, he decided to eat in his room. The waiter handed him a tab for eight dollars. Walter was aghast. "I can't eat out, I can't afford to eat in my room," he said, fuming. "What can I do?" The waiter murmured, "May I suggest, Mr. Reuther, that you bring your lunch?"

Walter didn't bring his lunch in Detroit, but he did eat sandwiches at his desk. He avoided restaurants because, like resorts, they weren't easy places to work, and of all his stimulants work was the greatest. Some people believed he never did anything else. Before fences and guards became necessary he lived in a residential neighborhood. One day a neighbor glanced out her window and saw a man on the Reuther lawn, weeding like nobody's business. "May's got a wonderful new handyman," she told her husband excitedly. "Look at him go! I'm going to get his name." It was only Walter, on the ball as usual. He just couldn't loaf. May said that if she saw him sitting she suspected he was sick, and she was usually right. Even illness didn't stop him—in the hospital after his wound he became terribly interested in medical problems, and by the time he was released wearing a leather-and-steel brace he had a hospital-insurance plan all worked out. Like all Reuther plans, of course, it infuriated conservative critics.

The irony is that this bugbear of American industrialists worked like one of them. He raced around with a bulging briefcase, studied correspondence while commuting to his office, and saved time by flying whenever possible. Once Ed Murrow suggested they meditate together in Burma. Walter was nonplused. He hadn't time to go home, let alone Burma. In Detroit he was off beavering twelve to eighteen hours a day. If you took the bust of FDR off his desk he could have been the stereotype of the inner-directed tycoon, seated beneath framed pictures of his children, fingering his wedding ring, fastidiously dressed in a quiet gray or blue suit. During the Battle of the Overpass at the Ford Rouge plant in 1937 he went into action with a watch chain sedately looped across his vest, and he rarely unbuttoned his collar or rolled up his sleeves on the job. Rabbi Adler once served on a three-man Labor-Management committee with Walter and Charlie Wilson of General Motors. He felt very much the odd man because the other two "spoke the same language, and there was a tremendous amount of mutual admiration between them." "In his own way," the Rabbi added, "Walter is the head of a corporation, you know. I think Wilson understood that."

Some of the titans in Detroit's executive dining rooms wondered what it would be like to have the redhead's fantastic energy in their camp, a fact that tickled him; in his office he had a Richard Decker cartoon original of one executive telling another, "I'm not saying it will *work.* I'm just saying has anyone ever *asked* Walter Reuther to come in as a V.P. at a hundred grand." Nobody did. During World War II Wilson and Big Bill Knudsen suggested he become a boss, but he wasn't interested, and when he became a V.P. of the A.F.L.-C.I.O., holding the penultimate post in American labor, there was a question whether he would trade himself up or down. It was an idle question, because Walter could never have crossed over. The son of a brewery-truck driver, he was born on his side of the tracks—in a red-fronted two-family house in Wheeling's mill section, on Labor Day Eve, 1907—and he liked it there.

Those who had been taught to respect Rotarian values regarded him as a rebel. Considered against the background of his own childhood, however, his career was as traditional as his personal habits. As a child he wrote on a Y.M.C.A. questionnaire that he wanted to be either a farmer or a labor leader. There was nothing to surprise his family in either. His grandfather, Jacob Reuther, a bearded Social Democrat, emigrated from a German farm in 1892 to exempt his children from Prussian military service, and a decade later Jacob's son Valentine became a fiery leader in the Brewery Workers Union. In his early twenties Valentine was the youngest president in the history of the Ohio Valley Trades and Labor Assembly; in his thirties he joined Eugene Debs and ran for Congress as a Socialist. Late in life his politicking was confined to Lutheran synods, though he still got hot under the collar at the very thought of injustice. "He can make noise too," Anna Reuther once said to me, glancing slyly at her husband. Walter told me with a grin, "Every time I go to Wheeling he lectures me. I keep telling him, 'Look, I'm on *your* side.'"

When Walter was a boy his father had a kind of jurisdictional dispute with the local Lutheran minister, who held that the welfare of man was of no concern to God. Valentine, indignant, quit the church and organized Sunday debates for the family on social problems. At the time he had no thought of raising labor statesmen. College seemed out of the question for his sons. He was making $1.50 a day at the Schmulbach Brewery. His wife was often ill. Walter and Roy slept in one bed, Victor and the elder brother, Ted, in another. Until their little sister grew old enough to help her mother, the boys took turns at the stove—to the end of his life Walter still roasted turkey at Wheeling reunions—and did the housework. Like any other immigrant father, Valentine wanted his boys to have what his generation called "improvements." His hope was that each would become a skilled craftsman, which he wasn't. He thought Ted might make a cost accountant, Victor a plumber, Roy an electrician, and Walter, smallest of the four, a tool-and-die maker. Only Ted followed through. Ultimately he became a chief clerk with Wheeling Steel, and his brothers, all in the union, called him the "white sheep" of the family.

Nobody thought then that Valentine was miscasting Walter. At Ritchie Grammar School the boy had excelled in what was known as Manual Training—Anna kept a wastebasket he made then, and later May acquired a copper ash tray from those years—and he knew machinery. At sixteen he quit school to become an apprentice, and for three years he plugged along at Wheeling Steel making forty cents an hour. Then he left for Detroit, looking "like I fell off a green-apple tree." Somebody had told him there were plenty of good jobs there. Somebody was wrong. Ford was retooling for the Model A. Jobless thousands were walking the streets, and after relatives of a Wheeling neighbor had found him a room, the best Walter could do was a thirteen-hour midnight shift at the Briggs plant. He put up with it for twenty-one straight nights. Then he strolled over to Ford's Highland Park plant and applied for a job as a die leader.

This was preposterous. Die leaders had twenty-five years of seasoning; Walter wasn't even twenty years old. The man at the entrance told him to run along. The guard was the first representative of management to tangle with the redhead, and he lost. Walter just kept talking for two and a half hours, and in the end the gate was wearily opened. Inside there was another scene. The hiring clerk was about to have him pitched out when Ford's master mechanic walked by with a roll of complicated blueprints. Walter accosted him. Just for laughs, the master mechanic handed him the prints and was astonished to find that Walter could read them all. Two days later the intruder was hired at $1.05 an hour. Within five years Walter was among the most highly paid mechanics in the company, bossing forty men.

It wasn't enough. The yeast of ambition was working in him, and he was dreaming his father's dreams of social justice. Averaging four or five hours' sleep, he finished high school nights; Victor came up from West Virginia, and after setting up housekeeping together they enrolled at Wayne University. For a time they flirted with the idea of becoming lawyers. It passed quickly; after a day hanging around courts they decided there was little justice there. Walter thought vaguely of becoming an aeronautical engineer, but already he was deeply involved in politics. The two brothers had first tasted victory when, remembering their grandfather, they had led a successful student protest against R.O.T.C. Now it was 1932. Detroit was in the agony of the Depression. Norman Thomas was running for President, and Walter decided to make a speech for the Socialists.

Meetings were forbidden in Henry Ford's Dearborn. Walter, being Walter, had a plan. A fellow worker had conned him into making a down payment on a vacant lot a few blocks from the plant, and he already had a Ford coupe with a rumble seat. He built a platform on the seat, drove the car on the lot, and climbed up to speak. A crowd of idle men gathered. So did several policemen. They told him this was private property, and he confirmed it, displaying his deed. There was a moment of official consternation; then they drove four stakes on the corners of the lot and decreed that his audience could be so large, no more. "I told my father it was the most expensive speech I ever gave," he said. "It cost me three thousand dollars."

It also cost him his job. A few weeks later his pay envelope carried a pink dismissal slip. Victor was already unemployed, but they had been putting money aside, so after finishing their mid-semester exams they breezily chartered a trip abroad. If they were lucky, they thought, they might see something of what both then regarded as the exciting experiment in Russia. They were lucky in another way: they withdrew their savings from the Detroit Bank just ten days before it closed. One bitter morning in February they said good-by to Roy, who was living at the Y and working on a Briggs strike committee, and left for New York bearing steerage tickets to Cuxhaven, $600 in travelers' checks, and a sheaf of letters of introduction from Reuthers and friends who had relatives in Germany. They looked upon themselves as students of the European labor movement. In fact, they were two innocents heading into a world crisis.

Their first letter was from a member of Wayne's German department. The addressee was a Hamburg businessman who, since the professor last saw him, had joined the Nazi party. He had, indeed, just been assigned to recruit the allegiance of Germans in other countries, and his first two prospects—or so he thought—were a pair of nice Aryan boys named Reuther. There was a nasty scene. Ten minutes after meeting him the brothers were on the street, swearing. They called next on an unemployed dock worker, the uncle of a Detroit mechanic, and lay awake in his house that night, listening to gunfire. Storm troopers were riding up and down the streets, shooting at anti-Hitler placards in windows. Meanwhile, in Berlin, other Nazis were busy with matches, and the Reuther brothers awoke to learn that the Reichstag had been burned.

They took the first train to Berlin. Sharing their compartment were a worried trade-union official—next day they read he had been shot—and two young German workers. The workers were interested in Walter's account of American union activity. One invited Walter and Victor to share his house near the Berlin railroad station, and they went there after taking the first propaganda tour through the smoldering ruins of the Reichstag. It turned out their host was a dedicated anti-Nazi. The house was a political headquarters, and their second night there it was raided. The Reuthers, flourishing their American passports and talking loudly in English, managed to get their friend out and away to the Swiss border. Later he re-entered the country secretly, was captured, survived a concentration camp, and appeared unexpectedly in Victor's Washington office one postwar winter as a visiting publisher of Ruhr union journals.

Germany was not at its most attractive in 1933. The Reichstag fire had ignited blazes everywhere, and two young American idealists carrying letters to enemies of the new order couldn't help getting scorched. They arrived in Mannheim, their grandfather's hometown, the day before a cousin was arrested by the Gestapo. In Scharnhausen, a suburb of Stuttgart and their mother's former home, they saw a worker brutally beaten for protesting the confiscation of his union flag. One night they took two girl cousins to a Scharnhausen movie. The film was a Nazi propaganda picture. After it a swastika was flashed on the screen and the crowd rose for the *Horst Wessel Lied*. Walter, Victor and the girls, whose father was a typographical worker, remained seated. People around them became abusive, and passports and protests in English cut no ice here; they were cuffed and shoved rudely into the street. The next time a band struck up a Nazi song, they stood.

In Berlin the brothers had applied for U.S.S.R. visas at the Amtorg Trading Company. Ford was building a factory for the Russians in the Volga city of Gorki; American instructors were needed; they could find work there. The visas would take time, the Berlin agents explained, suggesting that they spend the interval seeing something of Europe. Buying bikes in Stuttgart, they cycled through the Black Forest, the old Verdun battlefields, northern Italy, and Austria, where they joined the last May Day celebration before Chancellor Engelbert Dollfuss cracked down. They crossed to England and then pedaled through Holland and Belgium, sometimes carrying messages across borders for friends in the anti-Nazi underground. Neither was caught, though Victor enraged a Roman crowd by taking pictures of Mussolini during the observance of his tenth anniversary as Duce.

Meanwhile autumn was approaching. They were running out of

money. Walter toppled off his bike and cut his arm badly, but they couldn't afford a hospital, so they bandaged it and he rode on, one-armed. In France one dark night they sighted what looked like an inviting haystack. Exhausted, they dropped their bikes and crept up to it, and awoke next morning in what was all too clearly a pile of manure.

When the Amtorg agency sent word that their visas had arrived, it was the dead of the Russian winter. In Gorki the thermometer was thirty degrees below zero. Wearing zippered jackets and knickers, and carrying only their tool boxes—they had shipped their bikes and trunks—they were, Walter recalled years afterward, "completely disorganized." Neither knew a word of Russian. A Red Army officer got them on the right trolley. It dropped them a mile and a half from the factory, and as they stepped off another passenger pointed wildly at Walter's jacket. He looked down. Someone with a knife had quietly sliced it open and lifted his wallet. Luckily his cash was in a money belt, but all the notes on their European trip were gone, and as if that weren't enough, when they finally reached Amerikanski Pasholik, the village for American workers, they found the factory was unheated. "It was my introduction to the workers' paradise," Walter later said dryly. Victor says today, "I still shiver at the memory of that cold."

They worked in Gorki nearly two years. Walter became a foreman again, leading a "brigade" of sixteen workers and winning bonuses. He liked Russian youth, but he disliked the Bolshevik management, which kept fouling up his production plans, and he was appalled at the working conditions. Safety precautions scarcely existed. Meals in the *stalovaya*, the factory lunchroom, usually featured weak cabbage soup, scooped up with wooden spoons, and afterward a girl tossed a towel on the table, leaped up barefoot, and wiggled the cloth down the boards with her toes. Once the Soviet bosses held a contest. There wasn't enough culture in the factory, they announced; everybody should think how to get more. The department next to Walter's took an early lead when it lined its walls with fake palm trees, but he won by machining two barrels of metal spoons out of fender metal. The trouble was, the spoons kept disappearing. They were badly burred, and if you weren't careful you got a cut lip, but in Russia they were sensational. More were made; all were swiped. At last the management announced that anybody who wanted a spoon would have to surrender his factory pass. To get the pass back, he had to produce the spoon.

The Reuthers thought they had left international intrigue behind in Germany, but when they boarded the Trans-Siberian Railway to leave Russia they fell in with a conspiring companion. He didn't look like a conspirator. Victor remembers him as "the spitting image of C. Aubrey Smith," and according to his own account he was a retired English officer manufacturing aluminum in Japan. Only after the war did Winston Churchill reveal to the House of Commons—and the amazed Reuthers—that until his death Lieut. Col. Haley Bell had been Britain's top secret agent in the Far East. The colonel pumped them about Gorki and chuckled quietly at their passionate advocacy of democracy. When the train reached Harbin he suggested they hail rickshas. "What?" said Walter. "Be carried around by another human being? Not on your life!" "Silly ass," the colonel murmured, and vanished into the crowd. Later that day Walter heard himself being hailed on a Harbin street. Here came Colonel Bell, erect in a ricksha and immaculately dressed in a white linen suit and pith helmet. As he passed by—and out of the Reuthers' lives—he doffed his topee and called in sepulchral tones, "Behold the British imperialist!"

The colonel caused Walter and Victor no end of trouble, because while they didn't know who he really was, the Japanese had a hunch, and anybody who had been seen with him was suspect. Whenever they were in Japanese territory the Reuthers could count on three places being set at their table each evening, the third for the local police officer, who had been told to stamp their passports and keep an eye on them.

Their Asian trip was, in fact, something of a nightmare. The worst of it came in Hankow. The Yangtze was at full flood, rice crops had been destroyed, and the Chinese were reduced to eating seed. Parades of children followed all foreigners, beating tin cans and begging food. Everyone knew there would be rice on the steamer, and when it sailed, starving men, trying to leap aboard, were clubbed to death by burly Sikh deck guards and tossed into the water. Farther down the river, the boat rammed a junk. The forty people aboard drowned as the Reuthers watched, and when Walter protested the captain turned away, muttering that Americans didn't understand China.

In Yokohama the brothers counted their money. They had just seven dollars and were 7000 miles from home. The American consul found them berths with the crew of the *President Hoover*. Victor had a pleasant Pacific cruise, polishing brass and chatting with first-class passengers while Walter toiled in the engine room, and in California they spent their sea pay on bus tickets home. It was nearly three years since they had seen Wheeling. Their father didn't recognize their voices when they telephoned ahead, and much in American labor was even stranger to them. The automobile industry was in a turmoil of wildcat strikes, blacklists and lockouts. There was little doubt that the workers were ready to be organized. The question was who was going to do the organizing. In Detroit shops the A.F.L. president was scorned as "Sitting Bill" Green. John L. Lewis had just parted company with Green to form the C.I.O., but he distrusted the politics of insurgent allies. Meanwhile tension was growing on the assembly lines. Walter, arriving from Wheeling the winter of his return home, felt what he later described as "a sense of little people marching." To Rabbi Adler the yearning for a union seemed to have become "a secular religion." In many ways it did resemble a faith. Among other things, it had a hymn resurrected from the days of Valentine Reuther's hero, "Big Bill" Haywood, and his I.W.W.:

When the union's inspiration through the worker's blood shall run
There can be no greater power anywhere beneath the sun. . . .

They still sing *Solidarity Forever* in Detroit. In retrospect the years that followed the birth of the C.I.O. have taken on a romantic glow for graying workers. Friends tell how May Reuther's brother, told to turn out leaflets, struggled with a balky duplicating machine and finally settled for the one big word, "Strike!"; Roy Reuther, the first of the brothers to work for the union, treasures the shirt cardboard on which he scrawled the plan to seize Chevrolet Plant 4 in Flint; men at Briggs describe his redheaded, bareheaded brother leaping on the hood of a parked car and scourging their wavering picket line with four-letter words until it rallied and held. To Walter the late 1930's always remained a time when he was young, "and the world was simple, and there was a frontier ahead."

It seemed neither simple nor romantic then. Management was dead set against organization. Machine guns were being brought into Flint; Harry Bennett, the former Navy boxer who had won the affection of Henry Ford, was recruiting a private army of three thousand men at Ford. Blackjacks were stockpiled in the union camp, and John L. Lewis's political worries were not entirely unreasonable, though few took them seriously then. It was a period of leftist innocence. When Victor's future wife, Sophie, won a scholarship to Brookwood Labor College, a neighbor told her to watch out for Communists there. "What's a Communist?" Sophie inquired. "They believe in sharing everything," the neighbor said. That seemed like a good idea to Sophie. Then she had a tremulous second thought. "Even toothbrushes?" she asked. The neighbor nodded solemnly, and when Sophie arrived at

Brookwood she brought two toothbrushes, one for sharing and one, carefully stowed, for herself.

Victor, who was lecturing at Brookwood for the Quaker Emergency Peace Campaign, began dating her at about the time his brother was meeting May Wolf on a Detroit streetcar. Walter's ears pricked up when May told him she was organizing fellow teachers on the sly, and they talked unions until her stop. During a three-month courtship they talked little else. After the wedding ceremony on March 13, 1936, they drove out of town—he had to address a labor rally in Mount Clemens that night—and back in Detroit he dreamed of attending the first U.A.W. convention in South Bend the following month. His local was weak; workers still feared reprisal. Only seven members showed up for the delegate election, and they picked him. The treasurer gave him five dollars—it was all the local had—and Walter hitchhiked to the convention, where he shared a room with five other delegates, ate hamburgers, and was elected to the U.A.W. international executive board.

It was an honor, but unfortunately no salary went with it. The union had thrown in its lot with Lewis; finances were shaky. Walter hitchhiked home and borrowed three hundred dollars. He hired a sound truck and rented an office, into which he moved a secondhand desk, a mimeograph machine, a typewriter and Mrs. Walter Reuther. May had been making sixty dollars a week teaching. He paid her fifteen, which she endorsed over to the union; she was, Walter later said, "the lowest-paid secretary in the city." She was also head of Detroit's office-workers' union. His own income came from a tool-and-die-making job. Until just before the next U.A.W. convention, when he became the last of the Reuthers to draw union pay, he was to serve as an unpaid volunteer. He and his bride moved into a tiny La Salle Boulevard apartment with her parents. It wasn't as crowded as it sounds, because the Reuthers were rarely home; they worked every evening and dined in a restaurant at 10:30. Supper was skimpy.

"I never knew people to eat less," May once told me. "I was so thin the mattress hurt my hips."

Walter's local was growing. He was president now, and several others on the West Side merged with it, forming Local 174. The sky was just beginning to look blue when he lost his job. He had been working in a small factory. One afternoon the foreman inspected a die he was finishing and congratulated him on it. Walter instantly asked for a raise. His pay was increased a dime an hour at seven o'clock the next morning, and at nine o'clock, in an inconsistency nobody bothered to explain, he was dismissed for incompetence. Somebody had heard that sound truck. He liked the die, so he polished it off on his own time and left that evening to discover that he had been blacklisted. There was no job for him in Detroit. It was frustrating, because he had evolved a plan and needed to be inside a plant to execute it. The only alternative was to install a reliable substitute. He put through an urgent call to his brother, still on the road for the Quakers. That night Victor alerted his new wife to travel, and the following afternoon he was in Detroit's Kelsey-Hayes factory, working a punch press for thirty-six and a half cents an hour.

Victor's mission was to persuade workmen to sit, at the right time, in concert with members of the local. Walter had picked Kelsey-Hayes because although half of Local 174's membership was there, the company's front office had refused to discuss speedup complaints with him on the ground that he didn't represent the workers. The sit-down seemed practical. The idea, of course, was to prevent strikebreakers from being brought in. There was nothing new in it. Two years before, groups of Welsh and Hungarian miners had refused to come to the top until their wages were raised, and an Akron tire-workers' local had just won the restoration of a pay cut by perching on the job. It was in Michigan, however, that the all-night sit-down was to become famous and spread until half a million American workmen were involved. Kelsey-Hayes was a curtain raiser. It was a historic moment, and it was only a moment, because Walter had briefed everyone by the numbers. One minute Victor was punching out a new piece every ten seconds; in the next a girl pretended to faint, key men pulled the right switches on the brake-assembly line, somebody shouted "Strike!" and when the uproar subsided there was Victor, standing on a packing case, telling everybody to join the union. A bewildered personnel man, plucking nervously at his cuff, suggested that he get them back to work instead. "Only Walter Reuther can do that," said Victor, and the man, as innocent of the future as Sophie, asked, "Who's Walter Reuther?"

Walter was sitting by his telephone and looking at his watch. When the expected call came from Kelsey-Hayes' front office he inquired blandly, "What makes you think I can help you? You told me I don't represent the workers."

"If anybody can do it, you can," said the front-office voice, adding that it was sending a company car over.

Entering the plant under escort, Walter mounted Victor's packing case and took up where Victor had left off. Fingers twitched at his pants. The anxious personnel man said, "You're supposed to get them back to work, not organize them," and Walter, eyes dancing, replied, "How can I get them back to work if they aren't organized?"

When negotiations broke down the workers sat for five straight days, and in the end an agreement was signed establishing a seventy-five-cent minimum. In six months the local's membership jumped from seventy-eight to 2400. Meanwhile, the sit-downs were spreading—even John L. Lewis, who wanted to organize steel first, was caught off guard —and the great General Motors plants were paralyzed. Walter rushed a gang of West Side volunteers to Flint, where wives were passing children through windows to husbands, square-dancing outside, and joining in the anthem of the faithful:

In our hands is placed a power greater than their hoarded gold,
Greater than the might of atoms magnified a thousandfold;
We can bring to birth a new world from the ashes of the old,
For the union makes us strong!
Sol-l-lidarity Fore-e-ever!

General Motors capitulated in February and Chrysler a few weeks later. U.A.W. membership was approaching a half million, a hundred-fold increase. One night Emil Mazey, the future secretary-treasurer of the union, met Walter at a meeting. He was going to introduce him as speaker. Walter drew him aside, carefully explaining how it was to be done, what his title was, and so forth. Mazey says he decided then "that this man knew where he was going." The commander of Henry Ford's militia reached the same conclusion a few weeks later. Ford had announced that he would never recognize the U.A.W., and Harry Bennett was mobilizing. The union was wary of Bennett. A Dearborn statute required permits for distributors of leaflets, so one was carefully taken out before the organizers made their first move. As it happened, the clerk who issued it hadn't fully understood what he was doing, but no one knew this at shift-changing time on the cloudy afternoon of May 26, 1937, when a band of U.A.W. members, mostly women, left streetcars bearing handbills and mounted the concrete steps of the overpass outside the Rouge plant. The leaders were Richard Frankensteen and Walter, who had finally made the union payroll. They had announced they were coming, and photographers, ministers and investigators from the La Follette civil-liberties committee were on hand to assure fair play. It looked safe.

It wasn't. Inside were fifty of Bennett's men armed with blackjacks, rubber hose and pistols. Nobody was in the dark about who Walter Reuther was now. The goons had, in fact, been told to single him out for special attention. He was still posing for the photographers when a voice rang out—"You're on Ford property!" Before he could turn, his coat was over his head and he was down. The gorillas bounced him down the steps, flattening him, standing him up, and slugging him again, and they didn't quit until he lay bleeding on the trolley cinders below. Frankensteen sprawled awkwardly beside him, and nearby was a writhing, sobbing group of women who had been kicked in the stomach. Down the street a man's back was broken, another's skull fractured. Bennett's torpedoes withdrew, doctors arrived, and John L. Lewis sent the victims a wire: "Keep your poise. It is merely an instance."

Less than a year later there was another instance. It wasn't public. The first had brought Ford bad publicity, and when Walter returned to the overpass with a new batch of pamphlets and a thousand husky union men, he was not molested. Ford hadn't changed his mind, however, nor Bennett his tactics. On the night of April 9, 1938, a group of friends and relatives were celebrating Sophie's birthday in the La Salle Boulevard apartment when they heard someone at the door. Since Hankow, Walter had had a weakness for Chinese food; he had ordered chop suey, and everyone at the party assumed the man from the restaurant was arriving. They were wrong. The door opened and two heavies entered, one holding a blackjack and the other a gun. The gunman pointed at Walter. He said, "Come on. We want you."

In the scuffle that followed Sophie threw a pickle jar, a guest named Al King edged toward the kitchen, and Walter vindicated his years of Y.M.C.A. training and blameless habits. Backing into a strategic corner, he armed himself with a lamp and waited for the man with the billy, who came at him, shifting, looking for an opening. They wrestled; Walter twisted the handle off the blackjack and tossed it toward his brother Roy. King, meanwhile, had reached the kitchen window. He leaped two floors, narrowly missing a square concrete incinerator, and in the darkness his shouts for police floated up to the tense apartment. The man with the gun blurted out, "Let's just plug him here." Roy said quickly, "If you do you'll never get out alive."

King's shouts were growing louder. A hubbub suggested a gathering below, and the visitors swiftly withdrew. Later an informer called, offering their names for five thousand dollars. Walter agreed to meet him alone in a seedy bar—"probably the first time," a friend says, "that Walter had ever been in a dive." Of course he didn't go alone. The bar was swarming with nondescript union members sipping drinks, but the informer was on the level; he had the right men. To the surprise of nobody, they were revealed as employees of Harry Bennett. In court they admitted almost everything. They swore, however, that Walter had hired them to jump him for publicity, and on the strength of that they were acquitted. In 1941, when Ford bowed to the U.A.W., one of the thugs telephoned a U.A.W. official, proposing that the two of them bring Walter and Bennett together over a friendly table. The official's reply was a volley of the kind of oaths heard often on Walter's side of the tracks and sometimes elsewhere. The caller was aggrieved. He said, "You guys didn't take that personally, did you?"

The strange thing is that Walter didn't. All his life he had an odd, objective air toward everyone outside his family, friend or enemy, and his attitude toward attacks on him was detached, almost analytical. Still, he could take a hint. After the Chop Suey Incident, as it became known to the Reuthers, he began carrying a gun. He had a hunch his life was still in danger, and as it turned out, he was right.

The house that Walter built had to be seen to be believed, but until his death only a handful of friends and union leaders even knew where it was. It lay in green country thirty-five miles northwest of Detroit, which didn't tell snoopers much; all you could see from the road was a nondescript white farmhouse, a tall steel fence in the backyard, and a padlocked gate. When the householder was in residence, it was no place to poke around. The white building was really a barracks, manned by armed guards, and the fence was watched by four big dogs, two in and two out.

This property was very private. Ed Murrow wanted to visit it for one of his first *Person to Person* programs, but although he was a good friend of Walter's, he was refused. May Reuther wasn't interested in publicity. She left the outside world to her husband and devoted her time to the local P.T.A., the Girl Scouts, and the domestic fairyland Walter had created behind the padlock.

Beyond the gate was the sound of quick water. Walter lightly called this "my moat." It was a thirty-foot-wide spring-fed trout stream that described three hairpin turns within a remarkably small area. The Reuther home lay in the elbow of the third bend, and to reach it you crossed two wide bridges. Walter made both. He also planned and made the long modern redwood house; an eminent designer drew up blueprints, but knowing his client, he signed them "Architect: Walter Reuther." Those sketches were, in fact, discarded. In the end everything, from the floating steps in the living room, each supported by a single hanging steel rod, to the white-pine paneling in the master bedroom, was Walter's idea.

An odd thing about the house was that the rain spouts were inside. That wasn't planned by anybody. Walter began with a one-room summer cottage. He started surrounding it with other rooms, attaching a kitchen here, a bedroom and study there, adding a second story, screening in a porch. After he had finished, of the original building only the spouts and the hand-hewn beams in the living room ceiling were visible. Except for heavy jobs like the stone fireplace and the big bullet-proof picture windows, he did all the work. He built the furniture, too, including an elaborate hi-fi set, and later he added a guest house to put up eminent people who had entertained him abroad.

Walter's home, like its owner, was supremely practical. Built-in bookcases were within reach of deep chairs: accordion doors of hinged walnut opened surprisingly on washrooms; low cabinets were finished with boiled linseed oil—so they would be easy to fix, he explained, if scratched. Walter knew all about things like linseed oil and flaring tenons and joists. He was impressive at housemanship, especially when his guest was a writer easily baffled by a leaking faucet.

Still, nobody lives behind a guarded fence for fun. For all its charm, the house had the air of a voluntary prison. Eternal vigilance was part of the price Walter paid for the liberties he took with the status quo in Detroit. It started when he took out that permit for a gun. Today relatives recall the awkward pause at family gatherings when Walter would arrive and carefully shelve his pistol on the mantel; and how, driving the lonely roads of northern Michigan on an outing, they would watch to see if they were being followed.

Die-hard bosses weren't Walter's only enemies. He had plenty in his own union. In the late 1930's and early 1940's Detroit swarmed with extremists. It was a stronghold of both the terrorist Black Legion and the Communist party; Father Coughlin was so popular in the Chrysler and Dodge plants that he was used as a drawing card at the first U.A.W. convention in 1936, while Ford Local 600, largest in the world, was controlled by Reds. For ten years these angry factions were to give union politics a Borgia tinge which was deepened, at the outset, by inadequate control at the top.

The first U.A.W. president, Homer Martin, was a former Baptist preacher with a gift for Biblical oratory and not much else. Everybody wanted him out, including Walter. The name of Reuther already had a certain force. The Communists had an eye on him. He had worked in Russia, was a Socialist, and had displayed political ambition by running for the Detroit Common Council on a U.A.W. ticket. They thought they might pull him over the Red line. After he had led a vain attempt to overthrow the preacher they offered to back him for the presidency next time, and Louis Budenz suggested he carry a party card.

Walter declined. He was preparing to call it quits with Norman Thomas, but was going the other way, to support Michigan's Democratic governor. The scorned Communist party decided he was poison, and a seesaw struggle opened. Twice Walter pushed anti-Communist resolutions through conventions. The Reds, striking back, defeated his brother Victor for a high office in the state C.I.O. and almost drove Walter himself from the U.A.W. executive board. They had a lot on their side—neither the C.I.O. leadership nor R. J. Thomas, the tobacco-chewing compromise candidate who succeeded to the U.A.W. presidency, was sensitive to the Red threat—but the Communists were handicapped by the rigidity of the Moscow line. In 1940 they joined John L. Lewis and other labor isolationists in rejecting Walter's call for aid to Britain, but once Russia was invaded no sacrifice was too great for them. To the dismay of the workers they called for speedups, a dirty word in the shops. Walter protested, and Earl Browder, the Communist leader, bought space in the Detroit papers to accuse him of trying to wreck the industry.

That was an odd stance for an old fighter, but the war put a strain on conservative union leadership too. The rank and file balked at the blanket no-strike pledge given by labor to Franklin Roosevelt. As vice president in charge of the union's General Motors division, Walter found the workers didn't always understand his problems. An approving Senate committee later reported that wartime strikes there took less than .0006 of 1 percent of total production time; the men, however, were not so approving, and they jeered him at U.A.W. conventions and waved tiny American flags. Nevertheless, he lost less popularity than the Communists and was in fair shape for a peacetime showdown.

It was a long showdown—in 1948 Henry Wallace was denouncing Walter as "the greatest single obstacle" to his Progressive party, and twelve months later the Reds were still trying to field a team against him at a U.A.W. convention—but the outcome was decided in the first two postwar years. Today the rout of the left seems to have been inevitable. It didn't seem at all that way then, because the battle opened with a brutal Reuther defeat.

By 1945 Walter had a reputation as a strike strategist. He had acquired it before the war, when, after careful study of General Motors schedules, he withdrew eight hundred key tool-and-die workers whose absence hamstrung production while the men punching time clocks still drew pay. Now he evolved what was to become celebrated as his "one-at-a-time" stratagem. It was based on the belief that competition among auto's Big Three—Ford, Chrysler and General Motors—was stronger than their distrust of the union. Separate one from the group, his reasoning went; none wants to be strike-bound while the other two seize its share of the market. It was a powerful argument, and it won the approval of the U.A.W. executive board. The years afterward vindicated Walter's reasoning, for this very tactic became his unbeatable weapon at the bargaining table, but it was crippled that autumn by two handicaps.

The first was of his own making. Until then custom had sharply defined the bargaining role of bread-and-butter unionists. They stood outside the gate of management's private domain and asked for X cents an hour or Y hours a week, but they never trespassed inside. Walter wanted to break down the walls. He contended that more money wouldn't help the worker if the corporation charged more for its cars, stoking the fires of inflation and raising the worker's cost of living, and he wound up asking General Motors to pay higher wages without raising its prices. This was an outright attempt to usurp the traditional prerogatives of the boss, and to make matters worse he asked to look at the corporation books so he could prove his demands were sound.

Other labor leaders were shocked; they held, with Philip Murray, then president of the C.I.O., that it was the union's job to win money and management's to decide whether the stockholders or the public paid the bill. Management itself was apoplectic, and in executive dining rooms there was a genuine, deepening concern over Walter's goals which continued to his death. General Motors rejected the proposal, saying he wanted it to "relinquish its rights to manage its business." He responded by giving marching orders to 200,000 workers. Harry Truman appointed a board of inquiry which included Milton Eisenhower, but when it began inquiring into ability to pay, the corporation excused itself from hearings. After three and a half months the workers were still on the streets.

Walter's second handicap was that the Communists were prepared to break his strike. They controlled the United Electrical Workers, which was also negotiating with General Motors, and when they settled privately he had to quit too. The Red ruse was clear enough. He had decided to run against Thomas for the U.A.W. presidency in 1946, and they thought they could torpedo him by tagging him with a lost strike on the eve of the convention. They nearly succeeded.

Atlantic City was bedlam that March. Both sides arrived with fists cocked. There were scrimmages on the boardwalk and in bars, where an informal troupe of Walter's boys performed a buck-and-wing and chanted, "Reuther, Reuther, rah, rah, rah!" On the convention floor leftists were hailed with "Quack, quack!" while the party faithful grimly fought to save Thomas. That round went to the right. Despite a snub from Philip Murray, Walter won the presidential balloting 4444 to 4320. Thomas stumbled from the stage weeping, and then, while Walter's dancers and quackers were out celebrating, the Communists captured his officer roster and two thirds of the executive board.

The Reuther victory could scarcely have been hollower. He was the captain of a team sworn to ruin him, and the year that followed was the zaniest in the history of the U.A.W. Emil Mazey, the strongest anti-Communist on the board, was in the Army and didn't even know he had been elected; his mail had been cut off as punishment for his leading of demobilization demonstrations in the Philippines. Walter managed to hire Victor as the union's educational director, but that was the limit of his strength. The board majority decided he was entitled to his paycheck and nothing else. He wasn't even to be told what was going on.

Communist propaganda was released to the press as official union policy statements—Walter read them in the papers—and whenever he tried to act, he was blocked. He tried to put through a bland resolution saying the workers should make progress with, not at the expense of, the rest of the community. The board majority not only defeated it; they formally petitioned Congress to change the name of the country's labor law to the Taft-Hartley-Reuther Act, on the ground that Walter was more antilabor than either Taft or Hartley. Wild rumors were circulated: Taft and Reuther would head the next Republican ticket; Walter was anti-Semitic; he was a crony of Gerald L. K. Smith. At board meetings he was pushed around—literally—and Murray, turning now, confessed that the struggle had "sunk to a level of complete moral degeneracy."

Walter had been getting close to Murray. They had reached the "Phil" and "Walter" stage; a state C.I.O. summer camp at Port Huron was being used to train anti-Communist speakers, who were to be sent to locals all over the country.* In Detroit Walter was talking, he

* The Students for a Democratic Society was organized at the Port Huron camp in June 1962, but Walter had nothing to do with that.

recalled afterward, "to thousands of guys all over this town." He was also studying union by-laws. The sources of Communist Party cash had always been something of a mystery. He suspected that dues were going astray. Discovering that checks weren't valid unless signed by the union president, he demanded control of the books. The Reds told him what he could do with his by-laws, so he notified the bank that no drafts on the U.A.W. treasury were to be honored until he had given the cashier the check numbers over the telephone. Every morning he held a numerical conversation with the bank while the Communists huddled with their lawyers. The lawyers advised them Walter was right.

The legal view, however, was that he couldn't delegate his authority, and a neat little rubber stamp was prepared with a facsimile of his signature, for use when he was out of town. Walter was ready for that one. He called in the chief Red panjandrum. Not only was union money going to be spent by the numbers, he said; unless he got a little cooperation he would stop signing the executive board's paychecks. "Those fellows hated my guts," he later said with a grin, "but they loved their checks. They came through."

Then one of them had a bright idea. The Communists dominated a little farm-equipment workers' union. Why not merge it with the U.A.W., give it five hundred delegate votes at the next convention, and vote Reuther out of office? The board voted for a union referendum on the merger, to be held that summer, when local meetings would be lightly attended and organization would count. As it turned out, the Reds were voting themselves into oblivion. Anti-Communist speakers deployed, exposing the flim-flam; Walter won the referendum two-to-one. At the convention he was swept back into office, and his slate took eighteen of the twenty-two board seats. Back in Detroit, he launched a campaign for a more perfect union, firing Reds and drones, driving lottery operators from the factories, and preparing for a militant stand at the bargaining table. It was all done with Walter's characteristic thoroughness. He offended a great many people that winter. One of them decided to liquidate him.

He and his wife were then living at 20101 Appoline Street. After five years in little apartments with May's parents Walter had saved $1265, and they had made a down payment on a $7750 brick-and-frame house with maple furniture, ruffled curtains and a basement workshop. There was an upstairs bedroom for their five-year-old daughter and another, downstairs, for her baby sister. The kitchen was in the rear. After a late meeting Walter would pace around it carefully, so as not to wake the girls, and describe his day to his wife while she prepared his supper.

At 9:30 on the cool evening of April 20, 1948, he had finished a dish of stew and was standing by the refrigerator, holding a bowl of preserved fruit, when May asked a casual question. He turned to reply. At that instant an assassin standing a few feet away in the darkened yard fired both barrels of a ten-gauge shotgun loaded with double-O buckshot. As the blast crashed through the house—the children, miraculously slept through it—Walter collapsed on the floor, calling out, "They shot me, May!"

That was the beginning of a year of horror—of "accidents," as they would be euphemistically called in Reuther households. Walter's right arm was in a traction splint, his condition critical. On Appoline Street curious crowds gathered. It was a free show; popcorn vendors set up shop on the sidewalk. The first Walter knew of the staring herd was when one of his confused daughters asked at his bedside, "Daddy, why can't they let us alone? Why can't I be like other kids?"

He decided to move to another neighborhood as soon as his condition permitted it, but meantime the killer had another diversion for the mob. Victor and his wife Sophie had begun to notice that their cocker spaniel was barking urgently in the yard nights. It wasn't much of a bark, however, because it wasn't much of a spaniel, and they were surprised when a policeman called to tell them an anonymous protest had been lodged; they would have to get rid of the dog. Next day, at the cop's insistence—there had been another anonymous complaint—they gave away the one sentry they had. That night they were sitting in the front room, Sophie mending, Victor reading the New York *Times* magazine. Sophie had a wifely complaint. Her light bulb was dead, she couldn't see to sew. Her husband had scarcely replaced it—"illuminating the target," Victor observes dryly—when another shotgun roared on the lawn. In the brief moment before he lost consciousness he thought the bulb had exploded; then everything went black. There were two pea-sized slugs in his throat, and one in his mouth; a fourth had destroyed his right eye. At the hospital Walter, still crippled, cried, "It's not possible, not both of us, not twice." Victor, who in a quieter way was just as game as his brother, said, "It's a good thing they didn't shoot out my tongue. I couldn't make a living."

This time the gunman had left his weapon in the shrubbery. Despite that, and despite a clumsy attempt to dynamite the union building a few months later, the police couldn't find enough evidence to make a charge stick. Five years later a hood confessed he had driven the killer's

car the night of the attack on Walter. He named two other men, but
before the trial he gave police the slip and left the country, ending the
case. Today the twin mystery remains a quarter-million-dollar question;
no one ever claimed the U.A.W. rewards for new information.

The lack of convictions accounts for the elaborate security system
the union set up to protect the Reuthers. Walter's office was approached through an intricate maze of narrow corridors; visitors felt
like balls in a pinball machine. He took a bodyguard everywhere—
when a priest called to say he was sending a ticket to Cardinal
Mooney's funeral, Walter gently reminded him, "I'll need *two* tickets,
Father"—and over the years he came to accept his armed chaperon.
There were problems, though. One night a family party went to see
Hamlet. Two guards sat in the row behind them, and during a lull on
stage the Reuthers heard a queer rumbling sound. They turned. It was
their escorts, snoring in concert.

Walter revolted against the union's protective measures just once.
He didn't mind the invasion of his privacy. He was worried about how
it looked. Appearances meant a lot to him, which is why he hunted out
the cheaper restaurant in a convention town and raised Cain if anybody on the union payroll bought an expensive car. It was an automobile that was at the bottom of his row with his security men. They had
Packard build an elegant $12,000 armored car to convoy him around.
The thing never worked properly. Ventilation was poor, the bullet-
proof windows didn't open, and on a long ride, with Walter working
on correspondence, the back seat literally became a sweatshop. Rides
were longer than they were supposed to be, because the car kept breaking down on Detroit streets. It was just too heavy. The motor couldn't
pull all that armor. Friends started calling it "the hearse" as a joke,
which on second thought they realized wasn't so funny. To Walter it
was always "the limousine." He had long ago formed an opinion of
men who rode around in limousines, and he didn't want to be one of
them.

"I can't be seen in this thing," he protested, and he wasn't. If he
went downtown to the movies, he dismayed his lookouts by insisting he
disembark in an alley, violating the most elemental security precautions. Once a governor directed his state police to escort Walter through
a stretch of New Jersey. The governor thought of it as a gesture, but
Walter wasn't flattered. Whenever they hit a town, sirens screaming,
the people on the sidewalks would peer out to see who the big slick
was. He squirmed in the back, feeling guiltier and guiltier. Finally he
ordered a stop and told the bodyguard in front to switch with him. The

rest of the ride was fine. Ignored by pedestrians, he chatted easily with the driver while the man in back gravely bowed and waved. The guard loved it, and everyone agreed he looked far more distinguished than the little redhead by the chauffeur.

The limousine reached the end of the road in Canada. One wintry morning the driver saw, through the thick slab of a windshield, that he was approaching a town. A meetinghouse was letting out; the street was jammed with automobiles. He hit the brakes. The wheels locked. The car, with its monstrous weight, kept right on going. Luckily they were just idling along. The only damage was a crushed fender—on another car, of course. Walter, however, had had enough. He jumped out, slammed the ponderous door, and snapped, "That does it. I'm not going another inch in that." He finished the trip by bus.

The spectacle of America's most colorful labor leader fussing over what people thought was diverting to many. Some thought it was also revealing. Walter, they held, was a true ascetic—a man who shrank from pleasure, even from normal conviviality. Company bargainers saw him as an implacable, humorless robot, a talking machine obsessed with doctrine. Even some of his friends wondered about him. "He never asks me about my family," one complained. "He speaks of eleven o'clock on Sunday morning as the most segregated hour in America," a clergyman said, "but he never thinks of the personal hurt in race prejudice." "Walter," said a wry admirer, "is a dedicated fanatic." In public he seemed to be infatuated with principles but indifferent to people. In private, however, he was a very different man. He was no machine to his daughters Linda and Lisa. And though May said that whenever she heard him speak she wondered how she dared to argue with him, at home she more than held her own.

On one of his rare fishing days he caught a great northern pike. He hadn't fished enough to know what a feat this was, but when he found out he was excited. The prize was shipped home in a box, and when it didn't arrive he called the express agency daily, inquiring. The agent who turned up with it asked, "What's in that box, Mr. Reuther? It must be pretty important." "It is," Walter replied. "It's my reputation." He had it stuffed and mounted it in his living room. It didn't stay there, though. ("How would *you* like a great northern pike in *your* living room?" a woman who knew May asked.) Somehow his wife got him to take it to his office. "The difference between May and her daughters," said another of May's friends, "is that Walter knew when the girls were pushing him around."

There wasn't much doubt with the girls. They weren't as subtle as their mother. Once Walter stopped off at Linda's progressive New England boarding school and invited her to dinner. She told him she'd really like to, she honestly would, but she was busy. In fact, she was so terribly busy she didn't have time to shop for some things she just had to have, and would he mind? Walter hurried off to buy her some jeans and underwear and then spent the evening alone in a nearby motel, going over papers. He hadn't minded at all, nor did he protest when little Lisa informed him, on his departure for the West Coast, that she had made up her mind that her classroom was going to win the P.T.A. attendance banner the evening of his return, even though it meant he must drive straight there from the airport.

He could outsmart goons and ginks and company finks, but he was helpless against this kind of exploitation. At home he lived with a menagerie—two parakeets named Misty and Chippy, a horse called Charlie, and assorted dogs and cats and goldfish—because the girls loved pets. The mosquitoes that teemed on his stream seemed to find him irresistible, but the only effective repellent he could find drove birds away, so he took it back and settled for a swatter. His daughters liked birds too.

Until they reached their teens they had a sheep and two lambs. Everyone agreed that this was too much, so Walter quietly asked a couple of the guards if they would like some mutton. Lisa heard him. There was a scene which didn't end until Walter reached an agreement with a neighboring farmer, who promised to treasure and caress them and feed them and, above all, not kill them. She even insisted this be in writing, and her father drew up a formal document, which the baffled farmer signed.

For a time Lisa doted on a dog she and her sister called Soapy—he had polka dots and had come from a family named Williams. When a car ran over him there was a solemn ceremony. Walter was soberly digging the grave when his weeping daughter suddenly pointed at him and cried, "Daddy! You didn't love him!" He insisted that he had, but she stamped an accusing foot. "You didn't either! You're not crying!" There was only one thing to do, and as a conscientious father Walter did it. He screwed up his face and sobbed noisily as he shoveled Soapy under.

The girls were responsible for the house on the creek. After the retreat from Appoline Street, the Reuthers lived for several years in a residential area that was turning Negro; values were dropping, and they got a bargain. Summers were a problem, however. In the past they had rented cottages outside Detroit during July and August, but now landlords were afraid the Reuthers might bring gunfire with them. Walter bought the place by the stream as a solution. Being Walter, he began wondering how he could improve it. Since he had abandoned his leather-and-steel brace, continual exercise of his right hand had become a necessity; his doctor told him that unless he kept stretching the fingers he would have a claw hand. He squeezed a ball for a while, and then hammered nails each day until tears came. Slowly the muscles returned. At the creek he had a chance to do something useful with them, and for four years he worked at making the cottage livable. At the end of the fourth summer Linda and Lisa announced that they wanted to stay there always. Walter wasn't hard to persuade—he decided he had always wanted to live on a stream lined with evergreens—and May enrolled the children in the local school. That September the expansion began.

In the beginning things were primitive. They all slept in the one room with Walter's power saw. As nights grew chillier the country rats moved in. By the end of the year he had the chinks sealed and the first bedroom finished; they celebrated Christmas Eve by moving the saw there. Then there was a hitch. Walter ran out of construction materials. The lumber yard kept putting him off. One Saturday morning he appeared there at seven o'clock dressed in denim and helped cut lengths himself. When the man delivered them and saw the skeleton of beams, he started. "Gee, Mr. Reuther, I didn't know you were living in the *open!*" he said. The family felt affronted. They thought things were beginning to look rather nice. After the edifice was complete, the saw and Walter's tool box—"my social security"—were stored in the rising guest house. The Reuther home was quite nice now, and quite finished, and sometimes Walter was even there to enjoy it.

At home he liked to squint out hungrily at the brown trout lazing in the stream, or kick off his shoes and dance with May or just listen to light opera, romantic melodies and Strauss waltzes. Walter's musical tastes were in dead center field. He never went to the Detroit Symphony; he preferred to sing German *lieder,* draping the honorary-degree hoods of Walter P. Reuther, LL.D., L.H.D., over the shoulders of visiting children and leading them from room to room in a stamping march. His family was his relaxation. When he left them he left contentment behind.

Walter's home rarely intruded on his career. After building it he had just two emergency calls from there. The first came when the stream rose a foot and a half over the bridges and water was within a fraction of an inch of the electrical circuits under the house. May suggested he'd better cancel his appointments until the flood was over, and he left his office on the run, standing up Clare Boothe Luce. The second call was from Linda. Anticipating an intensive period of collective bargaining, Walter had given a friend permission to angle for trout. The man arrived with a determined glint and a hat full of flies, and before the day was out he triumphantly yanked a six-pound beauty from the stream. Linda saw him. "You stole my Daddy's fish!" she shrieked and raced for the phone. She thought Walter ought to know what his so-called friend had done.

That was during the 1955 negotiations for the Guaranteed Annual Wage, and it is unlikely that any of the corporation representatives poring over the contract would have believed the rufous ogre opposite them capable of a tender reply to a child. At bargaining sessions Walter was very much in his Detroit role. The meetings were staged around long, brilliantly lit tables; outside there were switchboards, recording devices and private lines to relay new proposals from the other side.

The union negotiated with Ford, General Motors and Chrysler simultaneously, in different parts of town, but the tip-off that Walter had picked his prey came when he stowed his briefcase and toothbrush under one table.

After that things would get rough. The final stretch might last forty hours without a break—he once suggested cheerily that General Motors hew out a tunnel from their office building to his—and a man with his constitution had a big edge. It wasn't that he huffed and puffed so much. He just kept talking. Walter was voluble under any circumstances; after dominating a Mike Wallace interview and cornering Wallace outside the studio for an hour he said, "There was just one thing wrong with the program. The questions were too long."

Company men complained that his multiloquence made negotiations longer than they need be. Flexing his powerful jaw muscles hour after hour, he suggested this, recommended that, expatiated, rebutted, lost his temper, was contrite, turned accusing, and expostulated in a dry monotone until the others were numb. Sometimes they were too numb to say anything themselves; one vice president wearily dealt reporters printed cards which said "No Comment" in six languages.

For a quarter of a century the best minds of the industry pondered ways to beat him. Their predicament was that they were many and he was one, which in Detroit meant that the arithmetic was in his favor. His authority cut across corporation lines. The union could assess its million members two dollars a month, build a strike fund of twenty-five million dollars, and use it to support workers in the one plant struck. Under the Taft-Hartley law the lockout was an unfair practice. If a company had tried to outwit him by building, say, a hundred-day inventory, he could have waited until the other two brought out new cars and had his men strike then. The struck company would have had to go to market with last year's models.

Henry Ford II and George Romney of American Motors suggested industry-wide bargaining—one huge table, with Walter facing everybody. Now and then there were signs of a common front. Walter would write all the presidents, suggesting they cut prices or share profits with their workers, and the phrasing in their icy replies would be curiously the same. Identical proposals might even be handed across two tables; Walter would cry indignantly, "How the hell do you get a Chevy on a Ford assembly line?" Sooner or later, though, one corporation would decide it could get the drop on the others by making a deal on the side. Even if that competitive instinct could have been curbed, there was no guarantee that unity would be successful. Moreover, there would have been the dreaded possibility that a provoked public would have demanded Federal intervention, which was what many executives thought Walter really wanted. He may have quit the Socialist party, they argued, but he played pretty close to third base just the same, and he had been trying to take over the plants since 1940.

Walter's first big bright idea came in 1940. America was supposed to be getting ready for war, and Big Bill Knudsen's Office of Production Management was issuing grand we-can-do-the-job statements, but vigilant patriots were painfully aware that the job was not being done. One of them was Walter. Another was Senator Harry Byrd, who complained that America was manufacturing a thousand cars for every combat plane.

Unlike the Senator, Walter knew a lot about jigs, lathes and assembly-line combinations. He even knew a little about converting civilian shops to military production, because he had seen tank dies introduced in that Ford-built Russian factory. The upshot was a Reuther plan to abandon the design of new automobile models, freeing skilled mechanics for work on airplane tools. If industry pooled its resources, he insisted, the country could have its cars and still turn out—this was the title of his pamphlet—*500 Planes a Day*.

Hardly anybody took that figure seriously. Still, it was something when there wasn't much of anything, and when Walter assembled his men at Cass Technical High School on the dingy West Side and showed them a Rolls-Royce aircraft engine, they thought their first planes might be ready to fly in six months. Franklin Roosevelt was delighted. Management was vexed. Knudsen, a former president of General Motors, blandly told Walter he lacked authority to take him through a plant, and though Walter requested airplane-motor blueprints so he could break down the job, he never got them. One labor-relations man said bluntly, "Who the hell will pay attention to a squirt of a labor leader?" That was the crux of it. The patroons of the industry had reluctantly recognized the U.A.W. at the bargaining table, but this new business was ridiculous. If any breaking down of jobs was going to be done, it would be done by bosses.

That attitude became a trial to management after Pearl Harbor, when the union crowed we-told-you-so, but the position of Knudsen, Charles F. Kettering and their successors continued to be consistent. Somebody had to have the power on the factory floor. Either they were in charge or the notion of private property had to be abandoned and command transferred to the first clever worker who sat on his job and flirted with a friendly administration in Washington. They suspected that Walter was flirting outrageously with Roosevelt then, and they felt certain he was vamping Truman five years later.

In 1945 he not only wanted a look at General Motors books (this came out of the Reutherian euphonium as "democracy in the economic sphere"); on the national level, where he was feeling increasingly comfortable, he proposed that the War Production Board be replaced by a Peace Production Board of industrialists, labor leaders, farmers, and consumers. Naturally he had an idea of what it might do. He wanted idle airplane factories converted to the manufacture of twenty million cheap, prefab housing units. Once more he ran afoul of management by demanding that workers' councils share in determining consumer needs. This time his senatorial crony from Virginia wasn't on his side.

The years after that witnessed a proliferation of what one negotiator called Walter's "Alice-in-Wonderland things." Executives were increasingly nettled by his persistent attempts to give them advice. He was forever trying to be useful, submitting some suggestion for the good of the industry—changes in marketing patterns, five- and ten-point plans, labor-management get-togethers, a "fish-bowl" for prices—that ruffled their feelings. His helpful hints were hard enough to take, but what really set the conservative tocsin clanging was the way he transmuted so many of his dreams into the harsh prose of labor agreements. The simple world of January 5, 1914, when Henry Ford announced he would pay five dollars a day for eight hours' work, had vanished. Contracts were increasingly complicated by escalator clauses, supplementary unemployment benefits, pension provisions and productivity factors; it took actuaries and statisticians to figure them out. The U.A.W.'s Solidarity House stood on the old Edsel Ford estate overlooking the Detroit River, and union and Chrysler engineers were studying work speeds together.

All this came in with the Reuther era. Labor gadflies of the other days were dogged enough, but they were limited by what Walter scouted as their "penny-ante" philosophy. They were haunted by the memory of America's first labor organization, the nineteenth century Knights of Labor, which collapsed when it became entangled in political and social doctrines, and they clung to the tight little more-and-better unionism of Samuel Gompers' American Federation of Labor. Their tranquillity was shaken when John L. Lewis strode out of the A.F.L. in 1935 to found the Congress of Industrial Organizations, but Lewis, for all his Thespian effects, was a traditional fat-pay bargainer. He never rocked the managerial boat much, and when Walter was elected president of the Congress at the age of forty-five and merged it with the Federation, John L. was fit to be tied. "Mr. Reuther," he thundered, "is an earnest Marxist, chronically inebriated, I think, by the exuberance of his own verbosity."

He didn't call Walter a Communist. There was a bitter fringe which was convinced the Reuthers were secret Soviet agents, but the record read the other way. At the height of the Cold War the Joint Congressional Committee on Atomic Energy reviewed the FBI report on Walter and granted him clearance to see "the highest degree of secret information," and his only infidelity to the Democratic party arose from his fear that the Henry Wallace threat might be real. He wanted the Democrats to nominate Justice William O. Douglas in 1948. Like all other savants, he felt sure that Truman hadn't a chance. He expected the Democrats to fall apart after the election, so he and his union planned a liberal anti-Communist party, to be launched the day Dewey was inaugurated. When the fantastic happened in November, Walter slipped quietly back in line. He remained there ever afterward, an active leader of the Democratic liberal wing.

As a multitude of G.O.P. candidates noted from time to time, he was also active in the Americans for Democratic Action, the National Association for the Advancement of Colored People, and the United World Federalists. Some conservatives distributed a pamphlet identifying him as The Man Who Plans to Rule America; others just said he wanted to run the Democratic party. Their failure to thwart him only sustained their distrust of what they called Reutherism. "When a

Democrat gets defeated he says his wife didn't want him to run," Abe
Martin drawled, "and when a Republican gets snowed under, he says
the people are following strange gods."

Abe, a cartoon character in the Republican Indianapolis *News,*
also said that "if capital and labor ever do get together, it's good night
for the rest of us." To Walter there wasn't any rest of us, and even the
capital-labor split was wrong. He spoke mellifluously of "voluntary cooperation" between unions and corporations, advocating a sort of cozy
industrial togetherness in which bosses and labor skates would work
harmoniously as "architects of the future." His critics—and even many
who admire him—thought this a bit naïve. His own career brought him
blood, bruises, hooliganism and hard words, but very little voluntary cooperation. He liked to think that the character of management was
changing, and he regarded Henry Ford II, who ordered coffee and
sweet rolls served to pickets during 1958's six-hour strike, as a very decent man. Yet he must have known how many people regarded the
Reuther name as a bogy.

Late in the 1950's, he met Martin Luther King in Miami. Outside,
police whistles were warbling, and when Walter strolled to the window
he saw that the street below was thick with blue uniforms. He burst
into laughter. "What a couple of characters we are!" he called to King.
"We're really starting something!"

The cordon was a tribute to the fear of what Walter started and to
his eminence in public life, which made him a strong finisher. His national role had long ago transcended the leadership of an automobile
union. Because he was deeply involved in sensitive issues, and because
he moved swiftly on the advancing edge of the present, he also had a
substantial international following. British Labourites extrapolating
from their own political system—he would have been a Cabinet
member there—found him the most exciting man in America. In
Nehru's India he was a popular hero. Official Washington, seeking an
unofficial emissary to New Delhi in the Eisenhower years, picked
Walter. He proved poisonous to Indian Reds. Local papers doted on his
prim democratic quirks—at receptions he wouldn't wear a dinner jacket,
which he vaguely associated with limousines—and his speeches were
powerful Western medicine, laced with wit.

Even in the paneled boardrooms of Detroit, where his eloquence
was rarely appreciated, he was conceded to be fast on his feet. Once a
supervisor was showing him through a Ford automated plant which
could turn out an engine block, untouched by human hands, in less
than fifteen minutes. Walter, remembering the hundreds of hours that

went into each block during his early days in Detroit, was silently impressed until his guide said slyly, "Aren't you worried about how you're going to collect union dues from these machines?" "Not at all," Walter said instantly. "What worries me is how you're going to sell them Ford cars."

To him automation was one of the reasons nickel-in-the-pay-envelope bargaining was obsolescent. Its threat of a sterile society depressed him. "Every man needs a feeling of achievement," he would say, running his fingers along a cabinet in his homemade home. "I get it here, making things. But what accomplishment can a push-button pusher feel? You can't be in the image of God unless you have some creative capacity, because that's the basic concept. Suppose we do have the highest standard of living in the world; if the outer man strips the inner man, we've still been robbed of our sense of achievement."

Workmen's pride had become more important than take-home pay to him, because by the time of his death the pay battle had been pretty much won. By then young union members were making what their fathers had called Cadillac money. Economically the proletarian had invaded the middle class. Culturally he remained a pinball-playing hillbilly, however, so his leader brooded over the four-day week and the constructive use of leisure—and was prepared to strike for intangibles to get it.

A consequence of this was that other labor leaders tend to look upon Walter as a traitor to his class. He was born in a dingy West Virginia purlieu and came up through the Detroit shops, "but he acts like a priest," Jimmy Hoffa said. "Why? He just wants to win the war, like me." Hoffa, of course, affected the air of a sea wolf; Walter's benign colleagues on the A.F.L.-C.I.O. board didn't snarl enough for the Teamster boss. They did pledge allegiance to orthodox symbols of power, though. George Meany is a golfer and duck hunter, like Ike; Dave McDonald cultivated the profile of a steel tycoon. Walter, however, stuck with his intellectual predilections. He actually enjoyed books about atomic energy, and though he bought a TV set to watch the 1952 political conventions, it was seldom on. One night he forced himself to sit through a typical evening's programs. Long before bedtime he was appalled. When Ed Murrow attacked TV mediocrity Walter sent him a note. It read, "Hurray!"

The labor fraternity mocked him as "the egghead." He snapped back that at least he was not an emptyhead, but some of his own automobile workers wished he weren't quite so smart. In the swarming tenements of Detroit's Third Avenue district a man feels that lean meat and neat whiskey will generate all the creative excitement he needs. The working stiffs there rarely dream of pie in the sky, and they couldn't understand why a man with Walter's upbringing should scorn bread-and-butter raises and insist that their bowling leagues be interracial. They grumbled, but Walter didn't hark. He'd strike for intangibles inside the union too. He was determined to build "a labor movement that will remake the world," and much of the activity in Solidarity House reflected this. There was a monthly newspaper and a daily radio commentator to educate the workers, a school for new union officials, and a forward-planning staff of experts in such fields as slum clearance and recreation for the elderly. Walter always attracted men of ideas, not all of whom were shop veterans. After a memorable strike-strategy meeting, one of them took a girl aside. "Tell me," he whispered. "Confidentially—what *is* a tool-and-die?"

This may have confirmed those who suspected sinister figures in the union were designing a master trap for all of us. Walter, however, didn't give that impression. He was a thoughtful man, and he thought ahead, but his vision of the future seemed rather hazy. Either he hadn't seen the farthest reaches of his ideas or he wasn't talking about them, which in him would have been incredible.

He appeared convinced that socialism had become a weary doctrine, and he insisted that he was in favor of the free marketplace. Yet every triumph at the bargaining table brought him closer to the great keep of industrial power, and apart from expressing a wish for chummy relations with management all he would say was that he was a pragmatist. Walter was for what worked. After he had it, he stalked the next thing that would work, and then the next, feeling his way, pushing on toward an unseen horizon and saying little about the implications of the victories behind him. "Don't ask me what he wanted," says a man who knew him twenty years. "I honestly don't think *he* knew. But I'll tell you this. He would have gotten it."

In the grim spring of 1948, when Walter's condition was still grave, his mother went to the hospital and begged him to quit. Later she would recall sitting by her son's bed and saying, "Go into some other work. Give this up. You could write books, or go back to your trade. You would make just as much money." Walter, she remembered, looked startled. "I'd make *more* money," he said weakly. "Then do it," she pleaded, and there was a pause, and he said, "No. I'm all tied up in this thing, all involved. I must do it." He faltered—Anna caught something about "brotherhood of man," a phrase all the Reuther brothers heard throughout their childhood from their father—and his voice trailed off. Then May, sitting opposite, quietly asked her, "Don't you see he must do it? You must understand," and Anna left.

Understanding Walter stumped men less close to him than his mother. Why he did what he did, and what he really wanted, may remain conundrums to everyone. Still, there was this thing, and he was all tied up in it. It brought grief and terror to the members of his family, the only people he really cherished. Had he lived, it would have meant that he would have had to spend the rest of his life in a home with a padlocked gate, escorted everywhere by bodyguards, but that's the way it had to be. There was this thing. It may have been an Alice-in-Wonderland dream, a pie in the sky, or the brotherhood of man—that didn't matter. Whatever it was, he was all involved. He believed in it, and he felt that he had to do it, whatever the cost, which, in the end, turned out to be the supreme sacrifice.

Cairo After Farouk

IN THE SMALL HOURS of July 23, 1952, Jefferson Caffery, the United States ambassador to Egypt, was awakened by two eventful telephone calls. The first was from a young Egyptian army officer who apologized for the hour of his call but said he had news that could not be delayed—the army was taking over the country. Caffery thanked him and hung up. There wasn't much else he could do. The second call, somewhat later, was from His Majesty King Farouk I, or, as he was popularly known in Cairo, the King of the Whores. His soldiers had imprisoned him in his own palace, the king said, and he wanted American intervention to crush them. Caffery unsuccessfully tried to cut him off by every method short of hanging up, for knowing Cairo, he suspected that the line was tapped. It was. What's more, that appeal for foreign help ended Farouk's reign. When members of the Free Officers junta running the coup learned of it, they decided to force his abdication. In his place appeared an Egyptian major general named Mohammed Naguib, who was so little known in the Anglo-American community that only one member of it, a U.S. captain, had been introduced to him. Naguib's right-hand man was handsome, thirty-four-year-old Colonel Gamal Abdel Nasser. No Americans at all had met Nasser.

Cairo was a city of appalling cynicism then—the local equivalent of the college of hard knocks was called "Farouk U."—but by the following winter, when I arrived in the capital, General Naguib had become enormously celebrated and widely respected. He was probably the most pushed-around dictator in history. Week after week, he continued to work an eighteen-hour day, and authority had not corrupted that curious naïveté which was his most appealing and most puzzling trait. People with the lamest excuses could barge in on him—chiefly, one gathered, because he was terrified that they might think he regarded himself as a big shot. He was such an earnest little shot, except in a pinch, when he could be firm in a wry, whimsical way, that Americans in the capital were comparing him to Lincoln, a slippery parallel which nevertheless provides an inkling of his popularity then.

It was an extraordinary popularity. He had conspicuous enemies, of course, but while they were powerful, they were also few, being largely confined to the rich, fezzed former pashas who, until his rise, had divided their time between the Riviera and yachting on the Nile. They were not among the fellaheen, the illiterate, diseased descendants of the Pharaonic peasantry, who saw in his land-reform program the culmination of the hope of generations, nor were they in the dirty stucco streets of Cairo and Alexandria, where the general was a symbol of decency that shone particularly bright after a decade of the grossest corruption. They could not be found in the Western legations, either, for occidental diplomats trusted Naguib with a desperate faith born of years of dealing with a depraved king and crooked premiers.

An instance of Naguib's accessibility that winter occurred during the Fourth World Cooperation Tour of the General Federation of Women's Clubs. Fifteen of the women on the tour, headed by Mrs. Oscar A. Algren, of Whiting, Indiana, arrived in town and informed the American embassy that they would like to meet the general. The embassy put in a routine request for an interview, but without much hope, for Naguib was deep in negotiations with the British over the fate of nine million Sudanese, and therefore presumably fully occupied. But he invited the ladies over for coffee anyway. They arranged themselves on divans in the former palace of Princess Shewkar while their host, a chunky terrier of a man in his early fifties, settled back in his woolly uniform and discussed state affairs with all the eager innocence of an armchair political strategist, which is just what he had been a year earlier. After the chat one of his guests confessed that she had a hobby; she collected memorable coffee cups. Could she have hers? Certainly, said Egypt's premier, minister of war and marine, and chief of the country's only political party; take it along. Immediately the other fourteen clubwomen announced that they were going to take theirs, too, and keep them forever.

Naguib affected people that way, journalists among them. In a *New Yorker* letter from Cairo I noted that while Naguib had not engineered the coup of the previous summer—"actually he was only an instrument in the hands of a committee of junior officers"—it was reasonable to assume that he would remain in power a long time. One reason, I said, was his remarkable personality. Then I added for the ages: "Another, of course, is that in all Egypt there just isn't anybody else." After the general's right-hand man emerged from the shadows and shoved him aside, I remembered that someone had introduced me to Nasser in Naguib's outer office. Certain that this man would remain obscure, I had been brusque, almost curt, thereby forfeiting a matchless opportunity to interview him. Once I saw just how clouded my crystal ball had been, I felt very sheepish. I said as much to Arthur Krock. He advised me to forget it. "It happens all the time," said Krock. "I remember that just after the Armistice I was traveling through provincial Italy by train. A friend suggested that I get off at one station and meet the obscure editor of *Il Popolo d'Italia*, who was standing on the platform. I wouldn't do it. I knew Benito Mussolini wasn't going anywhere in Rome."

Years later I read in *Britannica 3*: "For more than a year Nasser kept his real role so well hidden that astute foreign correspondents were unaware of his existence." In reality none of us was astute, and that proved it. When he emerged as deputy premier and interior minister on June 18, 1953—actually a little *less* than a year after Farouk—we were dumbfounded. He had been lurking around, and we had seen him, but we hadn't read him right. It was a grave error, and a significant one. For years outsiders had misread, misunderstood, and misinterpreted the Egyptian power structure. They still do. Nearly a quarter century has lapsed; Farouk and Nasser are dead; Anwar el Sadat rules in Cairo, and it is a rare journalist who comprehends the long, tangled chain of events behind the Sadat government. The dethroning of the King of the Whores was a pivotal event in the history of the Middle East. Some grasp of how and why it happened is essential to an understanding of that corner of the world, whose destiny, as they used to say in Fitzpatrick travelogues, has become inextricably linked with that of Americans.

One must begin a century ago, with the British. Egypt was never fully assimilated into their empire, but the completion of the Suez Canal and imperial interests in East Africa led to the country being designated, in 1883, an English protectorate. Like all superpowers, Victoria's Britain tended to mask naked force with piety and cant. In 1888 Suez was grandly proclaimed a world waterway, to be open in war and peace alike, but as the Germans discovered in two world wars, there was a lot of fine print about the safeguarding of H.M.'s interests. Again, in 1899 London announced that the Sudan would be jointly ruled by Englishmen and Egyptians. In fact, however, that jungly country was governed by Britons, to the mortification of Egypt, whose troops had played a major role in its subjugation.

Theoretically the supreme being in Cairo was the native khedive, or viceroy. In practice the reins of power were in the hands of the English High Commissioner. That situation began to change on November 13, 1918, just two days after the Armistice, when three Cairo politicians called on Commissioner Sir Reginald Wingate and demanded autonomy for Egypt. They declared that it was their intention to lead a delegation which would plead their case in London. H.M.'s government refused to receive them and arrested their leader, Saad Zaghlul Pasha, but the Arabic word for delegation (*wafd*) dominated Egyptian politics for the next thirty-four years. It became the name of the country's largest political party, which triumphed in one general election after another and wrung its hands in frustration much of the time, as constitutional rights were frequently suspended and the nation was ruled by imperial decree.

The constitution, promulgated on April 19, 1923, was a direct outgrowth of the rise of nationalist feeling in Cairo. Demonstrations by Zaghlul's followers had secured his release from prison and the establishment of a constitutional monarchy. The former khedive was now a sovereign—King Fuad I—under whom the new nation was administered by a premier and a parliament, with some of the legislators appointed and the rest elected by universal manhood suffrage. Most of this was cosmetics, however. The British army remained, and despite the declaration of independence England retained control of defense, communications, the protection of foreign interests, and the person of Fuad I.

These matters were supposed to be settled in an Anglo-Egyptian treaty, but negotiations dragged on for over a decade with no tangible result. Then, in the mid-1930's, London suddenly became interested in reaching an agreement. Deteriorating relations between Whitehall and Rome over the Ethiopian question prompted the British to sign a pact in August 1936 under which Egyptian troops were admitted to the Sudan, England kept its naval base in Alexandria, and 10,000 tommies remained in the Canal Zone, with the provision that the number might be increased in wartime. Egypt was to become a member of the League of Nations. Fuad having died the previous May, his son Farouk, then still a minor, became the new king.

Some idea of the Egyptian constitution's precision may be gathered from the fact that everything Naguib and the Free Officers junta did, including the abolition of all political parties and the expropriation of vast tracts of privately owned land, was entirely legal. All the trappings of democracy were there, including a cabinet and a judicial authority, but because the electorate was so impoverished and illiterate—one in six could write—control fell into the hands of the country's peerage, the pashas and beys. One group of them haunted the palace and influenced the king; the rest ran the Wafd and, through it, the parliament. The leader of the Wafd was a square-faced, mustachioed old man named Mustafa en Nahas who succeeded to the party's leadership in 1927, when Zaghlul died. In 1934 Nahas married Zeinab el Wakil, more familiarly known as Zuzu, who may be remembered as the lady with the stickiest fingers in 5,000 years of Egyptian civilization. She was certainly the most unsubtle, which was one reason Naguib became premier, a job Zuzu's husband had held five times before his dismissal in disgrace after Farouk's abdication.

After 1936 the Wafd continued to thrive under the new king and the new treaty with England. Its success was based on a perfectly sound political principle: throw the British out of Suez and the Sudan. That was its high mission, drummed into the fellaheen in tremendous rallies every year. But as time passed and the tommies stayed, another, less lofty mission took over. The Wafd became little more than a huge graft engine. Corruption spread throughout the government; everyone knew about it, and anybody with influence had a hand in it. Farouk was the ideal king for such a regime. Between days of poring over his monumental collections of matchbook covers and American comic books, and nights of pleasure with adolescent girls he would choose at random while driving through crowds, the obese monarch managed to get his pudgy finger deep enough into the pie so that, when he finally fled the country, he had a quarter of a billion dollars in Egyptian holdings and enough abroad to finance his retirement to a twenty-room suite in Capri's Eden Paradiso Hotel.

The trouble with political principles is that if they are going to work, they must sound good, and if they sound good enough, they are liable to convince some able men that they are just. In the case of the Wafd's Anglophobia, the convinced were Egyptian army officers. There weren't many of them, but they were devoted patriots, and in February 1942, when a British general surrounded Farouk's palace with tanks and forced the dismissal of Premier Ali Maher, whom he suspected of collaboration with the Nazis, they were humiliated. That intervention was costly in other ways—it confirmed the king's hostility toward Britain, divided the Wafd, and stigmatized Nahas, who replaced Maher—

but its most profound effect was the mortification of the Egyptian soldiers who had been unable to defend their government.

Nasser, then in his early twenties, was posted to the Sudan. There
he met three sympathetic brother officers: Zakaria Mohieddene, later
vice president of the United Arab Republic; Abdel Hakim Amer, later
field marshal; and Anwar el Sadat. Together they formed the Free
Officers as a revolutionary organization. Its membership would be
known only to Nasser; its goal would be the expulsion of the British
and, if necessary, the Egyptian royal family. Meanwhile it would lobby
for reforms to strengthen the army. Certainly the army needed it.
Equipment was obsolete, discipline was a joke, and the entire military
establishment was as formidable as a palace bodyguard, which was really all it had been.

These were the troops Farouk sent against Israel in 1948, and
these were the officers—there were now eighty-nine in the clique—who
returned to Egypt burning with shame after the outnumbered Jews
pushed them all over the Negev desert and forced them into a degrad-
ing armistice. The world believed that the superior skill of the Israeli
soldiers had defeated them, but they were unconvinced, and for an understandable reason. Repeatedly their own shells had exploded prema-
turely in the field, killing Egyptians. Some of their leaders, notably
Naguib, had performed brilliantly under fire, but Nasser's experience
was more typical. He had served in one of three battalions which had
been surrounded for weeks by the the Israelis in a group of Arab villages called the Faluja Pocket. Repatriated, he rode home in bitter silence, set up headquarters in Cairo's Officers' Club, and started digging
for the truth.

In the summer of 1950 it started to come out, less as a result of his
efforts than because Egypt under the British had developed a strong tradition of crusading political journalism. *Akhbar El Yom,* the most enterprising of Cairo's newspapers, published signed stories by General
Fuad Sadek Pasha, who had been Egypt's commander in the Negev,
charging that ammunition had been defective. Nahas authorized an investigation. Then, rather short-sightedly, he left for Paris. Since the
king was on the Riviera, there was no one around with sufficient authority to stop the prosecutor general from peering into the bulging
safe-deposit boxes of the palace advisers. The facts, it developed, were
that munitions money had been misappropriated and misspent, and the
safe-deposit boxes contained the loot. Before the frantic pashas could
quash the inquiry, a dozen indictments had been handed down. Then
the government solemnly decided that the king's honor was involved,

and a successful cover-up began. Shortly thereafter a mysterious fire destroyed a surplus ammunition dump at Helwan, just south of Cairo, and everyone assumed that things would quiet down.

In September the eager prosecutors got out of hand again. This time they nosed around the cotton exchange in Alexandria and came up with evidence that Zuzu Nahas, the premier's wife, and Fuad Serag ed Din, the fat, flabby secretary-general of the Wafd and the cabinet's finance minister, had rigged the market. Serag ed Din began by setting a low minimum; sellers couldn't charge more than that. Prices dropped, and Zuzu bought. Next the minimum was jacked. Merchants had to buy from her. There were two difficulties with this cozy arrangement. The first was that Serag ed Din set his new minimums so high that British buyers from Lancashire and Yorkshire decided to go elsewhere, and the middlemen were stuck. The second was that Zuzu had an extraordinarily loud voice. Whenever she telephoned her associates, anyone who happened to be in the room could hear her over the phone, and since on the occasion there was a cabinet meeting in the room of the associate she was calling, everyone knew about the racket.

On October 14, 1950, the leaders of the Wafd's opposition formally asked Farouk to clean his house. Nahas, outraged at this impertinence, replied that it was high treason to speak to the king that way, and that if he were Farouk, he wouldn't put up with it. The king did nothing, but *Akhbar El Yom* stepped up its pressure. In November a mob tried to burn down the newspaper's plant (one demonstrator was killed, and Nahas closed Cairo's schools so the children could attend his funeral), and in 1951 the paper's editions were confiscated twenty-two times, but Mustafa and Ali Amin, the twin brothers who published it, merely put out two editions, one for the confiscators and another for their subscribers. The operation cost them $300,000, but in the autumn of 1951 they turned up two classic scandals, and the repercussions started the chain of events which ended with Farouk's abdication.

Nahas had announced that the government felt sorry for the fellaheen and was therefore distributing among the landless a couple of hundred feddans of prime land near Alexandria. A feddan is one and one-sixteenth acres, and in a land-hungry country it was quite a prize. *Akhbar El Yom* investigated and discovered that the land was not agricultural but residential, worth between $1,500 and $3,000 a feddan. They further found that, apart from a few minor children who weren't old enough to be pashas or pashas' wives, the twenty grantees could scarcely be called landless. The list consisted of three of Zuzu's brothers, three of her nephews, three of her nieces, two of her sisters-in-law, two of her cousins, her sister, her brother-in-law, the sister-in-law of one of her brothers, her great-niece, her lady in waiting, her secretary, and her husband's cousin.

Cairo was still marveling at this three weeks later when the Amins published a list of the winners of a recent lottery in which the government had raffled off twenty-two houses. Over 80,000 Egyptians had participated. The holders of the lucky numbers were led by one of Nahas' cousins, followed by two of his nephews, five of his secretaries, six of his aides, the switchboard operator at his home, the brother and son of the minister of communications, the brother of the minister of foreign affairs, the leader of the Wafdist Youth, the secretary of the minister of economy, another of Nahas' cousins, and, just in the money, the official who had been confiscating *Akhbar El Yom* every other week for a year.

Nahas agreed that this was an amazing coincidence, but his colleagues in the Wafd told him he would have to do better than that, and so, three days later, he stood tearfully in parliament and asked for the abrogation of the 1936 treaty, which he, as premier, had signed for Egypt. The British, he explained, had been behaving very badly. You couldn't work with such people. They would have to get out of Suez right away. Diverting public attention from internal corruption to foreign affairs was an old Wafd trick, but this time it worked too well. The Canal Zone was a bad place to wave the flag. For generations a small army of Egyptian thieves had lived off British stores, held in check only by native police. Now the police enthusiastically joined the pilferers, and on October 17, the day after the Wafdist parliament ratified the abrogation a British PX in Ismailia, a town about halfway between Port Said and Suez, was looted of $85,000 worth of stock and then burned.

Lieutenant General Sir George Erskine, the British commander, pulled his troops out of Ismailia to avoid trouble, but Serag ed Din, who had been promoted to minister of the interior after his spectacular feats in the cotton market, sent 1,000 auxiliary police into the town. They built it into a guerrilla base and sent raiding parties behind Sir George's lines. By mid-January of 1952 the situation was darkening every day, and when a stray shot, fired on the grounds of an Ismailia convent, killed an American nun, Erskine decided to go back and clean the town out. He asked the police to surrender. They refused. On January 25 he surrounded their barracks and poured lead at them all day. When the policemen who were still alive ran out of ammunition and gave up, there were forty-six Egyptian corpses inside.

The next day Cairo erupted in riots which killed seventeen foreign residents and destroyed Shepheard's Hotel, the Turf Club, and a half-dozen English movie houses. No one really knew who started the trouble—the Wafd, the British, the Communists, the Moslem Brotherhood (a vague, semireligious, semipolitical organization with fanatical factions), and Farouk were variously blamed—but the best evidence is that the outbreaks were spontaneous. A gang of students organized a protest march on the palace at 9 A.M. They walked right by Shepheard's without incident, but when they got to Opera Square they glanced into a cabaret and saw an army officer squeezing a belly dancer. The contrast between his laughter and the martyrs in Ismailia was too much for them; they broke ranks and swarmed in on him.

Afterward no one pretended to know the sequence of events which followed. There were flashes of incident—American women cowering in their hairdressers' closets, Englishmen at the Turf Club ignoring their twelve-minute warning and going out to face the angry knives—but coherence was too much to expect from the foreigners who survived. The confused mobs that welled out of the ancient slums behind El Azhar, the great Moslem university, were as disorganized as their victims, and they, too, lacked any clear idea of what had happened. Somehow the army kept them off Gezira Island, the city's most fashionable suburb, but when night fell at last they had destroyed $300,000 worth of property.

Farouk sacked Nahas and Serag ed Din, called in Ali Maher, the premier whose resignation the British had forced ten years earlier, and told him to put out the fire. Maher did a workmanlike job, for he was a good administrator, whatever his sympathies during the war, but within a month he was out and the king was playing politics again. Throughout the spring premiers succeeded one another with bewildering speed. In the country things were drifting badly. Here and there the fellaheen were shooting estate managers and burning plantations, and the cotton brokers were still stuck with the vast stocks they had bought from Zuzu.

Colonel Nasser and his Free Officers decided that they had had enough. By now the clique's leadership had shaken down to a nine-man High Committee. (Later the committee was expanded to thirteen.) After the arms investigation they had sworn to act if the country wasn't cleaned up by 1955, but lately they had been getting impatient. Farouk had been feuding with them since the previous fall, when he had appointed his palace pet, General Hussein Sirry Amer, commander of the élite Frontier Corps, passing over the respected Naguib. The officers had despised Sirry Amer ever since the investigations of 1950 had indicated that he had run guns into Israel during the Palestine War, and when Farouk compounded the insult by demanding that he be elected chairman of the Officers' Club board, they defiantly picked Naguib instead.

Nasser was later reported to have spent most of his time, on the day of the January riots, hunting for Sirry Amer in the hope of killing him in the confusion, and the Free Officers were still unreconciled to him in early July, when Farouk again backed him for the chairmanship. They reelected Naguib. The king struck back by dissolving the club and firing a premier who had wanted to go along with the committee and give Naguib the war minister's portfolio. Instead, Farouk insisted on a premier who would give it to his royal brother-in-law. That did it. Sirry Amer had lived by his wits long enough to know that the Free Officers had reached the flash point, and on the eve of the new cabinet's swearing-in he decided to get out of the country. In the middle of the night he rushed from his house in his pajamas, packed his family in his car, and headed for the Libyan border. Libya considered his dress too informal and wouldn't let him in. By the time he got back his enemies had taken over the government, and he was arrested for being out of uniform. Later the charge was changed to attempted desertion, and the following winter a court-martial stripped him of his rank, threw him out of the army, and sentenced him to life at hard labor.

The coup was so well-planned that a lot of people thought it might have been managed by a mission of fifty former German officers who had arrived the year before to give the government technical advice. The same people thought it highly significant that the emblem of Nasser's Liberation Rally, which replaced Egypt's dissolved political parties, was an eagle. Actually the Germans were confined to their quarters the night Farouk was deposed; when they were released and they looked around, they were just as surprised as everybody else. And the Free Officers' symbolic bird didn't look at all like the starved crow Hitler wore. It was almost North American, and it was certainly bald. The fact is that Egypt was made for a coup, psychologically and geographically. It wasn't particularly difficult to move a few tanks into Cairo and Alexandria. After that it was largely a matter of determining what the people thought.

The people seemed to think that it was fine. Nevertheless, the junta's High Committee continued to meet secretly in twos and threes at odd hours, keeping the names of the members' identity quiet, and their real leader remained out of the limelight. It turned out that Nasser's caution was entirely justified, but in the meantime Cairo was bewildered. Ali Maher was premier again, by order of General Naguib. Obviously there was a lot more to it than that, however, and everyone was guessing at the true character of the shadowy committee.

Some thought the Moslem Brotherhood was running everything. The chief reason for this was that one of the three regents appointed to sign papers for the new king, Farouk's tiny son, Fuad II, was a colonel Rashad Mehanna, a brotherhood member with an impressive record in the 1948 war. One of the Free Officers tried to explain the true nature of the High Committee to Hassan el Hodeiby, a quiet former judge who was the leader of the Brotherhood, but it turned out that the officer didn't understand it very well himself. *He* thought the committee was Communistic. His wife was a Communist, which may have been responsible for his delusion; in all events, when word of this exchange reached Nasser, Hodeiby's informant was spirited out of town, and the committee became one man smaller. The Communists were largely an unknown force, in Egypt as elsewhere, because it was hard to tell just how many people were making all that noise. It soon became clear, however, that they were out to embarrass Naguib and the junta.

Apart from a few obvious political reforms, such as the abolition of the titles of pasha and bey and the proclamation of a minimum-wage law, most of the new government's early work was devoted to cleaning up inefficiency. It is small praise to say of a dictatorship that it makes trains run on time, unless you happen to live in a country where they never have in the past. In Egypt it had sometimes seemed to be a remarkable locomotive which got away from the station at all. Naguib changed all that. He and the junta started with the army, giving Farouk's favorites the sack. Apart from Sirry Amer and a few other grudge victims who probably had it coming to them, the erring were allowed to depart in peace. In governmental agencies, improvements were spotty. Under the new administrators you could clear customs in five minutes without a bribe, but you could still spend five hours getting an exit visa. The most impressive early reforms were in the ministries, where the new work day started at eight sharp. There was a story going the rounds in Cairo then of an undersecretary who showed up a little late and found a captain sitting at his desk and studying his watch. "Good morning, Mr. Secretary," said the captain. "What time do you have?" "Eight-twenty," the startled diplomat answered. "I'm sorry to hear that," the officer said. "I had hoped my watch was fast."

At first Ali Maher was permitted to run the show. Naguib announced that he planned to abolish all censorship, issued pious messages urging the people to cooperate with Maher, and suggested that the Wafd clean its own house, which it fervently promised to do. But three weeks after the coup, 6,000 textile workers rioted in a village south of Alexandria, and the Wafd's dirty fingerprints were all over town. At the same time, Maher, under pressure from land-owning relatives, was resisting the general's proposals for land reform. On September 8, therefore, Naguib reluctantly took over the premiership with the junta's approval and retired Maher to write his memoirs. Then the general set out on a tour of the Wafd stronghold: lower Egypt.

Instructions went out to all government workers in the Nile delta, forbidding, under penalty of dismissal, the organized demonstrations which had always marked Nahas' trips there. This was just after it became generally known that Naguib was planning land reform, however, and no organization was necessary. The fellaheen, after generations of loving the land and not owning any, saw the man who promised to give them a little, and they almost tore him to pieces. American observers retired after the tour's first day, nursing bruises, but the general kept right on going, and when he reached Samanoud, the village where Nahas was born, with no slackening of the mob's enthusiasm, he knew he had the old man licked. He returned to Cairo and demanded that the Wafd get a new chief, which it speedily did. When the party's executive council told Nahas that he was through, he wept. Within six months he was senile and had developed a disturbing habit of falling into a deep sleep in the middle of a conversation. Zuzu hovered near, but her voice had become so soft, and she used it so rarely, that she no longer kept him awake. Wisely, she had decided that it was not a good idea to remind Egypt's new rulers that she was still around.

The problem with the new leader the Wafd got was that he was Serag ed Din; he immediately began planning a counterrevolution, and he convinced Colonel Mehanna, the regent, that there wasn't anything the junta was doing that the Wafd couldn't do better. Mehanna wasn't a member of the High Committee; he had been given a spot in the new government largely because Farouk hadn't liked him, and he was deceived by Naguib's simplicity and Nasser's obscurity. The Communists volunteered to help, and the coup of the bizarre coalition was scheduled for January 12, 1953. On that day, however, Naguib took a page from the Wafd book and snubbed the British ambassador at a social function. It was a minor maneuver in renewed negotiations over the future of the Sudan, but it forced a postponement of Mehanna's plans, and before he could pull his people together again, Nasser had found out about them. Over two dozen officers and civilians were arrested, and both Mehanna and Serag ed Din were sent off to bake in the desert sun at El Tor, a notorious Frontier Corps concentration camp on the Red Sea.

Four days after Serag ed Din and Mehanna were jailed, Naguib outlawed the parties in a midnight broadcast, designated the High Committee as his parliament, or Revolution Command Council (RCC), and appointed fifty civilians to draft a new Egyptian constitution. The RCC extended his powers for a year. On January 23, six months after the coup, the date he had originally set for his retirement, a quarter-million howling Egyptians packed Liberty Square, where the cream of Britain's East African troops once barracked, to honor him. He announced the birth of the *Hayet Al Tahreer,* or Liberation Rally, with himself as chief and Nasser as secretary-general, and invited monthly subscriptions of five piastres, or fifteen cents. Three weeks later 2,000,000 had joined.

It was widely assumed in those days that Naguib, like Kemal Ataturk, the founder of modern Turkey, wanted to create a single-party state, with himself as president. In practice, he turned aside supporters of a republic with vague talk of a plebiscite to determine the future of the monarchy. He didn't seem to know what to do with the royal family, but his intrigue with Farouk's mother-in-law, which resulted in the return, alone, to Egypt of former Queen Narriman, suggested that he was toying with the idea of developing the regency. Farouk had no intention of letting his small son go, however, and the value of the former queen without the little king was something of a puzzle. It was a puzzle that Naguib intended to play with for quite a while all the same, for despite his popularity, he didn't want an election just then— not with Egypt's sterling balance growing smaller and smaller and bankruptcy looming ahead. For the revolutionary leader of a xenophobic people, he was making extraordinary overtures to capital abroad, repealing a Wafd statute restricting foreign ownership of Egyptian stock, encouraging Anglo-American oil prospectors to explore the Gaza strip, and even talking about special tax privileges for foreign firms. He was doing everything he could to buy time for his sick economy, but he wasn't having much luck getting what he needed most— customers for his cotton.

Egyptians had once called cotton White Gold. Now they were

using ruder names. Every warehouse in Alexandria was jammed, and the bales were overflowing into desert depots. Naguib gave the most desperate merchants a $158,000,000 subsidy, but that merely transferred part of the debt from private to public ledgers. The country had unsold cotton worth $432,000,000. There were three reasons for this backlog—Zuzu's corner, a worldwide textile slump, and what amounted to a British boycott after the abrogation of the 1936 treaty. The British denied this, and said that they had heavy inventories, but they were buying long-staple stock from Brazil, and there was nothing in Brazil's cotton that wasn't in Egypt's.

Behind all this was the fact that Egypt grew too much cotton and too little grain. The British bore a heavy share of the responsibility for that; empires like to have colonies and protectorates where they want them—dependent—and one way to promote dependency is to encourage one-crop economies. There weren't many customers for Alexandria beyond England; she could sell a little to the Dutch and the Germans, but the Arab League was angry at West Germany for agreeing to pay Israel reparations, and the prospect of an Arab boycott of Bonn accounted for Naguib's rather desperate trade agreement with the merchants of East Germany, whom Egypt didn't even recognize. American Point Four technicians were trying to encourage the development of other crops, but Naguib's land-reform schemes, however desirable in other ways, made that difficult. Wheat and rice required a lot of farm machinery and irrigation equipment; they were practical only on large estates. A tractor wasn't economical on a little farm, and the general intended to cut the big plantations up into pieces of five feddans each. Nasser was thinking in terms of communal ownership, a form of collectivization; that came much later, however.

Egypt is deceptive on a map. It looks much bigger than it is. About 95 percent of it is bleak desert, and 99 percent of the people live on what is left, a 6,000,000-feddan strip that clings lushly to the winding Nile. Until the early nineteenth century, Egyptian farming depended upon what is called basin irrigation; at the peak of the river's annual flood the land was fed by rich alluvial water, and the fellaheen sowed. In 1820 Viceroy Mehemet Ali introduced the concept of dams, or barrages, as the nilologists call them, and started perennial irrigation, permitting two, and in some places three, sowings a year. During Farouk's reign a feddan that produced three crops a year was, when the country's economy was sound, worth as much as $4,500 a year. That was the source of the pashas' wealth. Some 2,000 landowners, one tenth of one percent of the population, owned 1,200,000 feddans, a fifth of the arable land. A man like Serag ed Din had feddans in the tens of thousands and a vast multitude of peasants working them. Naguib began reform by expropriating all individual holdings over 200 feddans and parceling them out for sale on the installment plan in little lots. The landowners were given bonds, redeemable in thirty years, and the fellaheen had even longer to repay the government. One ironic feature of the expropriation law was that in determining how much compensation a landowner got for his property, the new regime used the tax assessment records of the old, which meant that the more pull a pasha had with the Ministry of Finance, the more he lost.

Over 272,000 feddans were in the process of redistribution, and the program had created about 350,000 new landowners before Naguib left office. But there still wasn't enough land, not in a country where 2,000,000 fellaheen owned less than a feddan each and there was an average of a third of a feddan available for every Egyptian. When Mehemet Ali started his irrigation program, it was an interesting experiment, but it wasn't vital to the economy. By the early 1950's it had become absolutely essential, even though some observers thought that the multiple sowings would eventually exhaust what was once the richest land on the globe. Egypt's population had quadrupled since 1820, and when the Free Officers toppled Farouk it was increasing at a steady rate of two percent a year. Both Naguib and Nasser disapproved of birth control, claiming that its practice would violate Islamic principles. As a consequence, the country's population continued to grow inexorably under them. The most interesting demographic study carried out when I was there was run by a team from the Johns Hopkins School of Public Health. They picked an area with the highest reproductive figures in the delta, showed outdoor movies there every evening for a year, and cut the birthrate in half. But when they ran out of funds and left, the impregnation ratios started to climb again, and the Nile valley remained the most densely populated region in the world.

Naguib's Ministry of Public Works reclaimed about 1,500,000 feddans in the upper Nile, thereby assuring maintenance of the status quo between the growing population and the amount of usable land into the mid-1970's, but anything beyond that was a matter of conjecture. There were plenty of imaginative schemes for improving the fella's food supply. A progressive landowner named Hafez Affifi dumped a stew of chemicals into 200 feddans in the desert and created an oasis, but the formula didn't work elsewhere. Dreamers suggesting extracting the salt from Mediterranean water and pumping millions of gallons into the Qattara Depression, the big hole of quicksand and salt marshes in the desert which squeezed Rommel against El Alamein in 1942, but the idea was unfeasible. Naguib exempted desert land from his land-reform program for twenty-five years to encourage reclamation. The only project to prove practical, however, was concocted by Americans. Point Four agents found land once fertile under the Romans and now buried under two to four feet of sand. They fenced in several thousand feddans, sowed them with reseeding grasses, and reclaimed them for grazing. That was fine for farm animals, but it didn't help the fellaheen much. The outlook for the millions of tubercular peasants, crowded 2,300 to the square mile, living from day to famished day on their diet of black bread, rice, and leaf soup, remained very dark.

The Nile was Egypt's silent motive in negotiations over the future of the Sudan, just as Kenya, then still a British colony, was Whitehall's. Both Naguib and Sir Ralph Stevenson, the English ambassador to Cairo, droned out about the right of the Sudanese to self-determination, but all Stevenson wanted was a buffer for the British base in East Africa, and all Naguib wanted was water. It almost never rains in Egypt, and so the agriculture depends on the river, flowing from where it comes down in buckets, high in the green rain forests of interior Africa, 2,450 miles away, outside the country. Since better than nine out of every ten Egyptians are engaged in cultivation, the agriculture is the economy. Without the Nile there would be no fellaheen, no Cairo, no Naguib, no Nasser; just empty sands.

The sources of the river are many, and they vary from year to year, but before they get to Khartoum, the Sudanese capital, they are channeled into two—the Blue Nile, coming out of Ethiopia's Lake Tana, and the White Nile, crawling down from Lake Victoria and Lake Albert, in Uganda. They join at Khartoum. From that point onward there is just the one stream, winding toward the Mediterranean with extraordinary languor. It takes nine months for a drop of water falling in the Ugandan jungles to reach Cairo, where the river, at its mightiest before it splits up in the delta, is crossed by wedges of low-flying egrets and feluccas, the lovely Egyptian sailboats that tack between the eucalyptus banks. Because it is so slow, nilologists, studying their nilometers, can telegraph the river's strength downstream months ahead, and their colleagues at the Egyptian dams north of the Nubian Desert can decide how much water must be released to feed the next season's crop. A nilologist is a highly respected engineer, and nilometers have an honored place in Egyptian history. The oldest is at Roda, south of Cairo, near the spot where Moses is said to have nestled in the bulrushes. It goes back to 641 A.D., and though its accuracy is extremely questionable, no one has ever suggested that it be scrapped.

After January 26, 1885, when howling dervishes slaughtered British General Charles George "Chinese" Gordon at Khartoum, Englishmen convinced one another that they had a tremendous emotional investment in the million-square-mile Sudan. The fact that a great many Egyptian soldiers had died with Gordon—Naguib's maternal grandfather among them—was ignored in London. After Anglo-Egyptian troops led by Lord Kitchener retook Khartoum fourteen years later, the Egyptians were generously treated in the basic water agreements, but there remained an abiding fear that the Sudanese might siphon off more than their share. The Wafd exploited this fear endlessly, refusing to discuss the future of Suez until the Sudan was Egyptian. Farouk's rallying cry, his one appeal to his subjects, was, "Unity of the Nile valley—Egypt and the Sudan as one!"

England was in an excellent position to combat this sort of thing, for Egyptian imperialism had as little appeal to educated Sudanese as British imperialism, and the British civil service was doing a good job there. Their eight hundred administrators were highly popular with the jungle tribes in the southern Sudan, near Kenya, while in the north, among the native Moslems, they played the two religious leaders, Abdel Rahman el Mahdi and Ali el Mirghani, against one another in the great imperialist tradition of divide-and-rule. Both were knighted and wooed, though the Mahdi, posthumous son of the Mahdi who killed Gordon and his men, was much closer to Whitehall, chiefly because Mirghani's loyalty became suspect during World War II and the English decided that he was becoming altogether too temperamental. Sir Robert Howe, governor-general of the Sudan, would make occasional statements about Sudanese independence in twenty years or so. This wasn't much, but it was better than nothing, which was what Farouk was promising.

Naguib startled Khartoum, London, and most of Cairo by reversing the Egyptian position. He presented himself as the champion of either sovereignty for the Sudan or union with Egypt—the choice was up to the Sudanese—with the decision to be made within three years. In the autumn after the Free Officers coup the British asked the Mahdi to stop in Cairo en route home from his latest visit to London and straighten Naguib out. Instead Naguib converted the Mahdi, who came out of their conference to announce that the general had the right idea. Mirghani, already angry at England, came over immediately, and on November 2 Naguib formally presented Sir Ralph Stevenson with the new Egyptian government's plan for the Sudan. Then the general sent Major Saleh Salem, a dashing young member of the High Committee, into the tribal area. On December 31 Anthony Eden, then Secretary of State for Foreign Affairs, got his first stunning intimation of what Salem had been up to. A petition, signed in blood by several key tribal chiefs, arrived on Eden's desk in Whitehall. The chiefs had declared that Naguib's proposals had their enthusiastic approval. Ten days later the Egyptian major had a signed agreement with the Sudan's four political parties, threatening to boycott any pact that didn't follow the Naguib plan. A couple of weeks later a photograph was released in Cairo showing one of Salem's unorthodox diplomatic tactics. The picture was of him and several chiefs. They were dancing in the buff.

Major Salem's agreement with the tribesmen became public on January 10, and the same day Sir Ralph gave Naguib a reply to his note of November 2. The British still had doubts, but Ambassador Caffery privately advised them that if they couldn't strike a bargain with Naguib they might not have another chance to deal with a decent Egyptian government. Sir Ralph, who had become an admirer of Naguib, agreed. The ensuing treaty, which was signed by Englishmen and Egyptians in Princess Shewkar's old palace on February 12, provided for a Sudanese plebiscite. The ceremony was badly managed, as ceremonies were likely to be in Cairo, and for that reason it had a high flavor. Fezzed Arabs who had no business being there rushed in and out embracing one another and, when they could reach them, hugging Naguib and Salem, too. An Egyptian army officer, his face streaked with tears, held a trembling red candle aloft, pooling sealing wax on the treaty. After Sir Ralph and his entourage had left, Naguib brandished his pen, bowed to Salem, and winked at the crowd. Later he said that he would fly south soon to visit relatives—his mother was Sudanese—but that he wouldn't go "as Saleh did." An aide explained that the general caught cold easily.

There was a sense of urgency in the Sudan negotiations. Naguib needed a solution on his terms to satisfy the Egyptian chauvinism which had kept the Wafd in power, and Sir Ralph wanted the treaty out of the way so they could get on with talks about Suez. Five minutes after the pact was signed Naguib told Stevenson that he would like to start Canal Zone negotiations immediately. Sir Ralph replied with a weary smile that the sooner they tackled them, the better. In this matter, Nahas unwittingly did Naguib a favor, for although the rioting after the Ismailia massacre gave Zuzu's husband a black eye, it weakened the British base and sharply cut its value.

Until then, Suez had possessed the three essentials of a major military base. The docks at Port Said, the city of Suez, and Adabaya could hardly have been improved upon. Internal communications were superb, with the canal itself running north and south, the Sweetwater Canal running east and west, and road and railroad networks stretching in all directions. Finally, the zone had a splendid labor force of 60,000 Egyptians, for which the English paid a wage bill of a half-million pounds sterling every month.

After Ismailia most of the 60,000 vanished, which was the chief reason the British were anxious to settle their differences with Cairo and get out. Nahas forcibly evicted eighty-five percent of the work force and dumped the laborers in upper Egypt, where it was almost impossible for them to return. A year later they were drifting back into the zone at the rate of 500 a month, and some 10,000 Royal East African Pioneers had been brought in to supplement them, but that wasn't nearly enough. The British reinforced their garrison to 60,000 men, interpreting in the broadest possible fashion the 1936 treaty, which allowed them 10,000 combat troops, 400 pilots, and "the necessary ancillary personnel for administrative and technical duties." They could struggle along with those in peacetime, but military bases have to be prepared for war. If the Russians had started south, which in those years seemed possible, the zone would have needed a quarter-million workers right away, and clearly they weren't going to get them from a hostile Egypt. The only answer was to cooperate with Naguib.

The general knew this, and he was making his own ground rules. The Suez Canal Zone, he said in speeches delivered for home consumption, was Egyptian territory; the British had to leave, and that was all there was to it. There could be no package deals, no conditions for withdrawal. Nasser, then just beginning to show his hand, threatened the English with guerrilla warfare if they didn't go. Privately Naguib took a different line, however. He was, he reminded those around him, a military man. He knew that neutrality in the Cold War was impossible then, and he had decided long ago to cast his lot with the West, provided the British would do things his way.

Already, in that first year after Farouk, it was obvious that the Suez dilemma would remain unresolved for a long time. Essential to NATO's defense plans, the Canal Zone was a gigantic military storehouse manned by a corps of technicians, including several thousand radar experts. Naguib agreed that he couldn't replace those experts, and British officers said they couldn't withdraw them and leave their equipment in strange hands. However, most Egyptians, including Naguib, had developed a tendency to talk of the canal as an internal waterway. Sometimes, in fact, they did more than talk. Since 1948 they had confiscated a lot of cargo bound for Israel, including some which could scarcely be called military.

None of the correspondents then living in Cairo foresaw the day when gigantic tankers would render Suez obsolescent, but even the dullest among us realized that a resolution of the Israeli problem would be the greatest possible boon to Mideast peace. It was also, of course, the least likely. John Foster Dulles was grandly assuring Israelis that they would be welcome to join the Middle East defense organization he was trying to put together, but the Arabs, with 95 percent of the region's population, didn't feel that way at all. "Egyptian recognition in Israel is about as likely as American recognition of China," I cabled home that winter. As we discovered two decades later, it was actually less likely. Compared with what had gone before and what would come later, Israel's relations with her neighbors were serene in the early 1950's, yet U.S. ships were being routinely blacklisted in Cairo for carrying cargoes to Tel Aviv, and Egyptian authorities, including Naguib, found it necessary to assure the Palestinian refugees from time to time that they would all go home someday.

The center of anti-Zionist sentiment in Cairo then was the Arab League, the federation which Anthony Eden had encouraged and afterward learned to detest. Ostensibly the League was devoted to the study of "major problems in the social and cultural spheres," but it was also interested in the Zionist atrocity sphere, and one poisonous little pamphlet which I picked up at its headquarters described the desecration of Moslem mosques, the bayoneting of pregnant Arab women, and the Israeli use of bacteriological warfare, which, it charged, had been responsible for cholera epidemics in Egypt and Syria during the 1948 war. The leaflet concluded that "a people who can commit such outrages upon innocent human beings and show contempt for the houses of God have placed themselves once and for all time outside the pale of humanity."

Cairo continued to be a nervous city under Naguib, partly because of the city's history, partly due to the Egyptian national character, and partly, I suspect, because paranoia is endemic among the makers of revolutions. There were plainclothesmen in every bar, listening; cables and foreign mail were censored; phones were tapped; and any foreigner walking up the Nile to the British embassy could expect to be shadowed. Suspicion is infectious; at least one correspondent cultivated the habit of taking the second, not the first, cab to drift by his hotel. A lot of others wondered whether all the intrigue was really necessary. Clearly Naguib was a militant democrat, and highly esteemed by his people. The Wafd was broken. All the key Communists were in jail. Apart from the embittered landlords and the fanatics in the Moslem Brotherhood who objected to the drafting of a new constitution because "the Koran is our constitution"—some two hundred of them forced their way into the first meeting of the drafting committee, shouting just that—the moderate regime appeared to have no enemies of consequence at large.

Its most dangerous enemy, as the passage of time revealed, lay within its own leadership. In retrospect General Naguib has taken on the aspect of an Egyptian Kerensky, while Nasser seems to have been more of an Arabian Lenin. Like Lenin, Nasser allowed his predecessor to take the first steps toward the future. Naguib was a stronger man than Kerensky, however, and more of an activist. He ended the brief reign of little Fuad II, declared Egypt a republic with himself as chief of state, put corrupt members of the previous regime on trial, and outlawed the Moslem Brotherhood. Then Nasser prepared his big move. In February 1954 he came out of the closet to take over the premiership. That November he put Naguib under house arrest, and in 1956, the same year the Sudanese opted for independence, he promulgated a new constitution, with himself as president.

The history of modern Egypt, with all its agonies, dates from then. Looking back, one cannot avoid concluding that events in the Middle East might have followed a different course if Naguib had remained in power. The man was wise, learned, temperate, fair, and, above all, decent. That, of course, was precisely the trouble with him. That was why he, and that entire region, was foredoomed to the Mideast madness of today.

Envoi

My Old Man

The Last Years of H. L. Mencken

"THE COOKS HERE DO A SWELL JOB with soft-shell crabs," Mencken said in a gravelly voice, peering at me over his spectacles. Beneath the old-fashioned center part of his white hair his pot-blue eyes gleamed like twin gas jets. "They fry them in the altogether," he rasped. "Then they add a small jockstrap of bacon."

It was June 2, 1947. We were in the dining room of the Maryland Club. The meeting was our first—I had just flown in from a Midwestern graduate school, where I was writing my dissertation on his early literary criticism—and it was the beginning of a seven-year friendship, an April–December relationship which I cherished, and cherish still, despite the dirty tricks fate began to play on him eighteen months after it began.

"This is a very high-toned club," he said over the crabs. "Nothing but men. Any member who suffers a heart attack must be carried outside to the front steps before a nurse can attend him."

He was in fine form that Monday noon. The thought that he himself might fall the victim of a seizure and wind up in the hands of nurses was very far away. At sixty-six he was still at the height of his remarkable powers and had, in fact, just completed the most productive period in his career. Since 1940 he had been feuding with his paper, the Baltimore *Sun*, as a result of the *Sun's* support of what he had called "Roosevelt's War." Holed up in his study at 1524 Hollins Street, he had written *Happy Days, Newspaper Days, Heathen Days, A Christmas Story, A New Dictionary of Quotations,* and two massive supplements to *The American Language* and was, when we met, at work on *A Mencken Chrestomathy*. His machete was still long and sharp and heavy, and he had never swung it with greater gusto.

Face-to-face with the man himself, I was enormously impressed.

Alistair Cooke once observed that Mencken had "the longest torso on the shortest legs in the entire history of legmen," and Mencken himself said there would be no point in erecting a statue to him, because it would just look like a monument to a defeated alderman, but actually he was a man of great physical presence. To be sure, his torso was ovoid, his ruddy face homely, and his legs not only stubby but also thin and bowed. Nevertheless there was a sense of dignity and purpose about all his movements, and when you were with him it was impossible to forget that you were watching a great original. Nobody else could stuff Uncle Willie stogies into a seersucker jacket with the flourish of Mencken, or wipe a blue bandanna across his brow so dramatically. His friends treasured everything about him, because the whole of the man was manifest in each of his aspects—the tilt of his head, his close-fitting clothes, his high-crowned felt hat creased in the distinct fashion of the 1920's, his strutting walk, his abrupt gestures, his habit of holding a cigar between his thumb and forefinger like a baton, the roupy inflection of his voice, and, most of all, those extraordinary eyes: so large, and intense, and merry. He was sui generis in all ways, and the instant I saw him I wanted to write his biography.

After reading my thesis the following summer, he agreed. ("I marvel at the hard work you put into it," he wrote me. "It tells me many things about my own self that I didn't know myself. . . . You will be rewarded in Heaven throughout eternity.") He did more. Swallowing his pride, he asked the *Sun* to give me a job, so that I could support myself while working on the book. My journalistic career was launched that September, and while I was unlikely to match the trajectory of his soaring star—at my age, twenty-five, he had been a managing editor—it did give us something else to talk about.

Beginning that autumn, we talked a great deal, sometimes at the *Sun,* which he now began visiting with growing frequency; other times in his club, his home, the Enoch Pratt Free Library, Miller Brothers' restaurant, and on long walks through downtown Baltimore. There was, of course, no pretense to conversation between equals; I regarded him with the special deference of the fledgling writer for the master. The high-ceilinged Hollins Street sitting room, with its cheery fireplace, dark rosewood furniture, and Victorian bric-a-brac became a kind of shrine to me. I treasured his letters to me, which were even more frequent than our talks, for he loved correspondence, always preferring the written word to the telephone. And I kept elaborate notes on all our contacts, which, he being Mencken, really were notable.

One warm day I covered a fire in his neighborhood. He appeared friskily at the height of it, carrying a pencil and perspiring happily. "I'm like the hippopotamus," he said in greeting, "an essentially tropical animal." Like the hippo, he was also a creature of exaggeration. He never asked me just to join him for a beer; I was invited to "hoist a schooner of malt." He couldn't order sweetbreads at Miller's without explaining that they were taken from "the pancreases of horned cattle, the smaller intestines of swine, and the vermiform appendix of the cow"—thereby causing me to choose something else. Anthony Comstock hadn't merely been a censor; he had been "a great smeller." Mencken was forever stuffing letters to me with advertisements for chemical water closets, quack-remedy broadsides, and religious pamphlets. Once, while showing me his manuscript collection in the Pratt Library, he said he was worried about its security; the stack containing it was locked, but he wanted a sign, too. "Saying 'KEEP OUT'?" I asked. "No," he said. "Saying: 'WARNING: TAMPERING WITH THIS GATE WILL RELEASE CHLORINE GAS UNDER 250 POUNDS PRESSURE.' "

By the spring of 1948 he was a daily visitor to the *Sun*. In the paper's morgue he advised a man updating the Mencken obituary to "Leave it as it is. Just add one line: 'As he grew older, he grew worse.' " One afternoon on Charles Street we encountered two sedate women from the *Sun*'s library coming the other way, and Mencken cried out heartily, "Hello, girls! How's the profession?" Later one of them said to me, "Of course, he didn't mean it the way it sounded." I knew that was exactly how he had meant it. By then, though, it was clear that he was yearning for a consummation of his rapprochement with the paper. The feud formally ended the following summer, when he arrived in Philadelphia to join the *Sun* men covering that year's presidential nominations and write happily of "the traditional weather of a national convention . . . a rising temperature, very high humidity, and lazy puffs of gummy wind from the mangrove swamps surrounding the city." Of the three political parties then taking the field, he preferred the Progressives, because they were the most preposterous. After Wallace had been nominated, he received a delegation of young Progressives in the hotel suite housing the *Sun* delegation and proposed that they join him in singing "The Star-Spangled Banner." He deliberately picked the impossible key of F Major. After crooning a few bars in his rasping tenor, he dropped out, waiting to hear his guests crack up, as was inevitable, on the impossible high E. When it happened, they looked appealingly to him for help. He just stuck his cigar in his mouth and beamed back at them.

My best recollection of the campaign which followed is of a

Wallace rally in Baltimore's Fifth Regiment Armory which I covered with Mencken. By then everyone in the audience had read the old man's *Sun* articles taunting their hero, and they knew the old man would be there that night. After the speeches, a mob of them crowded around the press bench, where, incredibly, he had unsheathed his portable typewriter and set to work. He had decided to knock out his piece with them watching. I know of no other writer who could have performed under the circumstances. There were perhaps a score of hostile, humorless men and women in an arc behind him, peering over his shoulder, and behind them were others who were calling out, "What's he saying about us?" The outrageous phrases were called back, the crowd growled—and the old man hunted and pecked on, enjoying himself hugely. He even hummed that catchy little ditty, "Friendly Henry Wallace."

Mencken was immensely amused, as the *Sun* hierarchy was not, by Truman's unexpected victory. He felt that it justified his assessment of democracy as a comic spectacle. He returned to Hollins Street, refreshed, to tackle a new book. Meantime I had written the opening sections of my biography, and he had read them. On September 27 he had written me, "It seems to me that, as they stand, the first two chapters are excellent. Some of your generalizations surprise me, and even horrify me, but they are yours, not mine. Don't let anyone tell you how to write it. Do it in your own way. You are obviously far ahead of most young writers, and I have every confidence in you." Thus we were both busy with thickening manuscripts as winter approached. On Wednesday, November 24, we were to take a break. A luncheon reservation had been made at the Maryland Club for four—Mencken, Evelyn Waugh, a Jesuit priest, and me. Waugh and Mencken had never met; the priest and I had arranged everything, like seconds before a duel. The encounter never took place, however, because disaster struck the old man the evening before.

Mencken was fascinated by the frailties of the human body, his own and everybody else's. He was constantly studying medical journals, reading up on diseases of the bronchial tubes, gall bladder, etc., and he was the most considerate visitor of the sick in Baltimore. Acquaintances who, in health, would not see him for weeks, found him at their hospital doors each evening, as long as they remained bedridden, fascinated by their progress, or, even more, by their lack of it. His letters to me and to others reflected his preoccupation with illness and anatomy. "Imagine," he wrote typically, "hanging the stones of a man *outside,* where they are forever getting themselves knocked, pinched and bruised. Any decent mechanic would have put them in the exact center of the body, protected by a body envelope twice as thick as even a Presbyterian's skull. Moreover, consider certain parts of the female—always too large or too small. The elemental notion of standardization seems to have never presented itself to the celestial Edison."

He ended another note: "As for me, I am enjoying my usual decrepitude. A new disease has developed, hitherto unknown to the faculty: a dermatitis caused by the plates I wear for my arches. No one knows how to cure it. I shall thus go limping to the crematory." He was always having a tumor dug out of his foot, or entering St. Agnes Hospital to have a folded membrane in his rectum investigated, or, depressed, shipping out samples of his body wastes to all the Baltimore pathologists he knew, which meant all the pathologists in the city. (A note of desperation here: "I begin to believe that in the end, as the hearse approaches the cemetery, I shall rise up and give three cheers.") Some weeks not a screed would go into the mailbox without some complaint, such as, "I have a sore mouth, can't smoke, it is 90 degrees, and at least twenty pests are in town," or, "My liver is swelled to a thickness of seven inches, and there are spiders in my urine." Other times he would audit his agonies—"an onslaught of pimples, aches, razor cuts, arch pains, and asthma," or, "asthma, piles, tongue trouble, hay fever, alcoholic liver, weak heels, dandruff, etc." Once he wrote George Jean Nathan:

My ailments this morning come to the following:
  a. A burn on the tongue (healing)
  b. A pimple inside the jaw
  c. A sour stomach
  d. Pain in the prostate
  e. Burning in the gospel pipe (always a preliminary of the hay fever season)
  f. A cut finger
  g. A small pimple inside the nose (going away)
  h. A razor cut, smarting
  i. Tired eyes

Nathan, feeling that this was too much, sent him a set of false teeth, a hairpiece, a cork leg, six bottles of liniment, and a copy of *What Every Boy Should Know*. In the return mail he received a querulous note asking why a bottle of asthma medicine had been omitted. "I am hacking and wheezing like Polonius."

It seemed to me that his hay fever sufferings were no greater than those of other victims, though they may have been exacerbated by his willingness to try every nostrum on the market. ("My carcass is a battleground, and I am somewhat rocky. Hay fever pollen is pouring into my nose by the quart, but in my arteries it encounters the violent opposition of hay fever vaccine, and as a result there is a considerable boiling and bubbling.") This tendency had increased with the years and the advent of other complaints. In his preface to *Supplement Two*, published in the spring of 1948, he wrote that his readers must not expect a third supplement, because "at my age a man encounters frequent reminders, some of them disconcerting, that his body is no more than a highly unstable congeries of the compounds of carbon."

By that autumn he was convinced that the end was near—with some reason. His friends had long ago written him off as a hypochondriac, for he had been crying "Wolf!" as long as they could remember, but a real wolf had been quietly stalking him for ten years. On April 12, 1938, he had suffered a slight stroke. Two years later his doctor had found evidence that his cerebral circulation had been impaired. Mencken immediately started a journal to document the stages in his disintegration. By the evening of November 23, 1948, when he called at the apartment of his secretary, Rosalind C. Lohrfinck, preparatory to taking her to dinner, his deathwatch on himself amounted to a thick sheaf of typescript, some fifty pages in all. There were to be no entries after that, for that was the night his preoccupation with afflictions stopped being funny.

He was having a cocktail with Mrs. Lohrfinck when, in the middle of a lucid sentence, he began to babble incoherently. Alarmed, she called his physician. When the doctor arrived, Mencken was pacing back and forth, ranting. At Johns Hopkins Hospital it was found that he had again been stricken by a cerebral thrombosis affecting his speech center and paralyzing his entire right side. He hovered for days at the threshold of death; then, slowly, he began to improve. The disability in his right side eased gradually and, after a month and a half of extensive treatment, left his arm and leg completely. But his speech center remained affected, and he could neither write nor read. Since boyhood his life had been built around the reading of the written word and the expression of his reflections. Now everything which had given meaning to his existence was gone.

The burden of caring for him—and it was to be a heavy one—fell on his unmarried younger brother August, a retired engineer who looked and sounded uncannily like him and with whom he shared the

Hollins Street house. After Mencken's fifth week of hospitalization August brought the old man home. His condition was appalling. In conversation he tried again and again to summon the right word, and failed. Sometimes he would resort to pantomime, raising an imaginary cup to his lips when he could not recall the word for drinking. Other times he would try circumlocutions, saying "the thing you cut with," for example, when he meant "scissors." And occasionally nonsense words came forth: "yarb" for "yard," "ray" for "rain," "scoot" for "coat," etc.

It was a bitter blow for the author of *The American Language*, and the worst of it was that he was fully aware of what was happening, understood the extent of the brain damage, and knew that his aphasia was incurable. In the Hopkins he had threatened to kill himself, but for all his thundering prose he had never been, and was not now, capable of violence. What actually happened was that he sank into a dreadful depression. He would stand in his study window, looking across at Union Square, on the opposite side of Hollins Street, saying almost inaudibly, "I wish this hideous existence would stop," saying, "How can anyone so stupid live," saying, "That a man like me, able to produce something, with the drive I had. . . . It's comic; it's just comic." In that first year of his disability he refused to allow anyone to read to him, refused to look at magazines with enlarged print, and wouldn't even listen to phonograph records. In one of his few remaining flashes of humor he hoarsely told me, "When I get to heaven, I'm going to speak to God very sharply."

Each time I called at his home I thought it was the last time, but he lingered and lingered. The 1940's became the 1950's; my biography, *Disturber of the Peace* was published—in an act of conspicuous gallantry, he had managed to initial his approval of every quotation from his correspondence—and still his agony continued undiminished. Late in 1951 he suffered a massive heart attack. Again the Hopkins put him on the critical list, but after five months in the hospital he was released once more. August asked me to lend a hand, and together we brought his brother back to Hollins Street.

During the next two years I rarely saw the Menckens, for I was moving up at the *Sun*, which meant assignments farther and farther from home. The ultimate outpost, for me, was New Delhi. After the better part of a year as the paper's Indian correspondent, I returned to Baltimore, and I had just finished covering the Army-McCarthy hearings when August told me that his brother's mood had changed slightly. He was now willing to be read to. Did I know anyone who could spend mornings as his companion? I hesitated for a moment. By then love had died between me and the *Sun,* and there was no hope of a reconciliation. So I answered August: "Yes. Me."

In those twilight years Mencken's day began at 8 A.M., when Renshaw, a hospital orderly, arrived at the house after an all-night shift in the Johns Hopkins accident room. "Rancho," as the old man always called him, gave him a rubdown in his third-floor bedroom, helped him wash and dress, and entertained him with vivid stories of colorful cases he had seen during the night. Meanwhile August was preparing his brother's breakfast downstairs—fruit juice, two soft-boiled eggs, and a slice of bread. Mencken ate this in his second-floor study, swiveling his chair around to the window so he could watch elementary school pupils trooping to school while he drank his coffee.

Children had become dear to him; unlike their parents they were natural in his presence, unembarrassed by his condition. He enjoyed trips to the barber because he could admire a kindergarten class playing across the street while his hair was cut, and two small boys who saw him almost every day were five-year-old Butch, who lived in the house next to his, and Alvin, a six-year-old Negro from down the street. He would stroke Butch's rather emaciated little dog—all pets look starved on Hollins Street; since Mencken's own childhood the neighborhood had gone downhill and was, his own home apart, virtually a slum—and congratulated Alvin on the racing speed of his pet turtle. Emma, the Mencken cook, nearly always had cookies for the boys. And each Christmas the old man distributed huge sacks of candy to all the children who lived around Union Square.

After breakfast Mrs. Lohrfinck came in. Together the two of them went through the morning mail; painful though all communication had become for him, he insisted that everyone who wrote him receive some sort of answer. Then she would riffle through miscellaneous notes in his files, reading them to him, and he would make a simple editorial judgment over the suitability of each. (The resulting collection was published four months after his death as *Minority Report.*) At ten o'clock she left. Her employer accompanied her downstairs to the front door. Then, unless the weather was impossible for him, he turned, trudged through the house, took his cap from a peg in the dining room, and went outside.

For Mencken admirers, the geography of the backyard at 1524 Hollins Street is often clearer than scenes from their own childhood. To the left, as you came out the kitchen door, stood a high brick wall which he had begun building after the First World War. In it were set various tiles, with a concrete replica of Beethoven's life mask and the first five bars of his Fifth Symphony at the far end. To the right of the back gate was a green-and-white shed which had sheltered Mencken's pony when he was a boy, and which now housed August's tools. In warm seasons morning glories blossomed over the shed, raising their lovely green fingers against the West Baltimore sky. Beside the shed, sloping toward the house, was a workbench and a woodpile splashed with outrageously bright colors. Nearby stood a child's wagon; an unsuccessful thief had left it behind one night, and it, too, was splotched with purples, yellows, greens, and reds. Between these giddy hues and the kitchen was a brick terrace over which, on sunny mornings, the devoted August would hoist an awning. He would work at the bench, puffing a pipe and glancing up at the sky from time to time while his brother sat on a canvas chair, his hands lying in his lap like weapons put to rest.

When the noon whistle blew, they reentered the house and Emma prepared lunch. Afterward they sat in the yard again until the children returned from school. Mencken then napped, and after an early supper they drank two martinis and retired. Often friends joined them for the evening cocktails. August controlled the social calendar. He excluded those who he thought might upset the old man and everyone he regarded as trivial—which, August being a misogynist, included all women except Blanche Knopf. The most frequent visitors were Louis Cheslock, Dr. Arnold Rich, Hamilton Owens of the *Sun*, and me.

There were variations in this routine. On sultry mornings, for example, Mencken went through an elaborate stage business with the backyard thermometer, inspecting it and denouncing it. The brothers had no use for dry cleaning, and once I found them in the yard washing their suits and coats with a garden hose. Saturday afternoons Mencken listened to the Metropolitan broadcasts. Saturday evenings the brothers called on the Cheslocks. And at least once a week they went to a movie. This was a new medium for Mencken. Had he retained his ability to read, he would have finished life without having seen more than a half-dozen films, but now his disability left him with little choice. Despite his disability he retained his scorn for artistic dishonesty; he enjoyed Walt Disney full-length cartoon features, Alec Guinness comedies, *Show Boat*, and *Lili*, but he despised melodrama or mawkishness in any form, and positively loathed anything about sports.

Starting in June of 1954 I arrived each morning as Mrs. Lohrfinck was leaving. Usually Mencken was ready for me. If he wasn't, and the sun was shining, I would wait in the yard. Balmy weather was a good sign; he would greet me cheerily, saying, "Well, it's very nice out today; that should make us feel good," or "It's not too bad, we might be able to do a little work today." Even if rain was falling, we could sit in the shed, provided the day wasn't actually raw. When the weather was impossible—when it was sleeting, say—I would approach Hollins Street with dread, knowing that his mood would be grim. "Did you ever see anything like this? Isn't it ghastly?" he would groan, or "I feel very wobbly this morning; I'm going to pieces." At such times August would intervene, raising a hand like a traffic policeman and growling back at him, "Look, you don't feel any worse than I do." And his brother, instantly concerned, would say, "Is that right? Don't you feel well, August?"

Our sessions always began with the *Sun*. If it was the hay fever season we always started with the report of the pollen count. Otherwise, as I leafed through the paper, he would ask, "Well, what's been happening? Any good stuff there, anything rich? Any murders or rapes? Any robberies?" Complex events—Germany's entry into NATO; McCarthyism—were beyond him now. He tried to grasp the tumultuous changes in China, but he couldn't, so we settled for small calamities. Sometimes there were none, and I would tell him so. He would stare at me, his eyes wide with amazement. "What?" he would say. "It's hard to believe. I don't know what's wrong with people nowadays. They're not killing one another any more. August, did you hear that?" And his brother, usually in the midst of painting some object a ghastly orange, or repairing a model boat for Alvin, would lay down his brush to echo his astonishment.

One day the *Sun* carried a story about a husband who had killed his wife, her lover and himself. "You know," Mencken said, "it's probably the only decent thing he did in his life." Another high point was Dr. Samuel Shepard's trial for the murder of his wife. For Mencken it had everything: high theater, the physician who wasn't really a physician, the pillar of the community exposed as a hypocrite. Of Mrs. Shepard, Mencken said with a deep sigh, "Well, she's a goner now. She's up there with the angels." We sat for a moment in meditation, contemplating the sublime fate of the doctor's victim. Then Mencken gestured impatiently at the paper. "Come on," he rasped. "How the hell did he croak her?"

On less favored days we turned to serious reading, and in retrospect I marvel on how much we got through that year: all of Twain and most of Conrad. I was struck by his observation that *Huckleberry*

Finn breaks down at the point where Huck is reunited with Tom; Hemingway had said the same thing. Apart from that, both felt, it was a perfect novel. The most moving book we read, however, was Conrad's *Youth.* Conrad never mastered our idiom, Mencken said; he was translating Polish into English. Yet he admired the Pole more than any other writer of his time. The rich prose of *Youth* evoked memories of his own youth. I too was deeply affected. I had first read the book in college and hadn't understood it at all. Now in my early thirties the torrent of energy with which I had written my first two books was beginning to slacken. I glimpsed what lay ahead—literally glimpsed it, for there was Mencken beside me—and deeply felt a profound sense of sadness for the irretrievable stamina of the receding past.

One morning I stumbled over a hi-fi set in the front vestibule. It had arrived the previous afternoon, a present from Alfred Knopf, and the thoughtful dealer had included the latest Liberace record. Both brothers were exasperated. They didn't know how the thing worked. My own mechanical IQ is very low, but I can remove an appliance from a carton, stick a plug into the wall, lay a plastic disc on a turntable, and flip a switch—which was all that was necessary. We played perhaps thirty seconds of Liberace; then Mencken muttered something obscene and I switched it off. That evening I loaned him my Gilbert and Sullivan collection, however, and he was pathetically pleased by a new source of pleasure. Later, because *The Mikado* was his favorite, I bought him the album. I also introduced him to FM music. He had begun listening to AM stations before retiring and had been complaining sourly about their programing. August and I found the best FM stations for him, and that helped.

Apart from the reading, there was no fixed schedule for our mornings, but certain patterns recurred. Twice a week, after we had left the kitchen to Emma and settled in the yard beneath the gaudy awning, we would hear the distant clatter of garbage can lids. "Ah!" Mencken would breathe, brightening visibly; "here come the professors!" Watching the trash men empty his own cans—each of which was gaily painted "1524 Hollins Street" in red and yellow—he would remark, "You know, they do that very well. The professors are really very elegant men." Now and then visitors came to the front door. They rarely saw him. He ordered William Randolph Hearst, Jr., turned away, and shook his head when I suggested that I ask John Dos Passos to come in from the York Road and visit him. He still had his pride; he didn't want strangers or slight acquaintances to see him in this condition.

Often he was even uncomfortable with August and me. His aphasia came and went. When it was bad, he couldn't remember simple words or terms. He always recalled his brother's name, but there were times when he couldn't think of Mrs. Lohrfinck's, Emma's, Rancho's, Butch's, Alvin's, or mine; and he despaired. Those sessions were grim for all of us, most of all for him. At his best, however, he was very like his old self. He described with gusto his vasectomy at Johns Hopkins when he was younger, and the fecund woman in New York who had voluntarily tested the success of the operation from time to time over the next year. He also told me that he knew twenty men, none of them braggarts, who had told him in confidence that they had bedded a famous Baltimore beauty during what she herself had called her "fast" youth. To him all women were either ladies, to be treated with elaborate chivalry, or sex objects. There was no third category. He was particularly hard on female journalists. He would dismiss them with a snort or a few corrosive phrases. ("God, what an elephant," he said of one. "She makes you want to burn every bed in the world.")

Occasionally he would talk of two books he had planned to write, which would now remain unwritten; the first on the human condition, for which he had completed two chapters, and the second on American politics. And sometimes he spoke of other writers: of James T. Farrell, who was a good friend to the end; of Scott Fitzgerald, whose alcoholism had disgusted him; of Nathan, whose late marriage he regarded as highly comic; and of Sinclair Lewis's dermatological problems—"The only thing to do with Red," he reflected one morning, "was to skin him."

After reading and talking we would sit a while watching August wield his bright paintbrush, dabbing it dry from time to time on the outside of the woodpile. "Isn't that gorgeous work my brother's doing?" the old man would say from time to time. But he rarely sat idle through an entire session. He had to be doing something; even make-work was preferable to no work at all. Heaving up from his canvas chair, he would drop to his knees among the shrubs, stripping leaves from fallen branches for his compost heap and binding the twigs into fagots for the fireplace. On hot days he would periodically mutter, "Here, I'd better quit this or I'll fall to pieces, this is knocking me out." But after an interval he would start groping among the bushes again.

Our most strenuous activity—I shared in it—was adding to the woodpile. On bitter days his fireplace was his chief solace. Cutting wood for it, and burning the wood, gave him extraordinary pleasure; it appealed, he said, to the boyhood love of vandalism which lingered in every man. The gathering of the fuel was as important to him as feeding it to the flames. His friends ordered seasoned cords over the telephone. In his view it was far nobler to scavenge neighborhood alleys and then saw up the loot.

Rising from his chair he would say to me, "Let's see what we can find outside. You can't tell—we might turn up something really superb." Strolling down the narrow lanes with the child's wagon and poking among the trash cans, we would uncover a variety of burnable junk —piano stools, fence posts, broom handles, discarded chairs, hatracks, broken coffee tables, ancient lounge chairs. If I spotted a particularly hideous specimen of Grand Rapids golden oak, he would gape and say, "Wow! *Look* at that, will you!" As we returned from patrol, he would call ahead, "August, I found something really rich. Isn't that beautiful? It's simply exquisite." Then a shade of comic doubt would cross his ruddy face. He would ask us gravely, "But don't you think it's a shame to burn a lovely piece like that?" After deliberation his brother would say, "It's a shame, all right, Harry, but we've got a long winter ahead." "It seems hard," the old man would say worriedly, and August would make a great show of winning him over by promising to save it for a very special occasion. This was the quintessential Mencken, clothing the preposterous in the robes of high seriousness. A passing stranger would have taken him literally, and he would have been in good company; Mencken had misled humorless critics thus for a half-century.

He himself wasn't well enough to do much sawing, so he sat by the end of the workbench, making outrageous comments while August and I took turns sinking the blade deep. We had a ritual; the length of each piece cut was determined by a measuring stick which was the exact width of the fireplace within. A certain percentage of our output had to be backlogs, and if our alley loot didn't include lengths of the proper thickness, we would nail odds and ends together—two mop handles, say, affixed to a broken crucifix, the base of a peach basket, and the wooden remains of a dilapidated plumber's helper. The more absurd the result, the uneasier Mencken grew over the propriety of feeding it to the flames. When its turn came at the hearth, he would wrestle audibly with his conscience before flinging it on the grate.

Eventually everything combustible went up in smoke, with one memorable exception. One morning we were prowling in an alley, furtively lifting galvanized lids and looking, I'm sure, like refugees in postwar Europe searching for a scrap of meat, when he saw, standing against a fence, a shabby chest of drawers. The rats had been at it; we were far from Mencken's back gate; whether it was worth dragging all that way was questionable. As we were debating, a third figure joined us—a short, swart man in seedy khaki. He asked us whether we wanted the dresser. We told him we didn't know. He explained: his little daughter needed a place to store her clothes. If we weren't going to take it, he would.

Disconcerted, and beset this time by genuine pangs, Mencken stammered that we were merely hunting for firewood; by all means the child should have it. The young man brightened with gratitude. He would be back shortly, he said. His car was parked across the street; he would fetch it and whisk the dresser home. As he dashed off we reexamined the rat holes. They were really enormous. It was a marvel that the thing stood. It had seemed worthless; it still did.

"Poor fellow," Mencken said.

In the long silence that followed we contemplated the plight of a father reduced to scrounging among castoffs for his children's furniture.

Then the hush was broken by the deep-throated roar of a finely tuned engine, and into the lane backed the longest, fattest, shiniest pink Cadillac I had ever seen. The man leaped out, the chest of drawers disappeared into its cavernous trunk, and then the Cadillac vanished, too, gone in a cloud of exhaust.

Mencken's mouth fell open in amazement. *"Jesus Christ!"* he gasped. "Did you see *that?*" I told him I could hardly have missed it. "Think of it," he mused. "Imagine that man raising a family, sending his children off to learn the principles of Americanism, keeping his mother off the poor farm, raising money to cure his wife of gallstones— and driving around in a rose-colored hearse! *August!*" he hoarsed as we neared home. "We just saw the goddamndest animal in Baltimore!"

As the noon whistle sounded he would methodically measure the wood sawed. "Say, we got a lot of work done today," he would say, standing back and admiring the stack. "Look how high that pile is now." As winter deepened it shrank again, for unless there was a thaw the brothers laid a fire every night. Evenings when I dropped in to listen to their growing collection of LP classics, the three of us would stare into the vivid coals. Like everything else about Mencken, his fires were unique. Their colors ranged all over the spectrum, for he cherished a hoard of chemically treated wood which, when ignited, matched the rainbow. I never learned to share his taste for after-dinner martinis, but I was tremendously impressed by those spectacular flames, and I said so.

When warm weather returned in the spring of 1955, Gertrude

Mencken arrived from her farm and joined us for two nerve-wracking hours. I had never met the brothers' sister before, and I think I came to understand something of their attitude toward women that evening. She was pleasant enough, but she couldn't seem to stop talking. The monologue went on and on, while August stared gloomily into the purple and orange fire and Mencken swelled with frustration. When she had departed the old man turned to his brother. In a slurred, gritty voice he demanded, "Where's the thing that makes music?" August replied, "You mean the gramophone, Harry?" Mencken nodded grimly. He said, "I want the ghastly one. Lib—Lib—" "Liberace," I supplied, and August brought it from across the room. Mencken ordered, "Throw it on the fire." For once August hesitated. "It will make a terrible stink," he said. "Baloney," said Mencken. "It will be elegant. We need it to finish off this classy occasion." Into the flames it went. The stench was dreadful; after a while the old man stalked wordlessly off to bed and August removed the record with tongs. Even so, the odor was evident the next morning, and Emma had to air the house all day.

When summer arrived I said my last good-bye at Hollins Street. I was leaving Baltimore for New England and had found a Hopkins graduate student who would come in mornings and read the paper to Mencken. It was a wrench for me; he obviously didn't want me to go, and at first he said so vehemently. That evening August reminded him that I had my own writing to do, and the next morning the old man had swung around completely; he offered his congratulations and said he expected me to write some swell books. His generosity, and his pretense that he had changed his mind, were typical of him. I have never known a public figure who was so different from his reputation. His readers thought of him as bigoted, cantankerous, wrathful, and rude, and he was none of those things. He was the elderly friend of Butch and Alvin. He was the cripple who was always solicitous about his brother's health. He was the stricken man who forced himself to initial the pages of my first manuscript, who always asked me in the shed whether I was properly clad; who, when he was in the depth of his worst depressions, would excuse himself and retire to his bedroom because he didn't want to burden me with his troubles.

We both knew we would never meet again, for all our talk of reunions. He was failing rapidly now. Yet he rallied gallantly that last afternoon, and as I turned to leave through the vestibule he struck a pose, one foot in front of the other, one hand on the banister and the other, fisted, on his hip. "You know, I had a superb time while it lasted," he said in that inimitable voice. "Very soon it will stop, and I will go straight to heaven. Won't that be exquisite? It will be very high-toned."

We shook hands; he trudged up the stairs into shadow, and I departed carrying two farewell gifts, an Uncle Willie stogie and a piece of the treated firewood. Seven months later an Associated Press reporter called me in Connecticut to tell me that Mencken had died in his sleep. His ashes were deposited in Baltimore's Loudon Park Cemetery. Long afterward I read of his brother's death, and later word reached me that the Hollins Street house—"as much a part of me as my two hands," Mencken had once said of it—was now occupied by the University of Maryland's School of Social Work. That evening I carefully laid the piece of treated firewood in my own fireplace. I didn't expect much; after all that time, I thought, the chemicals would have lost their potency. But I was wrong. Instantly a bright blue flame sprang up. Blue changed to crimson, and after a few minutes there was another change. It was eerie. From end to end the wood blazed up in a deep green which would have been familiar to anyone who had ever held a copy of *The American Mercury*.

Fleetingly I thought: *If only the Mercury were still being published!* And: *If only he were still alive!* I remembered him lamenting the fact that there was no decent memorial service for nonbelievers. This little fire, I realized, was the closest I would ever come to one for him. Now his home had become a headquarters for a profession he had ridiculed. Miller Brothers' eating house, where we had drained steins of pilsener, was being torn down; the name of the restaurant lived on ignominiously in a sterile new Hilton Hotel. The Baltimore which delighted Mencken as a young reporter, when, he wrote, "the days chased one another like kittens chasing their tails," was swiftly vanishing, as the flames on my andirons were vanishing; soon the Baltimore I had known would disappear, too. Briefly I was near tears. And then I checked myself. I realized what Mencken's reaction to the maudlin fireside scene would have been. He would have split it into sentimental flinders with one vast gravelly chuckle.

Index